DETOURS IN PHILOSOPHY

PHENOMENOLOGY
& LITERATURE

Hans H. Rudnick
General Editor

Vol. 4

PETER LANG
New York • Washington, D.C./Baltimore • Bern
Frankfurt am Main • Berlin • Brussels • Vienna • Oxford

William Vaughan

DETOURS IN PHILOSOPHY

Controversies in
the Continental Tradition

PETER LANG
New York • Washington, D.C./Baltimore • Bern
Frankfurt am Main • Berlin • Brussels • Vienna • Oxford

Library of Congress Cataloging-in-Publication Data

Vaughan, William,
Detours in philosophy: controversies in the continental tradition / William Vaughan.
p. cm. — (Phenomenology and literature; v. 4)
Includes bibliographical references and index.
1. Continental philosophy. 2. Philosophy, European. I. Title.
B791.V38   190–dc22   2007030626
ISBN 978-1-4331-0088-8
ISSN 1524-0193

Bibliographic information published by **Die Deutsche Bibliothek**.
Die Deutsche Bibliothek lists this publication in the "Deutsche
Nationalbibliografie"; detailed bibliographic data is available
on the Internet at http://dnb.ddb.de/.

The paper in this book meets the guidelines for permanence and durability
of the Committee on Production Guidelines for Book Longevity
of the Council of Library Resources.

Printed in Germany

Table of Contents

Acknowledgments

I would like to thank the following people for their support, in ways which may not be immediately apparent to them: Russell Weaver, Douglas Chismar, Mario von der Ruhr, Paul Johnson, Richard Schacht, Lawrence Hass, Pirmin Stekeler-Weithofer, and Charles Fisher. Kristian Evans was wonderful in helping me format the text. The chapter on Heidegger's *Beitrage* first appeared in *Journal for Philosophical Research*. The lectures on Sartre and Levinas were presented before the West Virginia Philosophy Society. The lecture on Nietzsche was presented before the estimable College of Wooster Philosophy Roundtable, and a revised version was a Phi Sigma Tau lecture at Ashland University. The lecture on "De-Spenglerization" was first delivered at the Ringling School of Art and Design in Sarasota, FL. The chapter on Simone Weil was first delivered before the American Simone Weil Society in Toronto in 2002. I would also like to thank Beverly Heimann, John Sikula, and John Bee of Ashland University for their support and Ashland University for a Senior Faculty Study Leave in the Spring of 2005 which allowed this project to be completed, and for research in Germany and Wales which allowed it to be improved.

Introduction

When it comes to thinking, the shortest distance between two points is not always a straight line. The proximity of one text to another, of one idea to another, or even to itself, is never simply given but must be reinvented with every thinking. We often must take a detour in order to get to the point, because it is often the case that the detour *is* the point. Such is the case with the directions of this book. Its every detour is the setting out into a new direction, no one of which is liable to save one much time. The time *of* the detour in philosophy is as well the time *for* the detour. One's going out of their way often *gives* as much time as it *saves*. When there is no navigable meridian, we take the time for such detours because we hope that it will illuminate the philosophical terrain for ourselves or others.

This collection of essays is both an invitation to think and invest, a promise for some future advantage, and an impossibility, since the pure detour, the one that does not belong to the economy of expenditure and recompense, is impossible. Each of these chapters was drawn from various seminars, courses, and lectures and so bear the marks more of undergraduate teaching contexts than research institutions. They emerge as critical summaries of various topics, perhaps having no greater merit than to attest to some extended readings in the authors or issues investigated, and therefore should only claim to be reading notes or teaching tools, extended critical introductions to various theaters of European scholarly controversy. Indeed, I would like to think of this work as a testimony to the possibilities of *teaching* as each chapter has variously been employed in the undergraduate teaching of philosophy. It was composed during a period which will one day become known as the American hologram, when the entire country seemed in active revolt against secularism and in bitter rebellion against pluralism. My campus took its cue from the cultural drift: during the semesters of the book's composition, websites and blogs from various constituencies at my university showed both that European thinking was responsible for all environmental, racial, and ethnic oppressions of the earth, that the thinking of "old" Europe resulted only in death camps, and that the American war in Iraq was to be welcomed as a possible mechanism for showing that "people like Heidegger were wrong," as if the mere mention of the name signalled a treachery requiring no further investigation. It was also a semester in which my University's Board of Trustees unanimously voted to enforce long dormant religious requirements for all new faculty hires, in an attempt to silence non-Christian voices (an event which resulted in the cancellation of my inaugural lecture). Such a hologram is marked by a crusading spirit of evangelical Christianity, a faith-based politics, monistic in its drive to hegemony among the world religions, and a virulent neocon preemptive backlash against the politics of difference. Like Hegel's Owl of Minerva which takes flight at dusk, American foundational moral clarity thinks that the New Testament God has died in European consciousness, and that because of this it is to be replaced by a recombinant Old Testament God, a fusion of crusading politics, redemptive violence, and a domestic tutelary of panic insecurity born by way of an imaginary political covenant.

It would probably take another book to establish that in fact the opposite is true, that it is American ideals that are in decline, and that the completed nihilism of which Nietzsche speaks has been visited upon us in these times, any detour from which would be seen as a gift. The more modest goal of these pages, however, is only to locate the still functioning graces of European philosophy, to gauge its impact to still spark the minds of Ohio undergraduates, and to try to illustrate that at most we have barely even begun to scratch the surface of its resources. European thinking, even with *its* oppressions and dead-ends, continues to be the aquifer for any and all impulses of genuine American thought, a wellspring from which we may yet draw nourishment to a drought-stricken surface. The thinking of "old Europe" can still bestow a great many gifts. Perhaps in this sense a detour always has the structure of an annulled gift. Just as the gift is always given with the expectation of some future taking or returning, so too taking these detours provides the expectation of getting back on track further down the road or of returning older but wiser, with some greater appreciation for the road already taken.

In outlining the chapters of this book, it need hardly be mentioned that Martin Heidegger plays a prominent role throughout, as he remains the central figure of European thought, even 30 years after his death. All of his lecture courses from the 1920's are finding their way to publication in his *Gesamtausgabe*. One of the most pivotal and substantive of such recent publications has been that of the *Beiträge zur Philosophie*, published first in Germany in 1989 and in English in 1999. This massive and dense work has slowly opened itself to scholarship. In Chapter One, "Beinger than Being is Being Itself' A Primer for Heidegger's *Beiträge*," I take a single page from the manuscript and in the form of a dialogue between one defending Heidegger's project and one critical of it, illustrate the extreme difficulty but eventual possibility of understanding the basic concepts of the work.

Chapter Two deals with "Seriality and Sartre's Marxism." The encounter between French existentialism and Marxism was one of the more interesting intellectual dramas of the 20th century. Driven by the development of the cold war to take a position for or against Marxism, for or against the west, for or against the Soviet Union, for or against the French Communist Party, figures such as Camus and Merleau-Ponty devoted book after book to specifying their attitude toward Marxism and Communism. Then slower than all the others, comes the most formidable and most famous of French existentialists, Sartre. The intellectual colossus of post-war France initially does not seek to reject or go beyond or implicitly absorb Marxism, nor even distinguish his existentialism from it, but, remarkably, accepts Marxism as the dominant philosophy of the age, and situates existentialism as an ideology within Marxism. The major thinker of a great school of thought declares his own philosophy to be ancillary to the rival outlook he has been combating for years, and sets out to correct and properly found that outlook for the sake of its survival and flourishing. Not since Kant was awakened from his dogmatic slumbers by Hume had there been such a spectacle of seemingly philosophical reversal. This chapter argues that while Sartre's movement toward Marxism was unsuccessful, it was ultimately a necessary stage through which European thought had to travel.

The work of the Christian mystic Simone Weil has had a lasting impact on postwar France, but the scholarship on her work has at times resembled hagiography. That many would cringe at the comparisons should not, however, prohibit an exploration of precisely those fascinating interconnections of her thought with the postmoderns, of those proximities which more and more we see with Simone Weil and figures such as Heidegger, Bataille, Levinas, and a host of other writers and figures capturable under the general category of the postmodern. Chapter Three—"Indiscretion with Regard to the Unsayable: Weil to the Postmodern," takes some further steps in this direction, by focusing on a particular area of Simone Weil's thinking, her views on affliction and the relation of affliction to language, and those of the French postmodernist writer Maurice Blanchot and his writings on death and the representability of death.

Contemporary European philosophy has been marked by a renewed reflection on religious phenomenology, focusing on the meaning of gift-exchange, and a continued interrogation with the texts of various mystical traditions. Thinkers as diverse as Weil, Levinas, Derrida, de Man, Foucault, Blanchot, Bataille, Heidegger, Cixous, Irigaray, Benjamin, Adorno, and Marion all participate in this discussion, and have been caught up in and at times compromised by the perceived mystical and religious elements in their thinking.

Their work remains intimately connected to the themes, the vocabularies and the concepts variously discovered in the writings of Christian mystics. Had they been contemporaries of Plotinus, their work might not have appeared so problematic. Since the Enlightenment, however, when Kant declared that mystical illumination leads to the "death" of all thinking, philosophy has with few exceptions sought to formulate its visions of existence in terms immune to the charge of nebulous thinking that the word "mystical" implies. Chapter Four—"Mysticism, Gift, and Bataille's Theory of Expenditure" argues that all such sweeping claims for the exclusion of the mystical from modern philosophical discourse should be challenged. With emphasis on the economic theories of the French thinker Bataille, I show that so-called mysticism, as the repressed other of philosophy, lies buried at the heart of philosophical logic, unsettling in subtle ways philosophy's march toward a rational and ordered view of the universe. Independent of any particular mystical experience, contemporary European thinkers now successfully use mysticism as a weapon against the confining and reductive positivisms of traditional philosophy.

Chapter Five regards "Aristotle as a Proto-Phenomenologist." In the early 1920's Heidegger had the growing perception of the poor theological grounding of his students. In a letter to Löwith he mentions considering teaching nothing but Plotinus so as to shore the students up, but decides instead on an intensive teaching of Aristotelian metaphysics, which he begins in 1921 and does not let up until 1924. These Marburg lecture courses have now been published. Through the course of this intense teaching and lecturing on Aristotle, one sees how Heidegger's "Lutheran" motivations get sidetracked in favor of a newfound affinity between his own original phenomenological analyses and Aristotle's texts, both in method and in content. Of specific importance for Heidegger was Aristotle's phenomenological method. Bringing his earlier interpretations of the dynamized facticity of life to bear upon these texts, Heidegger found in Aristotle a kindred soul, a proto-phenomenologist of the first order, which in turn led to the even deeper comprehension of the nature of phenomenology. This chapter spells out these complex connections, and illustrates how Aristotle was to play a governing role throughout much of Heidegger's subsequent thought.

There is now a small scholarly industry devoted to the claim that Heidegger's thinking on ethics is faulty, and that his thought fails to address the ethical dynamic of the category of the "other." Thus it gets suggested that the work of Emmanuel Levinas provides the necessary supplement to Heidegger's thinking along these lines. In this chapter, Chapter Six—"Community of Those who are Going to Die: On Levinas," I argue that there is no need for such a supplement, for the criticism by the Levinasians, which has gained momentum in contemporary continental thought, has done so at the expense of de-emphasizing to some extent the thought of the later Heidegger, its intimate engagement with poetry and poetic language, and its continuing reevaluation of the problematic of difference and its metaphysical provenance. This chapter defends how Heidegger's late, poetic thought ends with a radical opening which charts possibilities of thinking otherness non-metaphysically, and that this dynamic can be read as a proposition of a profoundly moral hermeneutic notion of community which outlines its concerns and develops its terminologies in entirely different ways.

Chapter Seven investigates a scholarly dispute concerning Nietzsche. In a letter to Ernst Schmeitzner on February 13th, 1883, Nietzsche referred to his work *Thus Spake Zarathustra* as the "fifth Gospel." Owing to the confusion surrounding Part IV of the work, one might be tempted to bring to the task of understanding it a variety of interpretive schemes culled from biblical hermeneutics. Scholarship on Zarathustra has been enormous, and in regard to the difficulties of Part IV has been divided into two camps. The "literalist" interpretative camp holds that Part IV of *Thus Spake Zarathustra* is a fragmentary mistake by Nietzsche, that the actual ending to Part III contains the book's real conclusions, and that Part IV was added later as an unfortunate afterthought. An alternative "ironist" position has taken Part IV to be the integral and concluding section of the book, with satirical elements added to undermine the natural development of the sections which precede it. This chapter argues that the confusion surrounding the fifth gospel can be dispelled by articulating yet a third narrative which accounts for both the literalist and ironist readings, namely, that Part Four is no mistake at all, but follows the Dionysian festival requirement, always fulfilled by Aeschylus, that a trilogy of tragedies, or three act dramatic movements produced from the succession of tragic events, be followed by a more cheerful satyr-play based on the same mythological material.

Traditional philosophy often dismisses mere cultural criticism as inferior or fashionable movements of thought. However, it can be argued that the cultural movement of decline narratives conditions the major philosophers, and not the other way around. This chapter, on the "De-Spenglerization of European Thought," focuses on how Spengler's work *Decline of the West* had an enormous impact and unprecedented literary success in Germany, both among the academic elites and the larger reading public. It was the most popular work of European thought in the interwar era. The wartime generation of university-trained intellectuals was profoundly affected by Spengler's intoxicating combination of both western collapse and German resurgence, including Thomas Mann and Max Weber. This chapter spells out how two of the most widely recognized and influential philosophical geniuses of the day, Ludwig Wittgenstein and Martin Heidegger, were as well deeply impacted by the work, enough to see both the cultural significance of Spengler's accomplishment and the need for a certain amount of de-spenglerization to accompany it.

Chapter Nine involves "Wittgenstein's Phenomenology of Mathematics." Since antiquity it has been a common picture to think that philosophers draw on mathematical concepts as exemplars of absolute truth. The power and precision of a priori concepts presents us with features worthy of emulation—if only philosophy in all of its endeavors could match mathematics in terms of its precision, universal applicability, necessity and certainty. It must come as a shock then, to those who hold such pictures, that the general impulse of Wittgenstein's thinking concerning mathematics is to treat traditional ideas about the privileged epistemic status of mathematics and logic as if they represent, not an exemplar of genuine precision and clarity, but indeed as a unique danger to the achievement of genuine philosophical clarity. Such a shock no doubt carried over certainly to some prominent critics of Wittgenstein's views on mathematics. When the Vienna Circle first engaged Wittgenstein's views on mathematics, they dismissed Wittgenstein's views as simply confused versions of their own logicist position, of far less interest than the shattering announcements (at the same conference) of Gödel's theorem. Similar critiques steadily followed: that Wittgenstein had failed to understand clearly the problems he faced, and that his work in mathematics would not contribute to his reputation as a philosopher; that Wittgenstein's views as "difficult to take seriously" and "plain silly"; it betrays a "mental asceticism" devoted to the goal of "irrationality"; "… a surprisingly insignificant product of a sparkling mind." Even Gödel himself is said to have commented that Wittgenstein "did not understand, or pretended to not understand, my theorem." In general, this chapter argues that Wittgenstein's sparkle seems to have exceeded his critics, and by embedding his discussion in the larger issue of impossibility proofs in mathematics, and bringing into the picture Wittgenstein's remarks on geometry, in particular the remarks on the algebraic proof of the impossibility of the trisection of the angle, the negative receptions of his views of mathematics can be shown to be deficient in precisely the degree to which they fail to take his work as a phenomenologist of mathematics seriously.

Chapter Ten is on the notion of nothingness. In the 20th century, the whole idea of "nothing" for the western mind is either abyssal, or a tech problem whose complexity is solvable merely with increased IT funding. Even as a liberation its exhilaration is strenuous and desperate. This anxiety before nothingness marks the western tradition. It is the way of thought that cannot face the nothing without a shudder. This feature only stands out in confrontation with another possibility. There is endless anxiety, boredom, nausea, panic, not to mention endless technological workings with regard to it, that the thought of the nothing induces in the west. The anxious or technical nihilism of the west has little of the serenity or blessedness of the nothing of the east. This chapter illustrates how such tensions over the nothing burst forth in the last century in the infamous exchange between the German-speaking philosophers Heidegger and Carnap. In 1929 Heidegger gave his Freiberg inaugural lecture entitled "What is Metaphysics?" in which he essentially states that the nothing is at the center of all contemporary thinking. Carnap responded with a bone-crushing essay, "Overcoming Metaphysics through the Logical Analysis of Language," which dismissed Heidegger's remarks as meaningless. Indeed, some have called this exchange one of the pivotal moments of twentieth century thought, an inaugural moment of the analytic vs. continental divide. I argue that we can see their exchange as the philosophical expression of diverging directions of the schools of neo-kantianism of the day, and that the fissure of the analytic and continental divide was indeed over nothing.

Chapter Eleven addresses Adorno's views in aesthetics. Since its posthumous publication in 1970, Adorno's major work *Aesthetic Theory* seems to have raised more questions than it has answered, perhaps more than could ever be answered on its behalf. It was not surprising that critics on the right condemned its poetic obscurity and embrace of dialectics. What was interesting was its reception, and outright denunciation, from those on the left, who condemned it as an anachronistic cultural elitism. In the 1990's major critical reassessments of the work sought to locate its impact somewhere in the rivalry between modernism and post-modernism. Thus Robert's *Art and Enlightenment* situates Adorno's thought as consistent with the modernist project, whereas Habermas' influential critique paints it as part of the project which "gives up" on modernity. Other major works of outstanding scholarship followed, such as Zuidervaart's *Adorno's Aesthetic Theory* (1991) and Paddison's *Adorno's Aesthetics of Music* (1993), both of which aim at a comprehensive synthesis of Adorno's writings. Still later authors sought to capture Adorno's complexities while remaining wary of systematizing them, given their own anti-systematic impulses, such as the work of Hohendahl (1992) and Martin (1997). In this chapter I argue that these attempts to understand Adorno's work are misguided. One must engage in a kind of mimicry of what one is addressing in order even to address it on its terms, but this risks either replaying the original, or foisting a false unity upon the fundamentally dissimilar. By highlighting the influences of Benjamin's work *Ursprung des deutsches Trauerspiel*, on which Adorno's work is largely modeled, one can understand the posture of strategic essentialism marking its own de-totalizing sympathies, which is the only way (I argue) that the work can be addressed.

Chapter Twelve investigates Husserl and Derrida. The reception of Derrida's critique of Husserlian phenomenology was decidedly mixed. Some of the first generation of commentators saw Derrida's critique holding to the highest standards of scholarly rigor, a "first class piece of analytical work in the philosophy of language," and a "quite accurate criticism of Husserl's *Logical Investigations* and of his concept of *Kundgabe*." Other voices rejected Derrida's achievement, that it was "vitiated by inconsistent acknowledgments of some Husserlian teachings, and by clear misinterpretations of others"; that Derrida's most specific criticisms "fail to undermine any tenets crucial to Husserlian phenomenology." More pointed criticisms also emerged, such as John Searle describing Derrida's "low level of philosophical argumentation, the deliberate obscurantism of prose, the wildly exaggerated claims, and the constant striving to give the appearance of profundity by making claims that seem paradoxical, but under analysis often turn out to be silly or trivial." Kevin Mulligan derided Derrida's "inflationary Parisian fashion" in his well-argued but derisively titled: "How Not to Read: Derrida on Husserl." John Scanlon topped all other critics in molten language by describing Derrida's work on Husserl as a "sophisticated parody of a pompously pedantic exegesis of the first chapter of the first of Husserl's *Logical Investigations*, a bumbling product of a fictitious exegete whose reading is dictated throughout by a pedantic fixation upon the conceit that the text being interpreted must, in every respect, be subordinated to a mythic master text known as the metaphysics of presence." Despite the mutually abusive and score-settling soquacities of the secondary literature, my chapter takes a step back from point-scoring extrapolations of individual arguments or works and seeks to situate Derrida's critiques in broader interpretative contexts, since many of the initial criticisms stemmed from a violation of the basic hermeneutical rule of reconstructing the contexts of the discussions. I argue that Derrida's criticisms are certainly something more than satire, something less than a refutation of Husserl's arguments, and largely successful.

The year 2004 marked the fortieth anniversary of the publication of Peter Winch's celebrated paper 'Understanding a Primitive Society.' Winch's work exercised a profound impact across a range of intellectual disciplines, including philosophy, sociology, anthropology, and political theory. Winch's paper is typically understood as the quintessential statement of relativism: different cultural groups, at different times and places, have their own peculiar conceptions of 'reality'. These different realities are frequently incommensurable with each other, such that (some of) what is 'reality' for a member of a 'primitive society' is illusion and error for the modern Western individual, and perhaps vice versa as well. In a word, Winch was perceived as completely abandoning the notion of reality entirely and reducing it into as many different, incommensurable, realities as there were different systems of socially functioning beliefs and practices. In a famous line from Winch's article, he expressly states, after all, that "[R]eality is not what gives language sense. What is real and what is unreal shows itself in the sense that language has." Winch's critics, numbering in the hundreds, including such luminaries as MacIntyre, Gellner, Popper, Apel, and Habermas, have subjected his ideas to at times scathing critique, arguing that a pernicious relativism follows inexorably from his ontological and epistemic relativism. Because 'what is real' can only be known and understood in the light of rules and criteria internal to, and constitutive of, some functioning, ongoing form of social life, it is not permissible to evaluate or criticize aspects of that reality by reference to any external criteria of evaluation. In Chapter Thirteen—"Winch and the Charge of Relativism," I argue however that most of the criticisms against Winch have fundamentally misunderstood his philosophical goals, and careful comparison with some well-chosen German philosophers can help us see those misunderstandings more clearly.

Plato's *Philebus* has been accompanied by centuries of attempts to clarify its confusions. In this chapter I spell out how Hans-Georg Gadamer's work *Plato's Dialectical Ethics* is both forwarding an interpretation of Philebus which reconciles its various interpretive dilemmas, and well as portending an entire approach to how one reads all of Plato's dialogues. Indeed, Gadamer is giving a first version of an entire hermeneutic theory in relation to any text, and to human understanding in general. In this connection the importance for Gadamer of Heidegger's lectures on Aristotle during the 1920's cannot be underestimated, and how doing hermeneutics as a kind of phenomenology is central. What I seek to show in Chapter Fourteen—"The Mimes of Sophron: Gadamer's *Philebus*," is that Gadamer is involved in a complex movement akin to pulling Plato back from the Aristotelianism through which Plato has previously been interpreted; more specifically, Gadamer would like to retrieve the model of practical philosophy (phronesis) that was conceived by Aristotle, but in a certain sense would like to infuse that model with the spirit of universal dialogical openness that he finds portrayed, in an exemplary manner, in the Socrates of the *Philebus*. Thus Gadamer's work on the *Philebus* is at once an enactment of phenomenological hermeneutics as applied to a platonic dialogue, and an illustration of the proximity of such hermeneutics to *phronesis*.

Chapter Fifteen explores "Poetry and Founding in Rilke and Heidegger." While several authors have explored Heidegger's readings of poets, few have done so in the appropriate way. Most have addressed Heidegger as a critic of poetry, and look at the import of poetry from the point of view of Rilke and Hölderlin scholarship in order to demonstrate how Heidegger misconstrues them. The criticisms levied against Heidegger thus have more to do with how he reads them to his own ends at the expense of the poets themselves. These critics see such a strategy as criminal in general, and measure the worth of interpretations merely in terms of a zero-sum game wherein traces of instrumentality are grounds for exclusion. The critics invariably identify what are taken to be interpretive blunders in Heidegger's dialogue with poets, and object to what are variously regarded as Heidegger's phenomenologically unwarranted totalizing, or his violent projection of the history of being upon texts that resist the closure such a vision entails, or his idiosyncratic interpretation based on an arbitrary selection of texts. Of the many poets Heidegger has addressed, from Hölderlin and Träkl, to Mörike and George, many critics take his readings of Rilke to be the most problematic. Despite the steady stream of opposition to his approach, I remain sympathetic to what Heidegger is doing, and in this chapter defend what I take to the correct interpretation. Much of the opposition to Heidegger's readings of poets neglects looking at the matter of poetic founding. Just exactly what Heidegger is doing with Rilke can best be seen by detailing first of all an account of what Heidegger in general is looking for out of poetry. This can be spelled out along three trajectories; first, by reminding us of how Heidegger's thinking about language is connected to his concerns about global technology; second, that technology constricts writing in its most intimate levels; and third, that his conception of language can be seen when set in relief against other, more traditional conceptions of language. Only then will we be in better position to return to his specific remarks about Rilke.

My final chapter returns to the British thinker Peter Winch on the issue of the universalizability of ethical concepts. This idea entails that if we judge an action or decision right, then it is right for anyone who is not relevantly different. Winch famously argues against this principle with reference to Melville's class story of *Billy Budd*. In this chapter I illustrate how Winch is employing Melville to illustrate how works of literature help us to understand the strange phenomenon of concepts surviving outside the frameworks of life that made them intelligible in the first place. Following Kierkegaard, Winch writes so as to display how ethical decision-making can amount to finding out about what it is possible for one to do. I make some further connections with Winch's thought and hermeneutics along these lines.

As important as is all of the philosophical reflection of the emerging democracies of the continent, from the foregoing list one can see how this work understands the thinking of "old Europe" to be mostly French and German. Terms such as ineffable, inscrutable, incomprehensible, unsayable, obscure, and inaccessible, continue to accompany many of the bodies of thought from these areas. Yet what I hope to show is that this chain of signifiers also foregrounds crucial opportunities at the center of contemporary thinking. It is these problematic tensions, these generative contradictions and points of interpretive complexity, which form the points of departure for *Detours in Philosophy*. The goal is not so much to identify the constitutive features of European philosophy, by no means a straightforward task, but to seize upon key interpretive occasions, spell out the complex histories, and tarry over concerns and issues not normally charted in a linear genealogy. That the thinking of "old Europe" is a speculative investment can only be known if its author were in some perfect possession of philosophical understanding, as if the detour were mastered from the outset by a philosophical speculation that risks nothing of its capital. Detours are neither express routes nor dead ends. Detours though the thinking of figures like Sartre, Weil, Gadamer, Nietzsche, Wittgenstein, Levinas, Winch and Heidegger would signal neither impotence nor dialectical mastery, paths that are not simply located within the program of philosophy but in some sense situate the program itself, that would not take place within the time of the detour but would give the detour its time. The detour *from* the American hologram would give the time *for* the philosophical detours within that program, and a chance for a detour that would exceed that hologram. These essays are intended as well as detours within the thinking of old Europe that would open up the possibility of a detour that would exceed *that* program, that would, at the limit, show the philosophical program itself to have been a long detour that aims to return to the name of an impossibility. Such a project cannot be completed except only in and as the time of a detour.

I. Undelivered Inaugural Lecture: "The Gift of the Question"

The awkward title of this address will perhaps not be alleviated by the further awkwardness of the inquiry which it pursues. I will begin with an anecdote which has haunted me. I was in a computer room, and a student looked over my shoulder and saw the word "philosophy" on the screen, and preceeded to tell me that philosophy was not only irrelevant but in fact completed. Just as I was about to embark on a lecture spelling out how the very product at his fingertips was itself the product of philosophy, he continued by insisting that all significant questions had been answered, that there was no need for any further philosophy. Any question for which there was no objective answer was mystification—it shed no light. All one need do is look up answers on the internet search engines. He kept repeating to me "no light, no light," and then dared me to ask him a question which he could not find the answer to on the internet. I asked him his name, and he said it was Rich. I asked him: what is the meaning of Rich's mortality for Rich? In the immeasurably awful next few minutes, he began dutifully tapping in the figures to the device, in effect "googling" his own death.

Indeed, I would say that such a state of profound alienation is shared by many of his contemporaries. We are living in a time where the very act of questioning has become jeopardized, a time in which the University as a place where fundamental questions are asked threatens to become obsolete. Many universities today have no definable mission, and have no public sphere in which even to ask such questions. The over-arching mission of many a university has no specific content and no referent. Its fundamental meaning lacks theoretical definition. This disappearance of the locus of social meaning for the institution of the university has been met with various responses, on the left and the right, either seeking to defend and restore the social mission of the university by reaffirming a national cultural identity that has lost its purchase, or, perhaps emboldened by recent political movements, re-casting the university entirely in religious terms; or there is the attempt to re-invent the identity of the university so as to adapt to changing circumstances, a kind of multi-versity position.

The University once held a central place in the formation of human beings for the nation-state. Its internal structure of belonging or community was meant to reflect that culture. With the decline of the nation state comes a major shift in the idea that the university is a preserver of some national culture or identity. A de-referentialization of the university has occurred to where the grounds for which one might have characteristically made grand claims for the humanities has been undermined. It is not clear there can be an appeal to a transcendence that our actions struggle to realize. Certainly nothing in contemporary society makes it evident that individuals should be trained to ask questions. Responsibility for questioning has been relegated to what I will delicately describe as thoughtless domains.

Teaching philosophy is first and formost concerned with the preservation of the significance of questioning, with rendering questionable. This immediately makes philosophy the enemy of all who think they have the completed answers. I just want to say that nothing I can say today in this address conveys what it means to teach philosophy. Teaching philosophy is of the greatest difficulty, and is always the most fragile sort of teaching; it is this questioning that is the first thing that is destroyed when teaching is destroyed, yet nothing admits of its easy expression. I wish only to try to convey that teaching philosophy is ineffable, that it cannot be measured or compared, that it reduces to no model or method, and that I still have a long way to go to be a better practioner of it. Teaching philosophy is to get people in a position whereby they can remain open to the possibility of questioning, as it is itself a question, the most open of open questions.

Teaching philosophy means, at least in part, to never give up on the question. I would wish also to say, without making the point too precious, that the restrictions on us in my time this evening, on speaking too hastily about questioning, is precisely what threatens the question, in that we wish to get to it too quickly, that we want to see teaching only as a vehicle for the successful transmission of information. Americans spend more time on their abs than on their questions. And that this threat exists wherever teaching and learning is happening, that the question gets reduced to its basic elements for the purposes of efficiency, that it get reduced to outcomes, to computational models, to systems which distort it into a mere economic transaction. Or that what I am speaking about applies only to the teaching of something like philosophy, and not other subjects, as if philosophy was something other than other subjects, and not just those subjects at their deepest levels. As if philosophy cornered the market on the question, which is of course not the case. Indeed it is often the case that the question is best preserved in fields other than philosophy.

Today higher education's version of teaching the question is, to put it charitably, circumscribed. Universities tend to become a collection of programs and institutes, having nothing to do with each other, having separate ideologies, budgets, and ideals, with no unifying principles sustained by the values of questioning. If to most thinkers a university represents an island of intellectual anarchy, to the enemies of teaching it is an enterprise akin to a corporation staffed by team players who develop public credibility by the homogeneity, rather than diversity, of their speculations. The rise of "distance learning" reduces teaching to ephemeral digitalized transactions made by way of electronic screens. Boards of Trustees make the non-christian questions unwelcome. What is lost is a fidelity to the question.

I do not so much "teach philosophy" as I try to foster an experience with the question. This is the essence of thinking. Thinking is what happens when we enter into an essential solitude. What is it to think within this space? Thinking belongs to a language which no one speaks, which is addressed to no one, which has no center, and which reveals nothing. To belong to this region means to lose yourself, to enter into an indeterminate existence where one no longer occupies any site or position. To think into the question is not to put one's answer on one's resume, but is to live a kind of exile. The thinker does not live except in the space of this exigency. You do not ask the question, it asks you; it imposes itself; it invades the space that surrounds and protects you. It is an intervention, an interruption. The question is also an opening unto profound moral responsibility. Responsibility takes the form of an exposure, being exposed to something other. Thinking is foresakenness, not by others but by oneself. It is to be carried away by a worldless existence, being at a loss, wandering in a place that is not a world. It is exilic. It is fundamentally a detour. To be in the question is to be dispossessed, turned out of oneself, to identify oneself with errancy and drift. Thus teaching thinking, teaching the question, is not to promise some return on the investment with compound interest. To the myth of Odysseus returning from Ithaca, thinking opposes the story of Abraham, leaving forever. Thinking the question is a departure without return.

Thinking is located in proximity to utmost questioning. Heidegger in his inaugural address said: What is most thought-provoking in these thought-provoking times is that hardly anyone is doing any thinking. I would paraphrase in my own by saying: What is most questionable in these questionable-times is that hardly anyone is doing any questioning. Taking our cue from the highest office in the land, we somnambulate through a wounded world, pausing only to ask the most superficial of questions. Thus questioning is at once most important and most fragile. How can questions maintain their welcome? Does the University still welcome the question? How does one welcome that which is foreign to it, without requiring final answers? Would that not translate the question of the stranger into the answers of the host?

What does it mean to ask whether or not questioning has come to an end? This is a moment of the gravest perplexity. The attention paid to the question is today called forth by its forgetting. Too many among us have forgotten to question. Not the kind of questioning that occurs in which the answer is projected in advance: the pseudo-question. We must always identify what is highest and best in questioning. Being a guardian of the question is a kind of piety. The degree to which the question that I pose is welcome is the degree to which my inaugural address appropriately inaugurates anything at all.

My fundamental philosophical stance is one of questioning. I am not one who is seeking to provide many answers. Instead I teach people to ask questions. In order to be able to really ask a question, one must move away from the craving for certainty that pervades what passes for questioning today. My approach to teaching then is little more than an attempt to move towards the position where it is yet possible to question. If one seeks intellectual comfort, if one seeks upholsterings for their fully furnished worldviews, one should probably go elsewhere than my classes, and they usually do. Opposition to questioning is always great— as Simone Weil put it once, there are many who would rather kill another human being than to ask questions.

My fear is that questioning itself is in danger of coming to an end. That happens when questioning itself becomes no longer questionable. That we think we already know what it is, and we are bored with our command over the proliferation of our electronic screens. Imagine, a university without questions. Maybe the privilege of questioning itself has gone too long unquestioned. Perhaps we are at a time in which all significant questions have been asked, and now there is nothing but electronically stored information. The greatest possible vigilance is required here. What is highest and best in thought is the question. Yet there is a lack of interest, an indifference, a lack of need for the question.

Perhaps the most fundamental question is why question? The particular content of the question is, however, despite appearances, not of great significance. For if one could ask the question simply by muttering the words, there would be no reason why we could not provide an answer. The point of the question, one might say, is in its form rather than its specific content. To merely state the interrogative sentence, to merely type the keyboard figure, is not yet to question. The point of asking the question is thus to discover questioning, and the question chosen is not chosen because it is the question, but because it forces us to move towards this fundamental attitude. In choosing the question "Why question?" I hope to unsettle the normal understanding of a question as a query with a discrete goal and thereby open up a wholly new region of concern. The point of my philosophical life and teaching, so far as it has amounted to anything, has been to get students, if only for a brief time, not just to ask questions but to live questioningly.

Central to all philosophical questions is that they question themselves; by attempting to ask these questions, I attempt to ask the question that underlies any particular question. The question that underlies all questioning is a kind of self-questioning unlike any other. To question questioning looks like a frivolous repetition of the same interrogative formulation, like an empty and unwarranted brooding over words. No doubt that is how it looks. The question is only whether we wish to be taken in by this superficial look and so regard the whole matter as settled, or whether we are capable of finding a significant event in this recoil of the question upon itself. The point is to not perceive this question as arising rather irritatingly in a few abstruse areas of thought, but as being present everywhere anyone teaches if only it could be uncovered. Thus I seek not to bring attention to a tedious logical conundrum, which might be solved in the manner of a crossword puzzle; rather, I wish to indicate an arena which I believe remains hidden, although trapped within our present frameworks for questioning. I have learned to ignore the logical puzzles of self-referentiality of my more analytical colleagues: We ought not to permit the validity of our inquiry to rest on whether it can avoid a paradox, as though, like Oedipus, we could not find our way without first solving riddles.

To question at all is the question of all authentic questions, i.e., of all self-questioning questions, and whether consciously or not it is necessarily implicit in every question. It can never be objectively determined whether anyone, whether we, really ask this question, that is whether we make the leap, or never get beyond a verbal formula. It is in the light of this self-questioning that leads me to deny the possibility of easily describing the purpose or object of philosophy. There is no way of determining once and for all in advance what the task of philosophical questioning is, and accordingly what must be expected of it. Every stage and every beginning of its development bears within it its own law.

To question questioning itself is to open a space in which the possibility of questioning is examined and the experience of questioning described. The point of departure for any university student worthy of the name is legitimated first and foremost and only from the possibility, the experience, the structure, and the regulated modifications of the question. The role of a university should not be to furnish people merely with employment or with worldviews. How at a university, the only institution left which holds open the possibility of the question, do we, without confirming it a priori and circularly, question this inscription in the structure of that from which we will have received our most minimal and yet most secure determination?

It will now be apparent why an attempt to easily describe my purpose and the object of my approach to philosophy and its teaching is beset with fundamental difficulty, for at the root of the project is the view that the purpose and object of philosophy must remain obscure. As has been done, one might say that my aim is to question. As it stands, that appears similar in character to the common perception of philosophy. However, if it were known what questioning consists of, there would be no need to seek to question. My questioning involves the question of what it is to question, and in the unsettling return of the question upon itself we may yet capture sight of the nature of questioning. As the question returns it makes that which appeared clear now elusive, and in that elusiveness there is an indication of what questioning involves. This indication, however, must always recede, for as soon as it reaches the point of an understanding, it has lost the character of questioning.

We must always return to the question. In so far as the questioner must be able to effect in relation to what is questioned a kind of withdrawal, he or she is not subject to the causal order of the world. Every question is a detachment, a refutation of universal determinism. When one questions one sets oneself into question, effecting a relation to that which is questioned. Questioning itself plays no part in logic—it is not a grammatical part of propositions; rather, it is marked by a pre-judicative attitude. In posing the question I stand facing what is questioned and this relation to what is questioned is itself a relation of what is questioned.

Maybe it is better that questions be fragments. Questions are often outside of some whole, some community. When we believe everything has been said, the best question is fragmentary. In an accomplished system or totality of answers, an ideally completed ideology worthy of launching wars to defend, only the question maintains the possibility of thinking. The forbidden question is often the most important. Those who forbid the question of course do so because it is about them that we might end up asking.

I thus stand before you this afternoon to report that my philosophical orientation has been one wherein I find the greatest preservation of the question, in existentialism, in phenomenology, in hermeneutics, those orientations which do fullest justice to the sanctity, the piety, the sacredness, of the question. I wish to inaugurate a place that welcomes such a question, that both poses questions and allows itself to be put into question. I ask: is it possible to be inhospitable toward the question? That what is welcomed before all questions here at Ashland is not the primordial welcoming? Does this place still welcome questions?

Questioning is a gift. The question is the condition for the possibility of the university. A true gift is something for which one receives nothing in return. The gift interrupts the economy of exchange. The gift suspends economic calculation. The gift of the question is without relation. The question will always appear to us as a stranger. At Ashland I will remain the stranger from Plato's Sophist. The question from such a stranger, before it is thematized, before designating a concept, is the question of the stranger. Everything opens up over the threshold of the question. Does welcome consist in the questioning of the one who has arrived? Or does it begin with the unquestioned welcome? The question of the question is inseparable from the question of its welcome. The stranger puts forward the question of parricide, contests the Parmenedian thesis. Like every parricide, this one takes place in the family. A stranger can commit parricide only if he is welcomed as family to begin with.

I would then like merely to have my inaugural lecture inaugurate a welcoming of the question. That the kind of teaching and questioning I am about is not welcomed by measurement, undetectable by outcomes assessment, has nothing to do with method, and resists articulation, and what I entrust trustees to defend. That teaching of the kind I describe is yet possible at Ashland. Teaching is itself in question, it is something about which we still know very little, and yet is something on which almost everything depends. It is necessary that we grow toward meeting its possibilities, and that we take only the most difficult steps toward such a thought, for this is the fundamental manner in which we must hold ourselves if we are to do justice to its calling. To my computer-room interlocutor on whether or not my remarks have shed any light ("no light, no light, no light") I want to answer yes, but only a little. The best questioners are those who see just enough to prefer the dark. Shedding too much light tends to cast shadows.

II. Beinger than Being is Being Itself:
A *Beiträge* Primer

Jen: Another magnificent text from Heidegger has emerged in English. For years the *Beiträge* was discussed in hushed tones as being a triumphant and as yet untilled masterpiece by the greatest thinker of the 20th century.

Ben: Heidegger seems to have joined that rare circle of thinkers who become quite prolific after their deaths. As this is a Heidegger primer, I assume you have summoned me for yet another lunchtime lesson on how to read this difficult thinker. One problem I have always had, however, is that often the Heidegger scholar is as impenetrable as the original he seeks to explicate. Thus for our dialogue to continue I wish to restrict our discussion to one paragraph from Heidegger, and restrict your clarificatory points to but a few paragraphs at a time. If something cannot be said in a few paragraphs, it ought not to be said.

Jen: I am not sure about these restrictions on our discussion. Parsimony is not really the strength of many German thinkers, or of thinking in general, but I will try to accommodate you. Perhaps you could give me some signal if my paragraphs become too long.

Ben: Nor do I want any wisecracks about my attention span. If you wish this dialogue published, its expression must be economical enough for its medium. There is a larger philosophical point to my requirement, as a check against the needless, almost hurtfully obscure traffic jams of prefixes and suffixes into which usually anyone speaking about Heidegger falls.

Jen: If we allow the publishing medium to dictate the content of our thinking, then actual thinking is already at a disadvantage. I will agree on the condition that our discussion does not in the end fall to a reductionist analysis of Heidegger's connections with the NSDAP.

Ben: Now who is the one putting actual thinking at a disadvantage? I conditionally agree to these parameters, although such silences will surely haunt our undertaking. Here is the passage, from the *Beiträge*. As I know some German, I took the liberty of providing a man-on-the-street translation, which follows.[1]

219. *Die Fuge der Frage nach der Wahrheit*

Die Wahrheit ist das ursprünglich Wahre.
Das Wahre ist das Seiendste.
> *Seiender als jedes Seiende ist das Seyn selbst. Das Seiendste "ist" nicht*
> *mehr, sondern west als die Wesung (Ereignis).*

Das Seyn west als Ereignis.
> *Das Wesen der Wahrheit ist die lichtende Verbergung das Ereignisses.*
> *Die lichtende Verbergung west als Gründung des Da-seins; Gründung*
> *aber zweideutig.*
> *Die Gründung des Da-seins geschieht als Bergung der Wahrheit in das*
> *Wahre, das so erst wird.*

Das Wahre läßt das Seiende seiend sein.
> *Wenn das Seiende so in das Da hereinsteht, wird es vor-stell-bar. Die*
> *Möglichkeit und Notwendigkeit des Richtigen ist gründet.*

Die Richtigkeit ist ein unumgänglicher Ableger der Wahrheit.
> *Wo die Richtigkeit daher die "Idee" von Wahrheit vorbestimmt, sind alle*
> *Wege zu ihrem Ursprung verschüttet.*

219. The Fugue of the Question Concerning Truth

Truth is the originally true.
Truth is the Beingest.
> Beinger than any being is Being itself. The Beingest "is" no
> more, but essences the event of happening.

Being essences as the event of happening.
> The essence of truth is the clearing hiding of the happening.
> The clearing hiding essences as the grounding of the being-
> there; however the grounding is ambiguous.
> The founding of being-there happens as recovery of the Truth
> into the true which only thus becomes.

The true lets the being be.
> If the being stands thus into the There it becomes re-present-
> able. The possibility and necessity of correctness is grounded.

The correctness is an unavoidable consequence of the truth.
> Where correctness predetermines the "idea" of the truth all
> ways to its origin are blocked.

Jen: You have selected an interesting passage, and provide an admirable attempt at a translation. I will provide the translation from the version recently published in English.[2]

219. Jointure of the Question of Truth

Truth is what is originally true.
What is true is the most-being.
>More-being than any being is be-ing itself. The most-being "is" no longer but rather holds sway as essential swaying (enowning).
Be-ing holds sway as enowning.
>The essential sway of truth is the sheltering-concealing of enowning that lights up.
>The sheltering concealing that lights up holds sway as grounding of Da-sein; but grounding is ambiguous.
>The grounding of Da-sein occurs as sheltering truth in what is true, which in this way first becomes what it is.
What is true lets a being be a being.
>When a being thus stands in the t/here [Da], it becomes re-present-able. The possibility and necessity of what is correct is grounded.
Correctness is an unavoidable offshoot of truth.
>Therefore, where correctness pre-determines the "idea" of truth, all ways to its origin is blocked.

Ben: Now the passage I have selected obviously has to do with truth, and I wish to begin with the last few lines, and work backward. It seems clear Heidegger is saying something about what makes "truth-as-correctness" possible, that it is an unavoidable consequence, and that this "truth-as-correctness" may well block all ways to the origin of truth. So perhaps you could give me some background on this idea of "truth-as-correctness."

Jen: To put it simply, Heidegger believed that our thinking about truth had undergone successive subterranean transformations which had secretly dictated its course for centuries. His thinking might best be seen under the rubric of a critique of anthropocentric modernity; the essence of modernity appears to him as a narrowing of the domain of inclusion within which the basis of truth can be thought. If this narrowing ultimately gave rise to the contemporary placing of man at the center of all things and the overlaying of all truth with an anthropological significance, where, in a wholly humanized world, all extra-human references forfeit their meaning, the condition of possibility of this development must be traced back to the quest that distinguishes the modern character of the contemporary world. However distant the original aim of this quest might have been from a contemporary anthropocentric orientation, Heidegger seeks to identify the preconditions of modernity with the specific variation in the approach to truth, which required that man set himself up by his own means and with his own capacities to render certain and secure his human-being in the midst of beings as a totality.

This metamorphosis in the early modern world takes the form of a rethinking of the essence of man qua subject in relation to the truth of beings as a totality. Modernity signified a reinterpretation of the "idea" in terms of the constitutive activity of the subject as the foundation on which the representation of the object depends. On this foundation truth related in a different way to judgment as the locus of conformity (or correctness) between the idea and that which it apprehends, for the notion of conformity itself was at once conceived on a more limited basis and reinforced: the cognitive representation not only confirmed but, as its condition of possibility, constituted the objectivity of the object. In its modern guise the role of the subject became paramount with the ascension of the language of certitude -- the expression of the object in its bare relation to the representation of the subject -- to the capacity of designation of the criteria of truth per se.

Ben: So when in the last line Heidegger speaks of "correctness" pre-determining the idea of truth, what he means is that a "way of thinking" about truth has gotten covered over by an inferior, or at least a different, way of thinking about truth, and this covering has become encrusted so as to pre-determine our thinking about truth. It is interesting how Emad and Maly insert a "therefore," in this passage, as if this subjective poetic insight of Heidegger's conveyed a kind of logical inference.

Jen: The insertion of "therefore" may be simply to capture a certain movement of thinking in the passage. It would seem to me to be a mistake to reduce this insight to a mere "subjective poetic insight" of Heidegger's. The philosophical defense of this line of thought in regard to truth is spread across many of his texts, but begins in full force with Heidegger's famous treatment in *Being and Time* of the way logical assertions are confirmed with an interpretation of the

Greek word *aletheia*. There Heidegger sought to indicate how the traditional conception of truth as an *adequatio* or correspondence of understanding and thing arises in Avicenna, but presupposes, and thus could be shown to derive from, some more primordial Greek notion of truth. This was to be shown by phenomenological description: only if the thing shows itself can there be a comparison between understanding and thing. Heidegger recalls two passages from the first book of Aristotle's *Metaphysics* where Parmenides is described first as compelled to follow what showed itself in itself, the phenomena, and secondly as compelled by *aletheia*. In *Being and Time*, Heidegger reads *aletheia* as a privative expression— as *a-letheia*— so that the Greek privative alpha is taken to indicate that unconcealment always takes the form of a kind of robbery; that is, concealment is not simply opposed to unconcealment as if beings were snatched from truth; rather, concealment always accompanies unconcealment. I have sought to explain this to you over many a lunchtime.[3]

Ben: You call this a "philosophical" defense, but it is only an etymological defense. I see the connections, up to a point. "Correctness predetermining the Idea of the truth" is Heidegger's jab at the representational way of thinking about truth. So that is why he writes *vor-stell-bar* the way he does, with the hyphens, to emphasize how all thinking of truth as representation, idea, or correctness of proposition or judgment fails to think truth in its "originary" way. So that means that the earlier lines of this passage would suggest that there is a way to think truth without succumbing to any of these representational, metaphysical ways. Putting it in somewhat Kantian terms, there is a way of thinking about truth which can reveal that which makes "truth-as-correctness" possible.

Jen: Yes. A greater philosophical defense can be filled out and confirmed with recourse to the history of philosophy. Heidegger elsewhere provides treatments of Descartes and Plato, not to mention many other thinkers, along similar lines. To be certain is to be certain for the knowing subject. An entity is an *ens certum* insofar as it can be known with certainty, that is, insofar as it can be secured in representation. Descartes derives from his first great discovery, the indubitability of the *ego cogito*, the principle of truth -- that judgments about entities are true insofar as an entity is grasped clearly and distinctly. But the availability of the object for certain representation is the availability of the object for the subject's calculation. What manifests itself initially as a purely "theoretical" interest in secure knowledge is at the same time an interest in securing and calculating, for the object is only knowable with security and certainty if it is secure for the subject. That knowledge must be certain means that reality must be secure for the knower in order to be acknowledged as real. The knowledge in which the object is secure and certain for the subject, in which the subject secures the object, reveals itself in the modern tradition as the knowledge which is identical to the ability to manipulate and control. The object which admits of certainty, then, is an object which in principle lies within the domain of will. The ultimate certainty comes to power when the object is whatever it is willed to be. When Descartes turns inward, he discovers his self as a constantly present entity that guarantees the presence of other things. The self is always co-present with any other mental content. Its constantly available self-presence is paradigmatic of what it means for something to be. The self that Descartes discovers is not merely present; it actively affirms its own presence as the being that gives other things their measure. From this perspective the difference between Descartes's immaterial souls and material objects is less than would appear, since both kinds of entities have constant available presence as their fundamental mode of being. But the self goes beyond this in actively relating itself to itself. Heidegger contends that the modern self affirms itself in and through its mensurative capacities, in and through its giving measure to other beings. To be a subject in the modern sense is precisely to be capable of bringing things to presence before oneself as a collection of objects. This representation is a making present under the discipline of the subject's view to form an orderly picture of the world. Modern subjectivity exists as a subject when it imposes order. To impose a self-originated order on other things is an act of will. Modern subjectivity's self-affirmation expresses its power to control the conditions of representation; the modern self in its mensurative role affirms itself as will.

Ben: It is only by emphasizing the Descartes of the *Rules* over the Descartes of the *Principles*, however, that Heidegger can say some of the things he does. It is simply doubtful to my mind whether Heidegger successfully justifies his claim that the modern self becomes the central entity in all modern metaphysical schemes. In Descartes the self may be the first entity whose reality is assured, but it is not metaphysically basic in the order of causality or even in the order of analogy. This is true for other thinkers who, like Descartes, deploy the Aristotelian distinction between what is basic in knowledge and what is basic in reality. In this sense, Heidegger tries to make Descartes more "modern" than he really is. He no doubt makes recourse to further suspect etymological arguments regarding Plato's conception of truth.

Jen: Heidegger's analysis of Plato is controversial, but that something is controversial is not necessarily to reject it as suspect. According to Heidegger, the pre-Socratics were "intuited" or looked at by the entities themselves—they had a more originary relation to Being. With Plato, however, humanity took on the role of viewer. What became important was the way of catching sight of the *eidos*, the right mode of "seeing." The stages which marked one's journey from out of the darkness of the cave toward the sunlight, then, involved the forming (*Bildung*) of correctness of vision. Here there arose the idea of *homoeisis*, the correct correspondence between the outward appearance (*eidos*) and perception of that appearance. For Heidegger, Plato's doctrine of truth promoted "humanism," the view according to which humanity establishes itself as the authoritative entity among entities. Humanism, then, began the long process whereby humanity understood itself not in terms of a subservient relationship to being, but instead in terms of a governing relationship to entities.[4]

 Ben: I do not really want to get into a discussion regarding Heidegger's Descartes or Plato interpretations, as those are not the texts before us, although Heidegger's "method" in those discussions is probably as questionable as what is before us in the *Beitrage*. Of greater concern is this whole approach. I am not the first to wince at Heidegger's use of various strategies, specifically his use of etymological inquiry, and the weight he places on Latin mistranslations, all of which seem very questionable. How can he draw such serious conclusions from what appear to many to be merely little stories that he tells? Why could one not, for example, challenge Heidegger's remarks with similar "phenomenological" descriptions which yield the exact opposite conclusions? Glassy-eyed obedience to such etymologizing seems to have spawned legions of bad imitators. What is the status of such an enterprise, and how does one validate the truth of these claims? To what extent do we allow to go unchecked Heidegger's self-assurance that he alone was endowed with prophetic insight into the originary meanings of words? Surely no self-respecting classical Greek scholar would take such musings seriously.

Jen: You must not read a lot of contemporary theory! A famous example of a "self-respecting scholar" taking Heidegger's etymological insights seriously (during his lifetime) was with the Greek philologist Paul Friedländer's arguments against Heidegger in Chapter XI of his *Plato*, which elicited a nominal recantation by Heidegger of some of his interpretations of *aletheia* in the texts of antiquity.[5] Heidegger acknowledged that the word *aletheia* does not undergo a radical change in Plato, namely from unconcealment to correctness. The latter signification is present in archaic usage, in Heraclitus, Hesiod, and Homer. In his retraction Heidegger goes so far as to affirm that the noun never was understood to mean a process of unconcealment; neither in the poets, nor in everyday parlance, not even in philosophy, did it signify anything but correctness and trustworthiness. The word *aletheia*, which Heidegger translated as *Unverborgenheit*, essentially conceals itself, buries its roots. By Heidegger's reasoning, this concealment only confirms the presence of *lethe*, the presence of absence, of oblivion, at the "heart" of truth. Friedländer's attack on Heidegger's etymology he subsequently retracted, since new evidence revealed instances in the *Iliad* where *aletheia* does mean unhidden. He likewise recognizes this meaning in Heraclitus, whose *paranomasia* reflects a widely felt connection between *aletheia* and *lethe*, though this does not prove that the former signified unconcealment in Heidegger's sense. There is no suggestion in Heidegger's writings that the distinctive role of the Greeks in the history of being is one that can be established only by a detailed philological comparison of the verb "to be" in Greek and in other languages. Comparisons of this kind have been carried out, however, with results claiming to support Heidegger's general thesis about the Greeks.

Ben: Please direct yourself to my question of what the status is of such an enterprise, and how one validates the truth of these claims. Heidegger's interpretations of other thinkers are legendary for their doing violence to the traditional interpretations of texts.

Jen: It is not entirely fair to criticize Heidegger's interpretations along the same lines as other traditional interpretations. In fact such criticism only accuses Heidegger of doing imperfectly what he does not do at all. The complaint that he is unfaithful to the text or insufficiently sensitive to the context in which things are said fundamentally misunderstands the intention of his own project, which aims at recovering not what was thought but what was left unthought, not the intention of the author but the intention of being itself, as it were, as the dark and incomprehensible destiny that operates in and through the text and the context. This does not mean that we cannot criticize Heidegger's interpretations but only that we cannot criticize him merely on a textual or contextual basis. Instead, one must determine whether his whole mode and conception of interpretation is valid and whether it can achieve the goal he sets for it.

Heidegger's conception of interpretation is fundamentally bound up with his conception of being and history. It is concerned not merely with the right and wrong reading of a text or historical situation but with the fundamental ontological transformation that occurs in and through this text or situation. Heidegger thus strives to think not what was thought, not the "historical truth," but what was left unthought, what could not be thought because it was concealed by the prevailing goal and tradition. His retrieval of past thought thus always is the establishment of a new tradition that is necessarily at odds with the old one and so always fails to "do justice" to it. Interpretation or hermeneutics is in this sense an act of creation that is carried out in response to the revelation of being itself, and thus rises above the constraints imposed by the demand for historical accuracy.

Ben: A problem with this is that, in the first instance, a determination of what was left unthought would seem to presuppose the antecedent retrieval of what was actually thought. Without such a retrieval it is difficult to see how Heidegger could come to know that he has really come to the unthought. So while one cannot demand of Heidegger that he actually produce an accurate interpretation of what was thought, one might ask him what is the difference between the thought and the unthought.

Jen: Heidegger's response would be the following: not only is it unnecessary or inappropriate to try to recover the original meaning of a text or an event, it is in fact impossible, since the meaning or the significance of every text and every event is dependent upon the ontology that is itself characterized by the prevailing revelation of Being. The original meaning thus is no longer retrievable because both the text and context are no longer retrievable since both are no longer as they were. Similarly, our attempts to do so are in fact projections of our own technological way of understanding things. Heidegger's goal was to try to reflect back to us that very impulse.

Heidegger's hermeneutic rests upon the assumption that there is no eternal truth which can be grasped everywhere nor even an absolute moment out of which the whole can be completely comprehended. For Heidegger, every age understands the truth and therefore being. Each revelation, however, is exclusive and conceals all other ontological possibilities. Each age only understands one way of being and always necessarily reinterprets the truth of all other ages in terms of its own revelation.

Ben: So the original meaning of this *Beitrage* passage before is unavailable to us? What is it then we are bickering about? Heidegger's project appears in the light of a millenarianism dependent on a judeo-christian eschatology, pointing not to a single necessary future but the continual revelation of new futures by being. However, as far as being able to determine interpretation from creation, Heidegger has little to say. I have waited in vain for the rules that would allow one to differentiate an authentic revelation from mere caprice. Each revelation may be characterized by concealment and thus error. I know we are not to bring up the Nazism issues, but how one distinguishes a true revelation of being from capricious and demagogic ones is something to which Heidegger seemingly has no possible response. There is no standard of responsibility for authentic interpretation, since it is wholly given up to the service of "Being." One criticism which must stand against Heidegger along these lines is his messianic insistence that he alone possessed the insights into the secrets of being and the essence of language. In portraying all other accounts as superficial or derivative, he depicts his own accounts of Western history as the standard against which all other accounts were to be measured. Despite his criticism of the one-track thinking at work within metaphysics, Heidegger himself is guilty of it to a great degree, by reading all of Western history and all Western thinkers and artists and poets in a way that forced them into his powerful but limited conceptual grid. But let us return to our subject, which yields absurdities as in the third line of the passage we presumably are still discussing, where Heidegger mentions how "Beinger than being is being itself, and it being the "Being-est" thing there is," and so forth. Are you suggesting that we take such a line seriously, and not invoke the kinds of objections Carnap raised against such nonsense in the 1920's? What about all of this making up of words? Orwell must be turning over in his grave at such obscurantism. This fuels the objections which claim Heidegger's thinking to be a Clinton-like self-exculpation from Nazism.[6]

Jen: There are those who have understandably seen these etymological maneuvers as a means for Heidegger to reinterpret key philosophical concepts as he wishes, and undeniably there are times when his "arguments from etymology" are stronger than at others. However, surely one can see how the function of his interpretations runs parallel to his overall philosophical project.

By seeking the original meaning of a term Heidegger will often give the impression that he is thereby uncovering the true sense of the word. It should be apparent that Heidegger cannot be interpreted as seeking to provide a definitive account of the truth in any straightforward sense. The main function of his etymological analysis is therefore to shake one's reliance on immediately available concepts, and breathe life into what have become empty categories. Etymology is thus a means of escape from the vacuousness of contemporary language, including contemporary philosophical language. Etymology does not therefore provide a correct vision of the meaning of the term, but is employed by Heidegger to unsettle the husks of meaning that surround us. That comic third line is just Heidegger "twisting the knife" somewhat, loosening the grip we think we have on words like "being."

When Heidegger takes a word "etymologically," he takes it against the flow or grain of the idiom, an idiom never true to its origins. An etymology is, rhetorically, a figure of speech that consists in taking a familiar expression strangely, not that the strangeness takes the form of some repressed or forgotten "original sense." But neither does this mean that Heidegger is really privileging some originary sense. There never was such a sense if by that is meant a time when etymology determined use. There was never anything but idiom, there was no time of pristine, undisseminated or fixed meaning. I think what Heidegger means by "originary" here just is a sense of dissemination, a difference from the customary and fixed, as in obsolete words or repressed senses of expressions no longer in use, or in an unheard-of play upon words that comes out of the "infelicity" of speech. To imagine a people somewhere actually speaking etymologically is comic.

Ben: Heidegger's knife-twisting stretches my patience and charitability in following him beyond all limits. Returning again to the comic third line, why does Heidegger refer to *Sein* as *Seyn*? That word is not in my German dictionary. Is this going to be another word-invention or etymological maneuver concerning "being" by Heidegger for which I will need recourse to the Brothers Grimm?

Jen: Yes, I'm afraid. In *Being and Time* Heidegger had used the term *eigentlich* to refer to authenticity; in his lectures on Hölderlin, this becomes "relation to Being" (*Bezug zum Seyn*). Dasein always stands in relation to Being (*Sein*). Evasion into inauthenticity also belongs to that relation. *Bezug zum Sein* becomes *Bezug zum Seyn* if it is explicitly grasped—in other words, authentically lived.

Henceforth, and as can be seen here in the *Beitrage*, Heidegger writes *Seyn* with a "y" (a spelling in use a few hundred years earlier) whenever he means the "authentic" relation that deifies Dasein in this sense. He uses this term in other works of the period as well, such as the Schelling essay. To perform an etymology on a word is to take it as a pun. This is what he is doing with many of his etymologies, for example, in the case of *Denken*, *Gedächtes*, and *Gedanke* in *What Is Called Thinking?* where Heidegger hears the echo or hint of the Old German *Gedanc*, where thinking and thanking intersect. It is another way of making the point that thinking has more to do with receptivity and openness than with reasoning in the sense of representational-calculative operations of description and explanation. Thinking is more like listening than questioning or probing or proving or building or dismantling. Perhaps this explains your impatience.[7]

Ben: These interpretations and translations of Greek terms were evidently intended to preserve equivalence but for Heidegger failed to do so. Now when someone misinterprets and mistranslates a word like *aletheia*, it would ordinarily be said that that person has taken the word in question in a certain way that happens to be mistaken. This way of describing the matter imputes an element of agency to the person responsible for misunderstanding the meaning of the original word. But Heidegger does not seem at all willing to treat such erroneous renderings simply as matters of conceptual history understood as the takings and mis-takings of historical individuals. Rather, conceptual history is only the manifestation of a sequence of shifts that "Being" itself brings about, not the historical thinkers whose names have been associated with them, as for example that of Cicero mistranslating Greek philosophical terms into the Roman world. For Heidegger, if such a thinker mistranslates *aletheia* it is because "Being" has disclosed itself to him and to his age differently, and his translation merely registers that change. Thus for Heidegger "mere translations" occasion epochal changes of great magnitude -- in them unobtrusively speak the "destiny of being." This might leave one with the vulgar image that, when Cicero mistranslated various Greek terms for being, it was "Being" itself "guiding his pen" to mistake itself for something quite different.

Jen: That was indeed a vulgar image. You still seem hung up on how the central aim or goal of Heidegger's thought has been named Being, the being of Being, and the Being of beings. To name it with apparent simplicity, however, is to give the false impression that here one is to be engaged in the consideration of something which can be observed and described. Thus while it is true that Heidegger's work is in a sense concerned with that topic, it is also one that, you would agree, goes by many names. The difficulty one has in trying to define or describe the subject to which Heidegger addresses himself is due in part to the extent to which Heidegger toils to free his thinking from the residual effects of metaphysical thinking. When Heidegger speaks of "Being" the inclination is to want to know precisely what he means, even generally what he means. However, what Heidegger was at pains to show, and what this *Beitrage*-passage before us seeks to indicate, is that the meaning of Being is systematically elusive. It is at the same time highly determinate and totally indeterminate. There are times when one is then tempted to think that Being is almost defined as that which is hidden or elusive or ineffable. But any account or description of this central topic will be seen to undermine itself and appear in the process to disintegrate.

Ben: Your account of all of this then admittedly and immediately involves Heidegger's understanding of Being in logical contradiction. Any description of Being must fail since it is that which necessarily eludes our present mode of thought -- and even this negative description of Being, as that which cannot be described, must be equally unsettled by its own self-denial. It is almost as if this poetic negativity, if you will, which in *Being and Time* at least was kept within bounds and halted before it undermined the conceptual distinctions entirely, is slowly unleashed. While in *Being and Time* we move towards uncovering the meaning of Being and do not arrive, nevertheless Being itself appears to retain a coherent character. Seemingly from 1930 on, Being has taken on a more paradoxical character. It proves to be totally indeterminate and at the same time highly determinate. From the standpoint of the usual logic we have here an obvious contradiction.

Jen: You make it sound as if Heidegger were unaware of this hermeneutic circle. In point of fact, he would of course wish to make sure you were as well aware of the ontological commitments of your criticism, namely, that something that contradicts itself need not be taken seriously, that what contradicts cannot be. That Heidegger is questioning the metaphysical foundations of truth at work in contradictions should not be to grant him license to just tell stories, but neither need it consign his work to oblivion. With such a thinker, there will be maddening practices. After the war Heidegger uses the technique of writing the word "Being" with a line through it, to indicate that one is not to take the word as referring to an object that has a unitary character. Still later, the use of the term is abandoned, replaced with a series of alternatives. You are correct in identifying the gradual abandonment of the conceptual distinctions of *Being and Time*. That is co-extensive with Heidegger's increasing stress on the role and importance of language. The subsequent centrality that Heidegger gives to the topic of language is due not only to language's being seen to provide the space for Being, but also all that follows in its wake. For to make the claim that "it is in words and language that things first come into Being and are" is to use language. Only through language are we able to talk of "Being" at all. "Being" is only a word. If it is through language that we have Being, then it is language which gives Being to the word "Being." At this point it is no longer clear what is meant by either "language" or "Being." It is as if through language there miraculously is something, and yet it is unclear what that something is -- since we remain caught within language in our attempt to describe that something.

Ben: The word-plays, etymological maneuvers, and questionable readings tempt me to dismiss Heidegger outright, and our cursory glance at this *Beitrage* passage contributes to this view. These lines do not formally shape themselves as a questioning or inquiry that pursue its subject as it would a prey or quarry or even an object of thought. There is to Heidegger's writing no movement, no plot, no progress toward a goal, not even the suggestion of effort. No wonder the editors added a "therefore" to the end of the passage. Otherwise the insights would have an even greater unrevised look about them that exasperates me. It is as if what we are reading is an improvisation, a thinking-out-loud in which there is no looking back, no going back over previous ground in order to remove what does not belong. I take offense at granting such primordiality to a thinker who does not bother to clean up after himself, who leaves behind within the text itself, rather than in smudged manuscripts in the desk drawer, the *Nachlass* of uncorrected thoughts.

Jen: These writings shape themselves as a listening, in which nothing happens, certainly nothing like an argument is advanced. There is nothing so active or strenuous as an intellectual movement against an adversary or a problem. The point in doing this is perhaps that our norms of rationality accustom us to the idea that thinking is something dynamic and aggressive -- being tough-minded, making impregnable, solid, or rigorous arguments, tackling hard cases, probing complex issues, undertaking strenuous tasks, taking bold positions, having strong views, overthrowing established opinions. Heidegger's essays are a response to all of this -- they do not function, operate, or proceed; they have no linear or chronological progression; they provide no innovation or breakthrough, and thus no advance, no emancipation from obsolescence. Their structure is purposefully other than that of getting things together and under control. Heidegger is violating one of your bourgeois taboos. What is purchased is supposed to be finished, concluded, in accordance with the mores of the exchange of commodities, where the customer insists that what is delivered to him at full price should embody the full quantity of labor for which he is paying the equivalent. If there is anything left to be done on what he buys, he feels cheated. The conceptual effort Heidegger expects simply qualititatively surpasses every customary standard of reception, and you hold it against him. If I were a Marxist, I would say that the fetish character of the commodity is the imperative of your reading. So the first requirement for reading Heidegger might be perhaps to rid oneself of these deeply rooted habits, which the content of Heidegger's thinking shows to be false anyway.

Ben: Of course what you now mean by false is subject to question. I am trying to be sensitive to how Heidegger employs self-referentiality so as to avoid hypostatizing "Being." The problem is I do not seem to be able to appeal to much stability even from you Heideggerians and your translations. For example, many authors of your ilk translate *Ereignis* as the event, or as appropriation, or simply leave it untranslated. You will recall I sought to translate it as "happening," that Being is not a thing but rather just happens, that there is nothing to it other than "its" happening. Now your *Beiträge* translators have come up with enowning. I see also they seek to translate *Wesen* not as essence but as holding-sway. I guess I can see why they would not wish to propagate metaphysical connotations with "essence," but I dare venture the following question, knowing fully how your answer will spew forth oceans of verbiage: why translate *Ereignis* as enowning, and what exactly does Heidegger mean by *ereignis*, by holding-sway, by all of this?

Jen: The first part of your question is simple enough, since leaving the word untranslated leaves it impossible to translate the family of words which Heidegger is making use of in the text, such as *Ereignung, Eignung, Zueignung, Übereignung*, and so forth. So the English translators sought to capture all of the interesting things Heidegger is doing within the German language regarding *ereignis* in ways that other translations do not capture. The second part of your question is of course very difficult.

Ben: I can start the ball rolling. You spoke earlier of how Heidegger rejects the primacy of self-consciousness in modernity. Man does not first have awareness of himself and then move from some inner sphere toward things. Humanity exists as the openness to things revealing a particular world of significance. To be aware of things, and of himself, humanity must already have a preconceptual understanding of their mode of being. That is why he substitutes "Dasein" for humanity in *Being and Time* and again here in the *Beitrage* passage.

Jen: Yes. In *Being and Time* Heidegger spoke in terms of humanity's receptive projection of the dimensions of lived time, whereby humanity both receives and projects the possibilities that make the texture of the world. Later he decided that this language still sounded too subjectivistic. He began to speak of humanity standing in the open space of the world. The opening of that space was not due to humanity's projections. Humanity did not make this clearing; it is not his creation. Humanity does not first exist and then extend an awareness that creates or receives the open space. A receptive standing in that space is what it means to be human and aware. The way humanity stands in the open is not by having concepts or theories but by being involved practically in his significant lived world with its characteristic modes of the mutual interpenetration of the dimensions of time. A being such as human existence is needed for things to be revealed, but it is not exactly the case to say that the open space requires some conscious being. This would make consciousness prior to the inhabitation of the open, but Heidegger is trying to describe what is prior to consciousness considered as a subject-object relation. What is needed is not a perceptive consciousness but a receptive abode for the open space of possibilities that make possible ordinary "Being."

Ben: This parallels in some ways discussions in the idealist tradition about the need to have consciousness (or perhaps language) in order for the world to take on meaning. In these cases consciousness or language is usually taken as a property belonging to man conceived as a being complete in itself, a "subject" in both the ancient and modern senses. I can see already how Heidegger would claim that his analysis in terms of man's necessary standing in the open undercuts any talk of consciousness or language as a property whose possession makes us human and gives meaning to the world.

Jen: Man does not possess the open space as a property; nor does man possess a relational property of standing within it. Man exists as standing within that space -- humanity just is the clearing, that receptive standing there, and is nothing before this. There is no foundation or substrate in man's being to which this is added. Again, space is no longer to be thought in terms of Kantian transcendental philosophy, as the spatial horizon projected by the subject in which objects can appear. That is why he uses *"Da hereinsteht,"* a here and a there. Instead we must see humanity itself appropriated by a region or opening which transcends the merely human and makes possible a non-anthropocentric clearing in which entities may gather each other into a mutual play that constitutes the worldhood of world.

Ben: So, when Heidegger says "The most-being "is" no longer but rather holds sway as essential swaying (enowning)," the most important thing to say about enowning, taken on its own, is that there is almost nothing to report about it. If *ereignis* had qualities of its own, they would need to be made available, unconcealed, ascribed with an "is." It would be some kind of entity among other entities, and the event of unconcealment, this new truth, would be missed. *Ereignis* itself cannot be an entity or event or relation among other entities. To think it as an entity is to perform the metaphysical transposition of the "wonder of unconcealedness" into the question about grounds and causes.

Jen: Yes. Be-ing holds sway as enowning. If it is not an entity in its own right, enowning does not have a structure, inner necessity, or law, or anything about it that could come to presence on its own. This means there is nothing in it or related to it that serves as a foundation for its occurrence. Therefore there is nothing about it to understand, as that word is commonly used. There is nothing hidden in it to be ferreted out, nothing to be analyzed, nothing to be used as a first principle or ground or as basis for an explanation. The opening of this free space for the appearance of things is not something that happens elsewhere. It happens not beyond or behind beings but, as it were, in front of them, it holds sway. As an opening of the space for the encounter with beings, *ereignis* allows things to rise out of the darkness. Heidegger himself puts it best. What remains to be said? Only this: enowning enowns [*Ereignis ereignet*].[8] It happens; it holds sway; that is all. It is the belonging together of humanity and the unconcealedness of beings. There is nothing further to "understand" or about which to "theorize."

Ben: So the occlusive nature of this "whatever it is" is covered over even in the grammar used in its description. His point is that enowning enowns the way the rain rains. One normally does not say 'the rain rains'; rather, one says "it rains" or "it is raining", where the pronoun "it", however, has no referent. One does not ask what it is that rains, because "it" is not anything at all, it is not an object of which raining can be predicated. "It" is a phantom subject of the predicate "rains": the subject has, in effect, withdrawn into the predicate. Withdrawal is an apt word choice, because the 'it' cannot be conceptualizable. So also with enowning in Heidegger's nonphilosophical sense of the word: enowning enowns is a locution from which the subject of the predicate withdraws itself, refuses itself as a conceptual or objective entity -- conceals itself in the "enowning."

Jen: Next when he says "The essential sway of truth is the sheltering-concealing of enowning that lights up," we understand the following. Before the term *Ereignis*, and at times later, Heidegger used the word *Sein*, "being," to designate the opening into unconcealment, as well as to talk about the meaning or sense that beings had when unconcealed in a particular way. Speaking in that way, Heidegger said that "being" refused itself and then kept its refusal to itself. The refusal, the turning away of being was itself hidden. It was this double hiddenness, this sheltering-concealing, and not our careless thinking that made possible the Western metaphysical transposition of the questioning unconcealment. We do not come to experience *ereignis* itself, as if it were some basic entity or mysterious happening that until now had not been noticed. We experience rather its hiddenness, its withdrawal, its sheltering-concealing, which is to say its character as not an entity. Then in hearing "The essential sway of truth is the sheltering-concealing of enowning that lights up / The sheltering concealing that lights up holds sway as grounding of Da-sein; but grounding is ambiguous," our experience of being already involved within *ereignis* is an experience of finitude. *Ereignis* is not an indeterminate openness waiting to be filled in; it has a particular character in each epoch. It is finite and limited. Heidegger means to recognize its finitude without contrasting it with possible total revelation. Unconcealedness happens only as finite possibilities. In order to make this change in our thought, Heidegger suggests we avoid images of illumination, which have been since Plato involved in contrasts of part and whole. He takes the German word *Lichtung*, which can mean "illumination, lighting," and usually uses it in another of its meanings, "a clearing in the woods, a place where light comes through the trees." The event opens up a clearing, makes things less heavy and close, allows light. The "clearing out" can be thought without reference to illumination. This image of clearing offers less temptation to imagine that there is a total clearing to be performed. There is no totality, no total view, no first or last word.

Ben: Is anything to be made of the idea of "clearing," then? Does Heidegger ever "get clear" about what the "clearing" is? I can probably reply with my own pun: The clearing is neither that about which nor from which we ever get clear. How does the grounding of Dasein now play a role?

Jen: We can become aware of the opening up of that realm, the "clearing," the extending out of that space, its happening as an event that appropriates us and things in a determinate way, but only on its own. We can experience ourselves and things being gathered into a particular constellation of this en-owning. When Heidegger next writes "The grounding of Da-sein occurs as sheltering truth in what is true, which in this way first becomes what it is," one might recall his remarks about the limitations built into death and nothingness. The cleared open space of *ereignis* remains as precariously finite as any of the descriptions of Dasein's being-toward-death. In *Being and Time* Heidegger argued that man was not a consciousness with an indefinite receptivity for objects but a definite openness within a finite happening of lived time and possibility. Man needed to give up the illusion that he was an object with a sturdy nature. Man must embrace the intrinsic limitations of his mortality. Death does not close off an indefinitely open field of possibilities; it is the expression of the limitation that opens a finite field. In place of grasping for the infinite and pretending to participate in something that grounded him, man must attain authenticity by accepting the groundless, limited facticity of his birth, tradition, and historical situation.

Ben: Death is the absolute futurity; it is the unforeseeable future that can never arrive, that can never become a past, that never could have been, and so that which will never be for me. It is what life is: this pushing back against and back upon death, but it is silent in its absolute rebuttal—we can never get at it, nor get to it. That is something like *ereignis*?

Jen: In *Being and Time*, Dasein exists for the sake of accomplishing its own ground. Dasein stands outside of itself in a thrusting into its ground. But in attempting to accomplish itself as its own ground, Dasein casts itself off away from its ground. The ground of the being of Dasein is not that which is projected upon, but lies in the projecting. That upon which the primary projection of the understanding of being projects itself is the meaning of being, yet this meaning itself emerges from out of an abyss of meaninglessness. Such a projecting is precisely the lack of any appeal to ground. Dasein is the projector groundlessly grounding itself in its own groundlessness. Dasein is a meaning-projector, but there is no-thing that grounds the projection, no-thing projected. All there is is meaning projecting itself around and around itself in order to see that it is really being. But if all there is is meaning projections in self circling groundlessness, then that all there is is that there is meaning means nothing. Being all along has been just this free-floating disappearing act. That is why Dasein was brought on stage but to die.

Ben: I'm afraid I do not follow much of that.

Jen: Heidegger believes we live in the oblivion of Being. Thinking marked by wonder was followed by technicians who replaced Being with beings, inaugurating a tradition in which Being has been forgotten. Heidegger is engaged in a destructive retrieval of the essence of thinking. He wants to call us back to a remembrance of Being, to return us to the primordial astonishment in its presence. We must come home to Being, heal the sunderedness of Being and beings. What the Enlightenment wanted to demystify, Heidegger wants to re-mystify to some degree. What prevents us is the calcified, sclerotic philosophical tradition and language which comes down to us. It has become encrusted with the fragments and dust of a ruined past; it must be cleansed and purged to become a viable path to Being. Like ancient ruins, we must attend to thinking in an unheard-of way. Luckily for Heidegger, we still have German, the most powerful and spiritual of the remaining languages of the west (other than Greek) Heidegger mines this language for its etymologies.

Ben: That Heidegger wants to re-mystify is one of the few points I am willing to grant you unconditionally. The paradox is that he wants to say all of these elements, Dasein, being, presencing, the art-work, language in its essence, are clearings or are part of the clearing. If Dasein and its art-works are inherently plural and being is just as inherently singular and unique, it is not apparent how this is to be understood. The trouble is that it is difficult to abstract from the plurality of Dasein, and there is textual evidence to suggest that even later Heidegger continued to speak of Dasein as distinct from being. There is a continuing contrast between the openness of being and the openness of Dasein, and it is as itself open that Dasein awaits the openness of beings. Let us retrace some steps. In *Being and Time* Dasein had been declared to be "the clearing." But being was also said to be "the clearing itself"; and other descriptions of being as "the giving-itself-into-the-open" (*das Sich-geben ins Offene*) and the "locality of the truth of being" (*die Ortschaft der Wahrheit des Seins*) associate being with the attributes of openness and place that attached to Dasein in *Being and Time*. If Dasein is a clearing and "man" is also a clearing, and if being then proves to be a clearing as well, one may well wonder whether all these points are compatible with one another and whether the clearing in question is the same in each case. Man's being a clearing in the required sense is essentially connected with his being or becoming Dasein, and if that is the case then two of these clearings would be identical with each other. That would still leave the question of how the clearing that is Dasein is related to the clearing that is Being as such. Heidegger nowhere unifies all of this, but instead moves on with further delineations of "clearings." Thus with the withering of Dasein we have the definition of truth as *aletheia* and the identification of truth with *ereignis*, both of which are said to be a "holding open" of "the clearing" that exists in the service of what transcends all entities: being as such. Entities at that stage could still manifest themselves only through the "clearing" opened up by and through human existence. Similarly, in other texts, Heidegger suggests that the work of art could refine our ontological understanding in such a way that we could learn to "clear" things from their captivity in the matrix of instrumental dealings associated with industrialism spawned by technological metaphysics. He then went so far as to say, with the remarks on the fourfold world, that virtually any thing could play the world-gathering role formerly assigned primarily to Dasein, then to the work of art. Through his meditations on language, *ereignis* comes to be understood as the "clearing" of the space that allows things to rise out of the darkness of universal imposition. Now finally we get a further addition to the later Heidegger liturgy with enowning. And it is there where Heidegger in the end simply sets us adrift as to any precise articulation of what is being discussed.

My difficulty here is in being willing to follow you or Heidegger's move in all of this to facilitate the "withering of Dasein" -- how can Dasein itself be essentially open and yet require the kind of supplementation that the openness of being as such would provide? The notion of trying to move beyond the concept of Dasein by postulating another clearing to which the clearing that is Dasein is then somehow subjoined seems tenuous. The objection to any claim that the openness of Dasein might be in some way deficient and therefore in need of such supplementation is the fact that Dasein is by definition familiar with being, and if this is so, there cannot be, on the terms laid down by Heidegger earlier, anything more that another clearing could impart to it. The discussion of artworks, the infamous fourfold, language, simply extends this issue. The reciprocal implication of all of these regions in one another is just another way of saying such regions are open to one another. The reciprocal openness and fundamental mutuality normally thought to obtain only with fellow human beings is expanded to include things as well. Explaining exactly in what sense a chair is open to the wall against which it stands, to use an example from *Being and Time*, where any such openness was categorically denied, involves replaying the path through art to the reciprocal openness in the medium of language.

Jen: You are again very far from being a good reader of Heidegger. You simply lack the patience to be a good reader, even of a single page. Let's finish our lunch—this cheeseburger I ordered is lousy anyway—the cook left it under-done.

Ben: Thus violating one of your bourgeois taboos, that what is purchased is supposed to be finished, concluded, in accordance with the mores of the exchange of commodities, where the customer insists that what is delivered to him at full price should embody the full quantity of labor for which he is paying the equivalent. If there is anything left to be done on what he buys, he feels cheated.

Jen: Just for that, you can pick up the tab.

III. Seriality and Sartre's Marxism

1. The encounter between French existentialism and Marxism remains one of the more interesting intellectual dramas of the 20th century. The stature of the figures involved, the stakes and historical importance of the debates, and the personal as well as philosophical controversies generated, speak to its lasting influence. Driven by the development of the cold war to take a position for or against Marxism, for or against the west, for or against the Soviet Union, for or against the French Communist Party, figures such as Camus and Merleau-Ponty devoted book after book to specifying their attitude toward Marxism and Communism. Then slower than all the others, comes the most formidable and most famous of French existentialists, Sartre. The intellectual colossus of post-war France initially does not seek to reject or go beyond or implicitly absorb Marxism, nor even distinguish his existentialism from it, but, remarkably, accepts Marxism as the dominant philosophy of the age, situates existentialism as an ideology within Marxism. The major thinker of a great school of thought declares his own philosophy to be ancillary to the rival outlook he has been combating for years, and sets out to correct and properly found that outlook for the sake of its survival and flourishing. Not since Kant was awakened from his dogmatic slumbers by Hume had there been such a spectacle of seemingly philosophical reversal.

2. After the war, the French could not avoid seeing themselves as between the United States and the Soviet Union. With its huge communist party (PCF), its deep traditions both of political democracy and workers' revolution, France was deeply torn by cold war tensions. Perhaps more than anywhere else, the cold war seemed to pose itself as a massive existential choice to post-occupation France. Merleau-Ponty eventually accepted parliamentary democracy; Camus sided quickly with the West. Both were deeply critical of Marxism on most fronts. Sartre rejected their rejection, and, out-living them both by 20-25 years, seemed to have the last word. Yet surveying all of this today, some sixty years in retrospective lucidity, Communism is over, and Merleau-Ponty and Camus seem to have won the debates. No one on the left rejects parliamentary democracy. No one any longer sees history unfolding in the direction of human emancipation. The universal, eschatological, scientific ambitions of Marxism are finished. In his thirty years of engagement with Marxism, in Search for a Method, in Dirty Hands, in The Devil and the Good Lord, in The Communists

and Peace, in *The Ghost of Stalin*, in *Materialism and Revolution*, in his massive thousand page *Critique of Dialectical Reason*, in his six volume existential analysis of Flaubert, in his efforts to synthesize class analysis, his alignment with the PCF, his engagement with the Third World, his eventual denunciation of the Soviet invasion of Czechoslovakia, Sartre attempted to find some existentially-charged third way between communism and capitalism. Marxism however is now no longer a living movement. Its theoretical force seems to have been eclipsed, as Sartre himself was eclipsed by post-structuralism. Are we not then compelled to say that Sartre's encounter with Marxism was a failure? Did he only veer toward Marxism for several years before rediscovering his more fundamental impulses? Was Sartre's Marxism flawed because of its academic, philosophical character, or its lack of a social dimension? We will seek to go some distance toward answering these questions.

3. Sartre's engagement might first be set in relief against the intense backdrop of the post-war purges of collaborationist intellectuals in France.[1] In an attempt to judge those responsible for contributing to the horrors of the war, Resistance authorities engaged in trials of fascists and collaborators, with a swirl of contentious judgments, verdicts, and debates. Writers and intellectuals suspected of having supported Vichy and Nazi occupiers played a central role in this scene, having been visible public figures, and having left traces of their collaboration in writing. Writers and intellectuals carried an important symbolic weight in France, and public opinion focused intense attention on these trials. Many writers felt public condemnation for betraying the French soul, and some, such as Robert Brasilach, Charles Maurras, Drieu la Rochelle, and Abel Hermant all faced prison or firing squads for their collaborationist writing. This purge planted the seeds for French literary-philosophical thinking to have an incredible political effect. Never before had theories of literature been so massively mobilized to serve political ends. The status of writing and thinking during the purge trials intertwined some of France's greatest minds, and laid the foundation for the discussions of political engagement and commitment in postwar Europe.

4. That Sartre was the intellectual heavyweight in the midst of this purgation had an indelible impact on him. He often came to speak of his writings at this time in juridical metaphors. Indeed, throughout his entire career, Sartre was the ultimate postwar activist: he engaged in courtroom proceedings, advocated political causes, mimicked legal vocabularies, borrowed from the courts, and performed much of his literary activity in relation to the tribunals of the state.

He defended figures like Genet and Martin, condemned the US for genocide in 1967, supported Basque separatists during the Burgos trial. As arguably the most famous intellectual on earth, Sartre consistently assigned to himself the role of judge, plaintiff, defendant, attorney, and jury. The three objects of his existential biographies, Genet, Baudelaire, and Flaubert, all were at the center of celebrated court cases. Indeed, the trial remained at the heart of Sartre's work until his death. He saw philosophical writing as a tool that both could be used to defend certain cases, and as a trace that could in the end be used against the writer in a collaborationist tribunal. Sartre thus considered his own philosophical project to be a site of litigation, even considering late in life some of his own works to be eventual witnesses for the prosecution.

5. If Sartre emerged from the war as one of France's leading intellectuals, his sometimes ambiguous position in Occupied France became the focus of an important controversy in the late 1990's, having been the target of numerous re-evaluations by academics and journalists. For all of his Resistance credentials, Sartre's war-time activities reveal his French soul to be less than pure, and the degree of his commitment to the Resistance was perhaps less than he himself implied at the end of the war. The Germans looked favorably upon him while as a prisoner, given his proximity to Heidegger and Hegel; and Sartre himself had published articles in a collaborationist weekly publication. His publication of *Being and Nothingness* and the staging of *The Flies* were made possible only with the approval of the German censors, which Sartre courted. By the end of the war, however, he sought to neutralize this ambiguity by becoming one of the leading theorists of the purge. He participated in the National Writers' Committee, a group devoted to the purging of collaborationist writers. He published in French Letters, a publication devoted to identifying and denouncing collaborationists, and founded *Modern Times*, his famous publication which launched the postwar careers of so many French writers, and which returned again and again to the theme of responsibility and engagement. Indeed, one could argue it was less the Occupation than the purge which taught Sartre and the existentialists about writers' responsibilities. Sartre had transformed responsibility into an ethical and juridical category, realigning existential responsibility with the political betrayals in France.[2]

6. Sartre most powerfully equates responsibility to the literary project in his introductory essay to *Les temps modernes*, a short piece in which he both projects his post-war paths to Marxism and justifies the sanctions against

collaborationist writers in the recent past. In that work, to take but a brief example, he assails writers who attempt to separate their writing from their income, irresponsibility being in not acknowledging how one's writing is a source of money. He does this both to announce the socialist and class-based literary analysis of his new publication, and to recall some of the principle accusations of the purge trials. The writers at Sartre's *Modern Times* are committed because they acknowledge their place in a society of wage earners, no different than workers on an assembly line. At the same time, the courts in postwar France tried to prove an author guilty of treason by claiming he had received German money. During the purge trials any economic exchange with the enemy was the moral equivalent of counterintelligence. Sartre invokes this accusation early in the essay by evoking the writers who were being punished for "renting their pens to the Germans."[3] Later in the essay, in historical analogy to the collaborators of 1940-44, he holds Flaubert responsible for the repressions that followed the Paris Commune because "he didn't write a line to prevent it."[4]

7. Sartre's major literary statement after the war is, of course, "What is Literature?" in which he argues in favor of a politically committed prose. This famous essay expands and clarifies the ideas of his introducing *Les Temps Modernes* essay by classifying different literary periods and systematizing different literary forms. The literary form of poetry, for example, has no place in Sartre's considerations. For Sartre literature is a prose text engaged in revealing the injustices of the world through the action of disclosure. That to speak is to act, that words are actions, means that the ambiguity and indeterminacy of poetry does not protect it from the responsibilities of engagement. For Sartre a poetry of resistance should give way to a resistance to poetry, a move not without its own legal precedent. That even a poem is a political action could be traced to the definition of treason in Article 75 of the French Penal Code that holds language to be a form of direct representation, no more open to hermeneutic interpretation than any action would be. For the purge courts, literary style was invisible: an article denouncing a Jew was a denunciatory act, the equivalent of bearing arms. Sartre weaves this sense together with his powerful expression of existential responsibility. All speech (or writing) is a speech act whose language is vehicular, and political attention is to be focused on the content. Sartre is transferring into his political vocabulary a system of argumentation and an understanding of literature borrowed from the purge trials.[5]

8. "What is Literature?" holds still further clues to understanding Sartre's critical theory in relation to the purges of collaborationists as a prelude to his encounter with Marxism. It's title echoes an essay Sartre wrote for *La Republique francaise* in 1945 entitled "What is a Collaborator?" which was a psychological analysis of collaborationist intellectuals. What is interestingly taking place beneath these two articles is Sartre's attempts to create social cohesion within the working class.[6] Whether in the person of the nineteenth century aesthete, or in the NSDAP collaborator, Sartre condemns their mutual trafficking in the fiction of the loner, in that the former, in tearing himself away from his class and refusing to write for the masses, remains in the service of the bourgeoisie, while the latter as well abhors the bourgeoisie, their class or origin, without having the courage to join the proletariat. The collaborator and the nineteenth century aesthete are structurally equivalent in their rejection of bourgeois values without finding voice in the proletariat. Their inability to integrate themselves into society is also marked for Sartre by how both attempt to judge their actions not by the present but by some far-off future. Both poet and collaborator justifies his actions by looking back to win approval of the great poets or historical precedents of the past or to future judges. Again for Sartre we have the juridical model in his diagnosis of a psychology which seeks justifications for present actions by winning the trial on appeal, to some tribunal of posterity or posthumous fame. Just as the purge tribunals had judged and punished collaborators, so too is Sartre ready to judge and condemn his literary precursors. His work on some level is a continuation of the process of the purge by redefining the role of the philosopher as judge, the role of the writer as the accused, and the role of texts as witnesses for the prosecution.

9. When Sartre returned to France in late 1941, having escaped from a prisoner of war camp in Trier, he attempted to make contact with the communist resistance groups, but was rejected on the grounds that anyone who successfully escaped from such a camp could not entirely be trusted. By 1945-47, Sartre's relations with the PCF were tense and problematic. Part of the issue had to do with his relationship with Paul Nizan, a very close friend of Sartre's who had earlier been excoriated by the party.[7] Part of it had to do with Sartre's refusal to become a party member in order to join. Given his celebrity status, and the explosion of Sartrian existentialism immediately after the war, there was some animosity to Sartre. His fame and philosophy offered an alternative philosophical system to Marxism. The PCF was continuously upstaged by the

more libertarian existentialists, and they took this to draw attention away from what they considered to be most important. Basically the PCF were engaging in an intellectual war to win over the hearts and minds of the French people, and they could not compete with Sartrian existentialism, which they considered to be merely the latest form of bourgeois ideology.[8] So they did what many of course continue to do today, attack existentialism as decadent and depraved, at the time lumping it together with what the party perceived to be the nihilism of the American Arthur Miller. In 1947-48 the party publicly denigrated existentialism as the corrupting ideology of the oppressive class, or as the most virulent form of decadent nihilism, and then attacked Sartre as a fascist sympathizer for his connections with Heidegger. At times the party chose to defend itself in Resistance terminology, seeking to wrest that mantle from Sartre. Perpetuating the resistance myth and outlook was a tactical maneuver by the PCF to compete with Sartre. Finally, in 1950, with the outbreak of the Korean War, did Sartre have a sudden turn around and embrace the party for a period of 6 years.

10. Sartre remained convinced throughout his lifetime that violence was unquestionably justified during periods of revolutionary transformation. His initial theorizing on the origins of human violence in the *Critique* is taken a step further in his analysis of the boxing match in Volume II, in which he attempts to demonstrate the dialectical unity of history through the assertion that any particular boxing match incarnates, singularizes, not only all boxing matches, or all sports, but also all violence mediated by the structures of a class-driven bourgeois society.[9] Sartre interprets boxing to be the domestication of proletarian class violence. The boxing promoter commodifies the violence of a working-class boxer for consumption within the economic structures of bourgeois society. This was just the tip of the iceberg, however. For Sartre violence is not only a legitimate but a necessary weapon of social transformation. For Sartre, the revolutionaries of 1793 were insufficient because they did not kill enough counter-revolutionaries.[10] Indeed, with the victory of de Gaulle, Sartre looked away from domestics and more toward the revolutionary fervor of Cuba, Soviet Union, Algeria, and Vietnam in his thinking, accepting revolutionary violence as a legitimate and necessary part of leftist political action.[11]

11. Thus Sartre's postwar political itinerary in ideological and tactical terms is essentially the story of his relationship with the PCF and Marxism. While in

1950 he began to praise the PCF, he still was suspicious of the party intellectuals and militants. He seemed to be looking for some authentic political community, and finally found the post-68 French Maoists. Again it is important to remember that Sartre argued for certain procedural episodes of "organic class violence" and against "abstract terrorist violence." For Sartre violent acts cannot be isolated from the social conditions which produce them. Violence as an organized expression of class consciousness in a given moment is morally justifiable. As opposed to terrorism, retaliatorial violence by the working class is morally justifiable. It is also important that Sartre is arguing this in the framework that such violence is performed with the end of establishing a more just, and hence less violent, society. There is a route to the human via the inhumanity of the retaliatorial violence of the exploited in the ideas of the oppressed.[12] Thus when Sartre was called upon to intervene with the kidnappers of an employment officer at Renault, Robert Nogrette, following the labor related death of Pierre Overey in February, 1972, he condemned the move because it was not consistent with his theory of organic violence. Nogrette was released unharmed. Sartre also intervened in the notorious Baader-Meinhof gang, the German terrorists whom he visited in Stammheim Prison in Stuttgart in 1974. Again his interactions were based on the distinction between violence arising organically from within exploited groups and violence initiated from the outside by terrorist factions not organically linked to the exploited social groups themselves.[13]

12. For Sartre, sheer contingency is necessary to the social formation, but only when it is recuperated by a constructive, temporal dialectic. The problem lies in the contingency of violence. For violence to represent, meaning must be arbitrarily, forcefully, thrust upon it. That in fact is the major violence behind the represented violence of sacrifice. There is thus a process of the internalization of a radicalized violence, in the subjectivity of the committed writer, who continues to make possible the unification of the group through his or her interpretive practice. Sartre depends, in his depictions of a sacrificial social grouping, descriptions which themselves are meant to act as motors for a larger, extratextual social unification, on an arbitrary speech act that is fundamentally mechanical, neither subject to the control of human consciousness nor subsumable within a group in fusion. The *Critique*, whose central movement recognizes the recalcitrance of the blind and directionless performative precisely by attempting to formulate the "group" through the act's total humanization, runs into difficulties because it fails to recognize that the

plenitude of the speech act that guarantees the representation of the group's fusion is indistinguishable from the emptiness of the unification-through-dispersion of the series. The writer as a committed intellectual is split because accompanying his function of representation that undergirds the intellectual's activity (he or she represents the masses or some other group, the group represents itself through its proxy, the intellectual), there is as well the mechanism of the possibility of the representation-function itself, the empty, automatic functioning of language on language.

13. Sartre is interested in founding a viable community as an alternative to fascism, repression, and capital democracy, and which includes the features of a dialectic that is politically progressive and that entails the mutual recognition of desire on the part of autonomous subjects. In the face of the storm clouds of postmodernism, Sartre relentlessly treats the problem of the formulation of the dialectic and the establishment of a coherent social grouping out of and in relation to it. One signal as to the difficulty of such a project is that no one since Sartre returned to it until Habermas.[14]

14. Sartre's postwar works of fiction and drama speak deeply to his engagement with Marxism, such as in his never completed proposed series of four novels *The Roads of Freedom*. The original intent of the series was to show the growing, or maturing, political commitment of a number of characters—chief among them being Mathieu Delarue, a French schoolteacher and intellectual—through life in prewar Paris, the fighting of May and June 1940, internment in a prisoner of war camp, and finally life in Occupied Paris. The final volume, never completed, Death in the Soul, was to have taken the reader up the Liberation, with the various factions of the resistance united and in power. Mathieu himself was to have died bravely under torture during the Occupation, but even his death was meant to be a kind of victory, signaling his gesture of "making himself a hero," a huge change from the impotent and self-mutilating peacetime bachelor we see in the first volume, *The Age of Reason*. Mathieu's politics were to be a version of a Popular Front agenda that once again seemed possible during and immediately after the Occupation, when a broad spectrum of groups fought together to defeat the Germans. The leading character of course was never meant to be anything other than a thinly veiled portrait of Sartre himself, as he was, and as he hoped to be. The evolution of Mathieu during the war years would exactly parallel political developments in the postwar period; his maturation was to be mirrored by the society at large, which would meld the

socialists, who advocated and respected subjective autonomy, with the communists, who were the embodiment of the solidarity of the proletariat and who were the models of revolutionary discipline. Sartre clearly hoped his novel would prefigure as well as make possible the definitive accession to power of a united, libertarian left in the postwar period. Sartre's cold war drama *Nekrassov*, a satirical farce directed against the French anti-communist press, was a further attempt to challenge the implicit power structures of western democracies whose information was controlled and disseminated through technocratic capitalist means.[15]

15. It is Sartre's *Critique of Dialectical Reason*, however, which is his monumental effort to solve the problem of solidarity raised in *Being and Nothingness* in ways which Sartre's later fiction and drama was unable to imagine or conceptually represent. For Sartre, the dialectical process of history is characterized by a never-ending search for transparency, for full reciprocity between subjects and the mutual recognition of the other's desire, for the renunciation of the exercise of oppressive power by one subject over another (a power that results in the transformation of the victim into a simple object to be manipulated)—a transparency which, ironically, can never be grasped except through the mediation of opaque and obstructing matter. Sartre, like Kojeve's *Introduction to the Reading of Hegel*, saw the agency of violence and destruction as integral to the movement of history and to the completion of a larger historical reason. If the violence of the Hegelian master-slave dialectic is crucial for Kojeve, for Sartre this same violence is just as important when it is part of a praxis by which the social group, in a violent but "fusing" state, acts upon and against the inert force of political reaction that opposes it. Individual against individual, group against group, self against crystallized or gelatinous matter—praxis, in this tradition, is inseparable from a strategically applied violence that may lack a universal justification, but which in a contingent situation, must be indissociable from the movement of history itself.

16. The Sartrian group in fusion is understandable only as a necessarily ephemeral dialectical event, in opposition to a status and oppressive anti-dialectical milieu Sartre calls "seriality." For Sartre the dialectical union of subjectivities is just in history, not at the end of it, and is radically contingent. It is an evanescent group transparency that clearly motivates and justifies history's movement, but which is itself attained only momentarily. The *Critique* thus reads at first as a vast fresco of historical events which chronicles the rise of seriality,

its sudden and momentary overcoming in the group in fusion, and then its slow and inevitable decay as that group itself is institutionalized and serialized. This then is the just dialectical relation between men, a relation which is itself inevitably swallowed by a larger, anti-dialectical movement, but which in turn generates history and provides humanity with a legitimate goal despite terrible periods of oppression. To understand this moment of fusion one must first understand seriality, and the role played by a differential ordination within it: for seriality is nothing more than the social inscription of the injustice of the impersonal language event and of a differential, arithmetic system of ordering, separating, and instituting. The most important thing about seriality is that it is inseparable from an arithmetic ordering. One must see how numbering operates within the series, and what it implies for the serial "gathering."[16]

17. The best-known example of seriality in the *Critique* is the gathering of people waiting for the bus in the Place St. Germain, Paris.[17] Each person is alone; each is a solitary member of a social entity which is constituted only because of a "common interest." No one talks to or looks at anyone else. That interest—to find a seat on the bus when it finally comes—ensures that each person, for the Other is nothing more than an additional Other who also wants a seat. Each person for the Other is only a cipher; each has significance for the Other only to the extent that he represents a possible privation. Nothing "interior" to each individual could serve to distinguish him or her from the others; each is constituted as a member of the series only in that he is just another potential bus rider, a physical presence that will occupy a seat. The only "unity" of the members of this gathering is, therefore, the fact that each is an Other to all other members. Each member is the same as every other member—each member is part of a gathering—only to the extent that he is just an Other to every other member. The very anonymity of each one—his or her inert materiality, waiting, and nothing more—is what constitutes membership in the gathering, and the member's "unity." This facelessness comes to be internalized by each additional member, and to constitute his or her presence. This "identity as otherness," a scandalous absurdity, is the only possible unity in a social aggregate whose unification is the result of a praxis, a human activity, that immediately leads to the ossifying of praxis into an alienating inertia.

18. This series is determined by the inertia of materiality which for Sartre is never anything more or other than the resistance of scarcity. The practico-inert in the bus example comes from the scarcity of there not being enough places

for everyone. Scarcity defines each person as potentially in excess, as nothing more than another one who can be added or subtracted depending on the number of places available. Ordination is an arbitrary, mechanical way of uniting people by distinguishing between them, and is meant by Sartre to be representative of all processes of selection and group formation in bourgeois society. The originality of each comes only from what it is, namely from the one that precedes it in the series. This inert series, as practico-inert, absorbs the energy, the free praxis, of each of its members, and returns that energy to each member as power coming from another. Through the alienated series, in its inorganic materiality, the subject gets reified into a quantified digit whose meaning is nothing more that its difference from each other one, determined by addition or subtraction. There is no concept to the union other than as a differential marker in a larger recurring aggregate.

19. This numbering constitutes an "ordination" in which the subject is invested with a certain status (of complete powerlessness) within serialized society. The mechanical function of seriality, the assignment of everyone's numbered place in a "Gestell-like" grid, is accomplished through a designating act that accords one a certain numerically defined position. The series entails that the lucky ones who succeed, who manage to get on the bus or accomplish anything else in bourgeois society, are merely the exceptions that prove the rule, namely that the unity of authentic selfhood is excluded. The act which enables the subject to do something is only repetitious disinvestment. The serialization of society through a kind of arithmetic language or inscription is but the subtraction of the power of the intellectual function within that arbitrary and empty system, by means of that system. What remains is an emptied out, machine-like subjectivity, the sameness of the potentially infinite series of selves as digitalized others.

20. Another powerful example of how a certain materiality breeds seriality can be seen in Sartre's example of the otherness of radio listeners.[18] The radio addresses me specifically; it is an address that would ordinarily presuppose the possibility of response, applause, or objection on my part. At the same time, though, this act is the impossibility of the fulfillment of the act as an address as it is conventionally conceived, because the listener is addressed not as a possible respondant or interlocutor but only as an inert thing. The series determined by the "object" is the group of listeners who are "ordained" by the act—they are identified (to themselves) as listeners called, but also frustrated because they cannot respond to the voice. The listener is utterly powerless, not being able to

argue with the voice, and worse still, cannot address other listeners to convince them that the voice is wrong. These others, as in the case of the bus riders, are both the same and the other: their identity, their gathering together, lie only in their distance from, and their otherness to, each other. By the very nature of the group, no communication can be successfully carried out in this version of seriality. No one can any longer do anything with words. Even the radio voice is as powerless as the listeners united in their impotence. The voice of ideology leads apparently only to aimless serial violence. My otherness to myself, and thus the otherness of all others to themselves, as impotence becomes an inward turning violence; its aimlessness becomes a principle of false cohesion, like the "unity" of monadic drivers locked in highway congestion reduced to inarticulate window gestures. The noncompletion of the mechanized and indefinitely reproducible speech act results in a differential and incoherent series of micro-quanta each of whose energy is turned against itself as well as against all the others in the gathering, and which thereby itself only generates more inevitably aborted performatives. Language results in the purely impersonal addition or subtraction of quantifiable terms, whose completion is effected through an unsuccessful and interminable performative. Road rage is not restricted to the road but generalized over the field as an ordinated condition of impotence.

21. Were this to be the last word, things would indeed be grim. Sartre does argue, however, at least for the possibility, however rare, of a group-in-fusion which dialectically overcomes seriality. The issue now is in how subjects interact in such a way that seriality gives way to an authentic community, and for Sartre that is in response to a common danger, the dialectically felt need by all to remove a common threat. Sartre uses as an example the famous uprising in 1789 that led to the storming of the Bastille, a negative order of massacre that causes the group to find its inner coherence. Each resident in the St. Antoine quarter feels threatened by the potential violence of the king's troops, aimed at any person in the neighborhood, whether he or she is involved in the revolt or not. One sees the threat to the other as a threat to oneself. The threat of destruction, experienced by everyone in the neighborhood, previously a mere serial collective, causes each subject to recognize simultaneously the group of which he is a member. Subjectivity now reveals itself to itself through the Other as itself. Thus full subjectivity is possible not in isolation but only as a member of group solidarity. Sartre presents this change as a dialectical transformation of the "third." In seriality each person is a third in relation to each other and to all. The violence of otherness gets inscribed in the third; it is thus turned against

itself as well as against all others—that is its only identity with them. In the group-in-fusion, however, the violence is external; the third gets dialectically integrated into the group through its solidarity with the group against the alien force.

22. The sacrificial model is strong on this reading. Each member of the serial gathering was a third in that he was excluded, or that he excluded the Other and the larger collection of Others. He was other to himself only in that he was excluded in and through his very membership. In the dialectical model, though, the third is unified with, and sees himself in, each other and in all Others (in the group). Together they must fight an external materiality, in this case the soldiers of the king, who would pacify the neighborhood by killing any of its inhabitants, irrespective of what groups to which they belonged. Either one unites or dies, and dialectical unification takes place because everyone recognizes this. The group itself is unlike serial assemblage because it is not constituted as material inertia, or in otherness to itself. Instead the materiality that "constituted" seriality now gets externalized—the group is united against it. The group "fuses" in response to the now external potentially serializing danger. For Sartre the dialectical-sacrificial model of group formation overcomes the violence of seriality through outward directed violence, through expulsion and catharsis, a purge trial. Group solidarity can be purchased only at the cost of a violence no longer internal to the makeup of each group member but directed out of the group, against an Other with whom each member has nothing in common. And if the violence is externalized this means that inequality that characterized the hierarchies of the former serialized society will be banished as well.

23. Perhaps Sartre locates if only briefly the positive possibilities of socialism only here. In the group-in-fusion the function of the intellectual becomes a multiple subjectivity. The intellectual function becomes omnipresent in the group; everyone becomes the intellectual, and formulates what everyone will already have realized. Power is shared not as in conventional democracy but in a moment in which each person has power and gets totalized in free circulation between all members of the group. This circulation serves as a mechanism by which a full subjectivity-in-praxis is constituted through the reflection of the subject to itself in each other member of the group and in the group fusion itself.

24. It is difficult to see, however, why this process of group formation is any less arithmetic than seriality. In the series there was "always one more" to be added; but here in the group-in-fusion model there seems always one more to be subtracted. For what guarantees the power of the momentary "one" is someone, we know not whom, who is himself always subtracted as soon as he is added. For only if everyone's becoming the intellectual is authorless can it be my becoming; only in this way can I be the author, if only now. Only if the author removes himself as soon as he enunciates the political catch-phrase can I share its status fully. The group-in-fusion plays the role of a kind of point of absolute political truth, toward which any dialectic must strive. The speech act of the group in fusion and its full subjectivity are established, not dialectically but still arithmetically. The immediacy of the empty command becomes simply the zero, the mathematical placeholder function. Sartre, through the notion of group in fusion, is grasping at the utopia of language fully present to itself, a moment of radical reduction in which the inertia of a fixed language or a tyrannical intellectual imposing his will through language stands in the center. Sartre avoids the inevitable reification or sclerosis of the revolutionary watchword, its inscription in thickened matter, its Stalinization, if you will, only by posing an empty term. It is no longer the empty addition of serialization but now the empty subtraction of the zero-function, the purely formal term in a differential relation with other terms. The Sartrian group-in-fusion is in complete conformity with the differential series that would seem to be opposed to it. It is not dialectical opposition but repetition of earlier seriality. Nor does it conserve seriality while negating it, but only repeats it, differing from it only arithmetically. The relation between seriality and the group-in-fusion is itself only differential, not dialectical.

25. Beyond this connection between the group identification and the arithmetic relation of the series, one could note also the complicity between the sinister radio broadcaster who generates seriality on a mass scale, the embodiment of seriality, and the narrator of the *Critique* himself. If the *Critique of Dialectical Reason* is the only real example of the fusing of the group, if Sartre's book is the only thing that resists seriality, even it is locked in the differential relation with other signs. I cannot respond to this book, I cannot reason with it or refute it; like the radio personality, it issues vacant commands and statements and I am alone, and united with all other readers in my isolation, in my inability to confront Sartre and convince him that his thinking has failed. Of course I can get together with other readers, perhaps here at the West Virginia Philosophical

Society, but that will have no influence on Sartre—it will only lead to more disputes, serialized conflicts with other readers over differences or similarities in my interpretations. Sartre's book is like the radio voice, an absent presence, the origin of botched speech acts whose only function can be but to institute an other in each other, to constitute me the reader as an empty place holder fixed in seriality. And if seriality is indistinguishable from the dialectic, if the dialectic issues from the series, then the group-in-fusion can be preserved only through its re-serialization. Revolutionary dynamism can be maintained only through its dialectical opposite, the literal serial killing and violence of the Stalinist purges.

26. Thus re-serialization constitutes an affirmation of the necessity of Stalinism similar to the inevitable brutality of the Terror in Hegel's *Phenomenology*. The failure of Sartre's Marxism is not in its justification of revolutionary violence; even the American founding fathers could see themselves in Sartre's conception of organic violence. The problem is that there seems to be no way for Sartre's dialectic to incorporate mathematical serial violence, nor to guard against fusion recognizing itself in its dialectical other and losing itself in seriality. The momentary dialectical fulfillment in the group as a totalization that incorporates seriality in its operation must at the same time exclude it in order to constitute itself, since dialectical fusion is defined as the exclusion, the subtraction, of seriality. Either existentialized Marxism ends in Stalinized seriality, or class-consciousness is achieved, but only momentarily, and at the cost of making Sartre a theorist of a necessarily terroristic and violent dialectic that incorporates seriality into a dialectically viable whole. By this bewitchment would we have Sartre in basic agreement with the terrorist assassination attempts on his own life by the OAS via plastic explosives in the early 1960's.[19]

27. It has been said that "what remains serious in Marxism is essentially located today in Universities, where it is probably best that it belongs." Such a remark captures something about how Sartre's thinking was both destructive and beneficial to Marxism. Sartre's theoretical Marxism, like any Marxist theory, is dependent on events, parasitic upon movements and parties and states that call themselves Marxist. Existential Marxist theory was defeated by events beyond its control. Just as Lukacs' earlier dialectical Marxism never stood freely on its own but only existed in dialogue with the orthodoxy it critiqued, existential Marxism presupposes Soviet Marxism such that if the one falls so too must the other. Sartrian Marxism sought to remove dogmatism from Marxism; it was the contemporary western intellectual's contribution to that process at that time.

His thinking left no stable or unified structures—neither states nor parties nor theoretical codifications. But neither is there any question that it inspired a political-intellectual current which exploded into a movement. Studying Sartre's Marxism in University illustrates how we can speak of Marxism being over to the degree to which each of its political permutations, Social Democracy, Orthodox Marxism, Third-World Marxism, and Western Marxism, has exhausted its potentials, or can be demonstrated to result in nothing but unstable or re-serialized violence. Sartre's efforts to deepen and modernize Marxism at first delayed, and then only deepened, the process of Marxism's obsolescence. He removed Marx's certainties, opened it to greater contingency, destroyed its relentless objective logic, kept it alive for philosophical reflection and undermined it politically at the same time. In a world which saw Marxism's power to explain events diminishing anyway, Marxism could never be as spellbinding or compelling after Sartre's analysis of it.

IV. Indiscretion With Regard to the Unsayable: Weil to the Postmodern

My title is of course infelicitous. All serious readers of her are aware of Simone Weil's appreciation of the precision of language, and the possibilities of achieving truth through language. That precision of vocabulary was for Simone Weil the equivalent of a moral law manifests itself in her protests against the arbitrariness of language in certain forms of writing, in her condemnation of journalists in their inaccuracies with language, in her condemnation of the power by which linguistic constructs can control people's minds and utterly destroy their lives. Thus to bring Weil's thinking in proximity to the label of the "postmodern" runs the risk of my not having paid enough attention to her condemnations of the mystifying power of words, and how like Helen of Troy they can take on lives of their own that lead to disaster. That Weil herself, and the many fine readers and scholars of her work, would cringe at my aforementioned infelicity should not, however, prohibit an exploration of precisely those fascinating interconnections of her thought with that of the postmoderns, of those proximities which more and more we see with Simone Weil and Heidegger, Bataille, Levinas, and a host of other writers and figures capturable under the general category of the postmodern. I would like then to make some small further steps in this direction, by focusing on a particular area of Simone Weil's thinking, her views on affliction and the relation of affliction to language, and those of the French postmodernist writer Maurice Blanchot and his writings on death and the representability of death, an obvious choice since Blanchot himself deeply read and published on the work and thought of Simone Weil.[1]

That Blanchot was drawn to address Weil's thinking is an indication not only of the urgency of her views for him, but also of the distance between these two figures, a distance which manifests itself throughout in divergences of language and idiom, strategy and context. Difference here, though, does not necessarily constitute opposition, nor should one attribute the undoubted community of questioning that exists between these two authors to the influence of the latter upon the former. Instead, to read the texts of Weil alongside those of Blanchot is to be aware, perhaps beyond influence and opposition, of the singular rigor of a response to an infinite debt.

Infinite debt does not of course imply slavish repetition, but in this case almost exactly the opposite. Properly to pay tribute to another means paying tribute to another's difference; and this is achieved not by bridging distances but only by accentuating them, not by faithful repetition but in the recognition of a kind of necessary infidelity. A commentator is not being faithful when he or she merely faithfully reproduces the ideas or language of another. The provisional tactic Blanchot imposes is to achieve a kind of proximity to what Simone Weil sought to address, proximity only being possible from a distance. To write of this is then not so much to repeat key words or concepts but to instead attend to the internal demand, the exigency of Weil's writing. Language, under the effects of such an approach, testifies here not to the stability of concepts so much as to the movement that carries it beyond its own limits. In order to respond faithfully to a text, it is necessary to respond, not to those elements in a text, concepts, arguments, topics or themes, which are easily repeated, and which, once repeated, threaten to calcify, but rather to that in the text which cannot be named as such and thus seemingly resists repetition and appears as a misreading. What is at stake in such a reading is not the conceptuality but the writing, not the ideality of meaning but the transformation effected in thought by textuality itself. Blanchot insists both upon a significant "absence" of God in the contemporary world and upon the insurmountable finitude, passivity, and opacity of the human subject who during the modern age would have sought unlimited autonomy in the full light of reason. This twofold insistence provokes the question of how exactly the radical finitude of humanity in contemporary thought might relate to the seeming absence of God in Simone Weil, and how that relation itself might be compared, in turn, to the interplay of God's unknowability and the soul's annihilation in traditional negative or apophatic theologies. And this is why it is crucial in considering Blanchot's proximity to Simone Weil that we begin to read them side by side not simply for their arguments but with an attention to their own singularity in that writing itself is in proximity to affliction (*malheur*), that it is a place of attention to the thought of what cannot allow itself to be thought.

How writing can hold such proximity might first be glimpsed in Blanchot's own works involving the poverty of language about death. Blanchot is an heir to the negative logic of being-toward-death in Heidegger. In the analytic of *Being and Time*, Dasein exists for and in the fruitless sake of accomplishing its own ground. The analytic of Dasein reveals, however, that one can never capture the whole of Dasein. Death is the absolute futurity; it is the unforseeable future that can never arrive, that can never become a past, that never could have been, and so that which will never be for me. It is what life is: this pushing back against and back upon death, but death is silent in its absolute rebuttal—we can never get at it, nor get to it.[2]

In *Writing of the Disaster*, as in a host of other works, Blanchot explores literary forms and operations of this kind of Heideggerian negativity in relation to death that would subvert or devastate the self-transparent human subject that sought its glory in Enlightenment thought.[3] He suggests that the poverty of our language concerning death is not so much a pure emptiness or silence but rather marks the ever ambiguous edge where language wavers between its own production and failure, the unstable border where language is generated precisely with the aim of undoing itself. The very production of language that characterizes death depends upon, or ensues from, the impossibility of articulating what dying is, that which eludes the presence of any subjective experience. Moreover, that elusive dying, that unrepresentable passivity of the human subject, Blanchot ties to the thought of God. Indeed, there is a point at which the poverty of the language about God and the poverty of the language about death intersect. In this way Blanchot signals, from a contemporary perspective shaped deeply by the disasters of twentieth-century Europe, a point at which the impossibility of rendering death present within the experience and language of a self-present subject could prove indistinguishable from the impossibility of making present in experience and language a level of affliction which resists human articulation, or a God who ultimately remains inconceivable and ineffable.

The ties that the comparison of Weil and Blanchot suggest between an impossible death and an unknowable divine are both historically grounded and conceptually motivated. The historical ground can be traced throughout the mystical traditions, at least as far as the biblical God's assertion that "man shall not see me and live."[4] The biblical word proves crucial to countless apophatic and mystical theologians who seek a way to articulate the experience of God as the absence of all experience, to represent the return of God as the annihilation of the self, and to speak of the transcendence of God as the failure of all speech. Thus Pseudo-Dionysus, St. John of the Cross, St. Theresa of Avila, Meister Eckhart—all might be said to similarly relate the question of language both to the question of God and to the question of death.

Weil most closely resembles the via negativa in her views on affliction. For Weil, affliction is not merely physical suffering, but a physical pain accompanied by an interior suffering, an infinite remorse, an acute sense of uselessness and anguish. It is often accompanied by social degradation, as well as complicity with one's own wretchedness. Affliction includes a futural desire without an object, a projection in which we are reduced to pure receptivity, an opening or clearing. In affliction, one is crushed by time while living in the present. The realm of humiliation and pain where even false consolations become impossible, a state equivalent to the imminent approach of death, the horror of which is due to the impossibility of future compensations.[5] This state is incomparably described again and again in her essay on the *Iliad*. Lycaon kneeling before Achilles and imploring him for his life is no longer living, no longer the projection for any possibilities of being.[6]

Affliction is mute, nearly impenetrable to the perception of others. It devours the personality of the person before me. One cannot be face to face with affliction.[7] Those who are in affliction cannot articulate their condition, and those who have not experienced it cannot turn their gaze toward it.[8] Affliction always falls on an individual through the blows of blind and brutal necessity. For Weil, affliction cannot be perfected into redemptive suffering. The plenitude of affliction is to continue loving God in his absence:

> Affliction is a marvel of divine technique. It is a simple and ingenious device which introduces into the soul of a finite creature the immensity of force, blind, brutal, and cold.[9]

In her great essay "Human Personality," Weil speaks about words:

> "To put into the mouth of the afflicted words from the vocabulary of middle values, such as democracy, rights, personality, is to offer them something which can bring them no good and will inevitably do them much harm." "In order to provide an armor for the afflicted, one must put into their mouths only those words whose rightful abode is in heaven, beyond heaven, in the other world." "The test for suitable words is easily recognized and applied. The afflicted are overwhelmed with evil and starving for good. The only words suitable for them are those which express nothing but good, in its pure state." "There is a natural alliance between truth and affliction, because both of them are mute suppliants, eternally condemned to stand speechless in our presence." "Human thought is unable to acknowledge the reality of affliction."[10]

Human thought is unable to acknowledge affliction, but for Blanchot writing of affliction has its unattainable source in an experience of this inability, a movement of dying, and the extremity of this experience cannot be faced, as it would be intolerable to the human condition. The writer is therefore blind to whatever are the guiding insights of her work. To write on affliction would be to imagine a writing in which the operation of all of the forces of meaning will be reabsorbed into meaninglessness. These pages composed of a discontinuous series of words, these words that do not presume any language, can always, in the absence of assignable meaning, and through the harmony or discordance of sounds, produce an effect that represents their justification. Writing of affliction is somehow external to what is possible. The writer seeks nothing, the no that is not no to this or that, but the pure and simple no. What is more, this is not sought; it stands apart from all investigation. Writing belongs to this space of pure refusal; like that of the accused, having nothing to say speaks to the secret of his solitary condition. The figure then becomes one of the writer as someone who responds to accusations with having nothing to say. To write is not to belong to any totality but to experience what it excludes, a terrible alterity, as if this unknown were not something negative, not merely the absence of knowledge. For Blanchot how to speak the insufficiency of language is a task that proves infinite precisely insofar as impossible, and in that infinity and impossibility, death, affliction, and God might indiscretely meet. Where Weil's effort was one of reintegrating this inhumanity back into the human world, Blanchot's work is a poetics of the refusal of this reintegration.[11]

There is thus a proximity in affliction with violence and words. To give speech to affliction, for it to find words, is always the exercise of force. To write of affliction is already to belong to a network of powers of which one makes use. Language is the undertaking through which violence agrees not to be open. To die, then, to be in a state of affliction, on the one hand, and to see the invisible and speak the unsayable, on the other, are equally and in like manner paradoxical in that both can be tied to a thought and language of God as unknowable and ineffable. "God" here becomes a figure of the unfigurable around which a paradoxical language would be generated: an impoverished or idle language that would seek not to work, a language that would seek to undo itself in order to speak, without speaking, that which cannot be spoken. Such a language, whose paradox stands at the heart of all apophatic theologies, unifies Weil to the postmodern in facing the double problems of first, always risking saying too little (hence never appearing as language and resembling indifference) and second, saying too much (hence missing the ineffable that it seeks).

Blanchot seizes upon this tension in Simone Weil, and holds that she does not follow it out to its end. On the one hand her thought is marked by an invincible certitude and precision. I mentioned earlier how she proposes severe sanctions against journalists, writers, and others responsible for transmitting truth in public life, who neglect to do so.[12] In her remarks on oppression, Weil speaks of the power of single words "compensating for all sufferings, resolving all anxieties, avenging the past, curing present ills, summing up all future possibilities." The word has aroused such pure acts of devotion, has repeatedly caused such generous blood to be shed, has constituted for so many unfortunates the only source of courage for living, that it is almost a sacrilege to investigate it; all this, however, does not prevent it from possibly being meaningless. She speaks of wanting to "reduce the whole art of living to a good use of language,"[13] and how "to clarify meaningless words is to save lives."[14] She warns against the arbitrary use of the name of the Lord: "Not to speak about God (not in the inner language of the soul either) not to pronounce this word, except when one is unable to do otherwise."[15] She gives an account of the order of the world as an order of necessary relations, which involves a consideration of mathematical concepts and their application. The theme of geometric proportions permeates her thought with a precision that has drawn many to her work.[16]

Yet the pressure such a certitude exerts on her, in her assertions that we know nothing of the Good, nothing of God save the name, stands out with even greater force. For there is as well her requirement of "passing words through silence, into the nameless."[17] The idea of salvation, the belief in personal immortality, the conception of a beyond, all that would allow us to bring close to us what has truth for us only if we love it, all are part of a movement which authorizes no affirmation whatsoever. By taking possession of desire and abandonment, by making affliction her own, Weil is seeking to capture experience which for Blanchot cannot properly be called hers.

> "What Simone Weil says of herself we should say of thought. Thought cannot but be fraudulent unless it is thought from out of the baseness of this affliction… To think through affliction is to lead thought toward this point at which force is no longer the measure of what must be said and thought; it is to make thought one with this impossibility of thinking that thought is for itself, and is like its center.[18]

What Weil has in common with negative theology is a suspicion of language as determining the indeterminate. However, this indeterminacy for Blanchot is not transcendence, nor can it be reached by prayer or desire. There is no possibility of salvation for me, for the experience of affliction puts experience as my experience into question.

Here, a disanalogy with Weil emerges, and with it a fundamental danger inherent in the very idea of comparing her to the postmoderns, the danger of assimilating their perspectives too quickly. For in Blanchot we have a figure whose doubt is so severe that it indefatigably questions its own veracity, whereas with Weil there is a certainty so strong that it indefatigably answers such questioning. For Blanchot, Weil

> had become familiar with this way of thinking and proceeding not by proof or by
> doubt, but by affirming and by holding firmly without wavering to the movement of
> affirmation that by a pact unites thought, will, and truth. But this itinerary is different
> with Simone Weil. The kind of invisible effort by which she seeks to efface herself in
> favor of a certitude is all that remains in her of a will as she advances from affirmation
> to affirmation.[19]

Death cannot be made an object of possible recuperation within even the most dialectical conceptual scheme. Here there is a state of incommensurability, as death is something with which one cannot enter into a geometric relation, of which there can be no certainty. Blanchot radicalizes this notion in Weil, for there is no transference of ourselves into our neighbor when we feel his suffering as our own; there is no self-identification with the universe, nor with God, nor with the love of God in us. There is not to be found in relation to affliction-unto-death any proportional mean, nor an image of the christus mediator and his incarnation. Blanchot thus rejects the idea that would have language be merely a vehicle of self-discovery, a form of language in which the obscurity might be brought to light and presence of self-consciousness—a form of language that would convert the passivity of suffering into an activity of conscious knowing. Instead, by dint of such passivity, Blanchot discerns how our being in language renders us irreducibly opaque to ourselves, how writing becomes a figuration of the unfigurable or an image of the invisible that devastates the self, leaves it indigent and suffering that which never takes place in the presence of conscious experience or its language. It is "that thought which would not allow itself to be thought." His gloss on the biblical word: "The one who sees God dies: for "dying" is a manner of seeing the invisible, a manner of saying the unsayable—the indiscretion where God, become somehow and necessarily a god without truth, would give himself over to passivity .[20]

> "...another regret one feels [regarding Weil]. She says that we can reach truth only
> in secret ... She nonetheless lacks this secrecy. No thought has more rigorously sought
> to maintain God's remoteness, the necessity of knowing that we know nothing of him
> and that he is truth and certitude only when he is hidden, the hidden God. But she
> does not cease to speak openly of this hidden God, with assurance and with
> indiscretion, forgetting that this indiscretion renders nearly all her words in vain."[21]

Weil for Blanchot performs a necessary indiscretion with regard to the unsayable. For like the writer's vain and deceiving utterances of death, Weil wants to hold to the belief that I, a being who is without relation to God and incapable of doing anything to approach him on my own, can nevertheless live in such a way that I will die in God's presence. At a certain moment, in extreme affliction, we can be certain in our desire for the good, even if our writings only lie; indeed, even to express the lie remains impossible, for the inadequacy of language is uttered only in language, which thus unavoidably obscures the inadequacy. If she has such a certitude, will not her desire lose its purity, tainted by the particularized want of an unredeemed subject? With this comes the essential contradiction. Thought of the truth alone is enough to falsify the truth, just as knowing the rules required for salvation is enough to make one no longer capable of observing them because the very fact of thinking about them already constitutes their violation. The unsayable will not be said or unsaid. Weil's writing, that would say the unsayable by unsaying it, cannot succeed, cannot reach closure, for success would either say something, and hence say too much and so fail, or else say too little. There is thus committed an indiscretion through which Weil would have us pass in reaching toward that annihilation which she can neither articulate as such nor finally fully silence.[22]

Proximity to affliction is somehow outside of the self's mastery. It is proof that the subject is not merely closed within itself, but extends out into the horizons of the past and future. Death does not come out of me and my own existential projects, but comes at me. It is the other which does not yield a hard and fast conceptual distinction between other and the same. Thought revolts from contemplating affliction. In the language of Levinas, another postmodern with whom Weil's shares indiscrete proximity, the absolute experience of the other in affliction is not so much a disclosure as a revelation. To give meaning to one's presence with affliction is an event irreducible to evidence. It cannot become an objectifying cognition. For Weil, over and against her claims for the utmost precision in language, we must be wary that the language of concepts suppresses the other in affliction, reduces them in some logic of the same. The afflicted silently beseech to be given the words to express themselves. There are times when they are given none; but there are also times when they are given words, but ill-chosen ones, because those who choose them know nothing of the affliction they would interpret. In the language of affliction there is no precision possible: one must listen, only to be open for a possible revelation. To recognize the other is to recognize the face in its vulnerability. To recognize hunger, destitution, nakedness is not knowledge. The other in affliction is the equivalent of death in demolishing our being at home in the world.

Blanchot recognizes in Weil's contradictions the experience of what cannot be grasped through experience. To hold that it is Christian thought that gives Weil her power is to over-state what is at work, since for Blanchot "seeking and finding" God are unsuitable expressions to account for what is at work in her work. Instead, it is her status as a writer that centers her work. Blanchot marks the strange power of her affirmation in thinking, coercive at times, a certitude which somehow accompanies how for her we know nothing of God but the name. This affirmation comes from the insistent repetition of that which by definition her writings cannot say. The writer is bound by the inability to write, so there is only the task of repeating what is said as a process of endless repetition. Like the narrator in Blanchot's novels telling a story that never happens as an event present to itself, Weil can write of affliction as never happening to the extent that it is what has always already happened, in exactly the same way that death, precisely because it always belongs to the past, is only ever the non-event of its own impossibility. Affliction can be thought only as an interruption of thought. It introduces into language a distance that withdraws events or statements from themselves and re-inscribes them as only other than they are.[23]

The Good is too certain to be an object of faith, so absolute is it that we have no relation to it. Just the desire for the good is faith. Desiring not to possess but just to desire. The necessity, the order of the world, is absolutely empty of God, and the very purity of the emptiness is closest to divine essence, and our suffering this necessity is a consent to distress. Affliction is a kind of natural redemption. Her own mystical experiences are to reveal nothing, guarantee nothing. Blanchot pushes to where this coalesces as the tearing of Simone Weil.

> We come back to the question: if what tore her from herself is not herself, and is not God, then what is it? One must answer: this tearing itself. This response ... is what sustains her entire life and thought.[24]

Outside us there is affliction, time, aimless necessity; inside us, consent to affliction, obedience to time. Like a clearing, language is the place of attention for that thought of what cannot allow itself to be thought. From Blanchot's perspective these tensions between silence and language are precisely what drive the poet as well, thus allowing the possibility that we could read apophatic theologians as poets and poets as apophatic theologians. For the utterance of affliction, like that of death, would be an utterance of infinitude, precisely because it faces a task never to be resolved. Seeking to express, to present the unrepresentable, that which cannot come into the presence of any language, would fail insofar as it succeeds: if it seems to say something of this radical otherness, it has in fact deceived, since, recalling Augustine, that is not ineffable which can be called ineffable.[25]

In this trace of what does not take place, the radical passivity and mortal subject of language mirrors the ineffable, invisible God in a mirror play that proves abyssal. The subject, now undone of all self-grounding and self-transparency, proves as some point indiscretely close to the God of whom any image or language remains impossible, and seems to signal an important proximity. This refusal to speak is the starting point of Blanchot's poetics. It grounds his views about how we are so profoundly offended by the use of force called torture. Torture is the recourse to violence with a view to make one speak. This violence wants one to speak. Torture wants the speech to be, not the result of torture, but that of some pure speech, free of all torture. This contradiction offends us, and in the contact reestablished between violence and speech, provokes the terrible violence that is the silent intimacy of all speaking words. This can also be seen by Blanchot's reflection on the nature of suicide. One who takes his own life has the aptitude to die content, provided that one considers self-destruction as supreme self-affirmation. Blanchot's analysis of suicide revolves around the question of whether complete consciousness of death can be achieved. His conclusion of course is that it cannot. The suicide's attempt to domesticate death by taking their own life constitutes an act of power, a kind of constructive negativity, to master or personalize or even render it present, are futile. The writer falls into the same trap as does the suicide except that instead of taking one death for another, writers mistake the writing for the act. The perpetrator of suicide sets out with great determination to conquer and possess death, to make it one's own, when in fact the opposite occurs. In a similar way writers, although they may initially feel confident in their ability to have some control over the raw materials of their craft, undergo the same kind of dispossession. The more they write, the further they advance in literary space, the less clear their original project becomes.

Suicide and writing thus both have something in common: on the surface each of these activities purports to accomplish something, and yet each must ultimately be considered as failing to do so. Each activity represents an extreme situation, an experience of limits, the crossing of which implies entering a domain where power is not of prime importance. Both actions are attempts to render death humanly possible. Dying is a defective verb that cannot be conjugated, for it has no forms in the present, nor can any personal pronoun serve as its subject. Suicide, and writing, try unsuccessfully to force this impersonal infinitive into a personal paradigm.

Blanchot's thinking about language resembles that of Heidegger's *Origin of the Work of Art* in its comparison of art and failed equipment. What works of art and broken tools have in common is their capacity to disclose contexts of significance, the original being of things which has been covered up by their having been adapted to perform particular functions. Whereas for Heidegger poetic language has the power of a kind of ontological revelation, it is for Blanchot not of full light-filled presence but the presence of an absence, what Levinas calls the "*il y a*," the phenomenon of impersonal, anonymous being, an uneliminable moment of existence which is not conditioned by the negative.[26] If the truth of affliction is its emptiness, then the content of any language of affliction is revelatory only in the opening of its failure as a tool. One cannot speak sufficiently the insufficiency of language-before-death, even in and through negation, since negation itself still works as a tool in cooperation with the language it would seek to undo.[27]

The language of affliction / the affliction of language is in contrast to that which would have language be a mere vehicle of exchange. Such language disappears after having served its purpose. It is the result of the exchange which is important, not the way in which the exchange is carried out. Poetic language is not uttered with a view toward accomplishing a transaction, and so is not predetermined by any particular function to perform. Something about it does not fade into the result that was provoked. There is a remainder. So language used in its everyday sense differs from poetic language in that everyday language disappears into whatever it evokes, whereas poetic language annihilates the object that it names and represents its absence somehow, but does not dissolve into the meanings it creates.

People die, but language survives. It lingers on to prolong indefinitely the irresolvable tensions. It is as if language were infinitely endowed with a capability that human beings possess only briefly. The very condition of literary language is that it can do indefinitely what people can do only for the shortest of times. Language already has the capacity to go beyond the limit of the living. It's function is that of Charon, continually conveying passengers to the other side of death and returning alone, going to the other side of death and coming back. Writers, by accepting the conditions of the approach of the literary space, participate for a time in this movement, but in the end they fall to what language does without them anyway.

Levinas is another for whom the poverty of language in regard to God and the other in affliction, in which language would (almost) fail due to an indiscretion with regard to the unsayable, mirrors Simone Weil. For Levinas, to have knowledge of God, to reduce God to a concept, is to reduce his alterity. Discourse on the nature of God is onto-theology, making of God an essence to be revealed. Atheism gives all prestige to the logic of the same, in effect denying transcendence. Concepts repudiate the significance of anything that does not fall within its range, philosophy claiming for itself the full range of the meaningful. To understand God as a concept or as an experience is atheism. Is God a meaningful word at all? No, for it is to talk of something outside of being. God is what strikes thought from the outside, utterly irreducible to being and inconceivable in terms of the knowledge and experience of the subject. This other approaches us instead as does the stranger, the widow, the orphan. [28]

The difficulty for Weil is similar to that which Blanchot spells out in Levinas, one of elaborating a philosophy of self and other in which both are preserved as independent and self-sufficient, but also in some relation to one another. The problem is that it seems to be the nature or desire of the relation to bring the other into the sphere of the same. This makes it intelligible from the perspective of the self-same self, thus reducing its true otherness. *Human thought is unable to acknowledge the reality of affliction.* So too a lack of acknowledgment lies at the center of the problem of description posed by the relation between self and Other. To preserve the other as other it must not become an object of knowledge or experience, because knowledge is always my knowledge, and experience is always my experience. Blanchot pushes Simone Weil at where she would diminish alterity. He would have her describe and defend subjectivity, describe alterity which does not reduce the Other to the same; and finally explain or describe the relation between same and other that does not abolish either. Thus he does not even describe the self as different from the other, since that would entail some God's eye view from which their qualities could be compared.

What is the encounter with the absolute other? Neither representation nor limit, nor conceptual relation to the same. The self and the other are not in any recuperable totality or relation. Whatever we are talking of or toward cannot encompass the other, cannot include the other. Late in *Totality and Infinity* Levinas holds that the Other is the condition for the possibility of language; yet language cannot make its own possibility a totality, without violence. Are we not at that point where the encounter of affliction and language occurs? One does not have to wonder even what this encounter is, for it is the encounter, the only way out, the only adventuring outside oneself toward the unforseeable, without hope of return. The status of those in affliction is not subsumable under any genus nor any concept, not part of a totality so much as the disruption (or freedom) of totality. Indeed, independence from totality is possible only because the Other in affliction so exists. Their alterity constitutes the ground which makes separation possible. The self exists because the other is irreconciliable with it. Otherwise self and other would be greater parts of some whole which would invalidate their separateness.

This is a thinking toward the other without logic or concepts. Concepts suppose an anticipation, a horizon within which alterity is eliminated or reduced as soon as it is announced precisely because it has let itself be forseen. Blanchot perhaps sees in Weil an incomplete version of Levinas' overcoming of the Husserlian horizon of the same in that the other no longer even appears as the other for the same. It is not the insufficiency of the self that prevents totalization but the infinity of the other.[29] Religion is a relation without relation. The other is not a fact, not an obstacle. It is desire for the infinite which calls into question my freedom. The other is not a foundation of knowledge, does not issue in totality.[30] The idea of infinity has more to do with desire than cognition.[31] There is no meaning in speaking of knowing nor not knowing the other. The formal structure of language announces the ethical inviolability of the other, his holiness.[32] The face of the other is neither an object nor a metaphor. The nudity of the face of the other is not a figure of speech. It does not seem to be even an opening to the other. The term tries to destroy itself after its use, after serving to indicate something beyond itself. This nudity of the other's face, being neither theory nor theorem, is offered and exposed. The face of the other is not in the world. Yet it is the origin of the ethical, not by opposing me with another force in the world but by looking at me from an other origin in the world, not my own. The word affliction then itself trembles, for it is neither a common noun without a concept nor an adjective nor verb nor pronoun. It is the unnameable source of every proper word.

The events surrounding dying and the impossibility of dying, as lying beyond the limits of language, yet which everywhere is to be spoken, puts Weil and Blanchot in indiscrete proximity. What is true of writing and death is true of writing and affliction: that they know no opposite, that they cannot be cured except through their enactment, and that the only antidote to the limits of language proves to be the limitless exposure to those limits. Negative theology is that thinking which denies God can be described adequately by either positive or negative predicates, and seeks to abstract our attention from concepts of God to the true God who cannot be conceptualized but only approached, whose name cannot be pronounced except when one is unable to do otherwise. Those in affliction and their implication in language comprise the Other that resembles God without a participation. The Other as infinity is the God of the *via negativa* never to be known nor grasped, the untotalled absence which must be thought without the same. An approach to the unsayable somehow gets closer by knowing itself failed, never undertaking a proximity in the first place, for have we not committed an indiscretion in arrogating God to any conceptual category of the same? Recalled to us is the passage from Exodus which reads: "Thou canst not see my face: for there shall be no man see me and live ... thou shalt stand upon a rock. I will take my hand away, and thou shalt see from behind: my face is never to be seen."[33] I cannot "be" there when my death occurs, since death undoes me as the being I am, so I cannot "be" there to see the God who remains invisible or to say the God who remains unsayable. Affliction is in proximity to this "god without truth," the god that cannot be reduced to a presence for a subject of consciousness or language, the god in seeing whom one would impossibly see the invisible, in speaking whom one would impossibly speak the ineffable.

V. Mysticism, Gift, and Bataille's Theory of Expenditure

I.

Recently the United States recognized the first-year anniversary of the terrorist attacks on the World Trade Centers in New York. Among the many responses to the anniversary of the attacks there emerged a belated gesture in the gift of fourteen cows to the United States from the Masai of East Africa. The Masai had heard of the attacks only in the spring of 2002 through a young Masai returning home from medical studies in the United States. Various news agencies sought to articulate the sacredness of the act, how such a gift was variably quaint, backward, comical in its simplicity, profound, mystical, spiritual, the equivalent of two years' income for each animal for the average African worker.

To the Masai gift, the western impulse is, if not first to ridicule or humiliate, to return with an equal gesture, a rational circuit of exchange, compensation, and control. Sacred experience however never presupposes an original plenitude to be reestablished. The events of September 11th, 2001 may well be defined by the marking of an irrecuperable loss, a loss which brings only the intangible gain of a certain lucidity regarding loss. Writing of the event is pierced by the truth that none of us has time to live the true dramas of the existence destined for us. The uncanniness of having been too late, a belatedness which disrupts the inevitability of every destiny, dislodges every claim to mastery.

The general economy of the gift is a dispossession. What is to be recovered is not some prior purity but the very experience of loss as such. There are gifts that precede the give and take of property, that precede any accountable exchange credit. Such a gift introduces the burden that shatters every project of self-recovery. To recognize the sacred in the gift of the Masai is now almost impossible. The dubious distinction of the west is to have singled out economic motives as the constant traits of human nature, thus convincing individuals that interest and profit are in fact the dominant incentives for their actions. A theory of social action based on economic motives establishes hunger, gain, or self-interest as the guiding activities of everyday life. Its social institutions therefore sanction any means to attain their satisfaction. *Homo economicus* is either economic or non-economic—any other values manifestly at odds with those of economism are segregated. The utilitarians endowed the economic side of man's character with the aura of rationality: he who would have refused to imagine that he was acting for gain alone was thus considered irrational.

The gift of the Masai gives occasion to reflect on how contemporary European philosophy has been marked by a renewed reflection on and interaction with themes from the religious turn in phenomenology, to reflections on the meaning of gift-exchange, to a continued interrogation with the texts of various mystical traditions.[1] Thinkers as diverse as Weil, Levinas, Derrida, de Man, Foucault, Blanchot, Bataille, Heidegger, Cixous, Irigaray, Benjamin, Adorno, and Marion all participate in this discussion, and have been caught up in and at times compromised by the perceived mystical and religious detours in their thinking. Their work remains intimately connected to the themes, the vocabularies and the concepts variously discovered in the writings of mystics. Had they been contemporaries of Plotinus, their work might not have appeared so problematic. Since the Enlightenment, however, when Kant declared that mystical illumination leads to the "death" of all thinking, philosophy has with few exceptions sought to formulate its visions of existence in terms immune to the charge of nebulous thinking that the word "mystical" implies. By the end of the 19th century the word had lost all dignity and specificity that the concept of *intuitus mysticus* once enjoyed. Thus does William James lament that the words 'mysticism' and 'mystical' are often used as terms of mere reproach, "to throw at any opinion which we regard as vague and vast and sentimental, and without a base in either facts or logic."[2]

All such sweeping claims for the exclusion of the mystical from modern philosophical discourse should be challenged. On the German side of things, Heidegger went the furthest distance to show that so-called mysticism, as the repressed other of philosophy, lies buried at the heart of philosophical logic, unsettling in subtle ways philosophy's march toward a rational and ordered view of the universe. The impact of mysticism on French philosophy has been no less momentous, triggered in no small part, perhaps, by the French reception of Heidegger. Independent of any particular mystical experience, these thinkers have often used mysticism as a weapon against the confining and reductive positivism of philosophy. Similarly, those who react against all such writing are themselves reacting to an entire tradition of mystical thinking, which both in France and Germany has come to be seen not only as the enemy of philosophy and reason, but an enemy of the state as well.

II.

Standing almost at the head of a long line of sociologists and anthropologists whose work focuses on the phenomenon of gift-exchange was a work which had an enormous impact, Marcel Mauss' *The Gift*, which first appeared in 1924.[3] In explaining how people become exchangers of goods, Mauss turned to the potlatch ceremony of the indigenous peoples of the Northwest coast of North America and to the gift-giving practices of some Polynesian and Melanesian peoples, practices which exhibit the obligation to give and receive the purely sumptuary destruction of wealth in order to outdo others. Bataille's infamous war-time essay "The Notion of Expenditure" in *La Critique sociale* developed the concept of expenditure in close connection with that of sacrifice, drawing on Mauss's discussion of potlatch.[4] Bataille argued that the classical economic theories that focus their attention on categories of utility and production have failed to grasp a deeper dynamic underlying all economic and social arrangements, namely the principle of limitless loss or unconditional expenditure. Such unproductive activity, such pure expenditure, is the ultimate end of all human activity. As exemplary social forms of unproductive expenditure Bataille cites luxury, mourning, wars, cults, sumptuary monuments, games, spectacles, the arts, and non-reproductive sexual activity. The common characteristic of these diverse behaviors is that they are oriented towards no external purpose and have their ends in themselves. Expenditure stands in opposition to the productive mode, in which each action or element is instrumentalized in the service of an end beyond itself, which alone endows it with meaning. Expenditure signals the triumph of exuberant, useless waste over the principles of order and utility.

Not only does expenditure exist as an alternative to the productive practices and patterns of accumulation reflected in conventional economic theory, but expenditure commands production and accumulation as their real, though unacknowledged, reason for being. According to Bataille classical economic theories, even those of Marxism, have obscured this fact. *The principle of uselessness is thus a defining quality of the sacred.* Unlike Mauss or Durkheim, however, Bataille is not interested in the expenditure of the gift or the sacrifice as either a representation or catalyst of social unity, but primarily in the immediate violence unleashed in the act of sacrificial killing and in the opportunities for social disunity and disintegration that the sacred might afford.

III.

Bataille's thinking wound its way through initial challenges from the quarters of existentialism. Sartre is not often taken as defending a Kantian line, but his influential critique of Bataille's *Inner Experience,* first published in *Cahiers du Sud* in 1943, sought to cut off any resurgence of mysticism in postwar France. At this time, philosophy in France was attempting to play the role of spiritual advisor to a nation in turmoil, and politically engaged thinkers like Sartre thought mysticism was the last thing the French people needed. The values existentialism sought to promote were ethical ones of commitment, decision, and responsibility. The passivity of mysticism, its surrender to a higher force, ran counter to the critical tradition, which presupposed that a good dose of oppositional critique was better than a blind embrace of mystical experience. In the heady wartime context where Sartre was positioning his version of existentialism to rule post-war France, the need to distinguish (existential) philosophy from mysticism reigned supreme. Thus one of the initial concerns by Sartre is Bataille's perversion of philosophical terms toward supra-philosophical, mystical ends. Notions like transcendence, immanence, Dasein, and nothingness "in the works of Hegel or Heidegger" had precise significations, but are put to use by Bataille in the interests of presenting an adventure beyond philosophy. Donning a Kantian cloak, Sartre is anxious lest Bataille be mistaken for a philosopher, and that his "mystic *Discourse on Method*" be a sanctioned form of existentialism itself.[5]

Sartre claims that Bataille evokes temporality and history of the human condition only in order to attempt to escape from that condition through the instantaneous. He derisively calls Bataille a "new mystic" or a "pantheist *noir*" who claims to confront human contingency, history, and the death of God only in order to evade them in a flight to some new transcendence. By hypostatizing negation and nothingness as the unknown, Sartre claims, Bataille's experience of the void becomes a space in which the transcendent may yet emerge. Bataille simultaneously denies God and mysticism and returns to a transcendent reality and a new kind of mystical, atemporal communion with it, and for Sartre these contradictions demonstrate Bataille's bad faith.[6]

Sartre dismisses Bataille's desire to lose himself as exorbitant, without limits, uncontainable. Yet he as well immediately asks if Bataille is sincere in this desire, and then ultimately argues that he is not.

> ...ce qu'on entrevoit sous les exhortations glacées de ce solitaire, c'est la nostalgie d'une de ces fêtes primitives où toute une tribu s'enivre, rit et danse et s'accouple au hasard,

d'une de ces fêtes qui sont consommation et consomption et où chacun, dans la frénsésie de l'amok, dans la joie, se lacère et se mutile, détruit gaîment, toute une année de richesses patiemment amassées et se perd enfin, se déchire comme une étoffe, se donne la mort en chantant, sans Dieu, sans espoir, porté par le vin et les cris et le rut à l'extrême la générositié se tue *pour rien*.

When one glimpses under the icy exhortations of this solitary is nostalgia for one of those primitive festivals where a whole tribe gets drunk, laughs and dances and couples by chance, one of those festivals that are consummation and consumption, and where each one, in the frenzy of running amok, in joy, lacerates himself and mutilates himself, gaily destroys a year's worth of patiently amassed wealth, and finally loses himself, rips himself up like a piece of cloth, gives himself to death while singing—without God, without hope, carried by wine and cries and sex to the extremes of generosity, killing himself *for nothing*.[7]

Sartre begins by criticizing Bataille for confusing scientific and existentialist claims. Bataille writes a "martyr-essay" grounded in interior experience and revolt, but at the same time purports to speak scientifically and objectively about nature and the human condition. Moreover, he believes that scientific facts give rise to and explain human experiences of anguish and revolt. By continually reinterpreting Bataille's arguments in terms of German existentialism, even to the extent where Sartre implies Bataille's thought must be translated into German to be rendered coherent, Sartre suggests that what Bataille lacks is the existential-phenomenological method through which subjective consciousness can be philosophically described. In other words, to make sense of the quasi-existentialist aspect of Bataille's thought, there is needed the method and descriptive ontology that Sartre himself provides in his *Being and Nothingness*.

Although Bataille *pretends* to locate human beings fully in history, speaking of the human condition rather than of human nature and underscoring the contingency and historicity of human existence, he simultaneously claims to step outside of history in the instantaneous moment. Sartre not only condemns the contradictoriness of such a move, but psychoanalyzes it as a vestige of Bataille's own Catholic past. As in the Catholic tradition, history will ultimately be overcome through a salvific apotheosis.[8] Bataille asserts the death of God and the end of salvation but reinstates the transcendent as nothingness or the unknown and then claims a mystical union with that unknown.

En nommant le rien l'inconnu, j'en fais l'être qui a pour essence d'échapper à ma connaissance; et si j'ajoute que je ne sais rien, cela signifie que je communique avec cet être par quelque autre moyen que le savoir... Il paraît que cet abandon à la nuit est ravissant: je ne m'en étonnerai point. C'est une certaine façon, en effet, de se dissoudre dans le *rien*. Mais ce rien est habilement ménagé de façon à être *tout*.

By naming nothing the unknown, I turn it into an existence whose essence is to escape my knowing: and if I add that I know nothing, that signifies that I communicate with this existence in some way other than by knowing ... It appears that abandonment to this night is ravishing: I am hardly astonished. This is the way, in effect, to dissolve oneself into *nothing*. But this nothing is easily managed in such a way so as to be *all*.[9]

From Sartre's perspective, Bataille's desire to be all is itself a form of totalitarian thinking. Bataille's methodological confusions are intimately related to his "bad faith" concerning God, salvation, and mysticism, for his desire to stand outside the human condition and history is reflected in his claim to scientific objectivity. He "vainly attempts to integrate himself into the machinery that he has set up: he remains outside, with objectivity, with Durkheim, with Hegel, with God the Father."[10]

An additional argument Sartre makes against Bataille is that of claiming to wish to communicate while writing with a contempt for his audience that blocks communication. Sartre outlines Bataille's constant queries about how silence and interior experience can be communicated and suggests that Bataille, the one-time devout Christian, remains a crypto-Christian despite his overt atheism.[11] Bataille writes only for *"l'apprenti mystique."*[12] Ultimately like the evangelist possessed of truth that he is required to share, "the communication that he wants to establish is without reciprocity. He is in the heights, we are down below. He delivers us a message: he receives it who can. But that which adds to our trouble, is that the summit from which he speaks to us is at the same time the profound abyss of abjection."[13] For Sartre, to stand on the heights bestowing a message on those below is to stand outside the human condition with a truth one must convey to those still trapped within it. The injunction to speak or to write generates endless paradoxes, for Bataille must move from the singular experience of eternity back into time in order to speak to those still immersed within history.

IV.

While the effects of Sartre's critique were long lasting, they gave way with the ebbing of his existentialism. The locus classicus for much contemporary discussion of the problem is Derrida's famous essay on Bataille, and subsequent work on the gift.[14] The issue is initially cast in Hegelianism, in which these French theorists see a transparent translation of the foundational principle of a capitalistic market economy. Conversely, capitalism, from this perspective, can be understood as the outworking or incarnation of Hegelian spirit. In essence Derrida's argument is a fairly simple one: if a gift is encompassable within an economic system, it is not a gift in the strict sense of the term. To give a gift with the expectation of return is not to give a real gift but is just a form of self-interest. If a real gift were possible, it would have to fall outside every exchange relationship.

More specifically, all real giving is exchanging. It is as if the proposition "x gives z to y" automatically entails its reciprocal "y gives z to x." Both x and y already understand that z is not a free gift or that it has no strings attached. It is this expectation of a return that seemingly links the idea of the gift to the idea of exchange and sacrifice. In this formulation every act of giving, every gift, and every act of receiving a gift entails an expectation of an obligatory return of an equivalent gift. The seemingly inocuous "z" is actually the basis for what can come to be the calculation of equivalent values in the determination of what kinds of things will count as the same as z. In Derrida's argument, any anticipation or expectation of reciprocity as a return for a gift spoils the gift. Thus it is the subject and the dative positions in the sentence that are problematic, since they already signify the idea of the subject as a complex of psychological attributes, not the least of which is that the subject is always selfish and incapable of any altruistic act. The subject's relation to the other as a giver to recipient follows the classic pattern of Hegelian subjects who enhance their own identity by overcoming the identity of the other. Behind every gift lies the ulterior motive of the giver who expects a return, and it is the recipient's perception of that ulterior motive that impels him to give as good as he gets in order to be free of obligation, or to be locked into an ongoing relationship of reciprocal exchanges over time.

In developing this argument, Derrida turns to Hegel by way of Bataille with alternative readings of negation or negativity. Although probably no thinker in the history of philosophy had thought more thoroughly than Hegel about the negative, Bataille insists that he still had not thought radically enough. In the *Phenomenology*, Hegel famously writes:

> But the life of the spirit is not the life that shrinks from death and keeps itself
> untouched by devastation, but rather the life that endures it and maintains itself in it. It
> wins its truth only when, in utter dismemberment, it finds itself ... Spirit is this power
> only by looking the negative in the face, and tarrying with it. this tarrying with the
> negative is the magical power that converts it into being. [15]

Having recognized the power of the negative in nature and history, Hegel proceeds to double and thereby simultaneously negate and preserve negation. Or so he claims. Double negation is the logical structure of the Hegelian idea, and as such forms the foundation of the entire system. The magical negation of negation is the *recuperative gesture* through which every loss turns into a gain. This is on some front a philosophical rendering of the economy of salvation: resurrection always follows crucifixion, and loss is never final because the return on every investment is guaranteed by the one upon whom we can always bank.

Neither Bataille nor Derrida is convinced that the signature Hegelian operation of double negation actually preserves the negative. If spirit finds itself in and through its own negation, then the only thing that is truly lost through the long tortuous dialectical process is negation. Investment in the labor of history is prudent, because every loss turns into profit. What Hegel cannot bear is unredeemable expenditure. Since Hegel believes that loss is impossible and return is inevitable, Bataille labels this Hegelian economy *restricted*. Derrida explains Bataille's point:

> The phenomenology of spirit (and phenomenology in general) corresponds to a
> restricted economy: restricted to commercial values ... a "science dealing with the
> utilization of wealth," limited to the meaning and the established value of objects, and
> to their circulation. The circularity of absolute knowledge could dominate, could
> comprehend only this circulation, only the circuit of reproductive consumption. The
> absolute production and destruction of value, the exceeding energy as such, the energy
> which "can only be lost without the slightest aim, consequently without any
> meaning"—all this escapes phenomenology as restricted economy. [16]

So understood, the Hegelian economy works by securing a return on every investment. This is what makes the system of such interest, a *Bildungsroman with compound interest*. The Hegelian economy is restricted to and by the principle of principle and interest and the law of return, which lends, as it were, the circulation of both speculative currency and speculative philosophy their currency. The general economy, on the other hand, designates that which exceeds or falls outside the restricted economy.

Changing from perspectives of restricted economy to those of general economy actually accomplishes a copernican transformation: a reversal of thinking—and of ethics. If part of wealth ... is doomed to destruction or at least to unproductive use without any possible profit, it is logical, even inescapable, to surrender commodities without return ... Woe to those who, to the very end, insist on regulating the movement that exceeds them with the narrow mind of the mechanic who changes a tire.[17]

In his later discussions of the gift, Derrida locates one of many points of resistance to economic thought, to thought that tries to take account of everything. That there can be such points of resistance does not mean it is possible for us through them to escape an economy altogether, for we always find ourselves within at least one, but instead indicates that it is impossible to reduce everything to economic terms.[18] There are some ideas that exceed the capacity of economic thinking, and hence exceed the human capacity to achieve their reality. Such an idea would be that of the gift of the Masai. Economically speaking the gift simply does not work. It is resistant to calculation. It is structured as an *aporia*, a problem that resists being solved because it defies any usual frame of reference, exceeding our capacity even to hold onto it as a problem. It is resolved not by reasoning or by proof, but only by decision.[19]

Derrida's analysis the gift focuses on three elements, the donor, the recipient, and the gift-object. On the part of the donor, any recognition of the gift as a gift anticipates some kind of return. For whenever I intentionally give, I invariably receive. I may receive another tangible gift, or I may simply receive gratitude. Even if the worst happened, and my giving were greeted with displeasure or rejection, there would still be some return, if nothing more than the reinforcement of my own identity as a subject.[20] From the point of view of the recipient, any awareness of the intentional meaning of a gift places that person, too, in the cycle of exchange. When I receive something I perceive to be a gift, I have already responded with recognition. Even if my response to the giver is one of indifference, it would be in my recognizing the gift as gift, in recognizing that I am indebted, that I would have unwittingly entered the gift economy. The goodness of the gift is transformed into a burden as soon as I recognize it and therefore contract it as a debt. Considering the gift-object itself, we are faced with further difficulties. The gift-object may be a real thing or it may simply be a value, a symbol, or an intention. Again the problem is one of recognition, which always has a reference to perceiving subjects in the present. So the problem seemingly is that as soon as the gift appears as gift, its gift-aspect disappears. Its very appearance, the simple phenomenon of the gift annuls it as gift, transforming the apparition into a phantom and the operation into a simulacrum.[21]

The conditions of possibility of the gift are also its conditions of impossibility. Those conditions that make the gift what it is are also the very conditions that annul it. If to give a gift means to give something freely, without return, then in its identification as a gift in the present, no gift is ever accomplished. Derrida insists: "If the gift appears or signifies itself, if it exists or is presently as gift, as what it is, then it is not, it annuls itself ... The truth of the gift (its being or its appearing such, its as such insofar as it guides the intentional signification of the meaning-to-say) suffices to annul the gift. The truth of the gift is equivalent to the non-gift or to the non-gift of the gift."[22] One of the critical points of this analysis is that the investiture of a gift-object with an excess of givenness on its own does not suffice to make the gift possible as such. The question has not only to do with givenness or generosity but with whether or not the gift becomes part of a circle, or is reduced to the terms of a restricted economy. At the same time, it is impossible to imagine the gift in terms other than these, since it seems that they are all we have.

V.

Bataille analyzes a number of areas in which the principle of loss and uselessness is operative, such as religious worship and various forms of competition. Also art and literature: the term poetry, which is applied to the least degraded intellectualized forms of the expression of the state of loss, can be considered synonyms of expenditure. Poetry's meaning is close to that of sacrifice. But both Derrida and Sartre overlook how the centerpiece of Bataille's essay is the claim that the fundamental Marxist concepts of class struggle and revolution must be reread through these categories of sacrificial expenditure as well.

Essentially, Bataille's point is that class divisions spring from a sacrificial impulse inherent in society itself. If useless expenditure is the true end of human life, access to its most potent forms is a privilege jealously guarded by those with high social status. The celebrity-of-the-week's most recent wedding must not only be extravagant in its cost, but its press coverage must also be extravagant, and the cost of that coverage reported in its extravagance. It is to maintain their monopoly on the pleasures of waste and destruction that the rich exclude the miserable classes from all access to social, political, and economic power. In earlier historical periods, not only were the poor denied the right to engage in the ecstatic prodigality of expenditure, but they themselves, as captives or slaves, often were themselves the objects of that sacrificial expenditure for the pleasure of the rich. This same pattern remains operative in contemporary capitalist society with the difference that slavery is now called wage labor. The point of endless material acquisition and waste of the CEO's, to use another contemporary example, is not to oppress workers for their own benefit; both obey a larger impulse constraining society, namely to realize as tragic and as free a mode of expenditure as possible. The rich do not want to exploit workers, they literally want to sacrifice them. Under the force of this constraining impulse, the oppressed have few options, save vicarious participation in superbowl halftime shows.

The end of technological progress is neither grand utopia nor Spenglerian apocalypse, but pure uselessness. By purity is meant the degree to which the elements in question would *not* be used, would *not* be an active agent that either benefits or hurts humanity. It just would exist in and of itself with no function, literally free of humanity, free even of its own machine function, serving no practical purpose for anyone or anything. One can see such machines almost everywhere today, in home and workplace. So many have come to see technology as either a manifestation of advance or decline that the third alternative has been missed, namely that much of technology does nothing at all. Electronics filled with useless gadgetry are nothing more than an homage to uselessness. Like the computer chip which allows a VCR to be programmed a month in advance, the entire culture is a clock that only blinks 12:00.[23]

It is not ineffectual Bataillian mysticism which diagnoses how the perverse desires that consumers associate with utility are limitless. Driven by vast spectacularized engines of desire, consumers want more for their money, even if what they get is something they will never use. The central question of modern consumption is precisely that of whether or not I can get more for my money than what I could ever humanly use. The desire for the useless triggers the spiral which has consumers buying the privilege of not having to use, and to keep the apparatus of use as invisible as possible. The desire of consumer economy is useless expenditure, a need for excess beyond the possibility of human use. Pleasure is derived through negation—by *not* using the product, by never being able to consume it all. This form of excess is the privilege of those who enjoy the surplus of production. The upper classes aspire to total counter-production. Too often excessive luxury in the center realm of the visible is mistaken for the limits of excess, but the limits of excess go far beyond the visible. To comprehend extreme excess, one must go beyond conspicuous consumption. Excess will never be seen, but only imagined, and within this ideal space the margins can at least be understood. Whether it is useless chips in the bowels of discarded computers, or underground missile systems, the purity of the useless expenditure, the limits of excess, are not visible. The real deployment of power flows in absence, in the uncanny, nonrational margins of existence.

Utopian technology is that technology which has fallen from grace. It has been stripped of its purity and re-endowed with utility. The fall is necessitated by a return to contact with humanity. Having once left the production table, the technology that lives the godly life of *state of the art uselessness* has no further interaction with humans as users or as inventors; rather, humans serve only as a means to maintain its uselessness. The location of the most complex pure technology is no mystery. Deep in the heart of the american hologram is the computerized missile system. Ultimately all research is centered around this invisible monument to transcendental uselessness. The bigger and more powerful, the greater the mega-ton yield, the greater the expense of the upgrades, the greater the value. But should it ever actually be touched by utility, should it ever be used, its value becomes naught. To be of value, it must be maintained, upgraded, expanded, multi-theatered, but it must never actually do anything.

There are stopping points to this process. The fall of the Soviet Union had little to do with ideology. The US and the USSR were competitors in producing the best apparatus of uselessness in order to prove its own respective global mastery. As with all useless expenditure, there is no return on the investment of the trillions the arms race cost. The useless represents a 100% loss of capital. The compulsive desire for a new useless master is much greater that any lingering utilitarian strain. The US Government has to this day remained convinced that further progress can be made. Reagan and his Star Wars campaign issued a policy radically expanding the useless. Playing on cold war paranoia, he convinced millions that a *defensive* monument to uselessness was needed, just in case the *offensive* monument was not enough. He was successful enough in his original monumental vision to ensure that no one would be able to stop the inertia, that the apparatuses of uselessness would expand even if the cold war ended. This situation has come to pass with the second Bush administration. Currently the US has no competitors in the race to uselessness, but the monument continues to be maintained and even to grow though the cynical argument of deterrance is now dysfunctional. Even though the offensive monument to uselessness seems to be shrinking, missiles are being disused and cut apart with the care and order of high ritual, at a cost exceeding that of their original manufacture. Research continues, systems get their upgrades, although the missiles are now aimed at the ocean, so that even if they are used, they will still be useless. No enemy exists against which the star wars technology would protect US citizens. The American hologram has achieved transcendental uselessness, the highest manifestation of technological purity.

The policy of mutually assured destruction located useless waste and expenditure at the center of the framework. With the collapse of the USSR came the idea that American utility could save US citizens from the total annihilation certain to destroy the rest of the world, and so the technology became depurified, and the dissociation of death and uselessness took previously sacred elements of war-tech out of the privileged realm. To save the apparatus of the useless from stalling it had to morph into a generalized schemata. Thus George W. Bush reversed the Reagan poles, convinced the loyal public to create an *offensive* monument against terrorism just in case the *defensive* structures failed. Thus the purity of the offensive WMD continues to get enforced, however now it is that nations that do not understand the code of uselessness are the greatest concern. The US government is willing to take hostile action merely on the belief that WMD's now could actually be used. Nations that break the code, and do not subordinate themselves to the idol of the useless, will be sacrified as heretics.

The common wisdom of using variables of national interest and utility to explain the relationship between desire and power gives way to using the principles of anti-economic perversity, expenditure, and uselessness. Progress in the 20th century primarily consisted in western culture looking for new masters. The aristocracy was destroyed, as was the church with its spiritual hierarchies, but the primordial desire to serve the useless has never been affected. The so called primitive ritual of offering goods to an angry God in order to appease it continues to replay itself in the most complex capitalist economies. All things must be subordinated to uselessness, only today the referent has become virtual, empty signs, to which sacrifice has no limit. Along these fronts culture gets de-spenglerized, not so much in a narrative of *decline*, but of lawn-chair *recline*, a casual neutrality toward limitless waste.

VI.

Heidegger's use of the locution *es gibt*, which appears in *Being and Time* and is also found in later works, seems to be a crucial point upon which Heidegger's thinking turns.[24] The way in which *es gibt* is situated in Heidegger's thinking is outlined in the 1927 lecture course *Basic Problems of Phenomenology*:

> Perhaps there is no other being beyond what has been enumerated, but perhaps, as in the German idiom for "there is," *es gibt*, still something else is *given*. Even more. In the end something is given which must be given if we are to be able to make beings accessible to us as beings and comport ourselves toward them, something which, to be sure, is not but which must be given if we are to experience and understand any beings at all.[25]

The ambiguity of the phrase *es gibt* means that it can be interpreted both as "there is" and as "it gives." According to Heidegger's translator Macquarrie, the second sense is the stronger, and Heidegger's intention is clarified where, in the "Letter on Humanism," he insists that the French *il y a* ("there is") translates "*es gibt*" only imprecisely.[26] His point is to emphasize the aspect of (generous) giving in a way that also enables him to avoid saying that being "is." As Derrida observes, "we translate the idiomatic locution *es gibt Sein* and *es gibt Zeit* by *'il y a l'être'* in French and in English 'there is being' (Being is not but there is Being), *'il y a temps,'* 'there is time' (time is not but there is time). Heidegger tries to get us to hear in this the 'it gives' or as one might say in French, in a neutral but not negative fashion, *'ça donne,'* an 'it gives' that would not form an utterance in the propositional structure of Greco-Latin grammar." [27] As this comment indicates, Heidegger uses *es gibt* in speaking both being and time. [28] What exaxtly he means when he says this is not clear. What does it mean that being is given? What is the relationship between the giving of being and the giving of time, especially since neither being nor time "is" any thing? What can be made of the "it" that gives?

Being is a gift. Being gives itself. Being gives being. It is human thought that provides the locus for this event, this gift of being. "In hailing the thinker into Being, Being imparts itself to him as gift, and this gift is what constitutes the essence of the thinker, the endowment by which he is."[29] Such a gift would precede the give-and-take of property, every "present" of an accountable exchange. Such a gift would displace without mediating the opposition between giving and receiving. The relationship between man and time or being would become the mutual extension of an excess rather than the measured reciprocity of the debt-credit exchange. Such a gift would introduce the restrictive pressure of the potlatch, still the burden of an unnamed debt or guilt. A guilt so infinite no repayment could be thinkable. Once acknowledged such a guilt would disrupt the economy of exchange and the system of retributive justice which follows. Had such a guilt been thought through it would have shattered the appeal to self-recovery and self-mastery which had defined Heidegger's project at the outset, for the existential analytic had uncovered as the constituitive structure of Dasein a moment of radical obligation or indebtedness [*Schuldigsein*]; an unrepayable debt, the coming to owe something to others,[30] located prior to every recuperative transaction of exchange. Such exchange transactions could only determine time as the linear flow of empty now-points—the homogeneous stream that characterized the inauthentic. The time of authentic guilt, in contrast, would precede such linear determination: time as such would be the gift preceding every accountable advance, prior to the law of the tallying of debits and credits Nietzsche once linked to the mercantile economy of revenge. Guilt in this sense would be the debt prior to the circuit of possessions—the restricted economy of the marketplace and as an opening to the others would mark sociality prior to all exchange. Only such a being as Dasein could be capable of such sociality. The peculiarity of its death, the still outstanding quality of its ending, marks its finitude as the site of an obligation which will never be paid off.[31] Such finitude would link death inseparably to the others. A debt so infinite that no thanks could ever be enough. Gratitude itself would be no answer to the incommensurability of the gift, but just the mediating recognition which would discharge the debt by symbolic restitution, annulling the gift by reinscribing it within the intersubjective circle of exchange.

Recall how Heidegger, in *What is Called Thinking?*, defines thinking as thanking, a grateful response to a gift which is itself nothing, other than the ability to think. Thanking becomes simply the recursive, performative movement—a thanking which does not give thanks, but only thanks for being able to thank, which knows no object for its gratitude and thus has nothing with which to pay back. Here the two moments of exchange become indistinguishable—the closed circle of compensation twists open into the spiral of a surplus without end.

> "How could we give more fitting thanks for this dowry, the gift of thinking what is most thoughtworthy, than by thinking over what is most thoughtworthy? So that the highest thanks would be thinking? And the deepest thanklessness, thoughtlessness? Authentic thanks never consists in our coming with a gift and merely repaying gift with gift. Such thanking is not a compensation but it remains an offering."[32]

VII.

How then is this the endpoint in our rambling, uneconomical discussion of enlightenment modernity in the progressive technologization of experience? That the progress of the enlightenment has brought new and irreversible forms of domination: the reification of experience and the introduction of the abstract measure of utility; the reduction of qualitative difference to the quantifiable identities of the market; the increasing centrality of productive labor as the determinant of thought and action; the expulsion of the mundane sacred and its replacement by an otherworldly deity; the Newtonian determination of time as an inert continuum of exchangeable now-points; universal installation as it pertains to the intimate realm of the composition of written language and all concepts of intellectual property. Processes cumulate in the technological vicissitudes of the present—the reduction of the earth and thought to a standing stockpile of resources, the reduction of time to an accumulation of empty instants, the reduction of experience to the private self-possession of a transparent subject. Heidegger offers as countermemory to the tradition a repetition of the Greek experience of being as *aletheia;* having exhausted itself in the spiral of unleashed technology, metaphysics exposes a secret opening to its other in those momentary glimmers of an experience beyond the reach of calculation, recapitulating without restoring the early Greek reflection of being as the withdrawing gift of a time beyond the cumulative flow of indifferent now-points. As countermovement to the avaricious grip of reason there are experiences of laughter, perverse sexual activity, plagiarisms, unsober in the production of discourse, ecstatic gestures of human self-abandon. No longer wed to the fear of losing, uncaught in circles of self-preservation, unmarked by greed or concern with consequences. A vertiginous horizonality of the acephalic victim, the freefall of an unconditional Bataillean expenditure.

In *Being and Time* it is only *das Man* which seems prone to limitless loss, the dizzy and distracted nonself of inauthentic existence. Self-loss is that by which Dasein misses its station and plunges onto the slope of the everyday. Its drunken lurch a whirling, a groundlessness, an uprootedness, an entanglement, a falling, a distraction, a floating, a plunging. Even its death is not its own, referring that ownmost possibility to another, vicariously experiencing death as something for "them" to go through, relinquishing phenomenological propriety. Death is the paradigm of the zenith of private property which the faceless public can never steal or own. Immured against this wobbly state by no more than a thin wall and for no more than a moment, Dasein pulls itself together from this scattered confusion and reclaims its own self in the firm grip of resolution. It is time here to speak of a self-loss instead of self-possession, a slippage instead of a standing, a living death through the imposture of the others where Heidegger would protect the irreplaceable uniqueness of one's proper death. But this must be undertaken in a way aware of the logic of inversion—self-abandonment may be hollow where it remains reactive: underlying the disintegrative posturing may be just a longing for the old one. The ultimate usury here is where self-loss becomes the prelude to a higher recuperation, a negative theology of loser wins. Are we involved here in an easy inversion of the Heideggarian *Eigentlich*, the sheer negative to phenomenological self-disclosure? Mere inversion is still a metaphysical maneuver, reinforcing what it would surmount. If fundamental ontology can and must be inscribed within the circuit of reproductive consumption, the recovery of meaning which is philosophy's founding gesture, it would be no alternative simply to privilege what it excludes. The dispersal of the they would be a determinate waste within the system, a relapse to precritical immediacy, not overcoming property relations. Self-loss would become naturalized and sterilized as the philosopheme of pure identity.

Technological writing overwritten by the circuit of productivity and exchange is the corner Heidegger turns when in *Being and Time* he related the vitalist stream of experience to the homogeneous flux of accumulative now-points to a modality of the inauthentic. Such a stream could only isolate the present as the empty unit of exchangeability, creating the very need to ground perception in the self-givenness of the private subject. A givenness which would obliterate all the differences, yielding only the trivial self-identity of the immediate. Such is the uncanny "too late" which marks the structure of lived time as such. It is a belatedness which disrupts the inevitability of every destiny, dislodges every claim to mastery, disappropriates every comfort of being at home. This turn was for Heidegger nothing other than the general economy of the gift, a turning from the property of authentic dasein and towards a general dispossession of the ownmost self. The standing reserve becomes the security holdings of accumulated stock, so there was needed a turn toward, a receding origin, the absent presence which precedes every relation of property or propriety which calls for a radical letting-be. It will be a question of the experiencing of the tug of a writing no longer and not yet embroiled in the snares of productivity, prior to every manipulation and all control. No movement of regression could recuperate this, for what is to be appropriated is not the plenitude of a priori purity but the very experience of loss as such. For presence defines itself precisely as the withholding of the present: a gift which determines time itself as an epochal self-suspended sending rather than as a serial string of accumulated now-points which could be collected and held intact. It thereby divests the present of its atomic integrity, unraveling the possibility of all exchange, undermining every structure of appropriation by refusing to render present that which it offers as only a gift.

The consequence of the domination of economics and its rationality bias for theories of gift-giving can be felt here. The Masai act illustrates how economics founds its credibility on laws so general as to be nonrestrictive, spilling out into all areas of thought. What force is there now in the Masai gift given which may yet compel us to make a return, a debt so infinite that no thanks could ever be enough, gratitude itself being no answer to the incommensurability of the gift? In a restricted economy gratitude would be just the mediating recognition which would discharge the debt by symbolic restitution, annulling the gift by reinscribing it within the intersubjective circle of exchange. What is needed is a thinking which looks at excess rather than scarcity, consumption rather than production, that this writing is only of excess energy, translated into the effervescence of life. In order to determine the possibilities of this writing, we propose more of a pseudipigraphica whose sum transcends its accumulated parts and is not to be equated with a quantitive expansion of the scope of any traditional economics. Such a thinking is to disrupt the pattern of harmonious reciprocity. It is in the interest of thought to spend rather than save.

VI. Aristotle as Proto-Phenomenologist

In the early 1920's Heidegger had the growing perception of the poor theological grounding of his students. In a letter to Löwith he mentions considering teaching nothing but Plotinus so as to shore the students up, but decides instead on an intensive teaching of Aristotelian metaphysics, which he begins in 1921 and does not let up until 1924. This period also finds Heidegger responding to questions posed by Löwith regarding publication of the Bonn edition of Luther's works. Luther's vitriolic attacks against "the liar" Aristotle, who openly consorted with "that whore, reason," have as their constructive goal the restoration of the simple tenets of primitive Christianity, which accordingly must first be purified of the age-old Greek contaminations perpetrated upon it by medieval theologians. This theme of the corruption of original Christian insights by Greek neoplatonism played no small role in Heidegger's lecture course on Augustine as well. Through the course of this intense teaching and lecturing on Aristotle, Heidegger's "Lutheran" motivations get sidetracked, however, in favor of a newfound affinity between his own original phenomenological analyses and Aristotle's texts, both in method and in content. Heidegger thus later declares that his early work on Aristotle was decisive in the development of his phenomenology.[1] His estimation of the Greek thinker was enormous, to the point of saying that no one has ever surpassed the greatness of Aristotle.[2] Of specific importance for Heidegger was Aristotle's phenomenological method.[3] Bringing his earlier interpretations of the dynamized facticity of life to bear upon these texts, Heidegger found in Aristotle a kindred soul, a proto-phenomenologist of the first order, which in turn led to the even deeper comprehension of the nature of phenomenology. As we will see in our later chapters on Spengler and Gadamer, Aristotle was to play a governing role throughout much of Heidegger's subsequent thought.

Phenomena are the Starting Place

As opposed to the transcendent tendencies in Platonism and the abstract deductions typical of certain pre-socratics, Aristotle amounted to saving appearances. For him, investigation should always begin with phenomena as presented to us, through which the search for explanations and causes can properly proceed.[4] Phenomena are the "witnesses" and "paradigms" for philosophical inquiry.[5] Contrary to speculative metaphysics and aetiological stories, Aristotle insists that the "why" and the "what" of things cannot be examined before the "that" (*to hoti*) of things, which Heidegger might call their "concrete presencing;" to reverse this order is to "inquire into nothing."[6] Aristotle thus takes his point of departure, not from theoretical constructions, but from what is immediately apparent in perceptible encounters.

Premodern Alternative to Metaphysics

There are several ways in which Aristotle's thought represents a premodern precedent for Heidegger's alternative to the ontologies of modern philosophy and science. Aristotle was a thoroughgoing realist and naturalist, in the sense that human beings belong in the world and are at home in it. Heidegger also found in Aristotle's ontology a recognition of particularity, plurality, and movement, which was akin to his own phenomenological alternative to the metaphysics of constant presence that marked most of the western tradition.

Consider Aristotle's concept of *ousia*, the primary sense of being as the unified reference for descriptions. Heidegger points to the pretechnical meaning of *ousia* as household belongings available for us, which he calls "possessions" or "havings," in line with his sense of environmental *zuhanden* relations. As indicated in the examples of fabricated things illustrating the four causes, Aristotle understands beings initially as modes of productive use, not as bare objects.[7] Heidegger associates this sense of *ousia* with the "having" of language, which Aristotle himself takes as a kind of middle voice between self and world, which thus accords (somewhat) with Heidegger's holistic structure of being-in-the-world.

And *ousia*, for Aristotle, unlike the Platonic conception of being and the connotations of the Latin translation "substance," is primarily a "this something" (*tode ti*), an immanent, concrete presence in experience.[8] Species and genera are *ousia* in a secondary sense, in that they reveal something about being, but not in a primary sense.[9] The primary sense of *ousia*, then, suggests the radicality of the "that" over the "what," which Heidegger takes to mean the sense of presencing in temporal experience (the Greek word for presence is *parousia*). *Ousia* is a unity in the sense of being a stable reference point for an account of things, but there are as many unities as there are beings in experience, and the temporality of nature shows that *ousia* is in each case finite.[10]

Aristotle's is a Phenomenology of Movement

Aristotle's ontology does not set itself apart from motion and change, and thus it accommodates negation. Heidegger calls Aristotle's *Physics* a straightforward phenomenology of movement.[11] In this work Aristotle investigates the explanations and ordering principles of nature (*physis*), which is directly identified with movement and change.[12] Aristotle specifically correlates the notion of *physis*, being, *ousia*, and movement,[13] thereby separating himself from philosophies that had counterposed being and change.[14] Things of nature have an intrinsic principle of movement, as distinct from things brought into being extrinsically by production.[15] *Physis*, then, has to do with self-manifesting beings. The task of analysis is to make sense out of change and movement, which Aristotle accomplishes by way of concepts of matter and form, which are given a dynamic sense in the concepts of potentiality (*dunamis*) and actuality (*energeia*).

Both *dunamis* and *energeia* are active concepts for Aristotle. The two together represent a single model of process.[16] *Dunamis* as potentiality is not simply logical possibility, but an active capacity to develop, and *energeia* as actuality is not simply a finished state, but being at work (*ergon*) in the actualizing of potential. Form (*eidos*), then, cannot be understood simply as a static "shape," but rather as the active self-organization of a developing being.[17] Heidegger notices *energeia* and *dunamis* coordinated with *telos* in Aristotle's coinage of *entelecheia* (literally "having-an-end-in" one's being), so that the movements of *physis* involve a being-toward, a self-emerging being-on-the-way-toward a not-yet that appropriately can-be, that is to say, a presencing of an absence.[18] Being, then, involves a self-surpassing otherness.[19] In thinking of *ousia* as a concrete occurrence in natural experience, Aristotle is able to give movement, change, time, and negation their appropriate sense of being.[20]

Aristotle's Dasein

In Aristotle's text on the soul (*psuche*), we find a great deal that fits Heidegger's phenomenology of Dasein as an active, temporal movement animated by possibility. The soul is the form of the body's matter, but in the unified sense of being the actualization of potentials in a living being, an active capacity to function and develop.[21] Aristotle specifically identifies the human soul with all the elements that Heidegger finds so significant in Aristotelian phenomenology; *phusis, dunamis, energeia, ousia,* and *logos* (*On the Soul*, 412a20ff), all of which suggests a dynamic capacity to be-in-the-world. Heidegger shares completely

Aristotle's notion that the self is essentially an activity, not a static essence.[22]

Heidegger's alternative to subject-object bifurcations in modern philosophy also finds precedent in Aristotle's reflections on the soul, which offer a "bipolar" conception of self and world. The soul is potentially the same as the things it thinks, without being identical to them.[23] Thinking is nothing until it thinks something in the world and what it thinks must be in thought.[24] The actively thinking soul is the things it thinks.[25] The mention of activity (*energeia*) can direct us to sections in the *Physics* (III. 1-3), where we are told that in activity, the agent and the patient are the same, as a single process of actualization (illustrated by teaching and learning, building and a house being built). The agent is not something self-contained in an interior zone separate from the object of its activity. The potential of both is actualized in a single bipolar process. Here we have something very much akin to Heidegger's sense of being-in-the-world, as an ekstatic placement of the self in its environment. Such a construction also gives dramatic presentation of Aristotle's realism that in certain respects is carried on by Heidegger, namely, that the activities and disclosures of the human self are appropriated to the world and indeed can be called the world's own self-emergent activity.

Aristotelian Aletheism

As in Heidegger, the realism of Aristotle is not of a uniform kind. Aristotle offers a kind of pluralism that Heidegger takes to be significant. There is the plurality of being. Aristotle tells us that being is spoken of in many ways.[26] Whatever unity there is in the notion of being will at best be analogical, since being cannot provide a universal genus.[27] Aristotle also gives a pluralistic account of truth in book VI of the *Nicomachian Ethics* that was of enormous importance in Heidegger's early development. Aristotle mentions that there are two basic modes of the soul's "having logos" (*logon echon*): (1) that pertaining to beings whose origins cannot be otherwise (necessary being), and (2) that pertaining to beings whose origins admit of being otherwise (contingent being) and thus call for *bouleusis*, or deliberation and decision.[28]

The virtue of each mode is its own proper function or work (*ergon*) in being appropriated to the different kinds of beings by way of a certain familiarity with them.[29] This leads to a discussion of five virtues of thought: pertaining to the first mode of *logos* are *episteme* (scientific knowledge), *nous* (intuitive insight), and *sophia* (wisdom); pertaining to the second mode are *techne* (skill in making) and *phronesis* (practical wisdom or acting well in human affairs). Aristotle then identifies these five functions with five modes of truth, which are defined as the different functions and dispositions of the different virtues; indeed, the virtues are five ways in which the soul is *aletheuei*, or "in the truth."[30] As Heidegger puts it, Aristotle is here associating truth with Dasein's very being, the soul as *ousia*.[31] What is key for Heidegger is that truth is not limited to statements of scientific exactitude; it also applies to inexact modes of discerning appropriate action in spheres such as ethics. And truth understood as unconcealment is certainly more appropriate for this multiple conception of truth than is the correspondence model. For Aristotle, there is truth (appropriate disclosure) in matters of making (*poiesis*) and human living (*praxis*) that do not reduce to precise agreement with external objects or conceptual principles or statements.

Radicalization of Aristotelian Ethics

Heidegger also gives real attention to Aristotle's ethics and the prospects of an ethics inspired by Aristotle. The Marburg lecture course *Phenomenological Interpretations of Aristotle* offers some fascinating material regarding the relationship between Aristotle's thought and the possibilities for ethics in Heidegger's early ontology. Here Heidegger highlights the problems in absolutist, transcendental moral systems, owing to their detachment from a more worldly, finite, lived morality.[32] It is Aristotle's *Nicomachian Ethics*, particularly its critique of Platonic moral philosophy, that gives Heidegger a historical focus for a new beginning, both in ontology and in ethics. Heidegger suggests an ethics that will accord more with the human world, that will renounce the comfortable, undisturbed, lofty distances of moral theories that foreclose any realization of ethical possibilities in the actual experience of finite conditions.[33] Heidegger's primary interest in Aristotle's ethics was not in its articulation of a moral sphere, but in the avenues opened up for alternative conceptions of being and truth. In a discussion of book VI of the *Nicomachian Ethics*, Heidegger specifically brackets Aristotle's ontical ethical problematic in order to draw out its ontological implications—witness his characterization of Aristotle's intellectual virtues as modes of the "truthful safekeeping of being."[34]

Heidegger's radically finite ontology calls for certain modifications of Aristotle's moral philosophy. Aristotle's notion of *phronesis* shows itself to be an inexact ethical finesse that discloses appropriate courses of action with respect to desired ends, or that for the sake of which human beings act. The human good involves striving to actualize natural potentials through deliberative choices. Such an ethical field connects well with Heidegger's sense of pre-reflective understanding, which is associated with Dasein's potentiality-for-being and for-the-sake-of-which (*Umwillen*) animating Dasein's existence. Ethics for Aristotle involves human potentials and the means and conditions needed to actualize these ends. A similar kind of ethical developmentalism can be read out of *Being and Time*, although already in that text there is a radicalization of Aristotelian formulations. Kierkegaardian influences in *Being and Time* show an even more dynamic, open, contingent atmosphere than Aristotle would allow. For Heidegger's Dasein's potentiality is never filled up in any way or compensated by the comfort taken in any metaphysics of divine actuality. Dasein just is potentiality, so full actualization is ruled out in principle.

Heidegger stresses elements of absence and negativity that are only given passing notice in Aristotle. Despite Aristotle's attention to potentiality, movement, and desire-as-lack, despite his recognition of limits and the contingency of ethical truth, Aristotle still displays a (Platonic) preference for more stable modes of knowledge and the self-sufficient perfection of a divine realm. Thus Aristotle ranks *phronesis* lower than *sophia*, *nous*, and *episteme*, which provide necessary knowledge.[35] Human ethical life is constituted by limits, lacks, and needs, which is why Aristotle denies that the gods exhibit moral virtue, since they are completely self-evident, and they thus lack or need nothing.[36] The life and activity of the gods is identified with intellectual contemplation (*theoria*), which is wholly self-referential and needs nothing outside itself.[37] Accordingly, Aristotle names contemplation the pinnacle of human *eudaimonia*, since it is what is most godlike in humans—most self-sufficient and least burdened by desire, external needs and relations with others.[38] Although Aristotle, being a good phenomenologist, sees the human, natural world as constituted by temporality and limits, he nevertheless reaches for the compensation of a metaphysics of constant presence in the divine sphere.

For all Aristotle's recognition of limits in the sphere of ethics, perhaps it is the metaphysical comfort of his theology that accounts for a rather secure, undisturbed tone that resonates in his ethical works, the sense of a clearly defined, organized harmony that marks *eudaimonia*, and the relative ease and confidence with which the virtuous person seems to move through life. Heidegger would have none of that. His take on *eudaimonia* would no doubt include more openness to negativity, disruption, and unsettlement, thereby subverting aristotelian comforts. For Heidegger, the experience of potentiality highlights futural openness that marks the temporal structure of ethical decisions, and that therefore includes a more acute awareness of not being grounded or secured in any strict sense. Thus Heidegger's perspective on ethical decisions would not be restricted to various positive states, conditions, or dispositions. For Heidegger negative dimensions play an essential role in disclosing the meaning of existential conditions, and for this reason, Heidegger's approach would have to be quite suspicious of the seeming security of the Aristotelian good life. Aristotle may have been a proto-phenomenologist, but not a proto-existential phenomenologist.

Although Dasein is always situated in a social world and shaped by tradition, the dynamic of authenticity shows that the individual self cannot be securely grounded in a community, custom, or habitual practice. The disclosing of authentic care follows from the *Unheimlichkeit* of an anxious separation from familiar supports. Heidegger identified *phronesis* with his call of conscience.[39] Conscience, in Heidegger's ontological sense, calls Dasein to the nullity of its own being-toward-death, and accordingly conscience "speaks" in the manner of silence.[40] Such silence gives voice to Dasein's loss of actual supports, but it also prepares Dasein's discovery of its own possibilities. Heidegger therefore offers a radical finitization of Aristotelian *phronesis* and potentiality which gives the temporal content of decision a certain tremble. In a way we can understand Heidegger's ontology as a radicalization of Aristotelian teleology that inscribes creative openness into temporal development. Heidegger can affirm an Aristotelian *telos* as a being-toward, but also unsettle its confinement to the actualization of definable forms in nature and its ethical paradigm of *eudaimonia* as the full actualization of potentials in some organized harmony. For Heidegger, the ultimate telos of Dasein is death, which resonates to bring much more edge and unease to the seeming composure of aristotelian virtue in its unvexed naturalism.

Rethinking Ethical Naturalism

It is thus possible to employ Heidegger's radically finite ontology to revise and unsettle Aristotle's ethical naturalism. Usually a thing's "nature" or what is "natural" is taken to mean a universal kind or a fixed essence. Often post-modernists take this immediately to imply an essentialism that is oppressive of otherness or difference. But for Heidegger what is "natural" or intrinsic to being includes otherness, absence, movement, change, tension, and variation. In this way Heidegger departs from Aristotle by way of German detours first through Hegel's insights into the historical character of being, and second through Nietzsche's moving beyond Hegel's progressive, systematic conception of history. The natural then gets connected with Heidegger's unique conception of essence as the coming to presence that is constituted by openness rather than fixed conditions or outcomes.

There are interesting suggestions of just such an approach to nature in Aristotle's own thought. In the *Nicomachian Ethics* he discusses the distinction between nature (*physis*), understood as the invariant and universally valid, and convention (*nomos*) understood as the variable and relative.[41] But Aristotle suggests that there is a sense of *physis* that is changeable, that *physis* may be unchangeable for the gods, but in our world nature can admit change. With his example of developing ambidexterity to overcome the natural dominance of one hand, we see that his admission of change allows more than simply the process of development in natural forms toward a completed state; it includes the possibility of altering natural conditions. In the *Politics* Aristotle states that human beings are made good by nature (*physis*), habit (*ethos*) and reason (*logos*).[42] All three conditions must optimally be in harmony, but such harmony is often achieved by reason going against nature and habit. This passage offers some relief from Aristotle's supposed conservatism, and suggests a conception of harmony that unfolds by way of conflicting tensions (anticipating Hegel), and provides another angle on the variability of what is natural. This constellation of forces also anticipates the confluence of thrownness, das Man, and authenticity in Heidegger's thought. With Heidegger one can say in a more pronounced way that human nature can exhibit change, adaptation, alteration, and divergence.

Thus with both Aristotle and Heidegger one can at least suggest a conception of the natural that can challenge radical conventionalism and skepticism, as well as the theoretical habit of bracketing established conditions, without having to depend on some invariant order, causal necessity, or fixed essence. In both thinkers can be found a presumptive naturalism with respect to their phenomenology of what is given in everyday, ordinary practices. In ethics one can talk of a presumption in favor of norms and values that have taken hold in human practice over the course of time. This would not mean that such norms and values are justified as such, because we can admit the (equally natural) possibility of openness and interrogation. But the burden would be on the interrogator to show internally how and why certain norms should be challenged, modified, or replaced without the presumption of a theoretical framework that mandates a priori grounds for criticism. An ethical naturalism would be a presumption of immanence because it dismisses transcendent

sources, wholly alternative worlds, and radical divisions between reason and
nature such as we see in Kant, and so it proceeds on the assumption that nature
would not likely operate by way of wholesale errors.[43] Both human practices
and their possible alterations would be understood as emerging out of and
within the immediate lived environment.

These remarkable lecture courses at Marburg and Freiberg covered line by
line specific texts from many of Aristotle's works. Here we see Heidegger give
extensive and innovative translations, backed by meticulous and exhaustive
expository supplements, so as to loosen the sedimented expressions of the
tradition and draw out the context of meaning out of which the texts speak. For
the first time in Heidegger, with Aristotle understood as an original fount of the
western tradition, the problem of an original retrieval of Greek conceptuality
rooted in *aletheia* is posed. The result is the continuation of the destruction of
the tradition Luther had called for, only now performed with and against the
texts of Aristotle himself. It has often been said that when one reads someone
like Derrida, even with admiration, one is not encouraged to spend time with
the texts he discusses. It is the opposite when reading Aristotle through
Heidegger's phenomenological prism, as it forces one to confirm the thinking
for themselves while maintaining a profound respect for the tradition even
while reacting against it.

VII. Community of Those who are Going to Die: On Levinas

Philosophy cannot be grounded on techniques of proof and argument unless it is first seized by a kind of attunement that prompts questioning in the first place and continues to animate inquiry. My thinking about ethics has changed. I have not really made much of an effort in the last 10 years to think through it, in part because it struck me as permanently entrenched camps suppressing an openness to life. I also experienced a visceral discomfort with the cool, detached logical machinations of analytic moral philosophy, which in large measure was dominated by the theoretical pursuit of necessary principles that could ground ethical practice and that could survive the gauntlet of trial by standards of consistency, universality, and infeasibility. Something was telling me that ethics had been transmuted into the logistics of some academic practice; the "presumption to theory" had shorn ethics of its living roots in flesh and blood people, and millions were starving while philosophers scored points against proofs, of thousands dying in "justified" wars within the American hologram. For these reasons I had a sense of bemused disdain for ethics in general, taking my rhythms instead from the philosophy of "old Europe," not in its love for the spectacular, but in its attempts to return to the lived-world of average everydayness. I have always been drawn to how this approach to philosophy takes notice of the complex finitude of the lived world and the depth of language in ways that analytic philosophy either misses, underplays, or consciously ignores. There is a profound relation to the other that is at once prior to, and moves well beyond, what can be captured by traditional propositional categories in ethics. Perhaps this can be approached by revisiting a certain trajectory of criticisms of the so-called immorality of Heidegger's thinking.

For a brief time a few years back a guiding question in Heidegger studies was the idea that Heidegger had neglected specific details or discussion regarding the relation of the body to what he meant by "Dasein." Thus Alphonse de Waelhens suggested that Merleau-Ponty's work was filling a lacuna in the problematic of *Being and Time* by bringing the analysis of Being-in-the-world into the primary field of perception neglected by Heidegger.[1] The publication of a series of lecture courses given by Heidegger at Marburg subsequently occasioned a reappraisal of this criticism. Those lectures had in fact developed what is truly a phenomenology of perception and therefore illustrate that the problem was never really neglected by Heidegger at all; indeed, the materials reveal precisely what it was in Heidegger that so profoundly influenced Merleau-Ponty on the issue in the first place. The neglect was to be found not so much in the German philosopher as in the partial understanding of that philosopher by commentators.[2]

Similarly, the criticism arises from some quarters that Heidegger's thinking on ethics is faulty, and that his thought fails to address the ethical dynamic of the category of the "other." Thus it gets suggested that the work of Levinas provides the necessary supplement to Heidegger's thinking along these lines as well. I wish to suggest in turn, and once again, there is no need for such a supplement, for the criticism by the Levinasians, which has gained momentum in contemporary continental thought, has done so at the expense of de-emphasizing to some extent the thought of the *later* Heidegger, its intimate engagement with poetry and poetic language, and its continuing reevaluation of the problematic of difference and its metaphysical provenance. In response to the Levinasians, then, however important and effective their work is in reflecting on such questions, Heidegger's late, poetic thought ends with a radical opening which charts possibilities of thinking otherness otherwise—that is, non-metaphysically, and that this dynamic can be read as the proposal of another hermeneutic of otherness which outlines its concerns and develops its terminologies in entirely different ways.

The nature of community has of course been of great concern to moral philosophers for centuries, with Western thought long being interested in building new or discovering lost community. One such view was the idea that the rational form of knowledge "naturally" produces a common discourse. One might immediately worry over how it is that rational discourse is natural. Rational practice renders the natural world a practicable field of instrumentally organized pursuits. Today there are whole plantations where biologically engineered species of plants grow not on the earth but in water, fed by chemical blends. There are reserves now where genetics is producing new species of onco-animals to grow cancerous tumors. Today science projects structures onto nature as much as studies nature; or calls its own projections "nature." The table of elements is no longer an inventory of irreducible physical nature. The scientific rational community produces, and is produced by, its own projections. The community based on reasons produces the means of subsistence and the materials of its knowledge.

Within the vaguely Kantian outline, in the rational community, the imperative is placed in advance, that whatever is said, must be said. The rational community produces, and is produced by, a common discourse in a potentially debilitating sense. The insights of individuals are formulated into universal categories, such that they are detached from the particular index of the one who first formulated them. Rational discourse sets out to supply a reason, a theory, a more general formulation, an empirical law or a practical maxim, from which the observations and practices could be deduced. This distributes the insights to all, as it were. The rational system implicates the agent as a representative of those theories of rational discourse such that, when any rational agent speaks, he speaks as a representative of the common discourse. The law he formulates for his own understanding and practice legislates for the discourse of everyone, because the consistency and the coherence, the cogency, of the integrally one rational discourse imposes this statement.

Speaking as a representative of the common discourse of rational culture is what is called serious speech. The seriousness in it just is the weight of the rational imperative that determines what is to be said. Whatever is said gets implicated with the universal principles of the rational integration of knowledge. Anything else is to indulge in eccentricities.

Alphonso Lingus, however, following Levinas, has written beautifully on the possibility of another community. When people are near death, what speaks in such terminal moments is not the ego as rational mind, as a representative of universal reason that possesses a priori categories and the forms of the rational organization of sense impressions. To see in the impending death of the other is another sentient agent, her postures and movements directed to a range of implements and obstacles. To see her is to see her in a sense interchangeable with me. It is the sense of the death awaiting me that circumscribes the range of possibilities ahead of me. To see the other as one who has her own tasks and potentialities is to sense another death circumscribing the field of possibilities ahead of her.[3]

Prior to the rational community there is the encounter with the other. This encounter begins with one who exposes himself in the utmost extremity to the demands of what is other. Beneath the rational community is another community, one which demands that there be an exposure to that which he has, or to whom he has, nothing in common. This exposure takes the form of an interruption. This community takes form when one recognizes, in the face of the other, an imperative, one which sets in question everything with which one has in common.

This conception of community is meant as a critique of western rationalism. It is not only with one's rational intelligence that one exposes oneself to such an imperative. Our rational intelligence cannot arise without some first recognition. This exposure to that which is other is not just one of rationality, but with the nakedness of one's eyes. Even when the most rigorously trained medical scientist goes to help the sick, he or she first looks into the eyes of the sufferer.

When one recognizes the mortality of the other, community is born. Community forms when one exposes oneself to this otherness, to the naked, those in affliction, to those whose deaths precede ours. One enters into this community not by affirming oneself and one's force but by a renunciation, to powers outside of oneself, to death, and others who die. Thus in the midst of the work of the rational community there forms another community, a community of those who are going to die, and have this in common. But this is no common death.

In European philosophy, the turning point for the question of the existential ground for community in the 20th century can be traced to Husserl. Husserl was aware that any philosophy which takes the transcendental ego seriously as its first apodictic certainty must necessarily face the problem of solipsism. He raises the issue in the second of his famous *Cartesian Mediations* and attempts to resolve it in the fifth.[4] The difficulty arises from the primacy accorded to the transcendental Ego, which phenomenological reduction reveals to be the source of all experience. I can encounter other people as physical objects in the natural world, but I cannot presume that other transcendental egos exist because I can have no direct experience of them. Indeed, if I could have direct experience of them, they would by definition no longer be transcendental egos, since they would be part of the world as presented to and constituted by my consciousness.

There can be no direct unmediated experience of other transcendental Egos; but if I cannot experience them directly, why should I presume that they exist at all? In his attempt to overcome the charge of solipsism which might easily be made against this line of thinking, Husserl proposes a second *epoche*, which he infamously calls the reduction of transcendental experience to the sphere of ownness. This reduction is more radical than the first: having bracketed off the objective world in the first reduction, the phenomenologist now attempts to jettison all assumptions about other subjects. The point of this is to discover what is originally and indisputably mine. In doing so the phenomenologist thus discovers, according to Husserl, a stratum of experience that cannot be further reduced: in the sphere of ownness I find that I have an empirical self. So the transcendental ego possesses a body which interacts with the physical world, and as it becomes aware of its own empirical self, the ego can also observe that the world contains other bodies which act and respond in ways much like its own. Discovering itself to be embodied, the ego finds itself in a world apparently shared with very similar creatures.

The realization that the world is inhabited by other bodies does not yet in itself prove the existence of other transcendental Egos. However, the reduction to the sphere of ownness and the discovery of the empirical self allow an important advance in Husserl's argument. The other cannot be represented directly to my consciousness, but his or her body and behavior can be. Observing the changing but concordant actions of others can lead to what Husserl calls an analogical apperception or appresentation: the Other behaves in ways that I recognize as familiar from my experience of myself, so I recognize that the Ego of the Other may be, like mine, transcendental. Thus other Egos are not presented, but appresented, revealed by analogy; what I can experience gives me knowledge of what I cannot encounter without mediation.

For Husserl this apperception depends upon real presentations, as the physical appresents the psychical. The appresentation does not reveal other transcendental Egos, but it does reveal that such Egos are there, albeit in a state of necessary concealment from me. Husserl now claims that the problem of solipsism has been avoided and knowledge both of other selves and of the natural world is assured within his own stringent criteria of apodictivity.

Heidegger of course both praised the Husserlian insights and seized upon the Husserlian weaknesses almost immediately. The concern with this solution to the problem of other selves is that it does not preserve the otherness of the other. It is true that other Egos are not experienced directly, so in one sense they remain unknown and unknowable to me; in another sense, however, they are known even without direct experience because all Egos are presumed to be fundamentally similar, like Leibnizian monads. The ego of the other is appresented to me only because I recognize the behavior of his or her body as already familiar; in other words, I acknowledge the existence of the Other because he or she is already basically like me. Although I cannot see or touch the monadic Ego of the other, the very fact that I call it monadic implies that it is in all important respects similar to my own. Ultimately for Husserl the Other can be known by empathy, not because I can cast off my own self, but because all Egos reflect each other. Despite the attempt to demonstrate the multiplicity of transcendental egos, there is still in a sense only one—my own—which is the model for all others. For Husserl, regarding the alter ego, it is the ego, and not the alter, which is most important.

The other is a reflection of myself, and because each ego is a monad, reflecting, containing and contained in all other egos, the crucial terms of Husserlian intersubjectivity can be supported. No wonder there is harmony, community, empathy, and reciprocal recognition. The ego is no longer a *solus ipse*; rather, it is the universal logos of all conceivable being.

Even recapitulating Heidegger's reappropriation of Husserl's phenomenology would take us too far afield, but preliminary comparisons might be suggested in regard to conceptions of death. Heidegger's thinking in *Being and Time* requires owning up to the fact that no matter what one does to lead a fulfilling and meaningful life, a thriving flourishing life that contains philosophical sensitivities, it is all in vain, for the final possibility of existence is death, and that is the absolute loss of all meaning and meaningfulness.[5] To live the philosophically exacting life is to realize that the philosophical life deprives itself of all significance and value. But notwithstanding that, it is only by virtue of the fact that death is implicated in the constitution of Dasein that existence can be meaningful. The philosopher discovers that meaning upon learning how to die, or more correctly, learning that one is going to die. For what makes me disappear cannot find its guarantee there; and thus, in a way, having no guarantee, it is not certain. No one is really certain about their own mortality. It is not enough for me to know that I am mortal; I have to somehow become mortal, mortal twice over, sovereignly mortal, born again into my mortality.

This is the peculiar human vocation, our being infinitely mortal. In owning up to my own mortality—if I can ever in fact do that and not rather flee from such owning up—in owning up to my own mortality I make death double itself. There is my death which circulates among my possibilities, which is determined as the freedom to die and the capacity to take mortal risks; and there is the other death, the death which makes of me my other, the death which I cannot grasp, which is not linked to me by any relation of any sort. This other death is that which never comes and toward which I cannot direct myself.

Owning up to my own mortality is my feeble and frustrated attempt, my futile attempt, to eliminate death, to strip it of what is out-standing about it. But what is out-standing in my death is its absolute futurity: my death is an unforeseeable future that can never arrive, that can never become a past, that could never have been, and so which never will be for me. Death never comes until after its arrival. Death itself is my perpetual flight before my death; it signifies my radical inability to be honest about my mortality, it is what is dishonest about my own mortality. It is what makes of us mortals immortals who live pretending that they have the key to the backdoor. Death is the deep of dissimulation. It is what life is: we the living push back and back upon death and against it, but it is silent in its absolute rebuttal: we can never get at it; we can never get to it.

Heidegger defines my death as the possibility of my own impossibility. So it is a question of facing up to this impossibility. But as soon as my-death is confronted as the possibility of my own impossibility it is transfigured into the impossibility of all possibility, including, most notably, the possibility of dying, and so the possibility of dying into this impossibility. Death removes all possibility, makes of possibility the impossible. Nonetheless, confronting mortality's dishonor makes possible for the first time all possibility, if you will permit me to say, makes possibility possible. To face one's death is to open onto that region where death no longer appears as possible, but as the empty deep of the impossible, and out of this deep life becomes possible again, becomes possible for the first time, as that which is wholly unto itself, there being nothing else, and so as pure gratuity, sheer fortuity. Being-unto-death has a way of showing that it is getting born at all that is the issue, not death.

My death is my most extreme power, my most proper possibility; but it is also the death which never comes to me, with which there is no possible relation. Indeed, I elude my death when I think I master it through anticipatory resoluteness. Death is that which happens to no one, the uncertainty and indeterminacy of that which never happens at all. It is my own disintegration, vacant and auto-debilitation. Rather: one comes into one's dying, where, finally, one is free from both life and death, and finally free for life. The deaths of others in tsunami disasters do not cause a ripple—their deaths are not mine.

To die is to shatter the world. It is the loss of the person, and, insofar as appearing as something for the sake of which there is appearing, to die is the annihilation of being. And so to die is also the loss of death, and therefore the loss of significance this my-death bestows on my life, the absolute loss of the meaningfulness that mortality confers upon existence. When I die I cease being mortal, I am no longer capable of dying, and my impending death horrifies me because I will no longer then be able to die it. Then I see it for what it is, no longer death but the impossibility of really dying. The only thing worse than there being no death but dying it is there being death but my not dying it. I do not die; rather I die always other than myself. My death becomes for the other as his became for me, a secondary event, because it is not mine. One never dies simply of an illness from which one never recovers—one dies of one's death.

On the other hand, however, the activity of dying prevents my death from ever taking over. I am too caught up in the activity of dying to ever be dead, which is for others. My dying separates me from my death by an impossible and untraversible gap in time; for no matter how close I am to death, I still have a little more time before I am dead. My death is that which is always outstanding in my dying. It is that which dying forestalls. My dying proves that I will never be dead, for dying is something in principle I can never complete. Rather, death is the movement of always dying more, of dying immeasurably more. Dying is a task without term. Dying is never so much to die as to let go into the dying. Dying is to transform the fact of death, to expose myself to what of myself can never be exposed, to become the intimacy of such self-exposure, an intimacy with death where death no longer can be faced, where my death, death which is proper only to me, uniquely mine, becomes anonymous. In dying I do not die, I have fallen from the power to die. In dying they die, the television studio audience; they do not cease and they do not finish dying. In dying death is that which cannot be accomplished by dying, that which the accomplishment of dying can never realize.

Dying is a contradictory affair. Dying is an ontic affair which prevents the ontological event, my death, from arriving, from ever being possible, And the activity of dying and only the activity of dying can preclude the possibility of death from arriving; for the possibility of death is inscribed in the essence of every other activity. Yet the act of dying is the condition for the possibility of death; so dying is the condition for the possibility of that which it renders in advance impossible, And death, that final possibility, renders all possibility, including that possibility, dying, that is the condition for possibility, impossible. Death delivers me over to the impossibility of dying. Death is the condition for the possibility of its own impossibility as well as the impossible condition for its own possibility. After such a discussion as this, Husserlian subjectivity could never be the same.

Levinas' criticisms of Heidegger can now be seen in a more helpful context. He bases his objection to this account of being-with-others on the solitariness of Dasein: despite Heidegger's occasional reference to the collective possibilities (he makes frequent use of *begegnen*, to meet or to encounter, in the pages devoted to his phenomenological analysis of Mitsein), it is not at all clear that any real encounter with the Other is entailed or even required by the notion. Levinas takes Heidegger's conception of community to be based on the relationship of Dasein to Being rather than a relationship with anything truly other. So Dasein remains fundamentally solitary.

"Just as in all philosophies of communion, sociality in Heidegger is found in the subject alone; and it is in terms of solitude that the analysis of Dasein in its authentic form is pursued."[6]

Mitsein does not break the structure of *jemeinigkeit* (mine-ness) which characterizes Dasein's experience. The Other does not come from the outside to challenge the sovereignty of my possession and comprehension of the world; instead he or she is encountered (if at all) in the intimacy of Being, and the priority of the same is maintained. If, for Heidegger, Husserl's empathy showed the failure to conceive the Other as Other, then for Levinas Heidegger's *Mitsein* makes in some fundamental sense a similar mistake. There can be for Heidegger no community of those who are going to die.

Levinas needed to find some way of showing that an encounter with what lies outside Being, or the Same, or the Ego, may be possible. From this point of view, his own discussion of death in *Time and the Other* forms a pivotal moment in his thinking. As in *La Mort et le temps* (lectures given in 1975, first published in 1991), Levinas develops his own ideas partly through a dialogue with Heidegger. For Heidegger, in *Being and Time*, no one can die for anyone else in a genuine sense. The other's death can never signify. Dying is something that every Dasein itself must take upon itself at the time. By its very essence, death is in each case mine, in so far as it "is" at all. Death for Heidegger is always my own death; I cannot die in the place of anyone else, nor does death entail an experience of anything outside myself. Heidegger insists that, ontologically, death is constituted by *Jemeinigkeit*: it does not disturb the relationship with Being in which is contained the sum of my possible experiences.

Levinas argues that Heidegger's description of death, of being unto death, has missed the essential point of death. If death is part of the relationship with Being, then it is always comprehended (albeit pre-philosophically) by Dasein; but for Levinas death is that which lies irretrievably beyond experience, it is utterly unknowable and thus it marks "the end of the subject's virility and heroism which Heidegger's position maintains.[7] Death is not something that can be seen, known, and comprehended; it disrupts the subject's mastery of itself; it shows that an event is possible which I cannot assume as part of an intentional existential project. The approach of death shows the subject that something absolutely alien is about to happen, something that escapes the sovereignty of intentionality or the comprehension of Being.

> This approach of death indicates that we are in relation with something that is absolutely other, something bearing alterity not as a provisional determination we can assimilate through enjoyment, but as something whose very existence is made of alterity. My solitude is thus not confirmed by death but broken by it.[8]

Both Husserl's transcendental Ego and Heidegger's Dasein are, for Levinas, essentially solitary. Death breaks this solitude by establishing the possibility of an encounter with something outside the self. This marks a crucial point of departure from Levinas's phenomenological precursors: the Other is not another self, but is constituted by alterity; it is unknowable and therefore refractory to the metaphors of light which support the phenomenologist's claims to knowledge; and it disrupts the self-enclosed totality of a world described in terms of harmony and communion.

> But this precisely indicates that the other is in no way another myself, participating with me in a common existence. The relationship with the other is not an idyllic and harmonious relationship of communion or a sympathy (Levinas's translation of Husserl's *Einfühlung*) through which we put ourselves in the other's place; we recognize the other as resembling us, but exterior to us; the relationship with the other is a relationship with a Mystery.[9]

This is the crux of Levinas' dispute with phenomenology: in the phrase *alter ego* only the word ego has been thoroughly examined, whereas the alter has been suppressed. In his discussion of death Levinas demonstrates what he calls "the possibility of an event,"[10] that is, the possibility that something might occur which is not always already intended and known by the transcendental Ego or assumed within the relationship with Being. He eventually comes to admit that his procedure can no longer be qualified as phenomenological.[11]

What resources in Heidegger's thought can be marshalled in rebuttal? Independent of an interchange over a phenomenology of death, as is well known, the later Heidegger's increasingly modifies the initial parameters by which to think about Being. The later displacements within Heidegger's thinking, from the analytic of Dasein, through his hermeneutic critique of technology, his remarks on art, through the ontological difference to the history or the place of Being, to, finally, poetic thinking, *Ereignis*, and so forth, continue and amplify these initial implications.

Even if for many years Heidegger indeed thinks the disclosive event of appropriation side by side with the ontological difference, the undercurrent of his later texts show a radical departure or abandonment of the original "ontological" concerns. Such a possibility signals itself in *Time and Being*, where the reversal of the problematic of *Being and Time* implied in the title brings with it an explicit reconfiguration of the relation between *Ereignis* and the ontico-ontological difference. This acknowledgement of a need for a revision of his enterprise, an amendment amounting to thinking "being" no longer from the perspective of the ontological difference but rather without it, without beings, brings into focus how important it is to move into the later Heidegger's poetic thinking as an elucidation of how to think otherness. It would obviously be a mistake to take the statement about the necessity of thinking Being without beings as a call to forgetting beings, or for forgetting others. Questioning the unstable demarcation between Being and beings does not amount to a neglect of beings but instead aims at revising and remedying the difficulties in relating to otherness inherent in that demarcation. In order to let the otherness of other beings be, it is necessary to approach the question of Being otherwise, by disengaging the problematic of language and *Ereignis* from the ontological difference. Only then can "what has been called Being" be addressed, and in turn the otherness of other beings be acknowledged.

This undermining of the initial priority of the ontico-ontological difference is underscored by Heidegger's disavowal of the task of overcoming metaphysics:

> *Sein ohne das Seiende denken, heisst: Sein ohne Rücksicht auf die Metaphysik denken. Eine solche Rücksicht herrscht nun aber auch noch in der Absicht, die Metaphysik zu überwinden. Darum gilt es, vom Überwinden abzulassen und die Metaphysik sich selbst zu überlassen.*

> To think Being without beings means: to think Being without regard to metaphysics. Yet a regard for metaphysics still prevails even in the intention to overcome metaphysics. Therefore, our task is to cease all overcoming, and leave metaphysics to itself.[12]

In order to really think Being, it becomes indispensable not to overcome metaphysics but to abandon it. For leaving aside metaphysics and thus the ontological difference is the only way in which thought can approach what used to be called "Being."

Heidegger's later poetic thinking charts a possibility of thinking otherness. Indeed, the work is a veritable "hermeneutics of otherness" which outlines its concerns and develops its terminology according to its own dictates. It's orientation seeks not to erase the other's difference but to underscore its radicality. It is a thinking acutely, incessantly aware of the dangers of thematizing the other and thus turning it into a mere projection of the same. The clues that would facilitate the understanding of this late reconfiguration of otherness are interspersed throughout Heidegger's later works.

It is in this perspective that one would have to explore the stakes and ramifications of Heidegger's *das andere Denken*. It would be seen not as a thinking advancing positive statements or making cognitive claims but rather as a thinking of dislocations, simultaneously withdrawing itself from the paradigms of thought. The effects of such dislocations would pertain specifically to the modes of conceiving otherness, how language invariably mishandles the other, how a critique of the *Gestell*-structure of technology is required, and how the possibility of an "other" reading of the Greek *logos* could issue in the thinking from *Ereignis* and its linguistic character. As Heidegger's continuing preoccupation with the concerns from *Being and Time* demonstrates, this reconfiguration of otherness requires a rethinking of our ideas about not only "what has been called 'Being'" but also history, time, space, and language.

Time and Being is already a Levinasian text. The abandoning of metaphysics and the inscription of both Being and time into *Ereignis* suggests that Heidegger no longer ascribes priority to Being but rather approaches it as one of the dual givens of the disclosive appropriations. There is nothing portable from the writing. Everything cancels itself out. Nothing is said that is not also unsaid. Commentary on it from afar is somewhat pointless, as it would be reduced to idle or baffled quotation, repetition without identity, as if some relation between text and philosophical context were formulable into a relation of some third kind. It is a text of infinite discretions and dislocations, of speaking forgetfully, or by way of endless detours, reserving names, deferring the period. It is a text filled with moments that are barely words. The fact that Heidegger describes *Ereignis* as a "structuring" of *es gibt*—there is/it gives—shows clearly the impossibility of finding or writing the one, the correct, word that could name "what has been called 'Being' up to now." The text does not use, as is the case with the term Being, one word but a structure, which with its empty subject implies the refusal of naming. As in the grammatical structure "there is," what "means" is what comes after the verb, and the "there" (*es*) effaces itself and disappears behind the meaning, the word, the writing.

Foregrounding Heidegger's discussion of time serves here the purpose of establishing the displacement of the ontico-ontological difference suggested by the priority given in time in the essay's title and underscored by the earlier remarks about leaving metaphysics to itself takes place indubitably with a view to inaugurating the thinking of otherness as nearness. When Heidegger characterizes *Reichen as die nähernde Nähe und Nachheit* (the nearing nearness and nearhood),[13] he is not only proposing a revision of the understanding of time and its relation to space but, in fact, is recasting the enterprise of thinking apart from metaphysics into the terms of nearness, nearing, and proximity. The tensions and difficulties underlying such a transition mark Heidegger's own language in *"Time and Being,"* culminating in three completely untranslatable sentences:

a) *"[Ereignis] ereignet Sein und Zeit."*   a) The event unfolds being and time into their own

b) *"Zeit und Sein ereignet im Ereignis."* b) Time and being are unfolded in the event

c) *"Das Ereignet ereignet."*   c) The event of unfolding itself unfolds[14]

The proximity between noun *Ereignis* and the verb *ereignen*, which each of the sentences underscores, reflects the strain put on Heidegger's idiom by his attempts at dislocation. This polysemic proximity in fact questions and destabilizes the grammatical and syntactical categorizations into nouns and verbs or subjects and predicates, effectively dislocating, if not exactly escaping, the differential economy of signification. Do not ask: what is this "event"? It is neither something nor nothing, It is neither here nor there. It pronounces itself without there being a position of existence with regard to it, without presence or absence affirming it, without the unity of the word coming to dislodge it. It is that which is between two, or several, or all words, thanks to which these interrupt each other, without which they would signify nothing, but which upsets them constantly to the very silence in which they extinguish themselves. What Heidegger is doing, what is happening in the texts to which he assigned his name, is the disclosure of *Ereignis* as an empty subject, too close to what it gives to be determined as different from it.

What I want to indicate requires taking the detour to the latest of the "later Heidegger," in that there is a movement from the community of those who are going to die to the community of its saying and listening. The conflation of *Ereignis* and *ereignet* is on some level, then, an enactment of the logic of otherness. There is never a separate name or sequence of "argument" for it, but always an entire complex where the infinitude of language lets itself be taken in hand by a sequence of words, and yet seeks at the same time, in the never resolved tension between noun and verb, to fall outside language, without however ceasing to belong to it. And this is to mark how it is no longer a matter of the self-erasing difference between Being and beings but rather of the resistance to difference of the fold between *Ereignis* and *ereignet*. It is precisely this dimension of nearing that Heidegger repeatedly tries to describe through various terms, beginning with the meaning of Being in *Being and Time* and continuing through the history of Being into *Ereignis* and the way of language. What Heidegger is after, what underwrites his texts on poetry and language, is as close as thought can get to what is other than thinking. This gesture is perhaps most pronounced in Heidegger's essays on language and poetry, which consistently describe the way of language in terms of nearness and the occurrence of the fourfold. Perhaps the most well-known passage about the nature of this nearness in the context of language comes toward the end of "The Nature of Language," as an attempt to assemble into a figure the constituitive elements of the exchange called by Heidegger the neighborhood of poetry and thinking:

> "Saying, as the way-making movement of the world's fourfold, gathers all things up into the nearness of face-to-face encounter, and does so soundlessly, as quietly as time times, space spaces, as quietly as the play of time-space is enacted."[15]

What this establishes through the notion of nearness is a correlation, a link, the "same" of the unfolding of the world, its fourfold, and the translative way of the saying of manifestation into words. For at the same time that the essay expressly defines nearness as "the movement paving the way for the face-to-face of the regions of the world's fourfold *("die Be-Wëgung des Gegen-einander-über der Gegenden des Weltgeviertes")*,[16] it also claims the way making, *die Be-wegüng*, as the movement of language into words, which constitutes the very "essence", the way, of language. In the end, it becomes possible for Heidegger to maintain that nearness as *be-wëgung* rests in the saying,[17] or, even more strongly, that nearness and the saying are the same *("Nähe und die Sage als das Wesende der Sprache das Selbe sind")*.[18]

One could multiply here similar examples from any and probably all of Heidegger's texts on language and poetry, but it will suffice to note that these writings on language are the best illustration of the complication that *Ereignis* introduces into the thinking concerning Being. Heidegger goes to great lengths to emphasize this quandary in his own language, as is evident in "Time and Being," "The Nature of Language," and "The Way to Language," which employ the rhetoric of nearness and consistently avoid differential terminology allied as it is in this context with technological and calculative thought. It is precisely this strategy that produces the strangest linguistic moments in Heidegger's works, moments too often relegated to some poetic side of Heidegger and dismissed as not having philosophical relevance. One need only think of the infamous semi-tautological statements with which the texts on poetry and language proliferate, in phrases like world worlds and thing things and time times and space spaces and language languages, to indicate the complexity of the Heideggerian way of language. These locutions are not merely to be placed in some Orwellian museum of obfuscation but are the unsettling results of Heidegger's encounter with the poetic, and are bearers of the most provoking insights. The maneuvers of presenting the verbalization of nouns as a duplication of the noun into the verb not simply as undermining the syntactical distinction between propositional subject and predicate but as writing the nearness, the proximity through which Heidegger describes language. In an attempt to sidestep tautology and circularity, on the one hand, and difference, on the other, Heidegger elaborates the idiom of nearness, which carries the message of the hermeneutics of otherness perhaps even more persuasively than could ever argumentative statements expressly devoted to it. It is precisely in the perspective of how Heidegger's writing belongs to this event and are not its source; they are not its realization but a form of its aleatory effects, that his conception of language can be appreciated for its achievements, and its bearing on the debates about Levinasian otherness recognized.

These poetic-phenomenological insights reveal how our relation with language is now no longer one of cognition and command, but an interruption, a relation of proximity in which, although nothing is revealed, neither can anything be evaded. Heidegger's re-configurations of thought and its proximity to language and poetry are as well a proximity with other human beings. Language is the happening, the event, the *Ereignis*, of this proximity.

> *Im waltenden Gegen-einander-über ist jegliches, eines für das andere, offen, offen in seinem Sichverbergen; so reicht sich eines dem anderen hinüber, eines überlässt sich dem anderen, und jegliches bleibt so es selber; eines ist dem anderen über als das darüber Wachende, Hütende, darüber als das Verhüllende.*

"We tend to think of the face-to-face exclusively as a relation between human beings ... Yet being face-to-face with another has a more distant origin where earth and sky, god and man reach one another. Goethe, Mörike too, like to use the phrase 'face-to-face with one another' not only with respect to human beings but also with respect to things of the world. Where this prevails, all things open to one another in their self-concealment; thus one extends itself to the other, and thus all remain themselves; one is over the other as its guardian watching over the other, over it as its veil."[19]

A passage such as this harbors nothing short of a powerful reconfiguration of otherness, perhaps even made more legible through the prisms of Levinas's writings on alterity, rather than through the traditional hermeneutic concerns which Heidegger authorizes in *Being and Time*. Language is an interruption of subjectivity in which we find ourselves face-to-face with whatever is otherwise, not just other human beings. What matters to Heidegger is whether an experience with language can open the way for thinking as well as for poetry as a mode of responsibility. Surely this is what he means when he characterizes thinking as a listening, that calls thinking away from the propositional and the calculative into the proximity of the other. As he says elsewhere, "it is more salutary for thinking to wander in the strange than to establish itself in the intelligible" [*es ist heilsamer für das Denken, wenn es im Befremdlichen wandert, statt sich im Verständlichen einzurichten*].[20] These passages make clear that openness and concealment have to be thought side by side, together, near each other, in proximity. Heidegger's manner of thinking about openness does not preclude or exclude the re-trait, withdrawal, or concealment. On the contrary, openness can be thought as such only in proximity to concealment and veiling (with the same obviously true for concealment itself). The proximity these passages alert us to is of focal importance of the notion of the other. Heidegger's circuitous writing style keeps us constantly aware that any articulation of otherness has to be predicated on the play of openness and concealment. The text itself underscores the impossibility of conceiving otherness as alone openness or concealment. Instead we are asked to look into the mechanics of this proximal exchange between openness and self-concealment, and recognize the stakes in this undertaking.

Compare to Levinas:

"Discourse is ... an original relation with an exterior being ... It is the frank presence of an existent that can lie, that is, dispose of the theme he offers, without being able to dissimulate his frankness as interlocutor, always struggling openly ... The face itself is a language without words that works the work of language insofar as it disrupts my self-identity, exposes me to the magisterial claim of someone outside my here and now, situates me elsewhere as if depriving me of immanence.

"The relationship of language implies transcendence, radical separation, the strangeness of interlocutors, the revelation of the other to me. In other words, language is spoken where community between the terms of the relationship is wanting, where the common plane is wanting or is yet to be constituted. It takes place in this transcendence. Discourse is thus the experience of something absolutely foreign, a pure 'knowledge' or 'experience,' a traumatism of astonishment."[21]

In his "Language and Proximity" Levinas describes this relation as "the original language, a language without words, propositions, pure communication."[22] Interestingly, as he figures it in this essay, the difference between poetry and ethics is that the one is the "proximity of things" and the other is the proximity of a neighbor. He does not see it as the possibility of entering into proximity with both, a relationship independently of every system of signs common to the interlocutors, literally a language outside of language, an interruption even of ethics as first philosophy. If the ethical relation is a relation of language, a relation in which the other speaks to me, this as well introduces an overturning, not just of my speech, the propositional discourse of the ego or the same, but the ethical discourse of the other as well, a difference outside the alternatives of identity and difference.

Death is a similar interruption, a relation of impossibility. It is a relation that is closed to me as an experiencing subject, as a "self" who has experiences. Language is thus in profound proximity with death, a proximity all the more formidable for being a secret. As Blanchot hauntingly reminds us, "It is accurate to say that when I speak: death speaks in me. My speech is a warning that at this very moment death is loose in the world."[23]

There is thus an understanding of otherness disclosed by Heidegger's texts on language. What does it mean to say that the other could be absolutely foreign to me except by virtue of the way language opens? Language is a foreignness in which the other interrupts me. The other needs language in order to breach my self-sufficiency, because language already has situated me beside myself. If I were not already so breached, no foreignness would ever occur to me. "The peal of such stillness is not anything human." [Das Geläut der Stille ist nichts Menschliches].[24] The transcendence of words means that words do not originate here, with me; they are not mine or a part of me. They are perhaps outside of me. "Linguistic competence" is not the building up of language but the sealing off from its flow. Words are in short the presence of exteriority, the infinite, the elsewhere, the otherwise or the nonidentical as such. So the otherness of the other is only brought home to me in a word that breaks in on me. Language does not unite us, as if it were a bond or a whole that contained us both; rather it separates us because it is itself a fissure, uncontainable within any totality. It is the interruption of every union. This linguistic openness to the other does not amount to the disclosure of the content of the other that would simply result in the eventual thematization and technical absorption of the other. Both the other and the one who reaches toward the other open themselves as self-concealed. What maintains this movement is nearness itself, "which makes them reach one another and holds them in the nearness of their distance"[25]—not in a dialectics of self-recognition but precisely in proximity to their respective otherness. The other thus remains the other, its alterity preserved in openness, the presumption to theory resisted.

The passage earlier quoted makes abundantly clear that the limit that maintains the reciprocity functions as a kind of veil, preserving the other's alterity. The extension by which things come into their own with regard to this otherness is captured by Heidegger's German word *verhüllend*, a sheltering that makes clear that the openness in which beings find themselves with respect to one another does not cancel out their concealment. To the contrary, it is precisely in nearness that the other can open or conceal itself in its alterity. In a sense, the reciprocity of the exchange that constitutes each's coming into its own is the condition of both emerging to and withdrawing from the alterity of the other, of letting it remain veiled. Crucial to this also is the attentiveness and heed that beings grant to one another so that they can remain themselves. Heidegger employs the words *wachen* and *hüten*, which perhaps allude to the consideration of the care-structure spelled out in *Being and Time* and also to remarks in his "Letter on Humanism." *Wachen* means keeping guard or watch over something, but with the connotation not of control or possession so much as that of staying alert, mindful of the otherness at stake. Similarly, *hüten* suggests protectiveness, tending to the other.

One must of course proceed carefully here in determining exactly what the ethical might mean in such languaged contexts, bearing in mind that nearness is both a language phenomenon and a powerful reconfiguration of otherness. All the more so since Heidegger's own hesitation in using the words 'ethics' and 'ethical' and his consistent practice of placing them in quotation marks are well known, especially since "Letter on Humanism." It was almost too easy to mistake these works as a disavowal of ethics. Heidegger's answer to Beaufret's inquiry about the possibility of ethics, even though it often evokes disappointment and tempts misunderstanding, and even mixing in Heidegger's own personal wartime human failures, in fact provides a venue for engaging the problematic of the ethical in the context of thinking and language. Heidegger's caution in engaging the ethical is motivated not by his inability to compose an "existential ethics," as was once incorrectly believed, but instead, as the "Letter" suggests, by the apprehension about having his thought collapsed into "moral philosophy," with its presumption of theory and its didactic overtones.[26] Heidegger's circumspect use of terms related to ethics testifies to his unwillingness to separate the "ethical" inquiry from the problematic of language. Indeed, almost from beginning to end, Heidegger's thinking is an exercise in thinking otherness in such a way so as to not allow it to emerge in its own. This reluctance underscores neither a failure nor a lack of interest but, on the contrary, an attempt at recasting the problematic in thinking. Heidegger's later poetic thinking is no more a disavowal of the ethical than his deconstruction of onto-theology was a disavowal of what was properly to be thought regarding the divine.

VIII. Confusion in Nietzsche's Fifth Gospel

In a letter to Ernst Schmeitzner on February 13th, 1883, Nietzsche referred to his work *Thus Spake Zarathustra* as the "fifth Gospel."[1] Owing to the confusion surrounding Part IV of the work, one might be tempted to bring to the task of understanding it a variety of interpretive schemes culled from biblical hermeneutics. Scholarship on *Zarathustra* has been enormous, and in regard to the difficulties of Part IV has been divided into two camps. The "literalist" interpretative camp holds that Part IV of *Thus Spake Zarathustra* is a fragmentary mistake by Nietzsche, that the actual ending to Part III contains the book's real conclusions, and that Part IV was added later as an unfortunate afterthought.[2] An alternative "ironist" position has taken Part IV to be the integral and concluding section of the book, with satirical elements added to undermine the natural development of the sections which precede it.[3] I will argue that the confusion surrounding the fifth gospel can be dispelled by articulating yet a third narrative which accounts for both the literalist and ironist readings.

First to consider on the "literalist" side, there is evidence external to the text to suggest that the original *Zarathustra* ends with Part III and not with Part IV. (1). In the letters Nietzsche wrote immediately after finishing Part III of *Zarathustra*, he proclaimed triumphantly that *Zarathustra* was finished and complete. In these letters he describes Part III as the last part of the whole work, as the conclusion of his drama in three acts, and as the sublime finale to his symphony.[4] (2). When Nietzsche published *Zarathustra* as a single work, over a year after completing Part IV, he included only the first three parts.[5] (3). In his retrospective work *Ecce Homo*, Nietzsche wrote that he finished with the whole of Zarathustra when he wrote the third and last part.[6] (4). Notes written while Nietzsche was composing Part IV seem to show that he was then planning further parts which would depict events subsequent to the first three parts.[7]

Secondly, there is evidence internal to the text of Zarathustra itself to suggest that the original ends with Part III. (5). There are many thematic and symbolic ways in which the conclusion of Part III seems obviously designed as an ending to the entire Zarathustra. (a). The animals say it is the end of Zarathustra's "going under." (b). Zarathustra's private songs invite the harvester, the god Dionysus, whose coming brings the end of the old order (III.14).[8] (c). Zarathustra successfully concludes his courtship with life in his dance with her, and the midnight bell tolls the completion of his wisdom (III.15).[9] (d). In the final song, Nietzsche seals his book with seven seals that mark the doom of this old order and the dawn of the new (III.16).[10] (e). The sixty-six chapters of *Zarathustra* ends with a repetition of the apocalyptic symbol from the 66th and final book of the Bible.[11] (f). Zarathustra's final song, an "Amen Song," is a marriage song, another echo of Revelation bringing to a happy end his dance with life.[12] (g). Part IV, on the contrary, does not read like an ending at all. Its three-day action concludes with Zarathustra's conquest of his last sin and temptation—a conquest that seems to anticipate and imply subsequent events of Zarathustra's completed work and the arrival of Zarathustra's children and great noon.

All of this evidence points to Lampert's interpretation that Zarathustra, as it exists today, is a whole (Parts I-III), plus a fragment (Part IV) of a larger whole that does not exist.[13] Nietzsche did not publish Part IV because he knew that the existence of a fourth part would violate the ending of Part III.[14] Why else would Nietzsche have printed Part IV privately, kept this printing secret, have given copies only to a select few, then later wanted even these copies returned, if not because it was an abortive effort to further the original text?[15]

The ironist interpretation has grown in recent years, and has provided textually faithful treatments of Part IV as evidence of the correctness of this reading. The evidence external to the text is compelling. Nietzsche, they argue, certainly intended Part IV to be an integral and concluding section of his book. (1) Even before the completion of Part III, Nietzsche had made plans for a fourth part and had advised Overbeck of this quite clearly.[16] (2) That Part IV was the actual ending is echoed in letters he wrote shortly after completing Part IV—letters in which he now called Part IV the last part of his book.[17] (3) Further, Nietzsche, although he did not publish Part IV, announced the existence of a fourth and last part in his advertisement for the published collection of Parts I-III.[18] (4) Also, he quotes from this fourth part in his second Preface to the *Birth of Tragedy*;[19] and (5) he described its plot in *Ecce Homo*.[20]

Internal evidence for Part IV is also strong since Nietzsche himself also indicates Part IV to be the conclusion of *Thus Spake Zarathustra*. The structure and allusions of Part IV seem to indicate deliberate design as a parody of the three parts that precede it. In this respect it brings to completion some of the thematic elements of the first three parts. The ironist readers have also pointed out that the fictive narrative voice is more pronounced in Part IV than the preceding parts. This voice does not belong to the protagonist but rather to someone who is narrating at a later date than the time at which his story takes place. There is a distance between the narrator and the protagonist in that the narrator refers to the history books which contain information about his story, mentions earlier narrators that have told different versions of his story, and even raises doubts about the comparative veracity of his own story.[21] Moreover, Nietzsche lets us know that the fictive narrator of Part IV is familiar with the entire narrative of Parts I-III, even quoting verbatim verse-fragments from previous chapters. So we are led to understand that the chronological place of Part IV is still sequential in the sense that the time of its narration follows the time of the narration of the preceding parts with a complexity which could only mean Nietzsche intended Part IV to be completing the whole.[22]

Thus we are at an impasse. The literalist's reading of Part IV as a transitional fragment of a non-existent whole has compelling evidence, as does the ironist's take on Part IV. Both are only partially correct, however, and can be incorporated into a superior larger interpretive whole which explains them both. The larger narrative is this: Nietzsche's Zarathustra is a tragic novel in three parts with a satyr play as its conclusion.

Zarathustra as a Novel

It is significant that Nietzsche does not write Zarathustra as opera or play, but as a prose-poem or novel. A brief reference to the origin of the novel by Nietzsche in *Birth of Tragedy* can serve as a starting point:

> Plato has furnished for all posterity the pattern of a new art form, the novel, viewed as the Aesopian fable raised to its highest power; a form in which poetry played the same subordinate role with regard to dialectic philosophy as that same philosophy was to play for many centuries with regard to theology. This, then, was the new status of poetry, and it was Plato who, under the pressure of daemonic Socrates, had brought it about.[23]

In *Birth of Tragedy*, the greatest and most authentic art is tragic. It is the understanding of the split, tragic will of Apollo and Dionysus, a will divided fundamentally and irrationally between nature and art (objectification), rather than the apprehension of a *logos*. The dialogue form, however, and by implication the novel form which derived from it, are exceptions. They are under a *logos* and therefore are not authentic art.

By arguing that the Platonic dialogue provides the pattern for the novel, Nietzsche would say that the novel, like the dialogue, must be dominated by conceptuality and optimism, celebrating as it does a triumph with every conclusion. Optimism is inherent in dialectical philosophy, at the expense of art and truth; it somehow had to hide or repress or annihilate the tragic truth before the form could come into being, and that this annihilation was accomplished by means of Socratic irony. Socrates rejected all tragedy because it does not tell the truth and for addressing itself to men of little understanding instead of philosophers.[24] Socrates, that enigmatic ironist, substituted the pure *logos* in the place of tragic truth. But what this entails is that dialectical philosophy, along with the dialogue and the novel, hover over an abyss of irrational truth, nature, and art, unbeknownst to themselves.[25]

Socrates' contempt for tragedy was of such magnitude that Plato felt compelled to burn his youthful tragic poetry, banishing unreason for the sake of reason, in order to become a disciple of Socrates. Art, of course, survived this Socratic onslaught, but only in the inferior forms of the dialogues. The dialogues rescued the arts which Plato himself has consciously repudiated; Plato the thinker rescuing Plato the poet by detour.[26] The dialogue was a mixture of all extant styles and forms, as tragedy had been amalgamated now under the sign of reason, rather than tragic unreason. The Socratic principles that virtue is knowledge, that one only sins out of ignorance, that the virtuous man is a happy man are all basic forms of an optimism spelling out, for Nietzsche, the death of tragedy. To once again become authentic art, the novel and the dialogue would have to become tragic. They would have to sever their connection with the *logos*, substituting instead the truth of the Will. They would, in a sense, have to reverse back what was itself once a perverse reversal, and restore the mythic nature of art.

The fact that for Nietzsche the restoration of art to its truth would involve great struggle, with art and Socratism, tragedy and the *logos* locked in confrontation, resembles Lukacs' early conception of the novel and of novelistic irony. For Lukacs the whole question of irony revolved around whether or not it could be both tragic and ethical, unreasonable and logical. Could it acknowledge in-superable dissonance? Or would it acquiesce again to the despotic logic of Socrates, and ignore the negative ground on which its ironies are built?[27] Nietzsche and Lukacs are comparable here; although the *logos* with which Nietzsche is concerned is Platonic rather than Hegelian, and his concentration is on the dialogue form rather than the epic, Lukacs conception of the novel is similar to Nietzsche's, and provides a vocabulary by which to proceed. For Lukacs, the novel and the dialogue would differ precisely in that the diametrical opposition of art and Socratism does not hold in the novel; rather it reverses the dialogue's pattern of domination and submission.

Like Nietzsche, Lukacs construed his own topography of the Greek mind;

but unlike Nietzsche, the early Lukacs aligned himself with Hegel in conceiving of Greece as a world of sculptured depth and harmony that does not yet know any gap between meaning and being, soul and essence, inner and external life. For Lukacs there is no real history of the mind before that of the Greeks; it was they who gave birth to the great forms of the creative mind: the epic, tragedy, and philosophy. In the dawn of history there is a perception of the absolute immanence of the heroic age of Homer; as time progresses, however, integral substance withers (*entweicht*) more and more until, finally, the irremediable development toward philosophical alienation results in the rigid opposition of meaning and being confirmed by the unfortunate transcendence of Platonic thought.

Tragedy for early Lukacs, then, develops as well between the time of the great epic and Plato. While the epic is still capable of dealing with the magnificent essence of life, tragedy (in a moment of progressive alienation) has no other chance but to question reality.

> Great epic writing gives form to the extensive totality of life, drama to the intensive totality of essence. That is why, when essence has lost its spontaneously rounded, sensually present totality, drama can nevertheless, in its formal a priori nature, find a world that is perhaps problematic but which still is all-embracing and closed within itself. But this is impossible for the great epic. For it the world at any given moment is an ultimate principle; it is empirical at its deepest, most decisive, all-determining transcendental base; it can sometimes accelerate the rhythm of life, can carry something that was hidden or neglected to a utopian end which was always immanent within it, but it can never, while remaining epic, transcend the breadth and depth, the rounded, sensual richly ordered nature of life as historically given.[28]

Lukacs' is a closed ontology of the epic and tragic genres; the epic is unavoidably empirical because it aims at the particular, at the given condition of the world; drama, on the other hand, lives in the world of what ought to be, in a tension toward the future. Lukacs thus excludes the hero as he ought to be from all forms of the epic; Homer's Achilles, for example, is epically more valid than Vergil's *Aeneas*, motivated as he is by imperatives.[29]

Thus, after the epic and tragedy developed, Greek thought ossified in the harsh opposition of idea and being of Platonic philosophy. A great divide is reached; now art, as Schiller put it, constitutes a created totality that, detached from real being, must create an illusion to mask its fall from grace.[30] In this sentimentive epoch, the novel, as a second possibility of the epic mode, takes the place of the genuine, resplendent genre. But, Lukacs asserts, it is by no means the psychology of the individual writers that is responsible for this change in form; true to his Hegelianism, it is rather by a succession of supra-personal and objective events in the history of philosophy.

> The epic and the novel, these two major forms of great epic literature differ from one another not by their authors' fundamental intentions but by the given historico-philosophical realities with which the authors were confronted.[31]

The epic, as the incarnation of a harmonious life, formed a self-contained totality; it is the task and the cursed fate of the novel that it must go searching for lost integrity, suffering as it does a kind of transcendental homelessness.

The comparison of Nietzsche with Lukacs on the novel is a fruitful one. The novel struggles for equalization and confrontation. The struggle is the annihilating effect of irony passing over into tragic recognition. The novel becomes a conflict in which the Apollinian (in Lukacs, the epical form impulse) has to yield to the formless impulse of tragedy.[32] Lukacs suggests an inner structure to the novel that in principle separates the disharmonious life from the felicitous integrity of the epic. As a reflection of harmonious life, the epic has organic continuity, whereas the novel, as an expression of metaphysical tension, merely offers a heterogeneous, contingent disjunct. So too for Nietzsche the novel buckles under the strain of logical individualism and the abyss of psychological dionysianism in tense conflict, a revolutionizing of its old dialogic paradigm.

For Lukacs then, in *Theory of the Novel*, the novel, by its presentation of the vacuity and absurdity of the objective present, displaces the *logos* of the epic world. The novel's form restores pessimistic truth, although only ironically. Thus, whereas Nietzsche in *Birth of Tragedy* calls for the total repudiation of any unification with the *logos*, and repudiation of the novel's origin, Lukacs laments the disconnection of the novel from its origin, and even has suggestions for its repair. It is a difference of degree between Nietzsche and Lukacs in these two works; the Lukacsian conception retreating from dialectical optimism to the moment of annihilating irony, Nietzsche's retreat is one all the way back to tragedy.[33]

Solution: Zarathustra plus a Satyr Play

Nietzsche's retreat is to that of a tragic drama in novel form. His Fifth Gospel however ends with a satyr play. The solution to the interpretative problem then is to understand Part IV's satirical and parodic features as a comedy following the tragic trilogy of Parts I-III. I will supply my evidence for such a claim, and then show how such a narrative explains most of the confusions both internal and external to the text.

Nietzsche himself writes in his letters of the Dionysian festival requirement, always fulfilled by Aeschylus, that a trilogy of tragedies, or three act dramatic movements produced from the succession of tragic events, be followed by a more cheerful satyr-play often based on the same mythological material.[34] In the *Birth of Tragedy* Nietzsche writes of the Greek satyr chorus that was the centerpiece of the satyr-play and that seems the model for his invention in Part IV of a chorus of dancing, singing higher men that are stripped of moral pretensions, removed from civilization, and attending to a Dionysus-like Zarathustra.[35]

As is well-known, satyr plays hold an interesting position in relation to our understanding of ancient tragedy. Their role is something more than merely a leftover from drunken dionysian spontaneity. In the Dionysia on three successive mornings, the three dramatists who had been selected competitively by the *archon* earlier that same year each presented a tetralogy consisting of three tragedies and a satyr play. Thus, for example, in Aeschylus' tetralogy based on the Theban cycle of legends, *Seven Against Thebes* won first prize in 467b.c., with *Laius* and *Oedipus* completing the tragic series, with *The Sphinx* being the satyr play; the *Suppliants* was the first play in the tetralogy, with the *Egyptians*, the *Daughters of Danaus* completing the tragic cycle, with the *Amymone* being the satyr play.

Thus we have the unique example of primitive drama continuing side by side with the highest literary achievements, the greatest tragic dramatists writing silly folk plays out of essentially similar materials, as if Shakespeare had followed Romeo and Juliet with an episode of the Simpsons satirizing some of the scenes. The two surviving examples are Sophocles' *Ichneutai* and Euripides' *Cyclops*. The most obvious function of the Satyr play is to supply a release from the tragic tension of the preceding plays. The plays never became associated with comedy proper, either the burlesque types we see in Aristophanes, or the more politically tinged kinds like Menander. In style and theme the Satyr play never deviated far from tragedy, even if its spirit might strike us as being more allied with comedy dialogue or farce. The tragic diction was still used, except of course when the Satyrs themselves were talking; and the satyrs themselves were farcical figures, while those who in the preceding tragedies had been tragic retain most of their character. Thus Odysseus in *The Cyclops* remains heroic, even though Polyphemous is less the dreadful figure of Homer's epic than some fairy-tale oaf. In the fragmentary *Ichneutai*, Silenus is presented as a cowardly braggart, ready to betray either side, but also not entirely unlikeable.[36]

Nietzsche no doubt saw in the satyr play a sign of spiritual health following a period of tragedy, although to some degree writing *Zarathustra* constitutes a reversal of his views in *Birth of Tragedy*. The reason for this reversal has to do with the fact that *Zarathustra*, when addressed under the general rubric of a novel, turns more seriously and consistently toward the dialogue itself as a model, to the discovery that true dialogue is arbitrary, open, and nonlogical. In a true dialogue with others one cannot plan what will be said. Dialogue does not proceed from assumed propositions, but from propositions derived from each other according to an internal scheme that goes in unexpected directions. It is controlled, not by reason as the logical Platonic dialogue was, but by free association or the demands of the unconscious. At this core is a movement and interchange, without a logically apprehendable or definable goal. It is a speech demanding recognition by something other, but one is not certain precisely what.[37]

At first, *Zarathustra* hardly seems the place for dialogue; not only those secondary figures, but the reader himself, is in an inequal position and has to obey the authority of Zarathustra, a fact which always makes dialogue difficult. But the obvious parodic nature of the fourth part of the work immediately puts into question the hymnic sayings of Zarathustra. His (and the narrator's) use of formulaic expressions, archaisms, inversions in word positions, syntactical oddities and parables all mimic biblical style. Zarathustra's teachings are elevated to a messianic level, and are thereby authenticated. But since they are wholly directed against Christianity, they effectively negate the biblical messages by imitating and parodying the biblical style itself.

More significant than this parody of the style and parables of the Bible is Nietzsche's parody of Zarathustra's own style and his own teachings. It is this recognition of substitution and fiction, this self-derailment of his own strategic purpose, where Zarathustra's monologue with the world becomes more malleable and less absolute, becomes more dialogical in the sense that he becomes freer from his model and more creative in his relation to a reality which he now knows to be preeminently a world of substitutions. In the chapter "On Passing By" in Part III, Zarathustra encounters a foaming fool parodying his own phrasing and cadences in his speech. He is referred to as Zarathustra's Ape, mimicking and exaggerating Zarathustra's own word plays and parallelisms. But Zarathustra labors to keep his own image free from the fool's rhetoric:

> Here, however, Zarathustra interrupted the foaming fool and put his hand over the fool's mouth. Stop at last! cried Zarathustra; your speech and your manner have long nauseated me...

> They call you my ape, you foaming fool; but I call you my grunting swine: with your grunting you spoil for me my praise of folly...

> But your fool's words injure me even where they are right. And even if Zarathustra's words were a thousand times right, still you would always do wrong with my words.[38]

Zarathustra, through such dialogic interaction with the Fool, has given substance to his own views. He has to remake his own views in order to negate the vile liberties taken by the Fool. The Fool's statements, vengeful as they are, dictatorially create Zarathustra's own views and message, and system of communication to which others must yield, and everything does yield, except language which finds in dialogue a way to acknowledge both the real and the false. But the language that can acknowledge both is fiction, a language in which words have become dissociated from substance and truth. This language is the site of absences, but it is only in such a site that fictions can survive, as can all errors and lies. The traits of the classical novel are born in *Zarathustra* at the moment when language is dislodged from substance and truth.

It is the fourth part of the book where the major parody of Zarathustra's teaching occurs. The narrative point of view, the tone and the tempo undergo a striking change; Zarathustra himself speaks very little in the fourth part, whereas he has mainly spoken to the crowd, his disciples, or to himself in the first three parts. Most of the fourth part is taken up by the higher men and the ass, who parody Zarathustra's saying, and Zarathustra himself seems to join this parody of his own teaching. At least he does not so vehemently respond as in Part Three. In the section entitled "The Ass Festival" Zarathustra is seen not only joining in the braying of the ass, but is told that he could as well be an ass himself.

> And whoever has too much spirit might well grow foolishly fond of stupidity and folly itself. Think about yourself, O Zarathustra! You yourself verily, over-abundance and wisdom could easily turn into an ass. Is not the perfect sage fond of walking on the most crooked ways? The evidence shows this, O Zarathustra, and you

are the evidence.[39]

As we have observed, unobtrusive and effacing in the first three parts, in Part Four he puts into question the veracity of his account by suggesting several different versions of Zarathustra's life:[40]

> But the old soothsayer was dancing with joy; and, even if, as some of the chroniclers think, he was full of sweet wine, he was certainly still fuller of the sweetness of life and he had renounced all weariness. There are even some who relate that the ass danced too, and that it had not been for nothing that the ugliest man had given him wine to drink before. Now it may have been so or otherwise; and if the ass really did not dance that night, yet greater and stranger wonders occurred than the dancing of an ass would have been. In short, as the proverb of Zarathustra says: What does it matter?[41]

Where recognition that all of Zarathustra's teachings are put in question is most persuasive in the Magician's "metalinguistic" statements, which are grounded no doubt in part on Nietzsche's own insights into the nature of language.[42] The magician suggests that Zarathustra's teachings are mere metaphors, rhetorical tropes to be banished from all truth, and wishes to expose Zarathustra as equally a magician, a liar, a seducer who knowingly deceives.

> Suitor of truth? they mocked me; you?
> No! Only poet!
> An animal, cunning, preying, prowling,
> That must lie,
> That must knowingly, willingly lie;
> Lusting for prey,
> Colorfully masked,
> A mask for itself,
> Prey for itself
> This, the suitor of truth?
> No! Only fool! Only Poet!
> Only speaking colorfully,
> Only screaming colorfully out of fool's masks,
> Climbing around on mendacious word bridges,
> On colorful rainbows,
> Between false heavens
> And false earths,
> Roaming, hovering
> Only fool! Only poet![43]

The Magician is pointing out that insight into the nature of language makes any persuasive use of language impossible. It is the remembering of the problematics of language, the awareness of rhetorical tropes, which is the adversary of Zarathustra. And this passage is not merely an isolated moment. Repeated in the Magician's song are Zarathustra's remarks praising words as a means of forgetting. Back in Part Three, after Zarathustra's collapse, the animals conversed with him about the notion of eternal recurrence, the thought of thoughts now brought to language. They spoke to Zarathustra about his new insight in seductive words that tempted him to sheer intoxication.

> O my animals, replied Zarathustra, chatter on like this and let me listen. It is so refreshing for me to hear you chattering; where there is chattering, there the world lies before me like a garden. How lovely it is that there are words and sounds! Are not words and sounds rainbows and illusive bridges between things which are eternally apart?...Precisely between what is most similar illusion lies most beautifully; for the smallest cleft is the hardest to bridge...But all sounds make us forget this; how lovely it is that we forget...Speaking is a beautiful folly; with that man dances over all things. How lovely is all talking, and all the deception of sounds![44]

Zarathustra is very much aware here that his idea of the overman is only a poetic lie. He therefore repeatedly warns his readers of his poetic speeches, of his parables, "... that I speak in parables and limp and stammer like poets, verily, I am ashamed that I must still be a poet."[45]

Zarathustra's scenes most often function in imitation of the pattern set by the early 19th century novel; they work against the lead characters monologic self-objectification and his attempt at a dialogue with the world. It is as well true that these dialogic scenes remain subservient to Zarathustra's self-realization. The dialogue is rejected as a source of truth, or the speeches of the others are accepted only partially, or much later in the solitary self-dialogue. Also the main figure characteristically makes his recognition alone. The recognition rarely occurs in the dialogue moment or process itself, although the dialogue may precipitate it. This is true equally for Zarathustra: he does not profit as much from dialogue or live in dialogue. Zarathustra's repeated awareness of the necessary falsity of all signs leads him at times to claim that all his speeches are mere noise that hides his silence.

> It is my favorite malice and art that my silence has learned not to betray itself through silence. Rattling with discourse and dice, I outwit those who wait solemnly; my wit and purpose shall elude all these severe inspectors. That no one may discern my ground and ultimate will, for I have invented my long bright silence.[46]

The first three parts of Zarathustra are not yet true dialogues precisely because they are tied to recognition. They are not free, but have a function and a goal. The goal is not the Platonic but the subjective *logos*. The dialogue functions in a Hegelian sense, oriented toward the individual and not the general. The dialogue is as if secretly planned to contribute to self-recognition, to self-enlargement. The dialogue still maintains its dialecticality, though this is now the Hegelian dialecticality of self-development.

Thus, considered as a novel, the first three parts of the work constitute a dialogue not yet free of logicality, because the impasses, the tremblings, and the dissolution that Zarathustra experiences always lead to a further explication of his being. But the fourth part of Zarathustra comes closer to a true self-dialogue, as is indicated by the fact that it so often comes to an impasse of contradictions, negations, and self-parodies. Zarathustra uses every known ruse to authenticate his sayings and to persuade his readers. These textual segments, in which he posits his myths, are followed by segments that undermine the foundations of these myths. This play of building and destroying, of asserting and doubting, of using old myths and then parodying them, is dialogic in its displacement and repression. It seeks simultaneously to reveal and disguise; and this is invariably a playful element, for the playfulness is inherently the displaced, the other, for which metaphor or metonymy substitutes.

Nietzsche's Fifth Gospel is thus a modern replay of the ancient tragic tetralogy that ends with a satyr play. The solution to the interpretative problem then is to understand Part IV's satirical and parodic features as a comedy following the tragic trilogy of Parts I-III. Again, this narrative explains most of the confusions both internal and external to the text. Given this structure, the literalists were in fact correct to see the end of Part III of Nietzsche's Zarathustra as the culminating conclusion to a "whole" that begins with Part I and ends with Part III. At the same time, the ironist readers are right to insist that Nietzsche intended Part IV to be an integral part of this same whole. But it is no longer necessary to suppose, as both literalists and ironists do, that the whole consisting of all four parts is either somehow incomplete, or the fragment of some whole which does not exist. For this supposition, that Nietzsche's *Zarathustra* has a beginning but no ending, is a result of reading the story of Part IV as some chronological sequel to the ending of Part III. The same error would be committed were one to read into the *Ichneutai* of Sophocles some chronological sequel to the events of *Antigone*.

That Nietzsche now has something like a satyr play in mind is marked by compelling references to them in works during the composition of Zarathustra. In *Genealogy of Morals*, for example, written soon after the performance of the prelude to Wagner's Parsifal at Monte-Carlo in 1886, Nietzsche writes:

> Was this Parsifal meant seriously anyway? One might be inclined to suppose the opposite, and even to wish it—that the Wagnerian Parsifal was meant as a joke, as a kind of epilogue and satyr-play with which the tragedian Wagner wanted to take leave of us, also of himself, above all of tragedy, in a manner worthy of himself: namely, with an extravagant and wanton parody of the tragic itself.[47]

Wagner's work, obviously the object of parody in the fourth part of *Zarathustra*, would have been more successful as a satyr play, as this would have made Parsifal a secret, exultant laugh signalling the artist's final emancipation.

> This, as I have said, would have been worthy of a great tragedian who, like every artist, first attains the ultimate summit of his greatness when he clearly sees himself and his art beneath himself—when he knows how to laugh at himself.[48]

In a manner worthy of a great tragedian, Nietzsche's novel will laugh at itself in a way Wagner's Parsifal could not. Such would complete Zarathustra's own consecration of laughter in Part III. The one who "laughed the same day he was born" could, in the fifth gospel, both laugh at himself and to laughingly say what was most seriously to be said, overcoming the curse of the earlier gospels.[49]

I would add as further external evidence for such a reading that in the work which introduces the character of Zarathustra to the world, Nietzsche's *Gay Science*, the work immediately preceding *Zarathustra*, Nietzsche does something similar to a satyr play addition in miniature, in his concluding poetry in the Fifth book of that work.

Nietzsche's poetry in the appendix to the *Gay Science* is in relation to the late Greek pastoral poet Theocritus, well-known for his bucolic or idyllic poetry, to whom Nietzsche makes satirical reference. Theocritus' depiction of shephards would seem ripe for satire. Indeed, Nietzsche seems to want to replace all insipid shepherd imagery in contemporary culture with "satyr" imagery. Specifically, Nietzsche is targeting the third of Theocritus' idyls, called "Serenade." In the poem, the singer appears as a love-sick goatherd needing something a bit more randy than some sheep to herd. Nietzsche immediately begins the ridicule: the goatherd is not threatened by wolves but by bedbugs, the pains he feels are not those in his heart but in his bowels. In Theocritus' original poem, the singer lies in wait for his beloved at the mouth of a cave. In his poem Nietzsche's goatherd mentions the frustrations it generates, an indignant anger seeking an outlet in jeers. That he has his lover throw-up onions is another comic reference to Heine. It is clear, from the preface and elsewhere in the text, that Nietzsche is poking fun at all poets, himself included. Indeed, at times toward the end he seems interested in poking in the eye everything called untouchable in German letters, Goethe, Heine, Wagner, as well as the Bible, such as in his mentioning the "seventh hell" in the last stanza using the German word *Ubel* from Luther's German edition of the Lord's prayer.

To be "theocritical" is to assume a poetic—parodic position in relation to all the tragic and collosal philosophical criticism that has gone just before in the work. It is as if Nietzsche wanted to show that this thinker of the death of God, the great destroyer of all fixations and thought-systems, so much so that he cannot be contained by any one of them himself, was not crippled in the effort but remained *fröhlich*. That is, Nietzsche is himself not afflicted with resentment and twistedness after having thought these portentous events, but is lighthearted enough to end his book with a self- critique based on a satire of an idyllic Greek poet. Indeed, there is a play on the name of the poet, as Nietzsche is about as "theo-critical" as they come. Nietzsche also intersplices terms from his own philosophy so as to seemingly achieve distance on himself, satirizing even those philosophical moments in the book that came before.[50]

In contrast to the literalist and ironist readings, then, reading *Zarathustra* as a novelistic drama with a satyr play it is possible to see all the events in this narrative conclusion as fulfilled in the concluding chapters of Part III. Nietzsche's book is a completely self-contained work in which the life of the protagonist comes to a climactic end precisely as Nietzsche announced it would when he introduced it in the *Gay Science*. Zarathustra's death is the chronological finish of his book at the end of Part III As to why, after ending his book with Part III, Nietzsche should have chosen to add a fourth part that relates events which chronologically precede this ending. Nietzsche wrote *Gay Science* I-IV, then wrote *Zarathustra* I-III, then read Heine, saw Wagner's Parsifal, and recalled the idea of the satyr play, and then wrote Book V of the *Gay Science*, and then Part IV of the *Zarathustra* with this in mind. Nietzsche is letting us know that he himself did intend Part IV to be a leave-taking parody of the tragic aspect in the Parts I-III trilogy, thereby demonstrating his artistic triumph by laughing at himself and seeing himself and his art beneath himself. A triumphant finish to his *Zarathustra* would be the good health demonstrated in being able to satirize even this teaching, and his subsequent need to incorporate in this narrative a resurrection coda that would parallel the ending of all the Gospels, allowing Nietzsche to resurrect Zarathustra in a life-affirming way.

IX. The De-Spenglerization of European Thought

Cultural decline seems to be a major enabling condition for 20th century western European philosophical thought. Discussion about cultural decline and despair was heightened at the turn of the century by World War I, which further eroded the leading status of the liberal-progressive view of history forwarded by the neo-kantians, tending as they had to affirm Enlightenment cultural, political, and scientific values. This view had taken history to be the gradual development of more effective ways of controlling nature and of more enlightened modes of social organization and cultural self-expression. Opposed to this progressive view of history were two groups: those who believed that history had no direction, and those who believed that history involved a decline from great beginnings. Versions of these latter views we will amalgamate under the banner of *spenglerization*, which takes history to be the story of the inexorable decline and fall from the pinnacle achievements of earlier peoples. This phenomenon of spenglerization becomes so great that not even 20th century master thinkers would entirely de-spenglerize their own philosophizing.

Decline discourses are persistent and pervasive narrative structures that frame their subject often in the sublime contexts of the rise and fall of empires, the mythology of apocalyptic eschatologies, the categories of moral, racial or physiological decadence, and in the most contemporary of mass cultural and environmental theories. They have accompanied western philosophical categories almost since their inception. Hesiod already describes his times as a deterioration from that of Homer. The myth of universal empire sustained Roman imperial propaganda until the age of Justinian—any movement against its universal harmony constituted decline. This essential decline structure gets Christianized when Roman empire seemed to presage Christ's *katholikos* church. Augustine seized upon the fall of Rome to the Visigoths to announce a Christian world order. Charlemagne and the German Holy Roman emperors all strove to build such a Christian empire during the Middle Ages. Late medieval Christian eschatologies structure temporality into linear rather than cyclical frameworks, pushing humanity irresistibly forward to *parousia*. The Enlightenment brought great benefits of political freedoms, growth in commerce and affluence, and articulations of natural liberty, equality, and property, but faith in the law of progress carried with it an accompanying possibility of reversal. Thus Malthus, Gibbon and Montesquieu generate famous late-enlightenment secular collapse narratives. The Roman Empire's precipitous fall, according to them, came not from moral failure so much as economic and political crises of bankrupt ruling classes, an impoverished peasantry, and an overconfident army. These authors structured the "course of empire" to embody a cycle of growth, decay, and destruction. That all great cultures reach a point of no return, and could collapse despite material accomplishments, had an enormous impact on late 18th century imagination.[1]

While the 19th century saw prophets of progress thrive in the figures of Hegel, Comte, and Spencer, by mid-century counter-weights to the rationalist faith in progress began to emerge, such as in the artistic and literary movement of Romanticism. The early twentieth century provided new and improved versions of imminent doom and total despair cast in the various anti-enlightenment contexts of titanism, reactionary modernism, and instrumental rationalism. These movements, fueled by calamitous world events and by the millions of unburied corpses of the Great War, held the gestalt of modernity to be that of technical rationalism—organizing all of humanity's experience, behavior, and reality into thoughtless order, until human life became nothing other than an expression of this order. That humanity was in the grips of a perverted titanic technological gestalt was an objection to the unkept promise of scientific rationality, economic and political individualism, and industrial technology of the enlightenment. Human emancipation had not occurred; rather, people had become depersonalized cyphers who achieve freedom only by surrendering to the higher economic powers which dictate his existence. The unchecked advance of scientific rationality distorted human existence into preprogrammed topiaries. The myth of human progress led to the scientific ideology and exploitation of the earth and the manifestation of an enormous 'foundary' of which all human beings were put in place, and the transformation of the earth into a totally administered technological entity. Human beings were not in control of technology but were themselves ordered by the totalizing mechanisms. Specifically with regard to Germany, writers such as Jünger, Sombart, and Spengler fueled the pessimistic insight that the categories of the Enlightenment had succeeded simply in removing all traditional and religious obstacles to western humanity's secret drive to gain total control over nature via a now unconstrained technological will which had humanity itself completely in place. These reactionary modernist figures consistently claimed that only an apocalyptic socio-political transformation could save the German soul.[2]

The flagship figure, who galvanized and summarized a half-century of historical pessimism and cultural despair with an arcane vocabulary of metaphysical concepts, *Volksgeist*, and organicist views of historical development, was the extremely unorthodox historian Oswald Spengler, whose writings included the all-too-famous, ponderous and contradictory two volume *Decline of the West*.[3] The work struck all nerves and catapulted him into fame as the prophet of right-wing nationalist resurgence of the newly defeated Germany. One of its central themes is Spengler's notion of history as the comparative morphology of cultures. He held that history itself, when properly practiced, details the passing of cultures and shows that they all develop, mature, decline, and die out in discernibly similar stages. The entire content of history is nothing other than this unfolding of cultures. His intent is to show that all known cultures, with primary focus upon the classical (which Spengler calls the "apollonian), the Egyptian, the Arabian, and the Modern (which he calls the "Faustian"), all have developed, flourished, and exhausted themselves in accordance with similar principles, passing through similar sequences of stages. The major task of the *Decline of the West* is the attempt to identify and document these in detail, purporting to describe the stages that known cultures, and presumably every culture, have passed through. Spengler summarizes his purported findings in elaborate, graphic, fold-out sheets in appendices to his work. These foldouts outline the supposed prototypical sequences of cultural development in columns, and parallel columns outline the developmental sequences of actual cultures. The resulting charts and graphs purport to show how world cultures have actually developed along the lines of spenglerian prototypes. The shared patterns and stages in the development of different cultures are manifestations of a powerful internal principle of development that is embodied in every known culture.

This essential task of history Spengler reveals by a "comparative morphology of cultures." The expression suggests an analogy between the development of a culture and that of an organic entity or process. Spengler writes frequently of youth, maturity, decline, aging, and death with reference to cultures. This, he insists, is more of an aid than a detriment to real historical understanding. As a seed or infant develops in a vivid, predictable sequence of stages, so too do cultures. He also writes at length of the development of cultures in terms of the succession of seasons, and many of his conclusions are couched in these terms as well. Cultures have their spring in an early heroic period when life is rural, agricultural, and feudal. In the Apollonian culture this was the Homeric period, whereas in the Faustian age it was the High Middle

Ages. It is marked by seminal myths, inspiring epic, and powerful mystical religion. With summer comes the growth of towns not yet alienated from the rural settings, and great individual artists succeeding their anonymous predecessors. In Apollonian culture this was the period of the early city-states; in the Faustian age it was the time of the Renaissance, of Shakespeare and Michelangelo. Autumn witnesses the full ripening of the cultures' spiritual resources and the first hints of possible exhaustion, such as growing cities, spreading commerce, centralizing monarchies, and religion being challenged by philosophy and tradition by enlightenment. In the classical world, this was the age of the sophists, Socrates, and Plato. In the west this is the 18th century Germany, with Mozart, Goethe, and Kant. Transition to winter is characterized by the appearance of megalopolis, competing worldviews, a rootless proletariat, and growing skepticism and materialism. It is marked by growing imperialism and increasing political tyranny. Culture loses its soul and becomes mere civilization, where the highest works are those of administration and the application of science to industry. For Spengler, one need only look as far as one's own culture to see the morphological contemporaries of the Caesarism which marked Roman decadence.[4]

Spengler's passionate and controversial appropriation of Nietzsche's diagnosis of the crisis of western culture is also well-known.[5] Already by 1900 the publication of Nietzsche's works had triggered a profound search for the origins of decadence in European culture in the draining away of vital life forces necessary for the creation of values. Nietzsche had sought to diagnose the origins of decline in the spirit of Christianity and the Enlightenment faith in material progress. Equally as influential was Nietzsche as a philosopher of history, arguing that "useful" history can only be written from within a present sufficiently strong enough to destroy the passivizing weight of the past.[6] Although he came to value historical thought more highly in his later works and grew to distance himself from his earlier condemnation of historicism, Nietzsche never revered the historical method to the degree that Spengler did. Nietzsche held a dim view of anyone's seeking to pack the complexity of human history into a methodical system of historical philosophy, as exemplified in Nietzsche's unwavering opposition to Hegel. Thus Spengler sought to systematize, at least to some extent, essentially Nietzschean insights into history. Spengler maintained with Nietzsche that world history is ultimately a meaningless but aesthetically sublime spectacle generated by irrational forces. Over and against Hegel, for whom world history is the triumphant procession of a dialogically rational *Weltgeist*, Spengler was more a student of Hegel's archrival Schopenhauer in holding history to be the march of the tragic, irrational human will towards complete catastrophe. Hegel, and prominent representatives of historicism, like Humboldt, Ranke, and Droysen, had optimistically believed that the course of history conformed to a moral order of divine origin. Spengler followed Nietzsche's lead in rejecting this optimism.

> (Human history) is a spectacle, which is sublime in its purposelessness, without aim and majestic like the motion of the stars, the rotation of the earth, the alternation of land and sea and of ice and primeval forests upon her. One can admire or bewail it—but it is there.[7]

Just as great cultures live like organic realities, each as well are characterized as unique individual types. Spengler proposed his vital cultural types as hypostatizations of a metaphysical life-principle making possible the primary forms through which cultural reality is constituted. All civilizations pass through the same sequences but are otherwise autonomous. Since human history lacks any overall meaning or purpose, each civilization views things from its own perspective, establishes its own table of values, and thus constitutes a type. Each great culture has an *Ur-symbol* that governs the style of the whole expression of life. It lies in the form of state, in religious myths and cults, in the ideals of ethics, the forms of painting, music, and poetry, the basic concepts of every science. Decline sets in as this primal symbol loses its force.[8]

According to Spengler, it was in the nineteenth century that the West had finally entered into old age, the final stage of every historical culture. Mummified and parasitical, western culture had degenerated in its winter to a mere "civilization" which clings to its once living roots of culture. All of its achievements were the mere thrashing about of a dying world. Denying the experience of the sacred, the West now faces the collapse of values and identity, just as other extinct cultures did previously. The optimistic philosophies of Comte, Mill, and Marx had been negated by the skeptical pessimism of Schopenhauer, Wagner, and Nietzsche. The nineteenth century had to face "the cold, hard facts of late life." For Spengler the "type" embodied by western civilization is Faustian in its restless pursuit of knowledge and change. The West's chief product, science, is merely the concretization of the indomitable western will, which it then projects onto the rest of the world in mechanical, rather than organic, terms. The time and space conquering appetites of the Faustian imperialists doom the west to machinic servitude. Spengler insisted that the western mechanical view of time, nature, and history stood in stark contrast to the organic reality. The result was an illusion of limitless expansion and improvement over time, symbolized by space conceived as abstract markets. The western businessman's Faustian appetite, characterized by Cecil Rhodes' frenetic punching through the African jungle, enslaves humanity to its own industrial creations, the only hope against which was the rise of a new Caesarism.[9]

The Decline of the West was the first work of thoroughgoing, historical-philosophical pessimism to achieve fame in the German speaking world, and its vision conquered the continent. Spengler integrated into his major work Nietzsche's denial of the idea of progress, which found a receptive European audience conditioned by the decline in the belief in metaphysics, the growth of scientifically-inspired skepticism, and the imperialistic motives of the Great War. Critics however had a field day with the inaccuracies and contradictions of the work, not the least of which was its confusing notion of cultural insularity.[10] Despite the morphological similarities he saw between vastly different cultures, Spengler emphasized their insularity from one another, holding to the idea that earlier cultures never really influenced later ones, or that from within one culture one cannot really grasp the perspective of another culture, and that the Modern mind has not been influenced by and thus cannot understand the Classical mind. This alleged incommensurability and perspectivism poses certain problems for Spengler. Unlike previous cultural interpreters, who were always influenced by their culturally specific standpoint, Spengler claimed that he effected a Copernican revolution in historiography by achieving the objectivity of the natural sciences. Based on this allegedly objective standpoint did he confidently predict the decline of the west. He did not however adequately address two performative contradictions. The first involves his supposition that he could provide a culture-transcending interpretation of all cultures, even though he himself was a member of one particular culture. The second involves his description of his own work as objective, even though he declared that natural science itself, the model of western objectivity, has no grounds for making ultimately valid truth claims but instead was a working hypothesis in the service of the technical will.

How can Spengler, who presumably thinks from inside the unique and limiting perspective of a modern human being, come to understand the perspectives of other cultures, given his own viewpoint regarding cultural insularity? His answer is that the occasional intuitive genius can overcome the obstacles of cultural insulation. Spengler never seems quite comfortable with the tension between what he says about cultural insularity and his willingness to expound upon the prime symbols of other cultures. In commending his own historical scheme in comparison with others, he says:

> In opposition to all these arbitrary and narrow schemes ... into which history is forced, I put forward the "Copernican" form of the historical process which lies deep in the essence of that process and reveals itself only to an eye perfectly free from prepossessions. [11]

Elsewhere he states a need to view things not with the eyes of the partisan, the ideologue, or the up-to-date novelist, not from this or that standpoint, but in a high, time-free perspective ".. if we are really to comprehend the great crises of the present."[12] Yet again elsewhere Spengler describes that the results of his analysis "at last will unfold .. the picture of world-history that is natural to us, men of the west, and to us alone."[13] Such remarks seem mysterious, given Spengler's claims regarding the possibility of a perspective perfectly free of prepossessions and his suggestions that an individual's cultural boundedness can be overcome.[14]

Spengler's work had an enormous impact and unprecedented literary success in Germany, both among the academic elites and the larger reading public. It was the most popular work of European thought in the interwar era. [15] Some have argued that Spengler was inspired to write his account of the organic rise and fall of world cultures because of the storm of national protest that occurred when Germany appeared to back down from a 1911 confrontation in Morocco between France and Germany. When it appeared in print in April 1918, Germany was in the midst of its last great military offensive, but the wheels had fallen off by summer, and the last vestiges of Wilhelmine Germany had collapsed in violent uprisings. The wartime generation of university-trained intellectuals were profoundly affected by Spengler's intoxicating combination of both western collapse and German resurgence, including Thomas Mann and Max Weber. Spengler was even awarded the prestigious Lassen Prize of the Nietzsche Foundation by Elizabeth Förster-Nietzsche in November 1919.[16] Two of the most widely recognized and influential philosophical geniuses of the day, Ludwig Wittgenstein and Martin Heidegger, were as well deeply impacted by the work, enough to see both the cultural significance of Spengler's accomplishment and the need for a certain amount of de-spenglerization to accompany it.

Wittgenstein's De-Spenglerization

Wittgenstein, often at pains to acknowledge his philosophical predecessors, mentions Spengler on a list of intellectual influences, and Spengler's impact on the Viennese genius has been recorded by various conversation partners, biographers, and Wittgensteinian philosophers.[17] While it is pretty clear that Wittgenstein rejected much that was in Spengler, such as the whole idea of approaching the phenomena in question in terms of cultural morphology and the propensity to understand history in terms of moulds and prototypes, there is no outright condemnation. There is instead the suggestion that Spengler would have done better to cast the ideas in Wittgenstein's own terms of understanding cultural epochs as family resemblances. Thus Spengler's historical essentialism is for Wittgenstein a conceptual confusion which could be alleviated through some greater philosophical precision, not so as to dismiss Spengler's achievement as worthless, but to bring out what was *indeed important* about Spengler.[18] The notion of cultural insulation might have appealed to Wittgenstein for a time during his famous transition from the *Tractatus* to the *Investigations'* conception of meaning. Spengler was as mistaken as Wittgenstein took his own earlier thought to be, in thinking that historical meaning depended mostly on something like logical form. That Spengler might nevertheless be able to "teach something about the age we are living in" suggests that for Wittgenstein what was *not* to be de-spenglerized was precisely the tone and temperament of *Decline of the West*.

Thus it is the Spengler as bleak cultural prophet of doom which resonates in Wittgenstein's preface to *Philosophical Remarks*. Here European and American civilization are denounced in terms reminiscent of the titanism and instrumental rationalism of the reactionary modernist, Spenglerian as it is in tone, substance, and vocabulary. Both refer to civilization as something lifeless and terminal, a deterioration of something once living. What Spengler could teach Drury was that Wittgenstein shared the historian's sense of his own time as one of demise. When Wittgenstein comments on the bleak outlook regarding modern architecture, music, and the disappearance of the arts, Spengler's introduction articulates the same views.

> We are civilized, not Gothic or Rococo, people; we have to reckon with the hard cold facts of a late life, to which the parallel is to be found not in Pericles's Athens but in Caesar's Rome. Of great painting or great music there can no longer be, for western people, any question. Their architectural possibilities have been exhausted these hundred years.[19]

For Spengler, religion and philosophy are in much the same state as architecture and the arts, only more so. Once the dominant force in the early stages of a living culture, these wither to a point of virtual non-existence in the stage of civilization. Whatever religious feelings and practices that may endure in a civilization do so as pale shadows of what they once were in times of youthful living culture. For Spengler such a kind of religious spark lies at the heart of every culture and dies with civilization.

> Every soul has religion, which is only another word for existence. All living forms in which it expresses itself—all arts, doctrines, customs, all metaphysical and mathematical form-worlds, all ornament, every column and verse and idea—are ultimately religious, and must be so. But from the setting in of civilization, they *cannot* be so any longer. As the essence of every culture is religion, so—and *consequently*—the essence of every civilization is irreligion, the two words are synonymous.[20]

Philosophy for Spengler is as well quite circumscribed. Systematic philosophy, like the arts and religion, is no longer possible in a time of civilization. "Systematic philosophy closes with the end of the 18th century. Kant put its utmost possibilities in forms both grand in themselves and, as a rule, final for the western soul."[21] Spengler's characterization of a new philosophy for the times is to be marked by psychological procedures. He also attacks the tendency in Kant, and for any philosopher, to establish anything of substance for *all* people and for *all* times. The philosopher, for Spengler, must accept that even a work in philosophy must be rooted in, and its scope limited by, its historical setting. Interestingly enough, against this totalizing version of philosophy Spengler suggests more modest detours in philosophy, namely a philosophical program that accepts its own radical finitude and situatedness, a philosophy that directs itself against philosophy.

> Systematic philosophy, then, lies immensely far behind us, and the ethical has been wound up. *But a third possibility, corresponding to the Classical skepticism, still remains to the soul world* of the present-day West ... [T]his unphilosophical philosophy is the last that West Europe will know ... With that, the claim of higher thought to possess general and eternal truths falls to the ground.[22]

It is not difficult to see the congruence between such sentiments and the philosophical work of Wittgenstein. The *Investigations* delineates a purified non-cognitivist conception of philosophy, according to which there is indeed no system of philosophical *knowledge*. Instead philosophy converts to a two-fold activity: a quest for a surveyable representation of the grammar of problematic domains; and philosophy as a kind of cure for diseases of the understanding. The point of the former is to simply find our way out of philosophical difficulties. The point of the latter is to transform latent concealed nonsense into patent nonsense, almost along the model of psychotherapy. For the later Wittgenstein the task of the philosophical therapist is to have the patient self-recognize their affliction through their use of words. Thus repressed doubts and questions are to be brought forward and expelled by the realization of their grammatical origin. The student who asks "What is the cause of the entire universe?" would learn not to ask such questions, as they are generated by a misunderstanding of the use of the word "cause." It is also part of Wittgenstein's point to show how the source of some of the confusion is the will to illusion, the craving people have to generalize meanings. People find solace, often perverse satisfactions, in certain utterly misconceived philosophical pictures. There is the desire for new and untold mysteries of truth and mind. But for Wittgenstein there are no such mysteries, or at least nothing is hidden that philosophy as traditionally construed can meaningfully express. There is only the mesmerizing confusions engendered by our entanglement in grammar, although, as in psychoanalysis, there is an underlying motive for cleaving to such error. The task of actually doing philosophy is teaching oneself to abandon certain combinations of words as senseless. Philosophical error is the mark of a failure of character on some levels—Wittgenstein does not merely explain the conceptual mistakes that occur but constantly exhorts himself and his reader not to give in to the temptations to do so. On such a detour, at least in some small way, is there not only an attempt at correcting the philosophical errors but combatting the conditions of civilization that created the moral conditions for those errors.

Spengler's prescriptions for philosophy seem to fit Wittgenstein's thought rather well, with its decidedly psychological character and self-berating style. Nor is it hard to see how the idea of philosophy as nothing but therapeutic analysis seems to many a depressingly negative conception of philosophy, depriving it of its greatness and depth. We thought philosophy was the transcendent pursuit into the nature of things, into the essential structure of the human mind, into the conditions of the possibility of experience, into the essence of truth, language, and thought. These were nothing but card-houses, and for Wittgenstein the point of philosophical activity is to dispel such illusions. There can be no theories in philosophy, nor even any explanations. Mostly what philosophy does is describe the tangles in our word usages to cure philosophical illnesses. While cultures may grow or die, there is no advance or decline of philosophical insights.

Such Spenglerian tonalities shed some light on Wittgenstein's explicit comments in the prefatory material of the *Philosophical Remarks*, and numerous references elsewhere in recorded conversations, to the effect that he seeks in his philosophical works to somehow address his own times, to somehow illuminate them, to help his reader respond to them with more understanding. Although the depth traditionally associated with philosophy is an illusion, the illusions are not trivial. Human beings often invest their ownmost being and importance into these conceptual schemes. The supposition of depth rests on the misguided assumption that philosophy aims to penetrate to the language-independent nature of all things, to uncover the essence of everything. But with these pictures demonstrated to be grammatically generated, now the locus of profundity is in those who, in undergoing therapeutic analysis, come to understand more clearly what they previously craved. One self-understands the source of their own puzzlement, namely that philosophical theories are not false but nonsense. They cannot be combatted by denying them, or by defending their denial using argument, (since the negation of nonsense is just more nonsense), but only by delving into the sources of confusion and demonstrating their grammatical status. These general trajectories are Spenglerian, as is the expressed intention to somehow capture a sense of the times within a work of what remains of philosophy itself to accomplish.

In an indirect sense, Wittgenstein's thought completely conveys Spengler's characterization of a new possibility for philosophy in this time. There can be no progress or decline in philosophy, if that is understood as modeled on the physical sciences. The only progress comes in the 'perspicuous representation' of the grammar of philosophical problems. Expressions can once again be located together correctly; new themes can be relocated together in the face of new problems, generated by new ways of speaking. One can never foresee all of the new conceptual confusions around the corner. The invention of computers, for example, exercises a mesmerizing force upon psychologists and neuro-scientists which simply bewitch their language. One cannot anticipate all the future diseases of the intellect which will infect thinking, only provide ever new means and methods for their cure. The primary source of philosophical confusion is language, grammatical illusions and misinterpretations. Wittgenstein demonstrates this most effectively against mathematicians, logicians, and psychologists, but also to your friendly neighborhood metaphysician. The forms of the question: what is an X? is appropriate in some domains but not others. Forms of expression suggest certain stock forms of interpretation: verb forms link to activities; substantives suggest a correlative substance. But in the case of "numbers," the form of such questions leads philosophers to think expressions represent "abstract substances" or objects. The word "mind" suggests to many thinkers some substance, just as adjectives deceptively suggest that they signify qualities. This then gets applied to color words or words like "good" to refer to some non-natural quality. In all such cases, indeed in doing any and all philosophy, one assimilates dissimilar concepts. We are unaware of the prodigious diversity of our concepts, concealed as they are by the limited range of grammatical forms in our language. We generate philosophical confusion when we transpose a concept from one domain to another, unwittingly assuming that the connections of the one domain apply in the other.

So in these respects, it is true that for Wittgenstein philosophy should relinquish its throne as queen of the sciences, even more so on the basis of the *Investigations* as on the *Tractatus*. Philosophy has no claim to the deep metaphysical insights into the world, the necessary structure of mind, the foundations of mathematics or science, or transcendent truths of religion or ethics. It will be as difficult, however, not to use such cherished expressions as it will be to hold back tears.[23] For Wittgenstein, no doubt Spengler's own historical typologies were consistent with this craving for generality which marked bankrupt metaphysics, which in turn have resulted in the ludicrous isolation of human beings trapped in nonsensical pictures unknown to themselves. While rejecting this underlying picture, nevertheless Wittgenstein adopts the Spenglerian tonality which represents the conditions of culture giving way entirely to the worst conditions of mere administrative civilization. Wittgenstein does not-despenglerize so much as seek to complete the spenglerization process in having us recognize the absence of that cultural cohesion which makes great art, music, architecture, religion and philosophy possible. The recognition accompanying the completion of such a process would yet prevent the widespread fragmentation which conditions a dying culture.

Heidegger's De-Spenglerization

While Spengler's influence on Wittgenstein is apparent if indirect, with only sparse textual evidence for the connections, Heidegger made scores of references to Spengler, again indexed to various concerns of his own earlier and later philosophical interests. We might begin by characterizing Heidegger's early take on Spengler to be with regard to *Lebensphilosophie* and the philosophical problem of history. After the 1930's Heidegger continued to address aspects of *Decline of the West*, but now more as a flawed philosophy of culture that was appropriately bold in its dire predictions but ultimately too philosophically unsophisticated to recognize its ontological inadequacies, specifically tied up with Heidegger's own attempt to retrieve what to him was most essential in Nietzsche's thought.

Heidegger's early Freiburg and Marburg lecture courses (1919-1921) targeted contemporary ideas of "spirit," "tradition," and "culture," and the historical and historicist orientations responsible for the elaboration of these ideas since the 19th century. Already one can see how, from Heidegger's standpoint, these orientations obstruct the approach to the past necessary for the reformulation of the more originary question of Being. For example, he illustrates how "culture" gets understood in German thought in relation to themes of historical consciousness from Herder and Schlegel in terms of an accomplishment having resulted from a long process of historical development. This idea of historical development was spurred by the emergence of scientific consciousness and by the ensuing progress of natural science and technology. The result of this was to reveal how a one-sided focus on the development of culture had tended to obscure other interpretive possibilities which could not be readily measured in terms of cultural values.[24] Also targeted were philosophers who had most strongly influenced the idea of culture at the time, namely the Marburg and Baden Neo-Kantians Cohen, Windelband, and Rickert. The *Lebens*-philosophers as well were challenged for their affirmation of the ideal of universal validity in the study of objectifications of cultural life, despite Heidegger's profound respect for thinkers like Dilthey.[25] Spengler's all-encompassing typology of cultural forms in *Decline of the West* at this time demonstrated nothing more clearly than the groundlessness of these historical methods in the human sciences in their attempt to elaborate objective, universally valid criteria of judgment as a basis for comparison of typical patterns of cultural expression.[26]

Spengler's work blinded readers to the weaknesses in its thinking about history. Its popularity is not hard to see, since it concludes that, although the decline of the west was inevitable, there would arise a new Europe centered not on decadent powers of the 19th century but on Germany. Composing *Decline of the West* between 1914-1918, Spengler kept his passion for *imperium Germanum* through the war and presumed that Germany would win. The inconvenient fact of its defeat did not discourage Spengler from asserting that Germany could still temporarily forestall euro-decline and bring western history to perfection or fulfillment by becoming a world-dominating military power. The first sentence of Spengler's work, that it was "an attempt to predetermine history," seemed to embody Heidegger's worst fears in conceiving history as a predictive discipline raised to the level of the exactitude of the law-constructing natural sciences.

> "Spengler's basic lack: Philosophy of history without the historical, *lucus a non lucendo*. That Spengler does not understand what he wants shows itself in the fact that he becomes anxious before his own position and now sounds the retreat and weakens everything and pacifies those for whom the decline-perspective—even if merely in the "as if"—has gotten into their bones. It was really not meant so grimly, business can peacefully continue (expression of the soul of the time).[27]

A "*lucus a non lucendo*" was originally a grammarian's term of derision for those fancifully perverse etymologies which attempted to derive a word from a cognate of directly opposite meaning. *Lucus*, literally a shining i.e. open place in the forest, a clearing, derives from *luceo*, to shine, be light. But *lucus* can also mean a grove, bower, or thicket, a place into which little light penetrates, and there were among Stoic etymologists some bold enough to maintain the absurdity that the name *lucus* derived "from the fact that there is *no* light there" (*a non lucendo*). To retain the name "history" with regard to Spengler's predictions, from which he conveniently pulls back, Heidegger means to say, would be to give the word a sense taken from its very opposite.[28]

As we will soon develop further, for Heidegger, Spengler's doubts about modern western civilization had been anticipated several decades before, and in far more subtle and philosophically significant form, by Nietzsche. But Spengler's popular reflections on history had gained such an enormous audience that one finds Heidegger in lecture after lecture at pains to spell out both how they were derivations from more demanding thinkers, and how Heidegger's own thinking differed from it. Heidegger's thinking in the early twenties was often lumped together with Spengler's with regard to their affinities. Löwith, for example, lists Heidegger, Spengler, and Barth as analogous thinkers, as does even Gadamer.[29] Occasionally Heidegger, such as in his 1928 lecture course on Leibniz, felt it necessary to disavow speculation that his thought might be a mere reformulation of the Spenglerian worldview.[30] There was also a general affinity in the impact of both Spengler's idea of decline and Heidegger's destruction of the history of ideas, especially among theologians.[31] Finally, whereas other German historians like Troeltsch were attacking Spengler at the time, Heidegger saw *Decline of the West* as but a continuance of their views, which looked to many like Heidegger defending Spengler against their critiques, given their mutual disenchantment with presuppositions of self-sustaining transcendent values.[32]

The great difference lies in the fact that Spengler did not fully appreciate the truly unique and radical character of western history: that it began as a life-risking response to the groundless presencing of beings. Unfortunately, this original response degenerated into a search for a permanent foundation that would guarantee the security and survival of that culture. In that moment human Dasein turned away from precisely the insecurity required for truly historical existence. Again, the key is Spengler's relation to his own methodological scientific objectivity and presumed pre-suppositionlessness. This for Heidegger reveals a restricted ontology. His critique occurs in the context of a methodological dispute that occurred among early twentieth century German historians. Some favored explaining human history through natural scientific methodology, whereas others insisted that only mental-spiritual or humanistic methodology was appropriate for interpreting human history. The latter group refused to treat human history as in any way analogous or reducible to physical, chemical, or biological processes. Accordingly for Heidegger, Spengler is the surest expression of such a perspective.

In the early 1920's Heidegger's de-spenglerization can be seen to be part of this much larger game, namely the working out of a methodology appropriate to the entirety of meaning-formation without objectification by science, a self-disclosing discourse that knows itself to be of the same nature as that of which it speaks. It is the elusive search for the point where subject and object of knowing converge, and where the movement of meaning-formation itself is disclosed. History offered such a viewpoint. 19th century German historians had made great strides in establishing how history could be the object of a theoretical pursuit, as in historical science, in respect to which the subject of knowledge may adopt a self-sufficient posture. But history can also be something which the subject knows only by *being* that something itself. This is the case with knowledge of philosophical knowing of the past. In such historical knowing the subject brings about the object of knowledge in and through itself. It understands its history by *being* that history, and it *is* that history in understanding it. The point is that already Heidegger has a grasp of the magnitude of the stakes involved in philosophical disputes of historical methodology, preserving some original region from the objectifying effects of ordinary modes of discourse and description, while at the same time indicating a means to approaching it that could avoid such risks. This alone could provide historical understanding of the kind needed for eventful cultural renewal, nothing Spengler was saying.

Something of this attempt to safeguard the phenomenon of subjectivity from being alienated can be seen quite clearly in Heidegger's remarks on Jasper's *Psychology of Worldviews,* a work published at the height of Spengler's fame.[33] Heidegger's principle critique of Jaspers consists in pointing out how the essential concept of "existence" is never properly thematized because Jaspers' typological approach obscured the existential phenomena in question. Heidegger instead proposed an alternative which had subjectivity itself have a kind of access to itself which was never the experience of something given for inspection as a worldly object, but was an experience of a peculiar historical nature. Although Jaspers' work involved the correct methodology for an existential psychology, Heidegger projects the full force of his own concerns at this time, the formulation of the task of philosophy as a first science. Before the projects of either history or psychology can properly get off the ground, a region of being prior to either domain must first be explicated. Already with this Jaspers critique one sees a line of thought that would equally apply to the philosophically inferior Spengler, namely that historical or psychological typologies presuppose a mode of being which is not only *not* available to immediate inspection in the present, but which is covered over when approached in such a fashion. Unpacking that more original region of life-experience would safeguard the phenomenon in question from an inadequate objectified or naturalized understanding, in the spirit of the Husserlian ideal of presuppositionless intuition. When Heidegger wrote to Jaspers of the need to apply hermeneutic concepts in the service of explicating the existential phenomena of historical life, he was at that time advocating a specific method to a specific task; but the idea behind these remarks is a much more encompassing project.

The genesis of that project, which can be seen in another text of the time period, and which shows the unbridgeable distance between Heidegger and Spengler, is the lecture course *Phenomenological Interpretations of Aristotle,* in which he depicts how human existence (factical life) is both the topic of philosophical concern and a process or movement which encompasses this concern itself.[34] In this text Heidegger first shows how our very orientation with regard to understanding historical or philosophical texts must be understood out of a present which in turn is taken in the form of enacted factical life to which we do not have immediate access. It cannot be studied or described directly and in general terms: it can only be reached through a questioning, and ultimately a destruction, of its own motives and tendencies. In order to reactivate Aristotle's past ontological concerns as present, the legacy of established interpretations must be destroyed. However, the ground from which this destruction occurs, the clear understanding of factical life, is itself not accessible except through another destruction, which is aimed at the past elements in the present. That the past is only accessible through an active repetition in the present, and inversely, the present is only accessible through a critical repetition of the past, is the hermeneutic circularity to which Dasein is constantly subjected. This estrangement may be understood on one level as the lack of the proper concepts and attitudes for an explication of its own being, which it tends to understand in a naturalizing or objectifying mode. Spengler's project was completely silent on this historically mediated distance within Dasein itself, manifested by its tendency to repeat, unknowingly, inherited forms of understanding of itself. Dasein tends to "fall" in this respect for generally inherited models of thought, and perceives their inadequacy in terms of cultural decline. For this reason there is need for a hermeneutics of the destruction of historically inherited forms of understanding as a way for the present to come to terms with itself, which, in turn, is a prerequisite for a valid historical interpretation of, in the case of this lecture course, Aristotle. Before an audience fattened on Spengler's fame, the vastness of such a hermeneutic project cannot even begin, since such an engagement would threaten to replay and thus gloss over precisely the ontology of factical life needed to be spelled out in advance:

> Yet it is an odd undertaking, the attempt to refute Spengler by pointing out to him his inaccuracies. That we cling to such attempts, and base them on a threadbare, and pseudo-scientific, superiority, proves that we do not understand what is at issue. Above all, we do not understand that the consciousness of an era, an era itself, cannot be "refuted" by means of theoretical-scientific arguments and cannot be disposed of like some erroneous theory.[35]

Only by making explicit the being of the questioner, and the privileged point of departure of ontological questioning, can the meaning of guiding historical questions be clarified. This is the argument of fundamental ontology. It is no surprise that five years after the lecture course on Aristotle, Heidegger publishes his work entirely modeled on the scheme of this seminal lecture course, with only one really significant exception, namely that "Aristotle" has been replaced by "being." This work is *Being and Time*, after the publication of which most of

Heidegger's Spengler references portray him as just another metaphysically-contaminated popularizer of Nietzsche.

Not only was Spengler's type-ology an inappropriate application of scientific categories to history, then, but it was additionally fueled by what was for Heidegger Spengler's misguided naturalistic understanding of Nietzschean *Lebensphilosophie*. Again, from Spengler's perspective, cultures literally "live" like other organic entities, and are individually distinct, characterizable as individual types. For Spengler, influenced by Schopenhauer, Darwin, and Nietzsche, the West's original drive for control, and its subsequent decline, were related to cycles involving the struggle for life, and so his vital cultural types were hypostatizations of a metaphysical life-principle making possible the primary forms through which cultural reality is constituted, forms which were themselves but masks of "zoological happenings."[36] For Heidegger all of this was an unfortunate biologism, the result of a superficial interpretation of Nietzsche's doctrines, which Heidegger was later to famously and controversially try to correct in his own *Nietzsche* lectures. The decline of the west occurred not for biological, naturalistic, or racial reasons, but for metaphysical and spiritual ones. Any true de-spenglerization would initially require insight into an "ontological decline,"[37] an insight which could not be reached by mere "higher journalists" like Spengler whose work was based on a "truly vulgar" interpretation of Nietzsche's psychology.[38]

Consider this sampling of successive reminiscences on Spengler's impact, and on what Heidegger saw as the more profound relevance of Nietzsche. In 1937:

> What a revelation it was two decades ago [1917] for the multitude unfamiliar with genuine thought and its rich history, as Spengler believed himself to have found out for the first time that every age and every culture has its own *Weltanschauung*. However, this was all just a very skillful and spirited popularization of thoughts and questions that had long ago—and most recently by Nietzsche—been more deeply thought. These [matters] were by no means mastered, and to this hour have still not been mastered.[39]

This from "Anaximander Fragment" written in 1946:

> Are we men of today already "Western" in a sense that first crystallizes in the course of our passage into the world's night? What can all mere historiological philosophies of history tell us about our history if they only dazzle us with surveys of its sediment; if they explain, without ever thinking out, from the essence of history, the fundamentals of their way of explaining events? Are we the latecomers we are?... Nietzsche, from whose philosophy (all too coarsely understood) Spengler predicted the decline of the

west, in the sense of the western historical world, writes "A higher situation for mankind is possible..."[40]

Still later, Spengler's negativism is again addressed in 1951's *What is Called Thinking?*.

> We call thought-provoking what is dark, threatening, and gloomy, and generally, what is adverse. When we say thought-provoking we usually have in mind immediately something injurious, that is, negative ... This tune is familiar to us all *ad nauseum* from the standard appraisals of the present age. A generation ago it was "The Decline of the West." Today we speak of a "loss of center." People everywhere trace and record the decay, the destruction, the imminent annihiliation of the world... Nietzsche, who from his supreme peak saw far ahead of it all, as early as the 1880's had for it the simple, because thoughtful, words: "The wasteland grows."[41]

Spengler in a dramatic but superficial way had captured the obvious features of crisis: the growing alienation of modern life, the sterility of the urban metropolis, the soullessness of commercial civilization, and the decadence of modern values. But Heidegger's Freiberg lectures had refuted Spengler for his crude reduction of historical facticity to the mechanical patterns of cultural morphology, and Heidegger would continue to characterize Spengler's work as "arrogant," "cheap," "concocted," "coarse," and marked by a "notorious ignorance and the journalistic superficiality of the vulgarly educated modern rabble."[42]

> Only to an age which had already forsaken every possibility of thoughtful reflection could an author present such a book, in the execution of which a brilliant acumen, an enormous erudition, and a strong gift for categorization are matched by an unusual pretension of judgment, a rare superficiality of thinking, and a pervasive frailty of foundations. This confusing semi-scholarship and carelessness of thinking has been accompanied by the peculiar state of affairs that the same people who decry the priority of the biological thinking in Nietzsche's metaphysics find contentment in the aspects of decline in the Spenglerian vision, which is based throughout on nothing but a crude biological interpretation of history.[43]

After the 1930's Heidegger's de-spenglerization is inextricably woven together with his complex project with regard to Nietzsche, on whom the extensive lecture notes and essays drawn from his courses from 1936-1945 Heidegger finally published in 1961. Through his confrontation with Nietzsche, Heidegger had hoped to provide a detailed, comprehensive, and critical account, not only of Nietzsche's thinking, but of the history of western thought as well. Nietzsche represented the consummation of the essential core of western thinking: he was the last metaphysician of the West. This "history of being" was as well narrated as a process of decline, decay, darkening, and devastation, a movement away from some ontological rootedness in pre-socratic thought. Only through the overcoming of this epochal nihilism might the west be saved. Throughout the *Nietzsche* lectures, Heidegger will come back to this mythic and eschatological reading of western history in terms of its Greek origin.

Heidegger's Nietzsche lectures were also part of an on-going generational struggle with thinkers such as Baumler, Hildebrandt, and Horneffer, and the general National Socialist interpretation of Nietzsche.[44] No easy summary of these lectures can be given as almost *too much* is going on in them, what with Heidegger employing them as a way of asserting his own philosophical vision, as well as a means of confrontation with National Socialism and with the reigning scholarly and National Socialist interpretations of Nietzsche. Thus Nietzsche will come to signify for Heidegger a whole complex of mutually implicated and reciprocally countervailing forms of confrontation, of Heidegger with Nietzsche's philosophy; of Nietzsche's philosophy with the history of metaphysics; of Heidegger with the history of metaphysics in and through Nietzsche; of Heidegger with other Nietzsche commentators, and of Heidegger with National Socialism. Spengler continually gets lumped in with this vortex of issues for the rest of Heidegger's intellectual career. Nietzsche seems to be Heidegger's comrade in arms against National Socialism until about 1938, when he begins to see Nietzsche as a forefunner to the fallen and inessential versions of the metaphysics of will to power of National Socialism. Thus at first Heidegger uses his confrontation with Nietzsche as a way of purging the heresies of other Nietzsche commentators and interpreters, including Spengler. By the time his lecture cycle is over in 1945 Heidegger will have abandoned his search to work within any established National Socialist framework that included Nietzsche. What began as a confrontation with Nietzsche's thinking now becomes a polemic against Nietzsche and every metaphysically-ensconced Nietzschean, like Spengler. Similar to what we saw in Wittgenstein, the crisis-narrative of western thinking gets de-spenglerized, not of its pessimistic vision, but of its biological-morphological metaphors which had diverted attention from the genuine source of *an even deeper and more pessimistic problem*, the occlusion of primordial sources for thinking under the calcified structures of metaphysics.

Our contemporary scene is replete with decline narratives of the right and the left, from "Y2K" and "Left Behind" religious eschatological fantasies, to right-wing jeremiads of moral decay, to leftist calls for the collapse of everything western. As we have witnessed with regard to our European master thinkers, most de-spenglerize in the name of some further re-spenglerization, be it tonal or eschatological. What would a refusal to play such a game, any further or more complete de-spenglerization look like? Even a critique of decline narratives presages *their* decline, such that there seems to be no standing clear of the divide. If we understand that every decline narrative entails a progress narrative, that every end is usually accompanied by some further myth of origins, that every school of cultural pessimism bespeaks an ungrounded optimism, we can see that what we are addressing here is not merely a malady which infects only seers and German metaphysicans. What if it represents the very structure of our thinking itself, to where any more complete de-spenglerization constitutes a thinking through of the transcendental ground of history, a dissolution of the teleo-eschatologico-metaphysics? That thinking occur without discernible origin or destination would to many appear as if the decline had culminated in something approximating an end. Carrying signs that "the end is near" does not, after all, rule out its already having taken place. To hear the saving message in either the oldest (for Heidegger) or the most ordinary (for Wittgenstein) words requires the ears to hear how the oldest of the old, and the most ordinary of the ordinary, tells us what is coming so that we can understand the end as a transition to some new beginning.

X. Wittgenstein as Phenomenologist of Mathematics

Part I

Since antiquity it has been a common picture to think that philosophers draw on mathematical concepts as exemplars of absolute truth. The power and precision of *a priori* concepts presents us with features worthy of emulation—if only philosophy in all of its endeavors could match mathematics in terms of its precision, universal applicability, necessity and certainty. It must come as a shock then, to those who hold such pictures, that the general impulse of Wittgenstein's thinking concerning mathematics is to treat traditional ideas about the privileged epistemic status of mathematics and logic as if they represent, not an exemplar of genuine precision and clarity, but indeed as a unique danger to the achievement of genuine philosophical clarity. While he had the greatest respect for the achievement of Russell and Frege in modern mathematical logic, the general trajectory of Wittgenstein's thought in regard to mathematics is in diagnosing and describing the philosophical temptations to use these new tools in the service of developing "philosophical theories" which were themselves riddled with confusions. Thus Wittgenstein took Frege's, Russell's, Hilbert's, and Gödel's philosophical work to evince new forms of philosophical confusion, deeper and more difficult to expose than the excesses of traditional metaphysics. It is a serious problem when mathematical logic is used as the model for metaphysics—but it will take a different level of analysis to reveal the deep set problems when metaphysics masquerades as serious work in mathematical logic itself.

Such a shock no doubt carried over certainly to some prominent critics of Wittgenstein's views on mathematics. When the Vienna Circle first engaged Wittgenstein's views on mathematics, in a paper which Friedrich Waismann read at the 1930 Konigsberg conference "Uber Das Wesen der Mathematik," they dismissed Wittgenstein's views as simply confused versions of their own logicist position, of far less interest than the shattering announcements (at the same conference) of Gödel's theorem. Similar critiques steadily followed. Alan Ross Anderson subsequently wrote that Wittgenstein had failed to understand clearly the problems he faced, and that his work in mathematics would not contribute to his reputation as a philosopher. Michael Dummett condemned

much of Wittgenstein's views as "difficult to take seriously" and "plain silly."
Paul Bernays was contemptuously dismissive of Wittgenstein's work, saying it
betrays a "mental asceticism" devoted to the goal of "irrationality."[1] Georg
Kriesel notoriously condemned Wittgenstein's work in this area as a shambles,
"… a surprisingly insignificant product of a sparkling mind."[2] Even Gödel
himself is said to have commented that Wittgenstein "did not understand, or
pretended to not understand, my theorem."[3] Recently there have been attempts
to defend Wittgenstein, particularly on his remarks concerning Gödel's
incompleteness proofs. S. G. Shanker has argued that Wittgenstein was not
really concerned with Gödel's proofs directly at all, but with the accompanying
philosophical remarks, and that all of Wittgenstein's subsequent remarks on
mathematics must be similarly read. Juliet Floyd goes further and defends
Wittgenstein's understanding of Gödel's results by embedding his discussion in
the larger issue of impossibility proofs in mathematics, thus bringing into the
picture Wittgenstein's remarks on geometry, in particular the remarks on the
algebraic proof of the impossibility of the trisection of the angle. In general, I
would like to argue that Wittgenstein's sparkle seems to have exceeded his
critics, and that the negative receptions of his views of mathematics are
deficient in precisely the degree to which they fail to take his work as a
phenomenologist of mathematics seriously. Whether or not such criticisms are
warranted, as well as the attribution of a uniquely phenomenological approach
to the subject has merit, is obviously a question which we cannot hope to
consider until we have first established, however briefly, Wittgenstein's
approach to the philosophy of mathematics.

While the general disrepair of the *Nachlass* fuels some of these reactions, the
parameters of Wittgenstein's views on mathematics are not difficult to find.
Throughout the stages of his work on mathematics, Wittgenstein remained
opposed to and tried to undermine what he considered to be a misleading
picture of the nature of mathematics. According to this opposing picture,
mathematics is somehow transcendental: a mathematical proposition has truth
and meaning regardless of human rules or use. According to this picture there is
an underlying mathematical reality which is independent of our mathematical
practice and language and which adjudicates the correctness of that practice and
language. This plays a role for Wittgenstein's philosophy of mathematics as
does the Augustinian picture for his later philosophy of language.

One might begin with a remark in *Zettel*: "On mathematics: 'Your concept
is wrong—however, I cannot illumine the matter by fighting against your
words, but only by trying to turn your attention away from certain expressions,

illustrations, images, and towards the employment of the words.'"[4] This remark illustrates how Wittgenstein's concern is not with the role of mathematical propositions but with the penumbra of explanations, justifications, grammatical pictures, analogies, images, and resemblances with experiential propositions which surrounds their actual use in the activities of counting, calculating, and proving. The intention is one of exposing misleading accounts of mathematical propositions by dint of their grammatical sources, and by exposing, abolish them. So to call Wittgenstein a "logicist" or "realist" or "finitist" about mathematics is already to seriously misconstrue his views, which are but grammatical investigations which exhibit the fluctuation and fluidity of our ways of talking about various mathematical activities. To try to classify him regarding mathematics in one way or another is to ignore his rejection of generality and consequently his rejection of the idea that mathematics has no uniform grammar. There is no grammar of mathematics, only grammars, and associated with the different activities and different grammars of mathematics are various conceptual pictures which seem appropriate for some of these activities and misleading for others. The fundamental question Wittgenstein asks of mathematics is along the lines of: are these pictures concomitants of the activities of counting and calculating or are they projections of the grammar of what we say in explanation of these activities?

The *Philosophical Investigations* famously begins with a quote from Augustine describing how he learned to speak. "These words, it seems to me, give us a particular picture of the essence of human language."[5] A great deal of the *Investigations* concentrates on trying to undermine this picture. The picture unifies several seemingly isolated discussions in that work. Hardy plays a similar role for Wittgenstein's views on mathematics. The view that "to mathematical propositions there corresponds—in some sense, however sophisticated—a reality" constitutes a "false idea of the role which mathematics and logical propositions play."[6] Wittgenstein is not objecting to the idea of a mathematical reality, but to a conception of mathematical reality that is independent of our practice and language. The faulty conception is of a mathematical reality that is capable of overruling how we actually do mathematics. The problem is not within mathematics, but its office, its position in providing a foundation for mathematics in logic. There is a lack of fit between what we *actually* do when we calculate and what philosophers of mathematics *say* we do or have *alleged* we do in explanation of *what* we do.

In Hardy's famous book, *A Mathematical Apology*, there is the following quote: "I believe that mathematical reality lies outside us, that our function is to discover or observe it, and that theorems which we prove, and which we describe grandiloquently as our 'creations', are simply our notes of our observations."[7]   Hardy makes it look as if there were two criteria for whether 2+2=4: (1) the computation of proof; and (2) the further checking of whether the results of this computation or proof match something else, namely, mathematical reality. Many mathematicians would hold not only are there two criteria, but that the second is the real one: proofs are but psychological devices to get us to see the mathematical reality more closely.

Wittgenstein's conception of mathematics then is modeled on his concept of natural language. For just as language derives its significance from our forms of life so too does mathematics. What gives sense to our propositions is their use, and what gives sense to our calculi are their applications. For someone like Frege the applicability of the truths and relations of mathematics was to a class of logical objects such that mathematics had the character of discovery. To draw a line in geometry was to trace some connection already there. To follow a rule (like that for the expansion of a numerical series) was to proceed along a set of steps whose nature and direction were determined by the rule. For Wittgenstein the applicability of mathematics was to human activities like counting, adding, and calculating, all of which were inventions rather than discoveries. Following a rule was inseparable from interpreting it and, as a rule may be variously interpreted, the feeling of compulsion, of being determined, arose from a particular, though not a vacuous picture of following a rule.

The issue is whether sense can be made of anything overruling our mathematical language and practice, our proofs and computations. The picture is that contrary to our computation, it could be false that 2+2=4, or that contrary to our proof it could be false that there is no largest prime -- false in the sense that the computation or proof has failed to accurately represent mathematical reality. The picture with which Wittgenstein disagrees holds that the real criteria for the truth of our mathematical propositions is the nature of a mathematical reality independent from our practice and language. This implies that the meaning of our mathematical terms is also independent of our practice and language. But Wittgenstein holds that our terms and proofs are only meaningful in the context of our language.

Much of the attack of the Augustinian picture of language in the *Philosophical Investigations* sought to establish the importance of the point that expressions are expressions only in the context of a language. In such a case there is nothing special about mathematical language: just as 2+2=4 is meaningful only in the context of our language, my pointing to a desk is only pointing to a desk within our language-game. If meaning is a function of practice then there is no room for any determinations of meaning that are not part of our practice. The mistake is not in talking of a mathematical reality but thinking that the meaning of this reality can be independent of our practice, that we can say something more than the proof. Thus the picture of a mathematical reality adjudicating our practice has become a wheel that when turned turns nothing else. Even God can determine something mathematical only by mathematics.[8]

What is important and implicit in Wittgenstein's thinking on both language and mathematics is the rejection of generality utilized by philosophers. His myriad analyses of many different examples are specifically designed to counter this craving for generality that he saw as the source of so much mistaken philosophy. He works against the idea that the activities of mathematics may be generalized and justified in terms of something else. The problem with the explanation in terms of something else is that the something else may have an entirely different grammar.

One thing that can be said of the *Principia Mathematica* is that the grammar of arithmetic is translated into something else, namely, the grammar of classes, correlations, functions, arguments, propositions, logical constants, and so forth. Russell took for granted that each of these concepts comprised a uniform class of instances or operations and Wittgenstein called this into question by devising examples illustrating important differences within each of these classes of instances and operations. The attempt to define number overlooked the fact that what we call cardinal numbers, irrationals, and real numbers have utterly different grammars. According to Wittgenstein we should not ask about the definition of number so much as get clear on the grammar.

Consider school-children learning certain counting skills. Wittgenstein concedes that he seems to be saying that every proposition is different and thus denying the generality of mathematics as though we have many mathematics. But the generality of the ordinary arithmetic we learned in school is not in the least threatened, and this becomes clear if one looks at the way arithmetic is applied. Arithmetic is a calculus and is related to its application in roughly the same way as a paradigm is to what it is a paradigm of. Arithmetic is learned by counting beads or using physical objects for illustration. Later we learn to operate the calculus without reference to any particular objects. Thus he says that we learn arithmetic "in the proper way."[9]

The point is that the generality of concepts used by Frege and Russell may be variously classified in quite different ways and lack the uniformity that they attributed to them as logically secure foundations of mathematics. What Wittgenstein is asserting is that there is an incredibly ambiguous grammar of generality concealed within the notation of Russell's calculus. Russell's use of existential and universal quantification, for example, simply selects from language a particular use of the words "some" and "all" from a variety of different uses and generalizes this into the real or correct use.[10] When one writes _x one is using notation in a strictly defined calculus. But Wittgenstein's point is that this can only be maintained at the expense of the generality of the claim that one is giving the general form of propositions. These notations do not remove the ambiguities of our use of "some" or "all" in language.

Wittgenstein is quite convincing about this when (in the Ambrose edition) he alleges that there is an ambiguity within the notation of the calculus quite apart from that incorporated by transfer from ordinary language, as when Russell writes (_x)fx and takes the 'x' inside the bracket to stand for a thing that is a man. Wittgenstein sees this as seriously misleading in regard to writing generality.[11] He captures the point in a nutshell when he says that "the basic evil of Russell's logic, as also mine of the *Tractatus*, is that what a proposition is is illustrated by a few commonplace examples, and then presupposed as understood in full generality." [12]

The remarks on Russell's views on "correlation" are equally illustrative of this point. The fundamental notion of correlation for Russell is introduced via the idea of being equal in number through a notion of similarity. Wittgenstein points out that the sense of ordinary physical correlation as exemplified by placing cups and saucers one on the other and the sense of Russell's correlation by identity have different grammars. To say of cups and saucers that they cannot be correlated in this way does not mean that they cannot be correlated in another way. The peculiar property of Russell's correlation is that if correlation by identity does not hold, no other correlation could hold. With physical correlation, but not with correlation by identity, what counts as "correlation" may be variously interpreted. In other words Wittgenstein is criticizing Russell for putting the cart before the horse with respect to his account of similarity or having the same number. We could check our calculations by making actual physical correlations. It is easy to check 3+4=7 by means of drawing lines and making one-to-one correlations but we don't do the same with 3 billion + 4 billion =7 billion. Furthermore, if for large numbers we added and got one result and then correlated and got a different one, we would trust the addition rather than the correlation. As Wittgenstein puts it: "This is all I'm saying. We already have a calculus and we don't check up on it by some other method. Instead, if anything disagreed with this calculation we should reject *it*." [13]

This view again impacts on mathematical "realism." Although Wittgenstein understands the tendency to say that mathematics is about reality he does not seem to want to either affirm or deny this claim. Still less is he prepared to choose between the alternatives that either mathematics is about reality or it is about marks on paper, because he regards both positions to be misunderstandings. When mathematics and reality correspond it is because we project on to the world certain features of the grammar of our mathematical paradigm such that, in a sense, the world is a grammatical construction. For the realist, the applicability of mathematics is evidence of a correspondence with reality such that the structures of mathematical grammars are determined by the structure of the world. But Wittgenstein's point is that mathematical grammars are inventions whose applications consist of interpretations of reality according to particular paradigms and that is all that is meant by asserting a correspondence between mathematics and the world. Thus he can again be read as in constant opposition to the view that there is an underlying mathematical reality which our language and practice must mirror or be responsible to. His point can be put that there are no criteria for mathematical correctness outside of the rules of individual calculi. Later the point becomes: there are no criteria for mathematical correctness outside of mathematical practice.

This brings us to the idea of necessity. The view of the axioms of mathematical systems as necessary truths because they are based on laws of thought, or are self-evident, or correspond to reality, is countered with Wittgenstein's view that what is important with respect to axioms is not their self-evidence or their attachment to reality but our acceptance of them as parts of speech to which we assign a particular function. Having accepted our axioms and formulated our rules of transformation are we not compelled to accept as logically necessary the theorems derived from them? Wittgenstein ascribes to the particular use in mathematical logic of the verbs "to follow" and "to infer" the idea that following is the existence of a connection between propositions, which connections *we follow up when we infer*. Russell's claim (in *Principia Mathematica*) that inference is justified by a fundamental law of logic is made because he wishes to establish the correctness of the processes of inference employed. If the criterion of correctness of inference is some fundamental law of logic what criterion of correctness do we use to establish this law? If one appealed to self-evidence in justification of the law, in order to escape regress, then one might as well apply this criterion to the rule of procedure of inference

—if self-evidence is sufficient for the law it is sufficient for the rule. Thus the rule stands in need of no further justification. The sense of being fundamental is something given by the system of propositions, like the adoption of a system of measurement, and the correctness of propositions within the system is like the correctness of particular measurements within the chosen paradigm. Trying to justify the paradigm by identifying it with some fundamental law of logic is an example of a grammatical misunderstanding.

There is no better illustration of the cliché of how Wittgenstein approaches many philosophical problems in a way which seeks their dissolution rather than solution. Repeatedly he draws attention to the fact that a particular picture presents itself to us arising from a particular use of certain words that seems appropriate when we are doing philosophy. In this case the picture suggests that inferring is the following of steps linking propositions that are laid out in advance and from which we cannot deviate if we are to infer correctly. To break the fascination of the picture one needs something to get us to look at how we carry out inferences in the practice of language. There are many explorations of similar cases in *Remarks on the Foundations of Mathematics*, where logical necessity, compulsion, and inescapability appear to be forced upon us by such things as mathematical proofs. Also, *Philosophical Investigations* refers to many misleading philosophical analogues of our ordinary language games as pictures or images or representations of the grammar of our expressions. The use of the word "object," for example: when used to refer to a physical object the idea of spatial location may be said to be part of its grammar. When we talk of a mental object, however, we may be misled by the persistence of this grammatical picture and feel impelled to locate such objects in the mind or in the brain. What is needed to be seen is that the grammar of "physical object" and the grammar of "mental object" are quite different and that this is best revealed by a comparison of their respective uses. The grammatical picture of logical inference as a mechanical process is similarly dissolved by construing the grammar of laws of inference as more like systems of measurement. This might explain Wittgenstein's dalliance with (or better, resemblance to) finitist mathematics and behaviorist psychology. His interest in them is in their therapeutic function in exorcising the ghostly entities conjured up by mathematicians and psychologists from the grammars of infinite sets and mental processes respectively. But this is not to represent the conviction that either are foundations of or justifications for mathematics or psychology.

While we have previously noted that Wittgenstein was indifferent to acknowledging his intellectual predecessors, recent scholarship has left little doubt that Wittgenstein was influenced by the phenomenological movement, if only as a reference to insisting upon a completely descriptive analysis of phenomena themselves, although it is clear Wittgenstein saw his phenomenology as purely linguistic in orientation. His notebooks from 1929 on frequently speak of phenomenology and initially identifies his philosophical task as a construction of a purely phenomenological language, that phenomenology is grammar, and that one could say of his work that it is phenomenological. Spiegelberg's thesis was that phenomenology continued throughout all of Wittgenstein's later works as grammar. Ricouer claims that Wittgenstein's use of *Dartsellung* shows him to be close to the aims of phenomenology. Hintikka goes so far as to say that the *Tractatus* in its entirety is an exercise in phenomenology, emphasizing, among other bodies of evidence, the employment of phenomenological terminologies and categories by Boltzmann and Mach, whose version of phenomenology would be the grammar for the description of those facts upon which physics erects its theories.[14] G.E. `Moore's unpublished notes of Wittgenstein's lectures from 1930 reveal references to phenomenology. Passages in other collections hold frequent references to phenomenology: There was an entire chapter entitled "Phenomenology" in the Big Typescript of 1933, left out of the version edited by Rhees as *Philosophical Remarks*. Even so edited, the text holds many intriguing references, such as: "Physics differs from phenomenology in that it tries to set up laws. Phenomenology sets up only possibilities (Section 1) and "Isn't the theory of harmony (in music) al least partly phenomenology and therefore grammar? (Sect. 4).[15] After 1929 he comes to reject this as a possibility, but retains many of the phenomenological methods of descriptive analysis. "The assumption that a phenomenological language is possible and that only it would say what we must express in philosophy is, I believe, absurd. We must get along with ordinary language and merely understand it better." Even very late in life, Wittgenstein mentions how there is no such thing as phenomenology, but indeed there are phenomenological problems.[16]

A phenomenological reading of Wittgenstein's mathematical aphorisms would preserve their seeming intent not to be taken to amount to some theory. In a rule for the expansion of an infinite series it seems as if the truth conditions for every step in a series, as well as the steps themselves, are already determined by the rule. To follow such a rule is to traverse an endless row of mathematical entities stretching from here to eternity beyond and independently of our application of the rule. A rule of inference determines a sequence of propositions and leads inescapably to a conclusion the truth of which is guaranteed by the truth of the premises and the validity of the rule of inference. Clustered around our concept of following a rule are all kinds of notions of mathematical objectivity, logical necessity, behavioral determinism, and so on. But this is not to be taken as itself some consistent theory. The various examples of following a rule that he considers do not comprise some uniform class of instances falling under a single concept. To take them as such is to ignore the rejection of uniformity implicit in his rejection of the facile generality which he believed philosophers tend to invoke and which seems to be the source of so many problems. Nowhere is this tendency toward grammatical obsession more apparent than in treating the following of a rule as a uniform operation in all circumstances instead of seeing it as a family of instances with complex interactions. Thus Wittgenstein's views are not going to be consistent. How could they be, given the grammatical differences, the changing circumstances, the varieties of interpretation, the conflicting pictures, and the traffic jam of models and images attached to following a rule?

Addressing his dozens of explorations of this topic as phenomenological investigations thus does justice to seeking to set into question the "presumption to theory" which accompanies them. The fascination Wittgenstein has for it is that the explanations that are offered of how and why we follow a rule are prolific generators of a mythology surrounding our linguistic and mathematical activities. He does not deny that inexorability or compulsion are features of most of these explanations. Indeed, it is not so much their impropriety and consequent abolition that is the target than it is again their office. Wittgenstein is like Hume in questioning the necessary connection between causally related events. He wants to reveal the complex network of largely mythological imagery with which we shroud such activities as calculating, inferring, playing games, and so on. The crucial point is that "the rule compels us" is a variable that changes with the different perspectives we adopt. Inexorability and compulsion are pictorial representations of our grammar. The calculus that results from following a rule stands in no need of justification or explanation, just description. The activities of calculating and following a rule no more require explanation than mathematics needs foundations.

One of the most misleading ideas suggested by logical analysis is that there is something like a final analysis of our forms of language. This *Tractatus*-view led to further mistaken lines of thought; that the process of analysis was a search for greater exactness in our expressions, as though there were some state of complete exactness; and that the "essence of language" somehow lay beneath the surface of language that philosophical analysis brings out. Both of these are to be rejected. The proper role of philosophy is that of grammatical investigation directed to clearing away linguistic misunderstandings and misconceptions. Whereas logical analysis was intended to dig for hidden forms and structures, this "substitution analysis" surveys and rearranges what is already on the surface and open to view. Grammatical surveying replaces logical excavation as the method of philosophical investigation.

Saying precisely what comprises grammatical investigation is enormously difficult. In fact, it is as well probably a mistake to construe it in anything like a unity of method. Thus to interpret Wittgenstein as saying that "all philosophical problems are solvable by the application of the technique called 'linguistic analysis'" is absurd. To suppose that this technique consists of a compilation of lists of word usages, as though the panacea for philosophical perplexity is lexicography, is to crown the absurdity. Grammatical investigations may consist in any of the following types of inquiry:

Constructing analogies between aspects of language and -

games
pictures
geometric methods of projection
tools, instruments, machines
physical and mental phenomena
mathematics
physiognomy
the atmosphere
corona
a private "beetle"; a private diary
conventions, custom, institutions
signposts
gestures
illness
standards of measurement
musical themes
imagining consulting a dictionary in the imagination
imagining the ascription of pain to dolls and stones
imagining God giving a parrot understanding
imagining a person who could only think aloud
imagining a person being in pain but concealing it

imagining a person being in pain while a piano is in tune and saying "it will stop soon"

etc.

What is important about all of this, as any competent reader of Wittgenstein perhaps already knows, is that the range and diversity of activities comprehended by the notion of grammatical investigation shows that it is very misleading to treat this notion as equivalent to a body of doctrine about language. "Logic" is no longer the formal unity but the family of structures more or less related to one another; it had appeared to have a peculiar depth or a super-order expressing the essence of thought and language and revealing the nature of all things. Now however, the unshakeable ideal of strict and clear rules derives its sense of inescapability from a different source. We are inclined to hold this logic only because we predicate of the thing what lies in the method of representing it. The projection of logic on to reality and the understanding leads us to attribute a life to our symbolism, with the consequence that we mythologize thought, language and the world. Indeed, words like "language", "experience" and "world" have a use as concrete and humble as words like "chair" and "table" and "lamp". The same is true of the favorite ghostly-entity words of philosophy like "knowledge" and "meaning". These remain utility-words despite philosophy's investing them with mysteriousness. We are able to have certain feelings and to identify things in our environment as significant because of the mastery of the "grammar" or "logic" -- by which we can now understand the background articulation of our possibilities of understanding -- that pre-structures the language-games we learn in growing up into a linguistic community. "Grammar" is the system of standard connections and relations organizing our language which is embodied in the regular practices and contexts of communal life. Thus the framework or scaffolding that makes the activity of mathematics possible is found not by conceptual analysis but by describing the familiar life-expressions of mathematicians. "Grammar" might be thought of as a web of practices which like a grid or template guides our ways of speaking and taking things, a world-picture that makes up the tacit inherited background against which one distinguishes true from false, the system of taken-for-granted convictions that make identifications and discriminations possible. Philosophical confusions arise because of the tendency of certain expressions to conjure up pictures which we assume to be integral parts of their grammar on all occasions of their use. Philosophical problems are engendered by carrying over a picture that is appropriate for particular uses of a word to other uses of it where the picture becomes misleading.

Wittgenstein is arguing that the relation of mathematical propositions to reality was entirely different from that of experiential propositions. One of his concerns was how we could be seriously led astray by the similarities of grammatical appearance between mathematical and empirical propositions, and that those propositions hide from us their contrasting kinds of relation to reality. This was Hardy's error in comparing mathematics and physics. The idea is that, just as physics is about physical features of reality, so mathematics is about mathematical features of reality. Hardy's picture is of two regions of discourse, differing in subject matter, but within which language functions in parallel ways, namely in the description of the relevant subject matter. Wittgenstein's point is that similar-looking propositions can differ completely in use, and thus in what it is for them to be responsible to reality. He makes this distinction often in his *Lectures on the Foundations of Mathematics.*

If one talks about a reality corresponding to mathematical propositions and examines what that might mean, one must keep in mind how there is an enormous difference between reality corresponding to an experiential proposition and reality corresponding to a word.[17]   The source of much philosophical confusion about mathematical and logical propositions is that we imagine them to have a kind of correspondence to reality like that of experiential propositions, whereas, if we look at their use, we can see that correspondence to reality in their case is like the correspondence to reality of a word.

Part of what Wittgenstein means for there to be a reality corresponding to a word is for there to be things (about us, about the world) which make it useful to have the word as part of our means of description. There is a difference between activities in which we develop our means of description and linguistic activities in which we are using, in experiential propositions, the means of description we have developed. Mathematical propositions look like we were using a language of mathematical description to describe mathematical reality, but Wittgenstein is trying to get us to see mathematics as like other activities in which we develop the means of description used in experiential propositions.

Following this is a second insight, in that just as Wittgenstein asks us to note two entirely different roles for the idea of correspondence to reality, he also asks us to note two entirely different uses for the word "about."—two different ways of speaking of what a proposition is about. What is likely to mislead us again in philosophy is the idea that mathematical propositions are about numbers in the same sort of way as "Bill has green shoes" is about Bill's shoes. A proposition's "being about" something means entirely different things in mathematics and in experiential propositions.[18] If you are clear that 2 x 2 = 4 is not about 2 in the way that "Bill has green shoes" is about Bill's shoes, if you see that the numerical usage has more to do with helping prepare the number-sign "2" for its applications, then you will not imagine the reality corresponding to the mathematical proposition as some sort of realm of numbers.

It is now not hard to see how the particular phenomenological treatment by Wittgenstein of certain mathematical issues and problems was not well understood by critics. It is charged, even by Gödel himself, that Wittgenstein failed to understand the significance of the incompleteness proofs. But what Wittgenstein objected to in Gödel's theorem was precisely the philosophical uses to which it was put, and how such uses introduce a spurious epistemological dimension into an issue solely concerned with the logical grammar of mathematical propositions. At first blush, the proof poses a special difficulty for the idea that mathematical truth is dependent on particular modes of proof. Gödel's theorem is usually interpreted as demolishing the hope of ever identifying the notion of mathematical truth with that of mathematical proof in a single recursively axiomatizable system. Furthermore, he showed how to construct what are usually called true but unprovable sentences of arithmetic for any given purported recursive axiomatization. This would seem to validate the idea that our notions of truth and proof in mathematics do not and cannot coincide.

Indeed, when Gödel announced his theorem it was immediately seized upon by the logical positivists as the key to consolidate their crusade against metaphysics. In his autobiography Carnap recalled how it was precisely over this that the Vienna Circle had broken with Wittgenstein and the *Tractatus*. The impetus was the publication in 1931 of Gödel's second incompleteness theorem. By use of Gödel's method Carnap set about to demonstrate how even the metalogic of a language could be arithmetized and formulated in the language itself. Gödel's theorem in effect suggested to Carnap a means of extending the basic notions of meta-mathematics into the philosophy of language.[19] From the seeds of Gödel's theorem was born Carnap's theory of logical syntax. Hofstadter's well known book *Gödel, Escher, Bach* seems to be a more recent example of an encomium to the "philosophical" or "trans-mathematical" significance of Gödel's theorem with analogies drawn from music and art. It is precisely the target of Wittgenstein's concern as to whether such trans-mathematical or philosophical discourse regarding the theorem is possible in the first place.

Instead, Wittgenstein's phenomenological interests are in a much more general mapping of the grammatical terrain surrounding such questions as to what is a proof in the first place, what is it to search for a proof, or to try to produce a mathematical proof. Included in such an investigation would as well be the negations of these, such as what is not a proof, when something that looks so much like searching for a proof really is nothing of the kind, or what it means when people state that it has been proven that something is impossible to do. Thus it is indeed correct to say that Wittgenstein's larger interest is with the general terrain of impossibility proofs in mathematics, such as the trisection of the angle with ruler and compass, another favorite topic of his analyses. He appropriates these theorems, and endlessly, even maddeningly dialogues with them to confirm his own philosophical attitudes. The problem of the trisection of the angle is an object of repeated interest for Wittgenstein, addressed as it is in every lecture course for which we have records, and subjected to the same idiosyncratic treatment as Gödel's theorem, yet no one would say he has failed to understand its basics. When Kurt Gödel mentions that Wittgenstein seemingly "pretended not to understand" his theorems, he did not know how right he was, as the remark testifies not to Wittgernstein's misunderstanding of the theorem so much as Gödel's inability to recognize the dialogic nature of Wittgenstein's phenomenological interlocutions.

What Wittgenstein maintains is that all there is to mathematics is calculi, each of which is justified by itself, not legislated on by other calculi. Each calculus is an island unto itself, and cannot say anything about another calculus. There is no meta-mathematics or any calculus-independent proof. Metamathematical results like Gödel's proof of the existence of true but unproveable arithmetical propositions makes no sense to Wittgenstein. What is really wrong with Gödel's result from this vantage point is that it is metalogical. It supposes to say something about a calculus instead of being a result in that calculus.

Part II

Wittgenstein's philosophy of mathematics is in some way an examination of his own problems, a fight against his own conclusions brought about by the treacherous enchantment of language. Thus on some levels no light at all can be thrown on his views by discussing them in terms of the traditional foundation concepts, such as finitism, formalism, intuitionism, and so forth. There is no end of the evidence to suggest that Wittgenstein's reflections on mathematics are as well in part an intense reflection on his own philosophical activity, his own moral life. To those who would suggest it is the height of philosophical craving for generality that we link Wittgenstein's thinking on mathematics with ethics or religion, one need only see how the coded passages in his philosophical notebooks constitute an astonishing chronicle of self-examination, self-accusation, moral and spiritual agony. For it is also part of understanding his to be a phenomenology of mathematics to see an incredible obsession with the weakness of his own ideas, the precise theoretical counterpart to his obsessive concern with his moral shortcomings. He agonized fully as much about his logical sins and the conceptual temptations he experienced, as about his moral ones. Like the medievals Foucault describes, Wittgenstein does not merely confess his faults; he tries to deal with them, engages them, records them, as a logico-linguistic monk purging himself of dangerous mathematical sin.

To move toward understanding such a point, let us recall again how these grammatical investigations do not explain or justify ordinary language, but only describe how language must "be constructed to fulfill its purposes." As Wittgenstein puts it: "Philosophy simply puts everything before us, and neither explains nor deduces anything—since everything lies open to view there is nothing to explain. . . The aspects of things that are most important for us are hidden because of their simplicity and familiarity."[20] Language embodies a grammar which constitutes our sense of reality and grounds our beliefs and ways of doing things. But grammar itself cannot be grounded by appeal to any extra-linguistic facts. Language cannot be used to get outside of language. Since every attempt to justify grammar by appeal to "facts" about reality only succeeds in making use of some description of reality which itself presupposes the correctness of the grammar in question, any such attempted justification begs the question.

We are often surprised at mathematical results. We think things are revealed to us which were there all the time, such as properties of a series. We think of the mathematician making discoveries. Mathematics is not an experiment -- its results neither confirmed nor refuted by experiment. The results of a calculation are not related to the calculation as the result of an experiment is related to the experiment. Rather in mathematics process and result are equivalent.[21] What unfolds are not properties of numbers, but their roles in the system. "Learning" here recalls what the Greeks meant by *ta mathemata*, the learning of things insofar as they can be understood in terms of something that one knows already. Learning here is a taking cognizance of something as what one already knows it to be in advance. One begins to learn something not when he just takes over something that is offered but when he experiences what he takes as something which he himself already has. The most difficult learning consists in coming to know all the way what we already know somehow.

Heidegger says something similar in his phenomenological reflections. For him the mathematical is the founding discovery of a clearly delineated and closed realm of things for the sake of this discovery itself. Each realm of things has its own kind of possible discovery, verification, foundation, and conceptual determination which is typical of it, and all of these procedures are determined by the character and the mode of being of those things which belong to this realm. The mathematical makes no discovery but thematizes what is already present in the method of representation. For Heidegger, "theology is mathematical," implying a thing or realm of things which is already somehow discovered and to some degree present as a possible theme of theoretical presentation and inquiry. "Process and result are equivalent in theology" as well, since theology implies, in Heidegger's language, this positum is already present in a determinate pre-scientific form of our concernful dealing-with-things, in which that which is typical and characteristic for the realm of things and their specific mode of being manifests itself before any theoretical apprehension, and is thus already discovered.[22]

This theological metaphor might be inappropriate, but we might follow it a bit further to approach the Wittgenstein view from another direction. Consider the religious believer having read Wittgenstein. He has listened to and absorbed Wittgenstein's remarks concerning these tendencies for projection and cravings for generality. He has begun to reflect on his own religious thinking, the force exerted by certain forms of expression, and the influence of the implications of certain symbols. Not wanting to fall into the misunderstanding, misinterpretation, bewilderment, or seduction produced by language, he comes to perceive how the concept of a person in the grammatical context of ordinary language depends on bodily criteria for its identification and application, and that theologians who say that God is a person or a unity of three persons are not invoking bodily criteria in making such a claim. The believer in other words realizes that we should not take the criteria for the use of bodily person and immaterial person as the same. He is aware now of the problems that arise because of the tendency of certain expressions to conjure up pictures which we assume to be integral parts of their grammar on all occasions of their use. The believer comes to see his thinking concerning belief in God as a person is confused, and begins then to reflect on how the depth of his puzzlement reflects the depth to which such pictures force themselves on his thinking. And the consequence of this investigation is that this issue, the issue of having conceived of God in terms of a person to talk to, loses its distinctive character of depth, persistence, and universality, which are themselves further versions of grammatical illusion. How are we to reconcile this with Wittgenstein's point about such investigations "leaving everything as it is"? Has not Wittgenstein said that there is nothing to explain here, and that what is hidden here is hidden because of its simplicity and familiarity?

Can one intelligibly characterize a belief to which one adheres as "true" if it cannot be supported by reasons or considerations of one form or another? If one is inclined to think not then he should be reminded of contexts where "true" carries no such implications. We all speak of logical truths and do not hesitate to acknowledge an arithmetical proposition such as "2+2=4" as true although we have no idea how we should go about proving or supporting this. Such a proposition *needs* no proof. If someone insists that still it can be proved, one could reply that the conviction we express when we call it true cannot be increased by such a proof were someone clever enough to devise one. As far as our conviction goes, such a proof is an idle wheel, a false support. Worse than this, it obscures the real source of the conviction which lies elsewhere, in the service which what we are convinced is true gives us in so much of our life and thinking, in the way it is interlocked with so much of what we accept and judge by. Its truth lies in the kind of understanding it makes possible for us in connection with so much that is of interest to us.

The point is the familiar one that there are contexts in which the notion of truth is not tied up with that of proof or verification. Socrates' faith in the idea that the story of Judgment Day is true (in the *Gorgias*) is an idea of truth that does not rest on evidence of the sort that would support an ordinary prophecy. His desire to live this sort of life is not conditional to what will happen to him in the future in the hands of judges. If Socrates' desire to live a good life were conditional on what would happen to him in a future life, then the question of evidence for his belief concerning that would be pertinent. But then the object of our desire is not to live that way but what living that way will secure for us if we are right in our belief about the future. In that case any evidence which undermines our confidence in this belief will also weaken our reason for wanting to live that way. So whether or not one has evidence and conforms to that way of life will make little difference to what one is like. It makes a difference to Socrates' life not in the way that someone's belief that he could not get away with cheating keeps him on the right path, but in the sense that it gives a life not on the straight path the kind of significance which makes him want to avoid it. There is a difference between these two lives even if they are outwardly similar, and neither do they believe in the same thing even if what they believe can be expressed in the same words. The difference lies in one's "standing behind one's words."

What about belief? Certainly we would say that we believe 2+2=4, much as we would say "I believe there is a chair beneath me as I sit." When we know a mathematical theorem such as this, there is something, some object, which we know; when we believe it, there is an "it" which we believe, and this is so equally whether what we believe is true or false. But there is a big difference between the roles of an arithmetical proposition and an empirical proposition. This is manifest in the different circumstances in which one says "I believe that 2+2=4" as opposed to "I believe there is a chair beneath me." What we require is a picture of the employment of mathematical propositions.[23] Believing a mathematical proposition might be compared with believing that a chessboard knight moves such and such. One does not believe a rule of chess, but that a rule of chess operates like this or that. To believe 2+2=4 is to believe this a proposition of arithmetic; "arithmetical proposition" signifies a role for the proposition in which believing does not occur.[24] The proof of a mathematical proposition is radically unlike the verification of an empirical one, and the calculation which yields the equation 2+2=4 and which informs our acknowledging it to belong among arithmetical equations is wholly unlike the grounds for an empirical proposition. The result of the multiplication is part of the multiplication, not something external to it. Thus even if it makes sense to say "Bill believes that 2+2=4," it makes none to say "Bill believes that 2+2=5," for here there is nothing to believe.

Socrates' words are "stood behind" in that they are the measure of life of the one who accepts them as the truth. The words characterize a measure filled with personal content. The truth of mathematical axioms is to be found in the way they are interlocked with so much of what we accept and judge by, so much of what we are agreed on. Many people would agree with others in saying it is true that 2+2=4. To deny this would be to exclude oneself from many activities. But when one resists the generality, not merely to resist, but that it goes "deep within him," he means something more than this in calling his beliefs true. He is speaking for himself in a way that he would not be doing when he affirms those mathematical truths which he takes for granted in their Russelian notation.

The difficulty with this involves understanding one's words in the first place. It seems that what one says on this matter is not our criterion of whether one speaks it as the truth. Thus two can say the same words, with the difference lying in their "orientation" toward those words. But how does one go about finding the sense of someone's words in their own life? Perhaps when one asks that person, and the person responds, "I find this indispensable for most of what I do -- my life would not make sense without this." Fair enough. But what of the words of people no longer alive? Do we have recourse to the secondary literature of their lives? Surely, no such secondary literature exists for many writers and thinkers, as well as for the great majority of the rest of us. It seems that when one is to learn whether someone has stood behind their words, one needs to look at their lives. But, like Socrates, looking at one's life necessarily involves understanding their words as having said the truth. Whether a person believes the beliefs she subscribes to, whether she believes them to be true, is a matter of what they mean to her, what she makes of them in her own life. But often understanding this necessarily involves recourse to the very words we wanted to understand the truth of in the first place.

The problem is that we come to see ourselves as participants in public language games which are not grounded on anything outside our lives, and yet insofar as they constitute our lives, are not something we create or can fully master. The background of intelligibility opened by our grammar is neither true or false but makes it possible to believe and say things that count as either true or false.

One might recall Phillips' distinction between religious belief and superstition.[25] To ascertain whether a confusion between the two is involved, one must look to what the people involved say about their actions, what the expectations are, what if anything, would render such actions pointless, and so on. The confusions show themselves in the way the belief or practice hangs with the larger surroundings. So the person praying to direct lightning to strike in a certain direction, or prayer thought of as an attempt to influence God to heal a child, confuses religious belief with superstition. Superstitious belief is understood as a means to an end, such as an attempt to bring about a different state of affairs in terms of causality. Following Wittgenstein, Phillips maintains there to be an absolute, non-tentative quality to religious beliefs which does not obtain with superstitions. In religious belief, "the whole weight may be in the picture,"[26] unstatable in any other fashion. Superstitions are contingent on the way things go. They are more akin to hypothesis because they are tentative, open to revision, and represent only an option—its religious character is reducible to its efficacy as one way among others of securing certain ends.

The religious character comes out in the role that the belief plays in a person's life, through the holding of a picture which regulates for all aspects of their living. The religious picture is said to be unshakable, held fast, not a means to a further end. It cannot be isolated from the rest of one's life. Superstitions play a contingent role in the lives of people, not regulative of all aspects, thus demarcated from the rest of life. Superstition has an external relation to the person, whereas religious belief is internal to the life of the believer.

Consider then a connection between mathematics and a delineation of the profane. What does it mean to understand the sacred as transcendent or timeless or God as a person or beyond our senses? These words of course ring familiar to the philosopher. Even Plato, in his dialogues, raised questions about the possibility of describing and understanding things that change, the kind of generality there must be in the words we use for the same word to apply to different things. The sense of certain phrases and words is to be found in the use they have in such a language and in the role this language plays in the lives of those who speak it.

When the sacred is described as God's having a body or existing beyond our senses, part of what is said is that the sacred cannot be found in this world, that it has no reality there. A believer who gave in to the claims of such a life and began to be enslaved by it would inevitably start to doubt the very intelligibility of God. This means that if these claims take root he can no longer look at things and respond to them from the perspective of the "love of the sacred."

The purity of the life depends on the hiddenness. If one identifies the sacred with anything worldly, or anything at all, if it is turned into a contrast between what is here and what lies elsewhere, then one either denies the transcendence or transforms it into something incoherent and confused. It is not something one can contemplate under the aspect of achievement. The only thing one can do is investigate one's motives so that one can give oneself to the sacred more fully, without reservation.

The inner life or inwardness here is not to be taken in some Cartesian sense. One might describe it instead entirely in one's relation to one's words. One's inner life is in that aspect of his life where this standing is active. Thus when Wittgenstein says that there is no objective mark of the happy life, he meant that not everyone would agree about the character of the life in question, however well informed. There is the possibility none of the objective features including the thoughts and feelings, daily conversations and words, could force them to agree on whether or not it is a happy life. The standing behind one's words is an opening up of the inseparability of how things are in their contexts of significance opened up by linguistic customs, conventions, and practices.

The sacred simply is not to be understood as anything like an object among or beyond the objects we know and interact with. This is not strictly to "doubt the existence of the sacred"; rather it involves what its existence amounts to. But verbs lose their traction with the sacred as their grammatical object. There is the word to consider in its use in religious discourse and what its use connects with in the individual lives of those who believe in or fear God. There is the word to consider in its cultural background and also those personal lives. Traditional theology is "mathematical" in the sense that religious talk shows how we can learn words only if we already have an understanding of the world, an understanding itself rooted in a prior mastery of language. What is basic is the preunderstanding embodied in our know-how, our mastery of standard patterns of discrimination and articulation as competent agents in a familiar world. Items in the world can stand out only because we have some mastery of the significance or importance of the ordinary situations in which we find ourselves.

The superstitious belief constitutes a debasing profanation, a desacralization. What is "delimited" is a profane realm; it is just what that which is most important in our lives is *other than*. Its sacrality is established by a desanctification of all that is less than it. It is the verdict of the mathematical -- as propositions (language) are models or pictures of the profane world, so metaphysical propositions are graven images which can only profane the sacrality of that which is delineated. Wittgenstein's views on mathematics are infused with something like this, the *Tractatus*-like distinguishing of a profane, logical sphere from a sacred, translogical one. But with the condemnation of the debasement there does not come an entreaty to reverential silence as a substitute.

Wittgenstein says that superstition results from fear.[27] This points to the external relation of the superstitious belief of the believer. Superstitions manifest themselves as ways for their holders to maintain some semblance of control over the way things go in the world. The holder of a superstitious notion would then be relying upon a belief as a means to an end, that of control. While the religious one trusts the picture which holds her, the superstitious one relies on the picture she holds at the time.

Consider now the following remarks by Wittgenstein on contradiction:

"I want to object to the bugbear of contradiction, the superstitious fear that takes the discovery of a contradiction to mean the destruction of the calculus." [28]

Then, later, in the *Investigations*:

> "The fundamental fact here is that we lay down rules, a technique, for a game, and then when we follow the rules, things do not turn out as we had assumed. That we are therefore as it were entangled in our own rules.
>
> This entangle in our rules is what we want to understand.
>
> The civil status of a contradiction, or its status in civil life: that is the philosophical problem." [29]

Wittgenstein is not so much getting rid of the problem of contradiction so much as he is trying to understand why a contradiction means the destruction of a calculus, of what it means to be entangled in our own rules.

Thinking that a calculus is a closed, self-contained system, but working against the view which holds there to be a mathematical reality adjudicating our practice, Wittgenstein works toward the harmlessness of a contradiction in a calculus. Our syntactical rules might allow the derivation of a contradictory sentence, but since the rules of the calculus itself are the only criteria for the meaning of the calculus' expressions, there is no problem. The rules cannot come into conflict with anything because they are not about anything.[30] Nor can they be said to conflict with one another, for if all we have are the rules of the calculus then the rules are the final court of appeal.

Very often opponents of Wittgenstein's thinking along these lines fall into a recapitulation of the standard motif in the Hardy example, the very theme that Wittgenstein had originally formulated his argument to expunge. Similar to that of religious belief, he is not commending a scepticism about mathematical certainty, but attempting to expose what he takes to be an incoherence in the attitude of someone who thinks that a proof of consistency makes things in some way more certain. But not only was Wittgenstein not commending a scepticism about mathematical certainty, he was trying to demonstrate the absurdity involved in supposing that any such possibility was feasible. It is not just that the conception of a consistency proof as a vehicle of mathematical confidence is under attack: it is the very premise that it makes sense to speak of the reliability of mathematical knowledge in the first place, let alone placing it on a more rational basis.

The Wittgensteinian therapy going on here is nothing pseudo-psychological, but consists in showing mathematicians that it makes no sense to speak of "refuting" or "setting such a doubt to rest" regarding contradictions -- the question is not how we can be certain that an axiomatic system is consistent, but is it even possible for mathematics to be inconsistent?[31] Hilbert's quest for a consistency proof is a paradigmatic example of the intrusion of sceptical worries into mathematics proper. Wittgenstein based his criticism on the fundamental theme that mathematical propositions are rules of syntax which fix the use of mathematical concepts rather than state mathematical facts. Hilbert's conception of "meta-mathematics," construed as a species of mathematical proposition, cannot be about anything, and *a fortiori*, cannot be supra-mathematical proofs about mathematical proofs. To argue that "meta-mathematics" constitutes a discipline whose "objects of investigation" are proofs rather than numbers is to introduce a new variation on the entrenched confusion that mathematical propositions are descriptive. Hilbert's undertaking was flawed due to the deep-rooted confusions concerning mathematical reality which gave rise to the spurious sceptical worries his undertaking was devised to correct. Hilbert accepted, like Hardy, the concern as to whether and if we could be certain that our "mathematical knowledge" was in harmony with "mathematical reality." His answer to the problem of whether we could be certain that the inferences in a system are truth-preserving was in consistency proofs. Wittgenstein's challenge was to the entire framework which precipitated the dilemma. He was not trying to refute Hilbert's version of the consistency problem (and in so doing argue for skepticism); rather, he was dissolving the issue by showing that Hilbert's anxiety resulted from a misguided conception of mathematical truth.

The important thing to keep in mind is that Wittgenstein adhered closely throughout his exposition of the innocuousness of contradictions to the quasi-formal definition of a contradiction presented in the *Tractatus*. Not only any actual state of affairs or occurrences but also any non-actual one, can be fully described without logical contradiction, for any "description" which is logically contradictory is in fact no description whatever, as it does not either truly or falsely describe anything at all; it is senseless as far as cognitive meaning goes (truth or falsity); but so likewise a logical contradiction does not have any cognitively meaningful negation. "Truths" like the principle of noncontradiction are not really true or false -- they do not report or misreport any actual facts; there is in fact no real state of affairs that such a locution describes, and consequently, there is no real limitation here on the power of anyone. A locution of this sort exhibits the rule-governed character of the language in which it is couched, but it does not strictly state anything.[32]   Thus a contradiction, like a tautology, does not say anything, So why should the former be any more worrying to mathematicians than the latter? Strictly speaking, since both types of expression function in exactly the same manner, mathematicians should be equally concerned that their axioms might one day land them with a "hidden tautology." [33]

"Why should a certain configuration of signs not be allowed to arise? Why this dread? Why this taboo?"[34] The essential move is to grasp that tautologies and contradictions must not be confused with rules. The two constructions are not at all equivalent, yet this is precisely the fallacy that has nurtured the consistency problem. The problem is that mathematicians have confused rules prohibiting certain forms of expressions, such as the "law of contradiction," with contradictions as technically understood.

Consider the following remark: "If e.g. in geometry I conclude from one proof that the sum of the angles of a triangle is equal to 180 degrees and from another proof that the sum of the angles is greater than 180 degrees, then this is in no way a contradiction. Both conclusions might hold at the same time and I can even imagine a case where we would apply such an axiom system: if the sum of angles of a triangle were by one method of measuring equal to one value and by a different method equal to a different value."[35] In this example we are dealing *ex hypothesi* with two different methods of measurement, which may or may not be "prohibited," depending on how we wish to use the system. For whatever reason we wish to prohibit this, then we simply create a rule forbidding this product. The mere fact that a proposition is contrary to a proposition from some other system, that we have different methods for measuring the angle of a triangle, which might yield different results, cannot *ipso facto* entail that the assertion of their product constitutes a violation of a rule. In order for this to occur there must already be a specific rule prohibiting the conjunction in question.

Mathematicians have failed to distinguish between contradictions and contrarieties, the distinction between an expression's being senseless and being forbidden. By confusing contradictions with contrarieties they have begun by arguing that it is possible to construct a contradiction in a calculus and concluded that such a result is disastrous because it is forbidden. But that in itself is a contradiction in terms, for if it is forbidden to construct a given contradiction, then it is logically impossible to do so, any attempt to do so yields nonsense. But contradictions have been confused with contrarieties -- it is possible to construct a contrariety, hitherto unthought of, and not forbidden in a calculus. What do we do in such a case? When faced with an unexpected contrary conjunction, we must simply determine whether or not to forbid such a result. And we do so according to whether or not there is any point to permitting it as considered from the purpose to which we intend to put the calculus. Restricting the understanding of calculi to be self-contained led to the fear of contradiction as a superstition. Wittgenstein came to the view that consistency was not an optional characteristic of calculi nor a superstition. One cannot isolate a calculus from at least one sense of activity—calculus implies already the activity of calculation. The minimum requirement is that a calculus not yield falsehoods from true premises. A contradiction in the calculus, and one can deduce anything at all. Wittgenstein wants to retain the capacity to describe the harm without falling into a mistaken picture.

What is wrong with a contradiction is not that it misrepresents mathematical reality; but in producing falsehoods from truths, it allows anything to follow; it fails to do what we want our calculi to do, namely to calculate; and this is similar to the way that what is wrong with a superstition is not that it misrepresents the sacred but that it allows the reverse, the profanation that one can judge the efficacy of the picture to see if it squares with our goals, or the larger surroundings and the common shared understandings of things and processes. If someone said there was a German aeroplane overhead, another person might say 'Possibly, I'm not so sure'; and in such a case we would say that they were fairly near in their beliefs. Wittgenstein contrasts this difference with that between a believer who says 'I believe in the Last Judgment" and someone who might conceivably say 'Well, I'm not so sure. Possibly'.[36] The two cannot be thought of as contradicting one another on some matter of fact. Religious beliefs have a role in believer's lives and this is what justifies translating people's beliefs as "religious" as opposed to "superstitious." Mathematics has a special role in our lives and special characteristics, and these are what justify calling alien practices mathematics. A calculus with a contradiction cannot serve that role. Wittgenstein meets the task of saving objectivity without paying the price of the profanation of a misleading external role of adjudicatory criteria.

The *Investigations* and later sections of the *Remarks on the Foundations of Mathematics* emphasize the role of growth in the language-games of mathematics. Instead of seeing mathematics as isolated calculi, they conceive it as a nexus of language games, related to each other and embedded in our form of life. Wittgenstein's immature view was that of seeing a mathematical system as completely closed, and that changes in its rules makes it a different game, that any revision of the rules means an entirely new calculus.[37] Since there can be no reference to anything outside of the rules, and since there is no basis to assert that calculi have anything in common, then all we can do is discuss individual calculi. Under that view one comes to a "superstitious fear of contradiction." The evolution of the three-point line and the shot-clock into the game of basketball did not turn basketball into a new game. The number system with irrationals is obviously different from a number system with only rationals, but it is an extension of the old system, not something new and different. Games evolve in ways not completely characterized by the rules themselves, such that we can say more about them than merely that they are "new games." Thus as far as the application of a mathematical system is concerned, Wittgenstein argued that the discovery of a contradiction at some later point would in no way affect the status of all the calculations that had hitherto been performed, nor need it irrevocably undermine any future use of the system in question.[38] This is entirely a matter of the nature of the contradiction vis-a-vis the application of the calculus. That a contradiction stalls a calculation is a matter of the bearing which the contradiction has on the nature of the application that is under consideration. If we decide in this situation that the presence of such a contradiction is intolerable then we must construct a new calculus, different from the preceding in so far as it contains this new rule. The mistake is to suppose that mathematics is composed of a single static calculus. On the contrary, mathematical systems, like language-games, are constantly fluctuating as we add or modify the rules. Thus I can imagine that at one time I prove that the sum of the angles of a triangle is 180 degrees, and another time that it is 182 degrees. We have laid down two different stipulations as to when to regard a measurement as correct, and one could imagine how to apply such rules, such as the one when measuring angles by a mechanical method, the other when measuring by an optical method.[39] If we want to hold fast to this concept of geometry then we must lay down such and such rules; we must adapt the calculus or construct a new calculus by stipulating a rule forbidding the contrary in question. But there is no compulsion to hold fast to a given system; there is no "geometrical reality" compelling us to follow this "uni-value" system of angular measurement. The essence of mathematics lies in the use to which we choose to apply a calculus.

This insight carries over into the discussion of superstitions in a parallel but opposite way, because superstition endeavors to make religion a question of science, or endeavors to induce change in a state of affairs. The picture going wrong in the connection it has to the larger surroundings signals profanation. Superstitious beliefs confusing people are seen in comparison with the religious believer held by the picture itself in an unshakeable way. The picture there is absolute, whereas the superstitious picture is contingent in its influence on things. The superstition carries with it an abiding fear of making sure the performance is correct. Similarly, fear of contradiction marks a grammatical reminder of the type of pictures we are confronted with. Wittgenstein's point in mathematics was not to bring out what we might do, but rather to clarify what we are doing: dealing with grammatical truths. And we must be careful to distinguish between saying "we must construct such and such rules if we want these results" and "we must construct such and such rules because we must have these results." The latter locution resonates of a Hardy-like mathematical reality to which Wittgenstein held we had no claim. Hilbert's argument that a contradiction can prevent us from attaining the results we want is flawed in that it is we who control the calculus, and not the reverse. In the religious context it is in turn just the reverse of this, in that something's threatening to undermine the results we want cannot be so summarily dealt with whenever it arises, for it is the very non-tentative, unshakeable quality of the belief system which distinguishes it from the profanation of mere efficacy.

To investigate Wittgenstein's views on mathematics and profanation means to look into what the people involved say about their actions, what the expectations are, what would render such actions pointless. Philosophical sceptical problems can make no sense in regards to mathematical truths, nor merely forbidden in regard to the sacred. Contradictions arising in mathematics are easily remedied by laying down new stipulations concerning the case in which the rules conflict. In religious belief such remedy cannot arise without destroying that which regulates for all in one's life, the sacred about which nothing can be said. With reflection on mathematics comes the entreaty to a continuance, on only one side of which are there no problems; with profanation comes the entreaty to a reverential silence, on only one side of which is there no sound.

XI. New Thought in the Clear Night of the Nothing

The Nothing is nothing new. Western metaphysics can be read as the story of the gradual and partial vindication of the nothing in the face of Parmenides' rejection of it. Leaving behind the Parmenidean dichotomy, both Plato and Aristotle reach an understanding of a complex interplay between being and the nothing. In medieval thought, the question of the nothing is applied to the relation between God and creation. With the major movements of the 19th century, negation and nihilism become defining possibilities for human life and consciousness, which must be acknowledged before they can be overcome. There is no easy summary of the history of the nothing in western thought, since the question of the nothing is interlaced with, and forms part of, the question of being, and so an overview of the history of the nothing would encompass the entire history of ontology in western thought. Suffice it to say, when the nothing bursts forth again on the philosophical scene in the twentieth century, it should not have come as such a shock but recognized as having done so out of a rich tradition from which to draw comparisons and conclusions about any so-called new thought of the nothing.

Twentieth century research on the nothing, following centuries-long trajectories, took the form of either scientific inquiry or advanced explorations of nihilism. After the collapse of Aristotelian science, research into the nothing in the sciences comes about by way of exercises such as Torricelli's production of airless space above a mercury column. Space devoid of air is not nothing enough, however. Gradually such questions merged into the physics of ether, which in turn gave way to Einstein's special theory of relativity. When the LEP accelerator at the CERN (European Council for Nuclear Research) laboratory for particle physics in Geneva causes electrons and their antiparticles, positrons, to collide at energies one hundred thousand times their rest mass, it is the nothing scientists are still seeking to understand. In the 20th century, the nothing of the west is either abyssal, or a tech problem whose complexity is solvable merely with increased IT funding. Even as a liberation its exhiliration is strenuous and desperate. This anxiety before nothingness marks the western tradition. It is the way of thought that cannot face the nothing without a shudder. This feature only stands out in confrontation with another possibility. There is endless anxiety, boredom, nausea, panic, not to mention endless technological workings with regard to the nothing, that the thought of the nothing induces in the west. The anxious or technical nihilism of the west has little of the serenity or blessedness of the nothing of the east.

The tensions over the nothing burst forth in the last century in the infamous exchange between the German-speaking philosophers Heidegger and Carnap. In 1929 Heidegger gave his Freiberg inaugural lecture entitled "What is Metaphysics?" in which he essentially states that the nothing is at the center of all contemporary thinking. Carnap responded with a bonecrushing essay, "Overcoming Metaphysics through the Logical Analysis of Language," which dismissed Heidegger's remarks as meaningless.[1] Indeed, some have called this exchange one of the pivotal moments of twentieth century thought, an inaugural moment of the analytic vs. continental divide. Here we can at least see their exchange as the philosophical expression of diverging directions of the schools of neo-kantianism of the day. The fissure of the analytic and continental divide was over nothing.

These neo-kantian schools had inherited from Kant the view that our knowledge or true judgments should not be construed as representing objects or entities that exist independently of our judgments, whether these independent entities are the "transcendent" objects of the metaphysical realist existing somehow behind our sense experience, or the naked, unconceptualized sense experience itself beloved by empiricists. Following Kant, the object of knowledge does not exist independently of our judgments at all, but is first constituted when the unconceptualized data of sense are organized or framed within the a priori logical structures of judgment itself. In this way, the initially unconceptualized data of sense are brought under the apriori categories and thus become capable of empirical objectivity.

According to Kant, we cannot explain how the object of knowledge becomes possible on the basis of the a priori logical structures of judgment alone. We need additional a priori structures that mediate between the pure forms of judgment comprising what Kant calls general logic and the unconceptualized manifold of impressions supplied by the senses. These mediating structures are the pure forms of sensible intuition, space and time. Thus the pure logical forms of judgment only become categories when they are schematized—when they are given a determinate spatiotemporal content in relation to the pure forms of sensible intuition. The pure logical form of a categorical judgment, for example, becomes the category of substance when it is schematized in terms of the temporal representation of permanence; the pure logical form of a hypothetical judgment becomes the category of causality when it is schematized in terms of the temporal representation of succession; and so on. For Kant pure formal logic (general logic) must be supplemented by what he calls transcendental logic, when the theory of logical forms becomes schematized in terms of pure spatio-temporal representations belonging to the independent faculty of pure intuition. It is precisely this account of schematization that is at the heart of the transcendental analytic of the *Critique of Pure Reason.*

How this applies to the nothing can be seen, without replaying too much of the archtectonics, in Kant's "table of nothing" passage in the first *Critique.* Kant says that his table of nothing is of no great importance and is added to the end of the Transcendental Analytic just to complete the system. Retroactively we know this now to be an understatement. The table indicates why Kant did not take the nothing very seriously. The highest concept of transcendental philosophy is that of an object in general, and the first division specifies it as either a something or a nothing. Since it is the thoughts of the understanding (called categories) that give the object in general its rational constitution, the type of nothing an object can be depends on its relation to those thought-functions or concepts. If the concept is empty, that is to say, without object, the nothing is a mere entity of reason. If the object is conceived but is itself empty (of sensory filler), it is a privative nothing. If the mere forms of sense (the intuition) are employed but without a real sensory object, the nothing is an imaginary entity. And if there is an empty object without any concept, we have a negative nothing, the true pit of nothingness. Here in general for Kant the nothing is the result simply of four different kinds of misfirings of the relation between thinking and its object. These "four nothings" have no business in a soundly conceived, cognitively accessible world. Since no one can have a determinate notion of a negation without having the opposing affirmation as a basis, the nothing does not even show up as a problem.

The wheels had started coming off the Kantian wagon late in the 19th century, perhaps locatable in the single word "*Vorstellung*" in Part 2 of the Transcendental Doctrine of Elements. The word, translated into English alternately as "representation" or "presentation," or even as "conception" or "thought," is the epistemological key, since "our cognition arises from two basic sources of the mind. The first is [our power] to receive (re)presentations (*Vorstellung*) (and is our receptivity for impressions); the second is our power to cognize objects through these (re)presentations (and is the spontaniety of concepts)."[2] The operative distinction lies in the contrast between a faculty of passive receptivity, through which objects are given to us, and one of active spontaniety, through which they are thought. Though he famously speculated[3] that these two stems may arise from a common but to us unknown source, Kant's view is that these two sources are independent faculties or powers of mind that play the distinct roles of active and passive in the synthesis that produces knowledge. The name "sensibility" was given to the faculty of receptivity, and the name "understanding" to that of spontaneity.

In the section on the Amphiboly of the Concepts of Reflection, Kant stressed that the two faculties are independent sources of cognition, where the objection is lodged against Leibniz that he intellectualized appearances and against Locke that he sensualized all the concepts of the understanding.[4] That only a synthesis of the two produces objectively valid judgments is the defining characteristic of Kantian epistemology. This independence of sensibility and understanding sticks out like a sore thumb in the section of the first *Critique* regarding the schematism, where Kant, due to the heterogeneous nature of the two faculties, notoriously posits a "third" to mediate between them that must nonetheless be homogeneous with both pure concepts and sensible intuitions.[5] Going back to Kant's earliest critics, this move, with all of its technical sophistication, has been seriously questioned. Kant has it that knowledge arises from the interaction between understanding and sensibility, but has so sharply divided these faculties that all interchange between them becomes inconceivable. If the understanding is intelligible, nontemporal, and nonspatial, how can it possibly coordinate its operations with the sensibility which is phenomenal, temporal, and spatial? With these problems do Kant's antibiotics wear off, and the "four nothings" threaten a virulent return.

By the turn of the century, thinkers in these Kantian waters had thus come to entirely reject the idea of an independent faculty of pure intuition. The a priori formal structures in virtue of which the object of knowledge becomes possible must therefore derive from the logical faculty of the understanding and from this alone. Since space and time no longer function as independent forms of pure sensibility, the constitution of experience described as "transcendental logic" must now proceed on the basis of purely conceptual, a priori structures. As Friedman's recent research has demonstrated, the one neo-kantian line of thought, from Cohen and Natorp, held that we explain the constitution of the object of empirical knowledge by the never-completed convergence of the methodological progressions of mathematical natural science, informed by the modern logical theory of relations developed by Russell. The other line of neo-kantian thought, following Windleband and Rickert, reacts against this, and rejects the project of Kant's metaphysical deduction.[6] What is most important is the already categorized real object of experience itself, and the subject matter of formal logic only arises subsequently in a kind of artificial process of abstraction, the entire realm of pure logic being nothing but an artifact of our subjectivity possessing no explanatory power whatsoever. Heidegger and Carnap can thus be seen as natural, if extreme, extensions of these neo-kantian trajectories, mutually fueled as they are, in the case of the former, by a powerful existential-hermeneutical variation on Husserlian phenomenology, and for the latter by the powerful mathematics and type-hierarchy of Russell's *Principia* and Wittgenstein's *Tractatus*.

Heidegger's Kant interpretation aimed to show that the first critique does not present a theory of mathematical natural scientific knowledge after all.[7] The real contribution of the *Critique* is rather to work out, for the first time, the problem of the laying of the ground for metaphysics. On this reading Kant argues that metaphysics can only be grounded in a prior analysis of the nature of finite human reason. Moreover, Kant's introduction of the transcendental schematism of the understanding has the effect of dissolving both sensibility and the understanding in a common source, the transcendental imagination, whose ultimate basis is temporality. This in turn implies that the traditional basis of western metaphysics in *logos* is destroyed. Carnap, following the Marburg neo-kantians, held that although humanity must begin with the transcendental imagination and thus with finitude, it is also clear that Kant gives us the mechanism by which humanity can break free from finitude into the realm of objectively valid, necessary and eternal truths in the mathematical natural sciences. For Heidegger, objects in their disclosedness are prior to all valid judgments and thus prior in particular to the notion of logical form. Indeed, Dasein's most fundamental relation to the world is not cognitive at all but is a more primordial orientation that is either disclosed or covered over. On this front pure logic loses its explanatory power with regard to the constitution of any actual empirical object. Pure formal logic is irrelevant to the existential analytic which must first be explicated by hermeneutic-existential methods. This analytic rests on some deeper analysis wherein both logic and the notion of valid judgment in general emerge as derivative phenomena. Logical objectivity is subordinated to the analytic of Dasein.

Carnap's work represents the by now familiar transformation of traditional category theories along the lines of the linguistic turn. Whereas in Aristotle we are concerned with categories of being, and in Kant with categories of thinking, the analyses of Viennese positivism pertain to the categories of language. For Carnap, all objects of empirical science are "constituted" by logico-linguistic means. The basic features of his criticism of metaphysics develops from his linking of formal logic with the principle of verifiability first worked out in Wittgenstein's *Tractatus*. The meaning of a sentence is supposed to be determined by its truth conditions, hence linked to the form of statements and is reduced to propositional meaning. Accordingly, normative statements are to be considered meaningless. In fact, the only statements that have sense are those that describe logically possible facts (in the sense of existent or nonexistent states of affairs). Already along these lines the statements of logic lack sense, not in a pejorative way, but merely as characterizing their status as logically true—as tautologies that say nothing about the world. Carnap however still sees these statements as meaningful because they are true solely in virtue of their form, and follows Kant in defining them as analytic statements which are valid a priori.

A hint of openness to a different "kind" of meaning can be seen by a consideration of the standard objection to the verifiability criterion sprung from the application of the verifiability principle to itself. This was intended to question the empirical verifiability, and therefore the meaningfulness, of the verifiability principle itself. This criticism cast doubt on the very possibility of an empiricist philosophy, based on verifiability as a criterion of meaning.[8] It does not work, however, since, for Carnap, the principle is meant as a criterion of *cognitive* meaningfulness; thus the application of the principle to itself establishes at most that it is not an empirical statement of fact. It is not necessarily nonsense, it just means what it does in a different kind of way. Most logical empiricists moved on to saying that, rather than an empirical statement of fact, the verifiability criterion should be construed as an imperative or a rule. Thought of variously as an "explication" or a "volitional decision," its justification lies, not in empirical or logical or any other kind of evidence that supports a claim for its truth. Instead, any justification must lie in the value of the results that accrue from its use. Rules can be validated or vindicated. One validates a rule by showing that it is a consequence of some other rule that we have already accepted. For example, the rule of conditional proof in first order logic can be validated by the deduction theorem, which shows that any conclusions drawn by conditional proof can be derived by use of the basic rules of inference of the system alone. Derivations using conditional proof are often much simpler than derivations of the same conclusions without conditional proofs. Among the basic rules of the system we may find *modus ponens*. We vindicate *modus ponens* by somehow convincing ourselves that it is truth preserving; that is the basic desideratum for deductive logic.[9] Thus Carnap is alert to how something important is addressed in metaphysics. He admits that language still has functions other than making statements, and comes to embrace a form of emotivism in ethics. He follows it up with a metalogical theory of syntactically meaningful languages such as the *Logical Syntax of Language*. In his desire to eliminate so-called metaphysical pseudoproblems from the sciences, he sought to formulate a standpoint that amounts to replacing ontology with logical syntax. The problem will be in the question of whether or not "replacing" ontology with logical syntax is not to replay ontology. The positivist cannot get past the spectacle of the inaugural address to see possible points of comparison.

Heidegger certainly twists the knife in his Freiberg lecture when he announces his famous sentence: *Das Nichts selbst nichtet*—the nothing nothings. This is an abyssal sentence, the meaning of which will be explained momentarily. From what we have spelled out, it is not difficult to see why Carnap lambasts this move. The sentence does have the same grammatical form as the sentence "The rain rains" a sentence which Carnap, or at least his translator, regarded as a meaningful sentence of ordinary language. But this harmless guise conceals severe logical blemishes. Heidegger treats the indefinite pronoun "nothing" as a noun, as the "name or description of an entity." When he says that the nothing nothings, he surely does not mean that there is a nothing that nihilates. He introduces the meaningless word "*nichtet*," which might loosely be translated as "to nothing" or "to nihilate," or as one translator would have it, "to noth."[10] According to Carnap, Heidegger implies, and later affirms, the existence of the nothing, when the existence of this entity would be denied in its very definition. If all this were not enough, the sentence is meaningless, since it is neither analytic, nor contradictory, nor empirical. It is metaphysical nonsense.

Let us focus for a moment on the abyssal *Das Nichts selbst nichtet*. It is common enough for German philosophers to convert what is ordinarily a pronoun into a noun. That is no reason for rejecting the device as a whole. It is not confined to philosophers. We often say that a person is a nobody, and we are unclear whether the nobody refers to some particular nobody or speaking in general about people who are nobodies, such as television reality-show participants, or even to some generalized anonymous Nobody, such as that to which, as Heidegger creepily claims in *Being and Time*, every Dasein has already surrendered itself. In German *Nichts* can be used in the same way as 'nobody'—to describe something, usually a person, as a non-entity, a nobody. In this usage it has a plural *Nichtse*, nobodies, non-entities. Then there is *the* nothing, the use of *Nichts* as a noun that has no plural, such as nothingness in English.

But Heidegger does something more—he coins this new verb, *nichten*. This is consistent with Heidegger's occasionally wanting to draw a distinction between something that is a being or entity (*Seiendes*) and something that, even though it still is a something, is not a being or an entity. Hammers and trees are entities, but the world in which they are the things they are, is not. Time is not an entity, not some thing that is, and yet it does not follow that it is nothing, that is, *completely* nothing. Something that is not a being cannot, on Heidegger's view, be said to be, or to be a such and such or a so and so. For to apply to it the verb 'to be' would imply that it is a being. Thus he often adopts, and sometimes coins, an appropriate verb for such things. He does not say that the world is, but that the world worlds. So too the nothing is not a being or an entity. Hence we cannot say that it is, but we can say that it *nothings*. This is not to be interpreted as saying that there is a *something*, and that this thing *is* the nothing, and that it nothings. We should not think of the nothing as something that sometimes nothings, but other times does not, or which does other things besides the nothinging it already does. That would be to think of it as a being, distinct from its possible activities.

Heidegger also holds that, if one is to speak of the nothing, the nothing must be given in experience. This poses some difficulties, since it is not a being, we cannot encounter it perceptually. Nor can we construct or define it in thought. For the concepts that we would have to employ to define the nothing are in turn made possible by the nothing. On some front the nothing recaptures the Kantian enabling gesture as what makes our discourse possible. However debarred we are from capturing the nothing in our discourse we nonetheless have encounters with the nothing, particularly in certain moods, most notably anxiety with regard to death.

But why say that the nothing nothings, rather than simply that it annihilates? There is a perfectly good German verb *vernichten*, meaning to annihilate. Why not say *Das Nichts vernichtet*? Because beings are not annihilated in anxiety, leaving behind some sheer nothingness. They are experienced as slipping away but not disappearing altogether. So we are left with *Das Nichts selbst nichtet*. Because of the affinity of *nichten* to *vernichten*, it is sometimes translated as "nihilate." Since *vernichten* is transitive, *nichten* has a transitive flavor. But Heidegger never gives it an object in the accusative, and its affinity to other coinages, such as *welten*, suggests that it is intransitive. The nothing just nothings.

Heidegger's nothing is abyssal. That is to say, it is a phrase that seeks not to represent anything but to *initiate an experience* of the nothing. This is an experience, however, totally at odds with anything recognizable to the logical empiricists. It is an enactment that is not designed to completely succeed, since the nothing cannot be *completely* experienced. Thus it is an inauguration of something that does not succeed, an experience that fails, without this failure being able to acquire positive value. This will certainly frustrate the scientistic mentality with its outcomes and deadlines. Carnap's thinking about the nothing remains on the level of beings and simply assumes that predication provides our main access to them. He is correct to suggest that Heidegger's nothing has something to do with intelligibility, but what he fails to grasp is that this unintelligibility is not just a failure to form propositions about some mysterious thing, but is an insidious insignificance that constantly threatens our entire capacity to make sense out of things, not only our assertions and negations but the whole of our existence.

The nothing vanishes if it awakens, and perishes if it comes to light. Earlier, in *Being and Time*, Heidegger had spelled out the nothing in terms of revelatory experiences of finitude Dasein undergoes, such as in anxiety and the call of conscience, and the basic traits that they display, as in death and guilt. The "nothing" here means Dasein's own existence as Being-in-the-world.[11] In anxiety, the world is revealed as meaningless, in that we recognize that we cannot base our identity on any of the things or objects on which we normally rely. The nothing as well manifests itself as the possible impossibility of Dasein, or death.[12] Dasein's wholeness does not then consist in eliminating this possibility of death; rather, Dasein authentically becomes itself only when it accepts and holds open the finitude of its potentiality.[13] The nothing is not some flaw that can be overcome if only we were raised to some more blessed state, or some scientific problem which could evince a technical solution. Rather, the nothing is the condition of finitude of Dasein—to eliminate any of its conditions would be to eliminate Dasein itself. Dasein's being is permeated with nullity.[14] There is a finitude that accompanies all ontological inquiry. The significance is that beings as such, and doing ontology at all, can become accessible only to us as finite Dasein. Thus the very event, the happening, that prior accessibility to propositions, must itself be characterized by temporal finitude, both experienced as and understood through, the nothing.

By the time of the inaugural address, Heidegger's thinking of the nothing has developed to where its display in anxiety can be more fully understood as the necessary precondition for all metaphysical and scientific inquiry. Whereas in *Being and Time* the nothing was directed to characterize the finitude of Dasein, in "What is Metaphysics?" the nothing is used to characterize the trembling fragility of Being. "Nihilation manifests beings in their full but heretofore concealed strangeness as what is radically other—with respect to Nothing. In the clear night of the Nothing Of anxiety the original openness of beings as such arises: that they are beings—and not nothing."[15] Heidegger is not making the nihilistic claim that beings have no meaning at all. He is claiming that their meaning must come to pass in a contingent way. It is precisely through our vulnerability and finitude in the face of the nothing that we are able to recognize that beings do have meaning, as Dasein just means: *Hineingehaltenheit in das Nichts* "being held out into the nothing."[16] Meaning is fragile and subject to re-interpretation, not fixed as in the sciences. This fragility is written into our inquiry standpoint and is the precondition for there being factual propositions at all. Being is finite in that it cannot be founded on the presence of some particular entity that serves as a ground for it. This means that it is constantly limited by the possibility of dissolution. *Das Nichts selbst nichtet.* Such a phrase sentences us to participation in that which can never finish with its own interrogation. The phrase cannot be brought out of the silence it bears.

Unfortunately Carnap completely disregards Heidegger's overall argument, which questions the basic presuppositions of Carnap's critique. Carnap's logical syntax affirms that beings are given (posited) in a way that conforms to the rules of assertion (logic). But this fails to ask how we have access to that prior opening which allows for the "givenness" in the first place. This prior opening is not primarily logical, because it cannot be founded on assertions. Indeed, propositional truths presuppose this more primordial unconcealment. True to his strain of neo-Kantianism, Carnap simply cannot imagine that the canons of propositional discourse are not the final arbiters of the question. His logicism understands any prior relatedness or opening to only be some function of thinking defined exclusively as forming propositional judgments. For Heidegger, of course, the flaw in such an undertaking is that our linguistics, logic and syntax are themselves merely calcified remnants of the very tradition Carnap is trying to criticize. Indeed, by way of the nothing, the roles of analytic and continental philosophy have strangely reversed moving into the 21st century. It is the continental tradition which struggles above all with the deconstruction of supposed remnants of old metaphysics, whereas a new metaphysics is celebrating its reemergence in the logically ingenious theories of analytic philosophy. Probably to his dismay, Carnap's *"Traum"* of the elimination of metaphysics through the logical analysis of language is *"ausgetraumt."* The order of the day for analytic philosophy is not the elimination of metaphysics through the logical analysis of language, but the establishment of ever new foundations *for* metaphysics *through* the logical analysis of language.

Although the tone of Heidegger's writing is unremittingly pessimistic at times, his work was informed by more hopeful orientations of the nothing. Two areas of twentieth century thought on the nothing which speak to this, areas which have long been in the proximity of the nothing understood in terms of blessedness or tranquility, are the current usages of medieval mysticism and the Kyoto School.

From the publication of his early lecture courses on the phenomenology of religious experience, to the notes for his abandoned course on medieval mysticism, much has been made of the Heidegger's use of the Christian mystic Meister Eckhart and his themes as *gelassenheit* (releasement) and *abgescheidenheit* (detachment).[17] Death for Heidegger is the *abschied vom Seiendem*: the fundamental experience of this 'not being' (*Nichts das Seiende*) is given in the stroke that relates to death in mortality, if it is true that death is the departure of beings. In Heidegger's understanding of death as an *Abschied*, a departure of or from beings, one can hear the resonance of *abgescheidenheit*, which in Eckhart indicates a mode of relation to God. Heidegger's understanding of death as a relation to the nothing, the *Nicht das Seiende*, resonates with Eckhart's understanding of *abgescheidenheit* as a relation to the God who is no-thing among beings.

Detachment and releasement in Eckhart orient the central theme of his vernacular sermons, the soul's return to God through annihilation, and they function according to the apophatic logic of Eckhart's overall theology. In order to unite with the God who remains beyond all created things, the individual soul must be detached and de-parted (*ab-geschieden*) from beings in the world. Beyond all the names and knowledge possible among created beings, Eckhart's absolutely simple God cannot be known or named; indeed, to the extent that we know or name created beings in their complexity, we miss God in his absolute simplicity, for "where the creature stops, there God begins to be."[18] In order, therefore, to receive God in his nothingness, for which there is no name, the soul must itself pass beyond all naming and knowing to reach (without reaching) the most radical poverty in which the soul "wants nothing, knows nothing, and has nothing."[19] In other words, Eckhart's negative theology, according to which God is a nameless nothing, implies an accompanying negative anthropology, according to which through the poverty of detachment the soul would approach the nothingness in which it might prove indistinct from God.

This self-diremption of the self, corresponding to the namelessness and incomprehensibility of God's nothingness, mirrors and informs Heidegger's own thinking through without silence of the relation between Dasein and Being throughout his intellectual career. It is not a stretch to say that many post-war, resolutely secular, even anti-Christian thinkers drawn to the excessive forms of Christian, Jewish, and Asian mysticism, have some structural connection to Heidegger's encounter with the nothing. This is especially the case when one reviews how French intellectuals look to mysticism as an encounter with an other that marks the apex of the religious or ethical life. Thus Bataille, Blanchot, Foucault, Derrida, Irigaray, de Beauvoir, Lacan, and separately, Sartre's own unique explorations, all effect a disruption of traditional metaphysical categories from deep engagements with mysticism or with Heidegger on the nothing..

A second venue of the nothing comes in a reflection on the connections between Heidegger's thinking and the renaissance of interest in the Kyoto school of philosophers such as Nishida, Tanabe, and Nishitani. These Japanese Buddhist thinkers had a front row seat to the post-Kantian happenings in German thought. Many of Nishida's students studied with Husserl and Heidegger in Freiburg in the 1920's and 1930's, such as Yamanouchi Tokuryu and Tanabe Haijime, along with dozens of others in Heidelberg and Freiburg. Rickert, Husserl, and Heidegger were familiar with Nishida Kitaro. Tanabe first introduced Heidegger's phenomenology into Japanese in October 1924, and became friends enough with Heidegger to have been recommended by him for an honorary doctorate at Freiburg in 1957. Nishitani studied under Heidegger in the 30's in Freiburg duirng his Nietzsche lecture series.[20]

Although faced with conditions of structurally similar war-time violence and fascist upheaval, Japanese thinking did not come to the nothing by way of a confrontation with nihilism in terms of a shaking of the foundations of its metaphysical traditions, as Europe had in relation to its Christianity. Instead, thinkers in this tradition, informed as they were by German thought, approach the issue through Buddhistic and Confucian standpoints of emptiness and nothingness. In his *Religion and Nothingness*, Nishitani adopts a similar strategy of overcoming nihilism by way of nihilism, a kind of spiritual ascent through descent into radical finitude. The first round requires an emptying of all categories of subjectivity through doubt and frustration. This is to be followed by a rigorous "nullifying" of all the beings one encounters. This nullity is itself nullified in additional rounds, eventually to be transcended in its negation in an awareness that the world of being is itself only a relative manifestation of nothingness. Beneath the world and all around it, there is an encompassing absolute nothingness that just is reality, which triggers an absolute emptiness which Buddhism names *sunyata*.[21]

Nishitani's complex working out of the standpoint of emptiness serves as a device by which to display the objectifying tendencies of western metaphysical categories. It eventually culminates in a vision of all of reality that is by nature self-emptying. In work after work that show a remarkable affinity with western metaphysical and religious sources, not to mention Eckhart and Heidegger, Nishitani examines the idea of creation of the world *ex nihilo*. This *nihilum* that is elemental in the human is not the negation of all meaning but only a negation of meaning that has been centered around the self as the *telos* of life. The nothingness beyond God of which the world is made is also the nothingness out of which God works. When he concludes that the nature of God is absolute nothingness, Nishitani finds common ground both with Eckhart and the 13th century Beguine Mechthild von Madgeburg in the shared horizons of Zen Buddhistic and Christian mystic thinking, tempered by Heideggerian insights into the nothing.[22]

From the inaugural lecture through dozens of other texts and lectures, Heidegger insists that the nothing is a legitimate topic for thinking, and uses it to refer to a wide variety of phenomena, including inauthenticity, uncanniness, guilt, meaninglessness, the withdrawal of Being, the possibility of the sacred, and the event of appropriation. In both his earlier and later texts, with enormous differences in emphasis and vocabulary, he uses these different senses of the nothing to awaken us to the temporal finitude that binds Dasein and Being. The manifestation of beings as such is ungrounded and ungroundable. It is finite, in the sense that it cannot be guaranteed or finalized. Being is a displacement that cannot be located or founded within the realm of beings, precisely because it is the happening that first opens up this realm. This means that we are as well displaced and can never define or control ourselves by appealing to any being that we encounter. In order to come into our own as Dasein, we must accept our own finitude. Far from leading to nihilism, such thinking is deeply spiritual, even necessary. If we quit tarrying with the nothing, then totality will make greater encroachments on finite and particular beings. If when thinking seems completed in the sciences, we continue to think; if when hope is gone we continue to hope, and write when there is nothing left to write about, and speak when there is nothing more to say, then there is at least the possibility of hope and speech and life. In this regard does the nothing preserve the possibility for thinking.

XII. Only Ruin is True: Introduction to Adorno's Aesthetics

1. Since its posthumous publication in 1970, Adorno's major work *Aesthetic Theory* seems to have raised more questions than it has answered, perhaps more than could ever *be* answered on its behalf. It was not surprising that critics on the right condemned its poetic obscurity and embrace of dialectics. What was interesting was its reception, and outright denunciation, from those on the left, who condemned it as an anachronistic cultural elitism. In the 1990's major critical reassessments of the work sought to locate its impact somewhere in the rivalry between modernism and post-modernism. Thus Robert's *Art and Enlightenment* situates Adorno's thought as consistent with the modernist project, whereas Habermas' influential critique paints it as part of the project which "gives up" on modernity. Other major works of outstanding scholarship followed, such as Zuidervaart's *Adorno's Aesthetic Theory* (1991) and Paddison's *Adorno's Aesthetics of Music* (1993), both of which aim at a comprehensive synthesis of Adorno's writings. Still later authors sought to capture Adorno's complexities while remaining wary of systematizing them, given their own anti-systematic impulses, such as the work of Hohendahl (1992) and Martin (1997).[1] One must engage in a kind of mimicry of what one is addressing in order even to address it on its terms, but this risks either replaying the original, or foisting a false unity upon the fundamentally dissimilar. We have in Adorno, then, another figure with whom we seemingly can engage only by way of a detour, here taking the form of a strategic essentialism which marks its own de-totalizing sympathies.

2. As is so common today, the very act of reading and interpreting Adorno puts us in utmost proximity to his thinking with regard to fundamental philosophical questions. Adorno wrote both impure, aphoristic philosophy and dense, academically rigorous works of teutonic philosophy. He gave radio addresses and composed music. His works are alternately ponderous and unforgettable. They combine romanticism with a kind of oceanic bitterness, a mix of joy and catastrophe theory. It was as if every thing he wrote had the tone of being evidence of, or decisive for, the entire fate of humanity. His work therefore appears to some as pompous and destructive, leaving no space for anything that was harmless. To others however his thinking does not disappoint their

expectation that philosophy should have a certain awesomeness, and instead of trying to soothe away the sense of astonishment from which the original impulse to philosophy springs, he tries to increase it. His philosophy consorts with the most dangerous aspects in contemporary art and seeks to extend them further. Thus our own introduction to his aesthetics requires us to splinter along with the fragments we study.

3. It will also pay to review some of the well-known features of and precedents to Adorno's work. It is of course most closely associated with the Frankfurt School, that group of high powered philosophers and sociologists associated with the Institute for Social Research at Frankfurt. Beginning in 1923, its founders expounded "critical theory" in their journal *Zeitschrift für Sozialforschung*, holding to the idea that only radical change could cure the ills of modern society, especially those of unbridled technology, and that every one-sided doctrine must be subjected to the acid-bath of ideology-critique, which was to include, first and foremost, Marxism. The Frankfurt school theorists were "marxians," rejecting the inevitability of proletarian revolution and Marxism's pretensions toward science. Theory never completely reduces to social conditions, but since it is the product of such conditions, critical theory must trace its origins in ways which, unlike empiricism and positivism, indirectly endorse the processes themselves.[2]

4. In general, while Adorno wrote on many different philosophical topics, for him it is art that is the last factor of resistance against the totalizing structure of society. Society had basically broken the promise of the enlightenment, because it has not overcome its inner antagonisms but merely appeased them. This appeasement in turn has led to the integration of all oppositional forces into society, which has become total. For the critical theorists, philosophy had not opposed this tendency toward totality but had indeed inaugurated it, imitated it, and ultimately ennabled it. In their devastating analysis of contemporary society *Dialektik der Aufklarung* (*Dialectic of Enlightenment*, 1944), Horkheimer and Adorno argue that total society has even eliminated all oppositional conceptual thought.[3] For Adorno only art carries the hope of escaping from the airtight totality of contemporary society. Philosophy could no longer guarantee any secure ground for the project that motivated the members of the Frankfurt Institute, namely the alleviation of social injustice. Adorno consistently locates *in art* the potential formerly attributed to philosophy, namely to show reality as it really is and remind us of greater possibilities.

5. Enlightenment thinking tries to subordinate all natural life to order and determination. Enlightenment is totalitarian in its unrelenting demand for system and unity, the same as the drive for equivalence and exchange which dominates in the commodity form of late capitalism. Everything is made comparable by getting reduced to abstract variables or magnitudes. Enlightenment sees its enemy as myth. Truth was not logical but capturable only with dialectics. All totalizations were suspect "after Auschwitz," to use Adorno's haunting phrase. Any attempt to logically intervene led to the alienating illusion of instrumental rationality, a self-deceiving surrender of bourgeois consciousness. Liberation from the world of totalized alienation was through a set of spiritual exercises of which art was one. Adorno thus engages in a comprehensive repudiation of everything the bourgeois world stood for, including every aspect of its conceptual identity. Art must be ferociously polemical. It must with every breath crush the petrified forest of the contemporary world.

6. After Auschwitz, which Adorno sees as the metaphysical completion of the West, art must struggle against the illusion of reconciliation with the inhumanity of the cultural logic of late capital. What is needed is art that shrugs off all traditional, socially uncritical aesthetic values of beauty and totality as complicit with fascism. The artist is the analogue to the Jew, the "other" resisting totality. The art which holds out hope as the last reservoir of genuine human experience and oppositional consciousness is that of the avant-garde, which is itself constantly in danger of being incorporated into the "profit loving tentacles of the culture-industry." Life in modern society is inhumane; any art which does not expose this condition is a betrayal; all allegiances with it are an "extorted reconciliation." Thus Adorno's aesthetic holds out hope of redemption from oppression only through radical critique. To resist the homogenizing tyranny of the culture industry, works must be ugly, unincorporable, hyper-useless, unexchangeable, anything that shatters the effortless reception of passive consumers. The purpose of art now must be to exceed the grasp of the "carceral gulag" of the culture industry. Given that mass-consciousness is insidious, popular art is bankrupt. Given that "the splinter in your eye is the best magnifying glass," confrontational art meets Adorno's criteria.[4] Art's expression must be inexorably negative, for as society is inhumane, art must be inhumane in its service to humanity. The shock value of the unintelligible reminds people of what everyone knows but no one will admit. Given that the

extermination of human beings became rational as Auschwitz, art cannot be whole or complete or rational but must contradict the "*Verblendungszusammenhang*" (delusional system) of culture. Work must be graffiti-like in its non-commodifiability, oppositional, with the soulless architecture of late capital forming its base, and the stolen paint further subverting and extricating itself from the world of consumption.

7. The forces of de-totalization are still often seen as the harbingers of destruction, as dangerous toxins which if unleashed would destroy civilization. Curiously today there is a sense in which such toxins are now available "over the counter, and without a prescription." Both ways of thinking neglect to recall how prevalent such categories of thinking were in the 19th century, which saw herculean efforts to de-totalize the Hegelian framework by Kierkegaard and Nietzsche. By the turn of the century, the deracinated fate of the modernist exiles becomes a kind of material condition for the emergence of a newly universalizing thought, one which having spurned the ambiguous comforts of the motherland now casts a bleak eye on all such historical legacies. Perhaps in discerning the hidden global logics by which all were governed, one might yet be able to make some grand narrative up as they go along. Turn of the century marxians argued that the commodity form is the secret villain in this scenario, in which the machine-like sway of exchange-value disintegrates reality into a multitude of irrational facts over which a network of abstract laws emptied of content is cast.

8. Adorno's scorn for mass culture mimics Schopenhauer in its pessimistic tone. Mass culture is not just folk art with millions of people: it is a culture industry devoted to the full-scale construction of commodity consuming subjectivity. The audience is meant to amuse itself, but this amusement is nothing but the systematic elimination of critical thought. Mass culture manipulated consciousness on an unbelievable scale, and could only be understood fully by revealing those who profited from the manipulation. His hostility was not from the idea that the revolt of the masses had polluted the temples of culture, but that the culture of the masses had been synthetically concocted from above. Rather than cultural chaos or anarchy, Adorno described only tight regimentation and control. "*Vergügtsein heisst Einverstandensein*" -amusement means agreement.

9. For our purposes, we can thus understand that for Adorno, modern capitalist culture had a completely disfiguring effect on art. Reacting against Benjamin, Adorno argued that "amusement" distracted viewing and listening which allowed for no sense of actual meanings to develop. Instead the focus of attention turns to disjointed individual stimuli—for example, in music, Ipods digitially indexing only memorable themes in a symphony. Such shortening of attention spans and the inability to mentally construct a whole leads to a kind of infantilization which carries serious political implications. For Adorno the culture industry systematically disables the development of autonomous, judicious individuals capable of independent decisions. It is fascistic because it literally destroys the conditions needed for a democratic society.

10. The products of the culture industry were not works of art turned into commodities, but produced from the very beginning as fungible items for sale in the market place. The distinction between art and advertising is obliterated. Cultural products now become created for exchange, not for spiritual needs. Modern music becomes nothing but cults of star performers, and the obsession of technical perfection in equipment, impoverishing the listening of those who could pick out nothing but famous melodies. Contemporary music had literally led to a regression of hearing. The growing inability to concentrate on anything but the most banal and truncated aspects of composition having an ever-same quality reinforced the status-quo. The incessant replacement of one fad with another was really a screen for the reproduction of sameness on an enormous level. Predigested formulae were replicated ad infinitum—even improvisatory jazz followed highly circumscribed patterns. The culture industry produced totally standardized commodities and pseudo-individualism that masked the sameness of the administered world. All mechanisms of style-revolutions were predetermined. Alternative music, poetry, film, all become absolutely suspect, each in their own way mirroring the relentlessly suffocating effects of the culture industry.

11. Similarly, Adorno attempts to provide a justification by showing the irrelevance of classical standards for its fragmentary creations and the retrograde ideological intention of beautiful, rounded works in the problematic era of modernity. In the struggle against the illusion of reconciliation provided by such works, de-aestheticized art embraces the manifestations of decline, society's ruins, as if in order to wake a somnambulate humanity from the nightmare to which it has fallen victim. Art must forsake the realm of beautiful

semblance for the sake of the accumulated suffering that is otherwise glossed over. The grotesqueries represent a testament to what modernity has forgotten.

12. By insuring that it is useless for all decorative purposes, the aesthetics of ugliness simultaneously polemicizes against the affirmative illusions of the culture industry. Modernism's thematization is a reaction against the dialectic of enlightenment, the logic of civilization and the principle of rational control. In order to elevate himself above the level of a merely natural existence and thus arrive at self-consciousness as a species, man must first learn to subjugate his own inner nature, become attuned to the renunciations demanded by the reality principle necessary for the level of cooperation required for the conquest of external nature. Yet the logic backfires in that the rigidification of the ego is ultimately so extreme that the original aim of the process, the pacification of the struggle for existence and the attainment of a state of reconciliation with nature, is eventually lost sight of; and the means to this end, the domination of nature, is enthroned as an end in itself. Ugliness represents an assault on enlightened subjectivity's horror of the unformed, its aversion in face of that which has escaped the leveling, identitarian stamp of modernity.

13. Thus for us it is now quite easy to see how Adorno's aesthetic thinking was in revolt against the leveling cultural mechanisms of capitalist society. So too would his own theory of art take as its premises a contrast to the commercial products of the culture industry. In philosophical terms this manifested itself as a revolt against the dominant category of aesthetics, that of beauty, in the modern world where the flow of life has been reduced to a series of minutely subdivided calculations. In direct response to the rationalized fabric of modernity, the predominant category of aesthetics becomes now one of dissonance. By virtue of its sinister qualities, dissonant art is that which alone retains the capacity to call modernity by its actual name. By simultaneously distancing itself from the conventions of modernity in an increasingly radical manner, by treating society as its adversary, dissonant art stands as an indictment of modernity, yet holding open hope of restitution. By virtue of its autonomy, art saves itself from incorporation into the reifying network of commodity production and also polemicizes against this sphere as being inimical to authentic human being. By shattering the omnipresent semblance of well-being, dissonant art lays bare the substratum of strife that lies beneath modernity's pretension to being Reason incarnate. In contrast to the essentially harmonious, rounded, totality-oriented great works of the past, modern art is

decidedly fragmented, problematical, and ruinous. In Adorno's de-aesthetic, only what is in ruin is true.

14. For Adorno, de-aestheticization is a consequence of art's avid utilization of new and advanced techniques, its self-conscious destruction of traditional aesthetic standards, and its unprecedented distance from social origins. Adorno considers the legitimate representatives of the progressive side of this trend to be virtually synonymous with the avant-garde. Through the process of de-aestheticization avant-garde art contests the counterfeit aura of reconciliation projected by affirmative art, the conciliatory notion that culture should serve as the ersatz domain where the ideals that are denied by a reified society can be realized. A trace of affirmation attaches itself to all art by virtue of its striving toward totality, its attempt to present the appearance of completeness or self-sufficiency, whereby fulfillment in art can substitute for the lack of fulfillment in life. The fragmentariness of de-aestheticized works of art originates in opposition to the concept of totality and the false recognition that concept implies. Radical de-aestheticization is the product of an era in which the contradiction between the symbolic reconciliation projected in art and the actual unreconciled condition of the world as a whole has become intolerable. This contradiction explains the unprecedented extremes to which modernism has recourse, its bombast, exaggeration and shock, in the attempt to divest itself convincingly of its affirmative character.

15. Adorno was similar to Heidegger in emphatically affirming the autonomy of the artwork from historical reality, and in his continued use of the concept of the work of art and its particular notion of its truth content. This manifested itself in Adorno's strange masterpiece *Aesthetic Theory*, complete with contradictory introductions. This work certainly weighs in as if it were a ponderous tome in German aesthetics seeking a systematic development of some grand theory. It is certainly a work for which 18th and 19th century philosophies of art, particularly Kant's and Hegel's, remained the unsurpassed models of aesthetic theory. From Adorno's vantage point, however, both had failed in their attempts to define the aesthetic through general concepts; more specifically they failed in an inevitable attempt to synthesize the moment of nonidentity of art with a philosophical discourse based on universal concepts.

16. According to Hegel's philosophy of the evolutionary advance of human spiritual life, in the modern era art has forfeited its former role as the pre-

eminent vehicle for the expression of spirit, the role it enjoyed in ancient Greece. Hegel defines art as the sensuous embodiment of the idea. The ideal balance between the moments of sensuousness and truth, represented in Greek sculpture, has been surpassed in the modern world in which the higher, more non-sensuous intellectual expression of truth, the concept, has come to prominence. Ours is the age of inwardness and intellectualization par excellence, ill-suited to the restful simplicity of the sensuous representation of truth in classical antiquity. Consequently art itself takes on a markedly cerebral, intellectualized guise that is fundamentally at odds with its essential formal (i.e., sensual and classical) requirements. Art itself becomes philosophical, a fact which underscores the need for a science of aesthetics to interpret it. This is Hegel's thesis concerning the death of art. It refers not the the literal disappearance of art, but rather to the fact that the classical symmetry of the "Ideal" has been irretrievably lost, that the old guidelines of artistic creation have entered into a state of crisis, and thus the superior form of spiritual expression represented by the philosophical concept. As Hegel famously puts it:

> In all these respects art, considered in its highest vocation, is and remains for us a thing of the past. Thereby it has lost for us genuine truth and life, and has rather been transferred into our ideas instead of maintaining its necessity in reality and occupying its higher place. What is now aroused in us in works of art is not just immediate enjoyment but our judgment also, since we subject to our intellectual consideration (1) the content of art, and (2) the work of art's means of presentation, and the appropriateness or inappropriateness of both to one another.[5]

17. Hegel's significant advance beyond the formalism of Kant's aesthetics was his recognition of the fact that all art necessarily possesses a truth content that makes it receptive to the methods of philosophical contemplation. For Kant, all intellectual judgments concerning art are forbidden, insofar as such judgments constitute a regression to heteronomy, to the cognitive sphere of "interest," which gives rise to the possibility of subjecting works of art to ignoble, utilitarian considerations, i.e., considerations that prove inimical to their cardinal status as formal, aesthetic objects. Consequently, according to Kant, the absolute canon for the "judgment" of works of art (although strictly speaking, all judgments are cognitive, and therefore inadmissible according to his criteria) is a feeling of "disinterested pleasure," a quickening of the faculties of the imagination and understanding vis-a-vis the aesthetic object which is, ideally, universally valid for every living subject who might encounter that object. According to Hegel, however, the emphasis on the feeling of pleasure in Kant's

aesthetics itself borders too closely on a relapse into heteronomy, insofar as it makes aesthetic judgment contingent on the "lower faculties" of inclination or desire. Consequently for Hegel art becomes a full-fledged member of the domain of absolute spirit, alongside the spheres of religion and philosophy. Through his conception of the truth content of art, the important convergence of works of art with the notion of philosophical truth, the crucial realization that, in addition to being objects of pleasure or enjoyment, authentic works of art represent significant forms of cognitive experience, becomes firmly established in the annals of the history of aesthetic judgment.

18. Hegel's conviction that works of art possess an essential cognitive function forms a point of departure for Adorno. According to him, the Hegelian hierarchy of the dimensions of absolute spirit incorporating art, religion, and philosophy seems to undergo a reversal; with art, on the basis of its having incorporated the moment of sensuousness into the framework of its cognitive activity, supplanting philosophy as the preeminent dimension. By virtue of the mimetic behavior characteristic of all works of art, the fact that their representation of physical reality is always sensual or intellectual, they serve as an important corrective to the ever-present tendency toward the hypostatization of abstract concepts inherent to philosophical thought. Through their somatic side—their thingly character—precisely that aspect of works of art that Hegel deems impure and therefore burdensome, works of art acquire an intrinsic, physical affinity with the external world they seek to represent and thereby show themselves capable of counteracting the "bad abstraction" that afflicts all pure theoretical conceptualization. Through their reliance on the mimetic faculty, works of art preserve the idea of a radically different relation of man to nature, a relation that ceases to be based on the principles of domination and control.

19. Adorno refers to the peculiar interlacing of sensible and supersensible elements in works of art as their enigmatic character. It is the enigmatic origin of their truth content, the fact that it inextricably issues forth from a determinate constellation of sensible elements, that differentiates the truth content of works of art from strictly logical, conceptual truth. For by virtue of its mimetic structure, aesthetic truth retains an affinity with the somatic side of things, with the ineffable dimension that remains occluded in pure conceptualization, the fact that truth can never be securely and totally grasped by thought.

20. The First World War and its accompanying 'spenglerization' compounded many thinkers' rejection of modernity and despair at the seemingly wrong turn enlightenment philosophy had taken. Already a century earlier German thinkers, other than Kant and Hegel, began to express concern about the consequences of an enlightenment movement then in its infancy. Schiller's *On Naive and Sentimental Poetry* bewails the orphaned state of homelessness in which modern "enlightenment" man finds himself, and his *Aesthetic Education of Man* sought aesthetic means to resolve the apparent dissolution of humanity. Novalis's *Christianity or Europe* (1799) echoes the despair of modern fragmentation brought on by the twin Reformations of Lutheranism and enlightenment rationalism. Both Schiller and Novalis demonstrate their negative idealism by turning to idealized projections of the past for solutions, with Novalis the romanticist constructing an image of Catholicism as a unifying force under the dome of the Holy Roman Empire; Schiller the Classicist seeing in ancient Greece the harmonious perfection of a time when humanity was unified with their world.[6] Though their selection of models was different, their idealization of those models was similar, as was their fundamental criticism of society. Their work had little to do with the reality of classical antiquity in any traditional historicist sense. As has long since been known, their work is itself an artistic creation, with questions of historical accuracy being replaced by questions of modern strategic function and intent.[7]

21. Antiquity functioned as a source to be emulated and not merely imitated: the ancient Greeks had succeeded, so it was claimed, in creating an authentic, indigenous culture, an important goal for mid-18th century Germans seeking answers to their own questions of national identity. It is with this yearning for a "totality" to culture that Lukacs began his *Theory of the Novel* (1916), with an elegaic invocation of antiquity: "Blessed are those ages..." This reinforces the emotional connections to Novalis's first few sentences of *Christianity or Europe*: "They were beautiful radiant times, when Europe was a Christian land, when one Christianity occupied this part of the humanely formed world."[8]

22. Lukacs' *Theory of the Novel* seizes on this notion of the lost original totality of antiquity. Christianity, according to Lukacs, had attempted an irrational but nevertheless somewhat successful effort at reestablishing a totality once the ancient Greek model had dissipated. This line of thought finds its theoretical foundation in Hegel's sparse remarks about the novel. Hegel had mentioned

that the existence of the novel was a manifestation of contemporary humanity's spiritual poverty as compared to the epic totality of the ancients. For Hegel, "what is missing is the originally poetic world condition, out of which the actual epic comes." The novel is the imperfect epic of this chaotic age, as compared to the closed harmony of antiquity. Such a split yearns for resolution and the restoration of harmony.[9] For Lukacs, the "form of the novel is, like no other, an expression of transcendental homelessness."[10] Novelistic narrative was an attempt to lead back to the harmonious world where the individual had allegedly once been integrated with society. In practice however this does not occur because novels could not portray resolution in a world where there was none. Characteristically Lukacs argues there have been two types of novels, the first depicting individuals who undergo a series of adventures in society, gaining knowledge and understanding through his experience; the second portrays the victim of modernity, an individual whose development is based on introspection bordering on self-absorption with a corresponding separation from the real world. Both types fail to achieve the genuine epic totality, the one because of the absence of any psychological dimension, the other because of the diminished social content. In essence, Lukacs combines Schiller's cultural pessimism with Hegel's aesthetic thesis.[11] Adorno took from Lukacs' work the idea that the novel was a reflection of objective historical conditions, and that the theme of cultural disintegration in art was connected to the reification of the historical process of decay which emptied meaning from inner life. But where Lukacs lamented modernity for its loss of epic totality, and waxed nostalgic for classical Greek *Weltanschauung*, for Adorno the project of reinstating wholeness by means of aesthetic form was to be abandoned. The ideology of cultural decline from perceived totality was nothing other than class privilege masking its own shock that its lofty goods might ever decay, "those goods whose eternity is supposed to guarantee the eternity of the class's own existence."[12] Lukacs' vision was too much under the category of a "theological awakening."[13] Rather than reconciliation, Adorno's thinking instead sought the explosion of all given forms, a detour without return.

23. Where Lukacs opposes the artefact to the commodity, Walter Benjamin tries to conjure up an entire aesthetics from the commodity form itself. Indeed, of all of Benjamin's many and complex works, their correspondence and personal relationship, I would argue that Adorno's aesthetics was influenced most by *Origin of German Tragic Drama*, particularly Benjamin's analysis of the art of the Baroque era in light of the concept of "ruin." The great achievements of

modernism and the Baroque consist in fragments rather than perfect or completed works. Both periods are eras of historical decline. These are both periods in which the "well-wrought work is only within reach of the epigone." The fragmentary works of modernism represent the contemporary counterpart to the ruins of the Baroque era: in an era of decadence, in which meaning is no longer immanent to life and the world thus becomes colored by an overarching sense of confusion, the creation of the beautiful, totality-oriented works of art can appear only illusory—a false consolation. Benjamin's study on tragedy represents a watershed in aesthetics, insofar as his critical rehabilitation of that lost and forgotten genre, for all its bombast and excrescence, serves to validate the idea of fragmentary art in historical ages of decline, in opposition to the traditional aesthetic values of allegedly timeless standards. Here the very unregeneracy of the situation holds itself out as a kind of hope: the more culture presents itself as mortified and devalued, as in the sluggish, spiritually bankrupt world of the German *Trauerspiel,* the more it becomes a negative index of some yet inconceivable transcendence. As with Benjamin before him, for Adorno, in a social order grown morbid and meaningless, in the empty, homogeneous time of commodity production, that which refuses the lures of the aesthetic, the fragmentary work of art, can yet hold out hope to figure truth by remaining resolutely silent about it all.

24. The intense, messianic idealism and the tortuously complex speculations of Benjamin's work on the *Trauerspiel* display both a surface and a depth. There is a capacity, at once gnomic and controlled, for recognizing the significance of the fragment and the detail, a talent for perceiving the tense relation between the fragment and the universal moment contained monadically within it. As anti-system, the philosophy in form and procedure acquires a tropism toward the fragmentary, the occluded, and the reflected, insofar as it approaches its object, the divine idea, by means of indirection or digression in representation.[14] It is theological conditions, not subjective ambition, that produces the philosophical treatise's mode of exposition. Indeed, there is a Kierkegaardian dispersion of the subjectivity infecting the philosophical system; the moment of authority of the treatise is reduced to where only the "authoritative citation" remains as the permissable intrusion of intentionality. If the philosophical systems of the 19th century bore unmistakeable affinities to the model of autonomous artistic genius who conjured up artworks full-formed and independent from the mysterious depths of inner spirit, the new model of philosophical procedure Benjamin had in mind was captured by the activity of mosaic construction:

"Just as mosaics preserve their majesty despite their fragmentation into capricious particles, so philosophical contemplation is not lacking in momentum (*Schwung*). Both are made up of the distinct and the disparate; and nothing could bear more powerful testimony to the transcendent force of the sacred image and the truth itself. The value of fragments of thought is all the greater the less direct their relationship to the underlying conception, and the brilliance of the representation depends as much on this value as the brilliance of the mosaic does on the quality of the glass paste. The relationship between the micrological processing of the work and the proportions of the sculptural or intellectual whole demonstrates that truth-content is only to be grasped through immersion in the most minute details of subject-matter."[15]

Thus the thinker sifts and sorts through the field of fragments, pulling out the correct piece, fixing it conceptually in place next to apparently heterogenous fragments, so that, as an ensemble, an idea may be momentarily represented. Benjamin's prologue is quite platonic in how the mosaic artist has some insight into the final product and some technical skill in reconstruction by way of material fragments. It is here where Benjamin introduces his famous central image of the constellation to clarify, if possible, the relation between phenomena, concepts, and ideas. "Ideas are to objects as constellations are to stars."[16]

25. The image of the constellation appears as a supplement to the analogy of the mosaic construction. The subject perceives individual objects, as in the vast canopy of individual stars. The imposition of concepts upon these disparate elements could have "systematic" ambition, dissolving the individuality of the discrete phenomena into the abstractness of a new conceptual structure. Benjamin's alternative is the moment in which the application of a concept effects a mediation in the relationship between the particulars and that which is implicit within them but cannot be grasped or possessed as an object itself. The idea is not what lies behind the phenomena as some informing essence, but the way the object is conceptually configured in its diverse, extreme, and contradictory elements. The thing must not be grasped as a mere instantiation of some universal essence, but instead one's thinking must deploy a whole cluster of stubbornly specific concepts which in Cubist style refract the object in myriad directions or penetrate it from a range of diffuse angles. Here again is a kind of return to totality: the emergence of the constellation out of the assembly of stars is the consequence of the imposition of conceptual patterns upon the stars by a community that finds not only the lessening of the once terrifying expanse of the night sky, but does so in such a way so as to annex the

images themselves to the purposes of navigation and mythic meaningfulness, rendering the mysterious cosmos known and controllable, producing the first possibility of rational control of natural features and processes. A "constellatory epistemology" sets its face against the cartesian or kantian moment of subjectivity, less concerned to possess or control the phenomena than to liberate it into its own sensuous being and preserve its disparate elements in their irreducible heterogeneity. The constellation refuses to clinch itself on some metaphysical essence, leaving its component parts loosely articulated in the manner of *trauerspiel* or epic theater, but it nevertheless prefigures that state of reconciliation which would be blasphemous to represent directly. In its unity of the perceptual and the conceptual, its transmutation of thought into images, the constellation bears a strain of the blissful edenic condition in which word and object were spontaneously at one, as well as of that of prehistoric, mimetic correspondence between nature and humanity which predated our fall into cognitive reason.

26. During the contemporary period of course reflections on language have assumed a growing importance for philosophy, and Adorno's thought is no exception. We have mentioned how Adorno's own works themselves manifest the fragmentary condition, refusing logical ordering. How else could a formal model which would challenge reified aspects of philosophical systems be presented without itself becoming reified? Thus his embrace of dialectical reasoning and blistering critiques are an ironic attempt to remain consistent with his main themes, namely to resist the counterfeit harmonies and retrograde ideological intention of the beautiful. Adorno self-reflexively sought to waken somnabulate humanity from the decorative purposes of art and thinking.

27. Such a constellatory approach finds confirmation in Adorno's sporadic views on language, often developed in polemical contexts, in which he singles out conceptualization as the linguistic topic with the highest philosophical significance. Conventionally conceptualization is supposed to hold together a series of phenomena, to situate and represent them, by definition and classification, within a scientific system. Nominalist conceptualization, for example, dissociates the phenomenon from its representation and sanctions its hierarchically determined recurrence within a conceptual arrangement. By shrinking the object to its token-like conceptualization, as it were, there is a kind of deprivation of its particularity. The abstract conceptualization enacts a kind of repression it does not reflect upon. The belief that the object can be

possessed by identifying or reducing it to its extensionless representation is denounced in almost overtly political terms as oppression. Against this Adorno directs his theory of the non-identical, which aims, in the last analysis, at the possibility of an identification with the object, but in a way which "brings object and expression close to each other up to a point of non-difference." Since only concepts can bring about what the concept precludes, the untruth of the identifying concept can be healed by increasing its number. The many cure the one. This treatment proceeds according to the category of the constellation.

28. The constellation is the point in language where a pictorial simultaneity enters linguistic sequentiality. The syntactic order of the constellation upsets the syntactic unit of the sentence, against which it adopts the fragmentary as the paradigm. Adorno's valorization of the fragmentary is based on its anti-systematic character; it resists the temptation of the closed, hierarchical system to which any finished sentence yields. In constellations the concepts gather around and surround the object, leaving gaps in between, because they fear to disfigure the object; this in its own way brings about the priority of the object.

> "Constellations alone represent, from the outside, what the concept severed within. By gathering around the object the concepts determine potentially its inner."[17]

29. The implications for aesthetic language follow suit. Insisting with Hegel on the truth-content of art, Adorno goes beyond Hegel in requiring aesthetic qualities for philosophical language. So as to resist advertisement for the world art must affirm what it negates. There is a partial affirmation that is a necessary prerequisite of any norm-centered critique; in another respect it condemns art to a ritualistic machine-like repetition of its negation. But Adorno, for whom "all works of art are a priori polemical," insists that "even in the most sublimated work of art there is concealed an 'it ought to be different.'" The artwork has to shrink from any participation in communication or even in the rhetoric of agitation, and the conditions for its existence are further restricted since "art goes to court against the work of art as meaning." In modernism the avoidance of communication extends to an avoidance of semantic phenomena: if art participated in the order of meaning it would already present itself as a form of knowledge whose guiding principle is identical with the principle governing society. If art is the social antithesis of society how can it still be invested with any critical function? Like J. D. Salinger mythologizing his own silence as an author, the muteness of the work of art retreats to an

uncommunicative for-itself, and shows its refusal to participate in the fraud which marks an integral part of the principle of exchange.

30. Art must maintain a complete distance from the social by renouncing communication and meaning. Art must differ from the social order to remain art. At the same time, however, it must at least be similar enough to its opposite in order to be possible as critique. These two conflicting demands with which modern art is confronted radicalize the critical bearing to where art must become a scene of subversion. As Adorno describes it:

> The works of art mimetically surrender to reification, their death-principle. Without an admixture of poison, virtually the negation of life, the objection of art against the repression of civilization is helplessly consoling. Art is forced by the social reality to a mimesis onto its counterpart. While art opposes society, it is nevertheless unable to occupy a standpoint beyond society; art's opposition only succeeds through an identification with what it revolts against.[18]

What we see here is an instance in which the distinction between affirmation and negation is suspended, and subverted in that suspension. Since critique can no longer serve as the reason for being for art, art now "finds its bliss in its ability to hold out." This perserverance implies a postponement of critique. This advances an "*Entkunstung.*" Art interiorizes the structures it opposes and techniques which belong to the sphere of dominating rationality are thus allowed to usurp it. Adorno's art is now that which serves as a repository for another rationality in the process of subscribing to the dominating one, an art "which does not imitate anything, but makes itself similar" and "seeks refuge in its own negation; it wants to survive through its death."[19]

31. Interestingly enough, Adorno describes Benjamin's ambiguous relationship to his contemporary philosophy as a process of *Schutzimpfung*, a kind of inoculation through the partial absorption of what is foreign. This is a means of defense which proceeds by artificially inducing a controlled outbreak of the disease in order to immunize the patient. In inoculation the protective measure is structurally indistinguishable from the disease itself: the difference between cure and disease is effaced. Accordingly, any outbreak of the disease can figure as an inoculation or defense against its next outbreak. The disappearance between cure and disease corresponds to the fact that in Adorno's ruined aesthetics the difference between affirmation and negation is suspended when one passes into the other. When art has finally surrendered to the principles of

rationality then the only conceivable cure would be that of disease curing disease. It undertakes the attempt to "heal the wound by the spear which caused it."[20]

32. The great tension in Adorno's work then is the attempt both to grasp the ultimate goal of speculative art theory, namely the truth content of the artwork, while at the same time preserving the impulse toward de-totalization. Thus the truth content of the advanced artwork can be demonstrated only through its negativity, in the way it subverts its own ground. And any work of philosophy would have to follow suit. A philosophical claim through concepts and arguments would violate the nature of the aesthetic. Adorno accepts and embraces the ruinous character of the work of art, in which all parts point to the same center but do not form a whole. In this respect *Aesthetic Theory* converges with the artwork by refusing purity and harmony, calling attention to its own contradictory nature. It seeks to sustain itself by its own impossibility. Thus the voices of Kant and Hegel, Lukacs and Benjamin, are not harmonized but used contrapuntally, each adding to the quality of the composition. In this way Adorno does not synthesize their positions in order to reach his own view as a final step of theoretical articulation. Instead, his book works out a pattern of oppositions and tensions, contradictions, and similarities, which suggest a totality without ever defining it. Hence the concept of truth is no longer stable but shifts according to a chosen perspective, while no one individual perspective is allowed to dominate the whole.

33. In this respect Adorno's aesthetic theory corresponds to the counterpoint constitution of the work of musical art, a combination of simultaneously sounding musical lines according to a system of rules. Here however one must take it as 20th century counterpoint, a corollary of the diminishing importance of tonal harmony. If the work of art is conceived of as a dynamic rather than a fixed constellation, its theoretical articulation as well calls for a perspectivist approach that can do justice to the dynamic mode of the category. No wonder the post-modernists saw in Adorno a forerunner to much of what is occurring in their theories.

34. Adorno's many works specific to music emanate from his general de-aesthetic conceptions, and follow a similarly pessimistic development. As a witness to twentieth century atrocity, Adorno locates analogous crises in twentieth-century music and correlates the two through a thesis of historical

discontinuity wherein modernism contrasts with its own traditional past in certain essential ways. The evolutionary thesis of historical development is, for Adorno, inadequate sociology because the twentieth century constitutes a betrayal of the earlier ideals of personal freedom and political equality. Equally, the thesis of formal continuity in music is inadequate aesthetics because modern music, in reaction to its own social matrix, takes on the function of criticism. Whereas traditional music signifies a certain accessibility of the work to its social institutions through performance and appreciation. For Adorno there can be no masterpieces in twentieth-century music because the imperative of protest inhibits accessibility and fosters alienation. The valuable modern work confounds the received practices of appreciation yet exemplifies the most advanced historical development of musical form.

35. Adorno construes the dialectic of musical development apocalyptically in that he sees it as having stopped, as being frozen in the extremes of its last antithesis -- between gestures of shock and a crystalline standstill. In the expressive content of radical music, passions are no longer simulated, but rather, genuine emotions of the unconscious -- of shock, of trauma -- are registered without disguise. If one goes along with the claim that music is concerned with truth, then the truth in radical music is not a pleasant one. About the general listening public, Adorno thinks that the dissonances which horrify them testify to their own conditions; for that reason alone do they find them unbearable. The inability to hear the sounds as music makes them unbearable, but then few can identify the form of appreciation that would make them music, and those few already understand the nature of the protest involved. Adorno's polarization of dialectical extremes, e.g., between "crystal" and "shock," also shows up in his distinction, within radical music, between expressionist and objective works. In one sense all radical music is expressionist in that its truth is obsessed with the ravages of the human psyche. In another sense expressionism represents the last historical stage of incomplete atonality, where vestiges of traditional form strain to preserve the music's accessibility for the general listener and thus render its expressive content both palpable and consequential. In this second sense, objective music is seen as a move away from the thesis of expression into the antithesis of indifference. Adorno says of Schoenberg's late works that they pose again the question of the content regarding subject matter, without pretending to achieve the organic unity of this content with purely musical procedures.

36. The attribution of "objectivity" to completely atonal works is surely supported by the systematic nature of the twelve-tone row. But if the row is not thoroughly articulate in, or cannot be retrieved from, the sound, the listener's volition to include the scored row in appreciation must be located elsewhere. This volition undoubtedly begins with an awareness of the music's context: the social and personal circumstances of its creation. But it proceeds through an incorporation of context into content by relocating these circumstances in the work. It concludes by relocating the work itself. The typical categories through which we distinguish appreciative ability, e.g., "layman," "connoisseur," "expert," are of little use here, for these categories are formed within the very institutions against which radical music protests.

37. The formal intransigence of the row correlates well with the seriousness of the protest. While use of the row does not preclude sensibility, it is not primarily governed by the appeal to sympathetic distributions of sound. Appreciation in atonal music cannot take as its primary function a progressive sensitivity to the quality of such distributions in performance. The historical development of radical music can be marked by failure of social accessibility. If one defines "social accessibility" as a situating of appreciation in performance, we can hypothesize that "musical protest" entails using the performance as a referent to something extraneous to it, something nonauditory which nevertheless completes and gives specific identity to the auditory. The imperatives that formed radical music necessitated relinquishing many characteristics of traditional music. These characteristics are not, as such, irreconcilable with atonality; e.g., the row can, in fact, be used to generate harmonic vertical progressions.

38. But the retention of such characteristics -- the pursuit of sympathetic sound -- produces a contemporary lie: the exaltation of feelings that accord with willful illusion, not actuality. In the expressionist phase of radical music the feelings projected are authentic, but they become increasingly hard to bear; they are fixed at their extremes. Reality is made more painful by the betrayal of hope: the failure of nineteenth-century social ideology in the situation of the twentieth. One way of coping with the pain can be found in play, in a retreat to illusion where other identities supplant or replace one's own. But in music Adorno sees this as a corruption of integrity, a historical recidivism to be rejected. Another way out is through a forced indifference to feeling, through an autodissection where feelings lose their interconnectedness in organic

subjective experience and are reconstituted in abstract arrays. Here even the desire for accessibility is relinquished, yet for Adorno this constitutes progress: another historical veil has been pulled aside and the value of what remains has been affirmed.

39.   Ultimately Adorno's thinking lies in his innovative points regarding dialectics. Normally under hegelian thinking one would anticipate the supercession (*Aufhebung*) of opposite terms, thesis and synthesis. Adorno stalls the dialectic in a kind of *zugzwang*; the autonomy of art lies precisely in this stall, this inability of the artwork to synthesize. Without synthesis, the movement falters, and the work's non-identity remains intact. And what is maddening is the degree to which Adorno's own analysis of this process with regard to the artwork initiates a negation ancillary to the negation implicit in an artwork's original non-identity. Add to this the insight that Adorno articulates his arguments from the position of art looking back in retrospect on moments whose falsity the work has already negated, like the cultural position of the art it describes, it follows that every social whole is already untrue. Adorno's philosophizing must be understood as an artwork as meticulous and as self-conscious as Nietzsche's *Zarathustra*.

40. The left rejected Adorno's *Aesthetic Theory* because its conclusions gave the appearance of adherence to a fixed conception of ethical autonomy. At first blush, since from the perspective of art that has already negated its social-historical context, it appears autonomous. The strategy of adopting the voice of art itself as a means of avoiding a reified concept of autonomy gave Adorno's opponents the impression that he had given up on political activism. But the fact is that Adorno's view could never have met such demands. There is no articulation of hypothetical alternatives, since that would sustain precisely the prevailing discourse by appealing to pre-tolerated avenues of dissent. Negation would be neutralized as quickly as the ad executives confiscating the most recent "hip-hop" innovations contractually composed for soap commercials. Rather, what is best is when the artwork stalls even this temptation to oppose. The futility of protest, in its false sense of beatitude, lies in the mistaken presumption that one can detach enough so as to actually offer an alternative that does not subscribe to the same repressive forces. Instead of offering already spelled-out alternatives through protest, ones in which the t-shirt industry is already poised with mass production printings for its pre-selected

sayings, Adorno sees in the "stall" a holding open of the crisis generated into an entirely unanticipated unknown.

XIII. Husserl's "Unthought Axiomatic" and Derrida's Critique

Derrida's first detailed criticism of Husserl's phenomenology was published in France in 1962. A revised edition appeared in 1974, and Leavey's English translation first appeared in 1978 as *Edmund Husserl's Origin of Geometry: An Introduction*. Rather than dealing with Husserl's specific essay, *Die Frage nach dem Ursprung der Geometrie als intentional-historisches Problem*, Derrida's was more a catalyst for confronting the entirety of Husserl's phenomenological project more generally. More expanded treatments of Husserl occur in Derrida's formidable *La voix et le phénomenè* and in an earlier essay "Genesis and Structure" in *Writing and Difference*, and in a host of earlier and later book reviews and essays.[1] As late as 1980 Derrida was declaring that the problems confronted in his work on Husserl "continued to organize all of the work he subsequently attempted."[2] The reception of Derrida's critique was decidedly mixed, however. Some of the first generation of commentators saw Derrida's critique holding to the highest standards of scholarly rigor. Thus Newton Garver described Derrida's criticisms of Husserl to be a "first class piece of analytical work in the philosophy of language."[3] Richard Rorty described the criticisms as a "first-class, highly professional job on Husserl."[4] David Wood described the criticisms in *Speech and Phenomena* as a "detailed and scholarly analysis of Husserl."[5] And Hans-Georg Gadamer took Derrida's accomplishment to be a "quite accurate criticism of Husserl's *Logical Investigations* and of his concept of *Kundgabe*."[6] Other voices rejected Derrida's achievement. J. Claude Evans, in a book-length study, concluded that Derrida's readings of Husserl are "condemned to failure" and "fail to live up to their own standards of rigor."[7] Alan White concluded that "Derrida's critique fails" and was "vitiated by inconsistent acknowledgements of some Husserlian teachings, and by clear misinterpretations of others."[8] Rorty has also said that "a lot of Derrida's arguments are just awful."[9] Dane Depp sought to demonstrate that Derrida's most specific criticisms "fail to undermine any tenets crucial to Husserlian phenomenology."[10] More pointed criticisms also emerged, such as John Searle describing Derrida's "low level of philosophical argumentation, the deliberate obscurantism of prose, the wildly exaggerated claims, and the constant striving to give the appearance of profundity by making claims that seem paradoxical, but under analysis often turn out to be silly or trivial."[11] Kevin Mulligan derided

Derrida's "inflationary Parisian fashion" in his well-argued but derisively titled: "How Not to Read: Derrida on Husserl."[12] John Scanlon topped all other critics in molten language by describing Derrida's work on Husserl as a "sophisticated parody of a pompously pedantic exegesis of the first chapter of the first of Husserl's *Logical Investigations*, a bumbling product of a fictitious exegete whose reading is dictated throughout by a pedantic fixation upon the conceit that the text being interpreted must, in every respect, be subordinated to a mythic master text known as the metaphysics of presence."[13]

Despite the mutually abusive and score-settling soquacities of the secondary literature, the next generation of criticism has taken a step back from point-scoring extrapolations of individual arguments or works and has sought to situate Derrida's critiques in broader interpretative contexts, since many of the initial criticisms stemmed from a violation of the basic hermeneutical rule of reconstructing the contexts of the discussions. This is no small task, since to reassemble all of the parts of the Husserlian philosophical project, and the contexts of Derrida's criticisms as part of his deconstructive program, is an immense undertaking. Thus anthologies devoted to Derrida's reading of Husserl have appeared, as have entire books on Derrida's relation to phenomenology more generally.[14] Some have even argued that Derrida's analysis of Husserl's "unthought axiomatic" can now be seen to be regulative for the entire deconstructive project. Many still hold that the frivolity of Derrida's project can yet be gleaned from these early Husserl texts "when Derrida still argued."[15] My modest goal will simply be to provide a further overview of a few of these contexts, and to try to get to a position to be able to see that Derrida's criticisms are certainly something more than satire, something less than a refutation of Husserl's arguments, and something different from being the lynchpin to explain deconstruction's having been invented.

Husserl's Philosophical Project

It is widely held that Husserl was not well served by historical circumstances. An assimilated Jew, his career coincided with the growth of German nationalism. He suffered from never being fully topical in his own country. Phenomenology was not publicly complete as a doctrine until 1913, and lost momentum in the war. Nietzsche was the philosopher of the German trenches, as phenomenology did not provide comfort under fire nor inspiration for self-sacrifice. Then, Husserl was unlucky in having the genius Heidegger as his protege, whose *Being and Time* supplanted attention to the master. The study of Husserl has fallen mainly to the study of specialized schools, although it has proved attractive to Catholic philosophers, who see in Husserl an erstwhile rehabilitation of Aristotelian categories. Husserl did not recognize himself in the project of Heidegger's *Being and Time*. He dimly saw how his attempt to refound the scientificity of philosophy was to be transformed into both a destruction of metaphysical rationality and a descriptive analysis of the elementary structures of existence. Before we can survey the terrain of all of the turns of the phenomenological movement foreign to his ideals of philosophy as a rigorous science, whether they be Heidegger's or Derrida's or anyone else's, we must again familiarize ourselves, at least in outline, with his overall philosophical project, and its emergence out of the general conditions of *lebensphilosophie*, in which consciousness was taken to be the basis for all experience. Somehow it is out of consciousness that the achievements of ideal, timeless meanings were grasped. Husserl was simply fascinated by this process, how out of consciousness we grasp transcendent truths and objects. And since consciousness is always particularized as someone or other's consciousness, philosophy must begin with the rigorous self-examination. He also came to work more on the shared sphere of understanding, the *lebenswelt* or life-world. But beneath this there is the project of first philosophy, the relation between being and knowing. His insight, taken from Brentano and James, is that consciousness was the condition of all experience, that it constituted the world, in such a way that the role of consciousness was obscured and not easy to isolate and describe. So the task of philosophy was to overcome prejudices in the recognition of a realm of pure consciousness. Husserl really saw himself as an explorer in the domain of the a priori science of pure consciousness and transcendental subjectivity.

Phenomenology is derived from two Greek words, "*phainomenon*" meaning an appearance, and "*logos*" meaning reason or word, hence a reasoned inquiry. An appearance is anything of which one is conscious. Anything at all that appears to consciousness is a legitimate area of philosophical investigation. For many phenomenologists, an appearance is a manifestation of the essence of that of which it is the appearance. In the 19th century philosophy was developing along the paths which attempted to treat consciousness as an empirical phenomenon that can be investigated by the quantitative methods of natural science. Phenomenology rejects this approach and insists that such methods are simply not adequate to treat the nature of consciousness for principally two reasons: (1) consciousness itself is not an object among other objects in nature, and (2) there are conscious phenomena which cannot be dealt with adequately by means of quantitative methods of experimental science. A merely scientific approach to the study of consciousness led to a severe constriction of the scope of philosophical thinking. The spectacular success of natural science in describing the physical world had given rise to the conviction that there was nothing about the world that was not capable of being investigated by empirical means. Just as philosophy was viewed as the handmaiden to theology in the medieval period, so now many took philosophy to be the handmaiden to the sciences in the 19th century; its role was not to question the assumptions of science or to clarify the concepts implicit in scientific activity but only to explicate certain problems arising in logic.

Husserl began as a mathematician with a "psychologist" bent. Psychologism was the effort to reduce philosophical and mathematical questions to psychology. For Husserl's purposes, it is the doctrine that all "science" is ultimately empirical. All concepts, a priori and empirical, are based on abstractions from experience. Thus there is no difference between necessary and contingent truths. Like Hume, a psychologist would claim that our knowledge of cause and effect is no more than a mental habit of association based on the experiences of constant conjunction. Similarly "validity" is explained not by appeal to rules of logic but by appeal to empirically well-founded laws about what people do in fact think. Psychologism seems particularly plausible if we regard mental phenomena as acts. An act, understood as an event in time, seems to fit well with the model of science as concerned with all things that arise within a time-bound causal nexus. Human thoughts arise as the effect of some cause or other, and proceed in their turn to have further effects. Logic, from such a standpoint, is merely the study and, perhaps, manipulation of such causal sequences. Husserl's dissertation was a psychological analysis of the concept of number, an application of Brentano psychologizing to one basic problem of the foundations of mathematics. The dissertation became his first major work, *The Philosophy of Arithmetic*, in which the concept of number and the laws of arithmetic were reduced to well-confirmed hypotheses governing the experience of counting.[16] A philosophical idea—the notion of number—is clarified by finding the experiential origin of that idea. Thus Husserl argues that the idea of number is derived from the idea of multiplicity, which in turn in derived from the idea of collective association, which is observed only through reflection of the psychical act through which totality is realized. The philosophical anaysis of number reduces to an analysis of this mental act. Husserl takes this idea from Brentano and basically applies it to all symbolic forms—geometry and logic as well as arithmetic.

Husserl's early enthusiasm for psychologism was destroyed by an assault on all types of reductions of arithmetic and logic to psychology by the great German mathematician Frege. In his *Fundamental Laws of Arithmetic* he gave a general argument against the psychologistic approach to studies in the foundations of arithmetic.[17] A psychological generalization depends on the contingent facts about what people happen to think; a mathematical law states what is necessarily true whether or not anyone happens to think it. The statement of the validity of the propositions of mathematics is independent of any inductive evidence in favor of a hypothesis. Frege thus argues that the laws of mathematics are a priori and not empirical, but against Kant argues that the laws are not synthetic a priori but analytic a priori. In 1894 Frege applied this attack on psychologism to Husserl's work, complaining that Husserl's use of the concept of "idea" confused the ideas or propositions of arithmetic with the ideas people had about arithmetic. Husserl's reaction to Frege's onslaught was admirable. So impressed was he that he stopped publication of the projected second volume of the *Philosophy of Arithmetic*, and completely abandoned his psychologistic training in philosophy.

Such an awakening from his dogmatic slumbers was this that a great deal of the rest of Husserl's work could be said to be marked by his reaction to his own former psychologizing. Now impelled to once again take up the Cartesian and Kantian projects to ground the empirical sciences, pure logic, and epistemology, Husserl argued that philosophy had to be defended against the aggressive psychologism of an empirical scientific explanation of intellectual operations. Psychology had begun to treat the activities of consciousness as objective facts, to be studied by the methods of scientific investigation. In order for it to do this, it was necessary to demonstrate the pure and a priori nature of logic. Scientific psychology could not explain what thinking was, since its activity depends on the formal principles and logical rules which determine all thought. Husserl thought he could accomplish this by embracing a science of phenomena more basic and more foundational than any knowledge possible by the existing sciences. The main project of the *Logical Investigations* was to demonstrate that science requires positing meaning unities that are irreducible to the factually occurrent entities of the physical world.[18] Now the idea that logic and arithmetic reduce to, or are explained by, the psychological acts wherein logical and mathematical concepts operate and originate, are under attack. Husserl now comes to see psychologism was a kind of betrayal of the very essence of logic, so it was necessary to separate the objects of logic, thoughts, from all factually occurring psychic processes. Psychology is a purely factual, empirical science of consciousness—its laws are generalizations from experience. The laws of logic however are universal, ideal, and exact. Furthermore logic is an apriori science, and hence cannot be based on some science of fact. Logic makes no assumptions about the existence of mental states. To collapse these distinctions is, according to Husserl, to embrace relativism and subjectivism, which is to collapse into absurdity (*Widersinn*). He also condemns it as a species of anthropology, that truth is simply relative to the human species. For Husserl truth does not depend on any facts, including facts of human nature.

In *Logical Investigations* he begins anew, then, agreeing with Frege that natural science could not establish the foundations of mathematics or philosophy, so he develops an entirely new source of such foundations, a new science of phenomena, a *phenomenology*. What is this science of phenomena? Husserl starts with conscious experiences, which he does not treat like an object of science, like a real datum in the world which merely bears the special mark of the mental. Rather, it is all a matter of a peculiar concentration on phenomena. The concept of phenomenology is thus to be understood principally in the sense of a method. *After all those presuppositions of existence which are regarded in the natural attitude of our consciousness as self-evident have been artificially excluded, the pure contents of what is present in consciousness are to be described.* We need to artificially disregard the interpretations of conscious experiences in our everyday life in the world by bracketing those experiences in the *epoche*, which then gives us the pure content of those experiences free of subjective modifications. Unfortunately Husserl refers to phenomenology as *descriptive psychology*. If logic rests on psychology, what was the point of making a critique of psychologism? Husserl spent a great deal of time defending that phenomenology and psychology were radically different kinds of projects. For him, phenomenology maps out apriori essences, entirely distinct from the factual embodiments of cognition in humans or animals.

Thus Husserlian phenomenology begins with the suspending of all immediate presuppositions about the objective world and the withdrawal into the subjective consciousness. But this does not lead to solipsism, because from the outset consciousness is conceived of as *consciousness of something*. The elementary structure of consciousness is so constituted that there is no such thing as a consciousness without a content. Consciousness fundamentally refers to something beyond itself, adopting Brentano's notion of intentionality.

Consciousness always involves a directedness on to something other than itself. For Husserl, a gaze directed on consciousness, free from contingent assumptions and subjective intuitions would not shrink into nothing but would give insight into the relatedness of contents of all kinds. In the *Logical Investigations* he characterizes phenomenology as a pure descriptive science of consciousness, which presupposes nothing about what it is describing other than what is given in intuitive evidence, a concrete science foregoing abstract speculative theorising like in traditional metaphysics. Constant employment of phenomenological reduction gives us access to a transcendental field of pure experience and prevents us from lapsing back into psychologism, naturalism and relativism. As he famously proclaims in the Introduction to the *Logical Investigations: Wir wollen auf die Sachen selbst zuruckgehen.* This is not some mere interest in scientific facts; nor is it a reference to the Kantian *Ding an sich.* His point is that we cannot be satisfied with employing concepts whose evidential basis has not been properly clarified by being brought back to their original sources in intuition. The things themselves are thus for Husserl immediately intuited essential elements of consciousness, viewed not as psychological processes, but in terms of their essential natures as meaning-intentions and fulfillments. The logical investigations are concerned with analysing the most basic elements which are required for any form of knowledge whatsoever. Phenomenology is the apriori investigation of the ideal meaning structures which are the ground for all other areas of inquiry.

By the time of the publication of *Ideas I*, Husserl was committed not just to the apriori realm of mathematics or logic but a science of essences which would provide the essential grounding for all fields of inquiry.[19] Phenomenology could describe not just the region of conscious experiences but all material regions of being, from geometry to morality, eventually addressing all conscious experiences, their correlates, and their essential structures. Phenomenology becomes a philosophy of the 'infinite task' of pure description. By now he had taken a transcendental turn. Phenomenology must explore not just the essential structures of all conscious experiences and their intentional objects but the rootedness of these essences in a transcendental realm. The goal was still to root out all naturalistic presuppositions about consciousness. Thus transcendental phenomenology gets purified of all naturalistic tendencies. In *Ideas* he gives his principle of principles: *every originary presentive intuition is a legitimizing source of cognition, that everything originally offered to us in intuition is to be accepted simply as what it is presented as being.*

Every rational activity begins with assumptions about the nature of its activity, the object being investigated, and the method appropriate to this kind of inquiry. Phenomenologists sought an avenue to investigate all possible presuppositions concerning the nature of what was real. Their approach is to seek to simply suspend all judgments about such matters until they can be founded on a more certain basis. This suspension of the "natural attitude," as Husserl called it, was labeled by him the phenomenological *epoche*, the multi-layered Greek word from Sextus Empiricus' *Outlines of Pyrrhonism* conveying an artificial maneuver of abstention, dislocation, exclusion, disregarding, or abandoning. Having performed this *epoche*, philosophy begins its description and clarification of consciousness unencumbered by the assumptions of the natural attitude. This was to give philosophy a starting point free from the presuppositions which mask hidden assumptions about the nature of reality. Like Descartes, skepticism's own lack of commitment to assertion could prove to be the very tool needed to overcome skepticism. We use it to suspend the natural standpoint. We switch off their thetic character—thesis, a proposal, an act of positing *setzung*. All features of conscious experience must be taken as they appear, without our attempting in the slightest ways to characterize them as valid, or real or true or illusory. It is the correlate to Descartes' notion of objective reality—performing the *epoche* gets us to the essential structures and contents of the experiences. Consider a phenomenologist before a desk. What is assumed at this point in the inquiry concerning a desk? Not the spatio-temporal world; none of the scientific theories which are used to interpret the world of existence; no independent or continuous existence; no other human beings; not one's own bodily existence; not the ideal science of pure logic. In short nothing is assumed, only the self-validating cognitive experience itself. Nor are such elements to be doubted—that would be a negative presupposition. The aim of phenomenology is to suspend all such questions while turning to the content of consciousness itself.

Husserl thus attempted to rekindle Europeans waning faith in the possibility of rational certainty. This universal phenomenology of consciousness is the same for every consciousness and can be made into an absolutely apodictically certain science. He was convinced we could gain access to the essential features of all phenomena manifest to consciousness, regardless of their actuality, without regard to the consequences of their being actual entities in the real world. Just like Descartes Husserl believes that mental acts such as thinking, believing, perceiving, imagining, etc., appear with complete self-evident givenness because they are wholly present to themselves. Even if the object of such acts is not presented in a wholly fulfilled fashion, the act itself is presented with complete adequacy. Husserl advances beyond Descartes by discovering an additional realm for which the evidence is adequate: the realm of senses. He defines this realm by performing a certain operation which he calls "transcendental" (or phenomenological) reduction. In lived experience one naturally takes the objects of perception to be independent of consciousness. Husserl's reduction neutralizes this assumption. One simply suspends belief in the actual existence of the world and brackets the existence-status of any object of any mental act; one regards all objects of all types of acts as mere suppositions, as possible meanings or senses, that can be used by the ego that survives the bracketing of the world. A "sense" is an object of any mental act taken as supposed, as purely intended. Senses, the objective correlates of mental acts, survive the suspension of the natural or common-sense standpoint; they constitute the reality of "phenomena" that is the principal theme of Husserl's investigations. In contrast to naturalism, Husserl believed all knowledge, all science, all rationality depended on conscious acts, acts which cannot be understood from within the natural standpoint at all, for that would be to fall back into psychologism. Consciousness should not be viewed as part of the world at all. Consciousness does not create the world—that would be idealism. Since consciousness is presupposed in all science and knowledge then the study of consciousness must be a transcendental one. Phenomenology is thus now the science of essences of consciousness and of the ideal essences of the objective correlates of conscious acts, and how to arrive at them without construing them psychologistically.

Heidegger's Critique of Husserl in *Prolegomena*

What much of the Derrida-Husserl scholarship overlooks is the degree to which Derrida's criticisms are indebted to Heidegger. Perhaps in turn this is due to an over-reliance on *Being and Time*, in which Husserl is only indirectly mentioned, and more often with regard to expressions of gratitude. The terms of these inquiries are instead laid down in the other major lecture courses of the Marburg era which reveal completely the nuanced and extremely deep analysis of Husserlian phenomenology. In *Prolegomena to the History of the Concept of Time*, a lecture course in Marburg in the summer of 1925, in many ways a first draft of *Being and Time*, and *Basic Problems of Phenomenology*, a course given shortly after the publication of *Being and Time*, Heidegger grounds his analysis of Husserl in terms of the works of Husserl then available in print, the *Logical Investigations*, the paper on *Philosophy as a Rigorous Science*, and the first volume of *Ideas*.[20]

These lecture courses reveal that the decisive categories Heidegger credits to Husserlian phenomenology are intentionality, categorical intuition, and the original sense of the a priori. Intentionality is the structure of lived experiences and not just a supplementary relation.[21] Husserl reveals how the basic constitution of intentionality is a reciprocal belonging together of *intentio* and *intentum*.[22] The area of categorical intuition receives the most attention, as it is the most modest of intentionalities, the perception of things, and the identification of the constituents in entities were designated as categories in crude form by the Greeks. At work beneath those apprehensions, however, was an identifying fulfillment of the intentional presuming, or intending. Such presuming or intending, empty at first, reaches fulfillment when what it aims at or intends, its intentional correlate, at first devoid of any intuitive givenness, achieves this givenness in the form of a state of affairs given in an original manner to intuition, i.e., to perception. When one considers the sequence of the initial empty intending and the intuitive seeing that provides it with a fulfillment, it appears that the seeing is an act of identification. In a long and complex analysis, Heidegger demonstrates that the founded act of categorial intuition, as a founded act, is not a formal repetition, at the level of ideality, of the founding act. Instead, categorial intuition allows us to see how sense perception is already intrinsically pervaded by categorial intuition.[23]

Heidegger's praise for Husserl's discoveries are accompanied with reservations that must be investigated more closely. Husserl fails to see intentionality as but an initial approach toward overcoming the uncritical application of traditionally defined realities. "If such a task is implicit in this basic concept of phenomenology, then "intentionality" is the very last word to be used as a phenomenological slogan. Quite the contrary, it identifies that whose disclosure would allow phenomenology to find itself in its possibilities."[24] If it were the case that the Husserlian exploration of intentionality was accompanied with the continuing acceptance of a certain number of traditional unquestioned notions, the whole notion of phenomenology as some presuppositionless starting point is botched. In spite of the stress placed on the pure seeing of the matters themselves and on the necessity of avoiding all non-critical presuppositions, Husserl's own presuppositions condition each and every step of his approach. We would be justified in applying to Husserl himself what he says of Descartes, that "for him, to discover and to abandon were the same."[25]

The list of presuppositions Heidegger reveals is complex, but a few preliminary remarks can spell out their scope. Husserl speaks of the notion of the "natural attitude" as though it characterizes the comportment not only of each and every individual in everydayness, but of the scientists as well. Heidegger asks: does man really experience himself as a ζοον, as a living being? Does humanity experience itself zoologically? The suggestion is that this characterization of humanity's spontaneous manner of experience phenomenologically is not seen in the phenomenon but is a determination projected by the philosopher on the basis of a well-defined theoretical position, in which every entity is taken a priori as a lawfully regulated flow of occurrences in the spatio-temporal exteriority of the world."[26] The very fact that ordinary experience is termed an attitude is already an admission of a posture that is nothing spontaneous but a comportment one adopts deliberately. Thus Husserl's so-called natural attitude is an artificial one, corresponding more to the way modern science has considered nature since Descartes than to the everydayness of humanity.[27]

This has severe ramifications for Husserlian phenomenology, which was to begin with a bracketing of what it calls the natural attitude, for Heidegger's analysis has seemingly revealed that the bracketing has precisely been motivated by what it suspends. What is bracketed is an attitude pre-secured for the completion of phenomenology as a science, and its prerequisite organization of experienced reality in sequences of spatio-temporal events taken from within a globally regulated totality of nature. This attitude is then supposed to apply not only to humanity's everyday experience, but also the theoretical comportment of the modern scientist in her exploration of nature, and to the epistemological theorist who adopts the comportment of the modern scientist. The *epoche* however is secretly guided by only one of these modalities, and by characteristics taken from what it brackets. It is no surprise that the only definition of metaphysics given by Husserl in the *Idea of Phenomenology* is the distinction between nature and spirit, between two ontic regions presupposing a metaphysics that can be satisfied with the Cartesian distinction between *res extensa* and *res cogitans*, a distinction reiterated in Kant, in Hegel, and in neo-Kantianism. The very distinction indicates for Heidegger that the thematic field of phenomenology is not a going back to the things themselves, just a going back to convenient traditional metaphysical categories.[28]

Heidegger continues his analysis of Husserl's ontological presuppositions in his discussion of the four characteristics of pure consciousness given by Husserl, namely, consciousness as characterized by immanence, as an absolute datum, as marked by the property of being absolutely given, and as pure being.[29] While this is not the place for detailed examination of these complex readings, in general the examination of these four determinations of consciousness shows that Husserl's delimitation of the thematic field of phenomenology and his use of the notion of Being for that purpose were not guided by any overt ontological concern but instead again by a scientific project, mapped on to the idea, Cartesian in origin, of an absolute science whose site is in consciousness. This lack of overt ontological concern in the end betrays a position of ontological neglect. The mode of access is phenomenological reduction which neglects that actual existence of our lived experiences, and abstracts from their individuation, from the property that each has of being mine. Were there an entity whose essence is precisely to be, and nothing but to be, then Husserl's merely eidetic seeing would be the most fundamental of misunderstandings.[30] Such an entity of course is precisely the one that we are, Dasein, an existing which is strictly individuated. By canceling at the outset the features of facticity and mineness of the intentional entity, Husserl neglects in principle the mode of being of the being endowed with intentionality in the first place.

> In elaborating intentionality as the thematic field of phenomenology, the question of the being of the intentional is left undiscussed. It is not raised in the field thus secured, pure consciousness; indeed, it is flatly rejected as nonsensical. In the course of securing this field, in the reduction, it is expressly deferred. And where the determinations of being are brought into play, as in the starting position of the reduction, it is likewise not originally raised. Instead, the being of the acts [the intentional acts which for Husserl are the *cogitationes*] is in advance theoretically and dogmatically defined by the senses of being which is taken from the reality of nature. The question of being itself is left undiscussed.[31]

Heidegger's criticism, then, is that each stage of Husserl's phenomenology confirms the persistence of the neglect of the being of the entity endowed with intentionality and the neglect of the meaning of being in general. These oversights inform one another, since it is precisely because it was postulated that there is no other meaning for being than occurring as a thing in the world understood as nature, that the question of the meaning of being of the intentional being is avoided.

Basic Problems also expresses the acknowledgement of the Husserlian legacy in fundamental ontology. This legacy is connected to the fact that the definitions laid out by the first of Husserl's *Logical Investigations* are important, especially in their distinguishing *Bedeutung* from sign, mark, and designation.

> The sign-function of the written as opposed to the spoken is altogether different from the sign-function of the spoken as opposed to what is *Bedeutet* in speech, and conversely altogether different from the function of the written, of writing, as opposed to that which is aimed at in it. Implicit here are a multiplicity of symbolic relations which are very difficult to grasp in their elementary structure and require extensive investigations. Some inquiries of this kind are to be found, as supplements to Husserl's investigations, in *Being and Time*, the orientation there being toward principles. Today the symbol has become a favorite formula, but those who use it either dispense with any investigation as to what is generally meant by it or else have no suspicion of the difficulties that are coincealed in this verbal slogan.[32]

Heidegger had praised Husserl's decisive discovery of *kategoriale Anschauung*, categorical intuition. *Anschauen* in German is the equivalent of the Greek *theorein* which is present in the core of the Heideggerian characterization of the *logos*, and is one of the focal points of Derrida's later discussions. The Husserlian notion that discourse is first of all enunciative, that it is essentially made of assertions and therefore falls within the philosophical competence of logic, forms a thematic totality Heidegger is far from endorsing. *Being and Time* had famously maintained (in Section 33) that assertion is not at all an originary mode of discourse and that discourse is primarily interpretive in nature, consisting in apprehending states of affairs as having this or that meaning, so that assertions are nothing but a derivative mode of interpretation. This criticism is foreshadowed in the 1925 lecture course in the insistence with which Heidegger maintains that discourse is a possibility of the being of Dasein and therefore "that the sense of a scientific logic is the elaboration of this a priori structure of discourse in Dasein the elaboration of the possibilities and kinds of interpretation."[33]

All of the seeds of Derrida's displacing of Husserl's doctrine of *Bedeutung* are to be found here. Inasmuch as it means something, (*bedeutet*) discourse depends on a complex set of idealities—forms and categories which are nonetheless offered to an intuition that is ideal, and no longer sensible, namely, the so-called categorial intuition. Ultimately, therefore, the *Bedeutungen* that discourse expresses are based on the intuitive seeing of these idealities. It is thanks to their *Anschauung* that discourse is capable of expressedness. As Heidegger puts it: "It is not so much that we see objects and things but rather that we first talk about them. To put it more precisely: we do not say what we see, but rather the reverse, we see what one says about the matter."[34]

Derrida's Critique of Husserl in *Origins of Geometry*

Just as it is often said that the entire 19th century is reacting against Hegel, so too could one say that the entire 20th century is reacting against Husserl. The German detours through the thought of Heidegger, Scheler, and Fink remain extremely influential. Now with 75 years of perspective on its brilliant French sequels, the original reception of Husserl in France appears to us to have been at once both an oversimplification and an explosion of exceptional talents such as Sartre, Merleau-Ponty, Levinas, and Ricoeur, doing intensely original things with a new methodology. One need look no further for this phenomenon than Sartre's brilliant and reckless existential appropriations of Husserlian categories in the thirties. In *Transcendence of the Ego* Sartre was detaching the Husserlian cogito from Cartesianism and attacking what he presented to be Husserl's return to the classical thesis of the transcendental. In his 1939 article on intentionality, Sartre cast Husserl's project in the most glittering and sensational colors, as "reinstalling the horror and the charm in things."[35] *Being and Nothingness* and the *Psychology of Imagination* proved to be extremely intelligent and provocative works, even if unfaithful to the master, stimulating phenomenological research and completely refertilizing French philosophy. After the war French phenomenological investigations continued to move phenomenological ontology toward ethical and political contexts. Ricouer's 1950 translation of Husserl's *Ideen I* reconvened reflection on transcendental idealism in France.[36] In the mid-fifties Merleau-Ponty anchors the investigations of his *Phenomenology of Perception* in Husserl's works on genetic phenomenology.[37] By the late fifties Levinas, in arguments very similar to what we will see in Derrida, questions the self-presence of the transcendental Ego and its ability to experience the world external to itself.[38] One must thus understand Derrida's thinking as parallel to and its tone the beneficiary of an entire generation of French scholars for whom phenomenology was both "heideggerized," and was not all of philosophy, and would not allow it to merely parade its merits or overestimate its possibilities.

Derrida's analyses of Husserl in *Speech and Phenomena* and *Of Grammatology* are connected with an examination of the effects of structuralist thinking in criticism, philosophy, and the human sciences. Philosophy has constantly sought the structuralist imperative, to try to fix the limits of discourse of knowledge and the truth claims of universal reason. What structuralism leaves out is precisely the excess of meaning over form, the fact that certain elements (like force or signification) always escape structural determination. This is why Derrida pursues relations between structuralism and phenomenology, interrogating Husserl in "Genesis and Structure." Husserl shows how both structuralism and phenomenology are caught up in an endless process of reciprocal questioning which allows for no final synthesis.

On the one hand Husserl wanted to establish that the truths of science like geometry were a priori truths, unchangeably vested in the nature of human reason. He thus set out to rethink its grounding assumptions in such a way that their history and genesis, the record of geometric discovery from Euclid down, could be thought of as somehow prefigured in its origins, simply awaiting their historical turn. For Husserl it is imperative to save such primordial intuitions by explaining (1) how their logic is reactivated in each subsequent reflection on that founding moment; (2) how geometry only has a history insofar as it involves thinking back to a pure origin or moment, and (3) how the a priori character of geometric truth is ideally unaffected by errors and distortions attendant on the process of historical transmission. In other words, Husserl thinks of geometry as a paradigm or test case for the method of transcendental phenomenology which might secure science and all forms of knowledge against the threat of unbridled relativism. This would point to the ultimate grounding of knowledge and perception which cannot be doubted since experience itself is unthinkable without them.

Derrida thinks of Husserl's effort to be at once a philosophy turned back toward its origins and seeking to enclose all the history of thought in a moment of pure, self-present understanding. His criticism turns on the fact that Husserl cannot conceptualize geometry or its source of its primordial intuitions without in the process deploying a language of inscription, writing, or graphic representation, and this affects not only the ideal objectivities of geometric truth but also that concept of a timeless access to such truths through a perfectly repeatable interplay of present intuition and past discovery. For Derrida it is only in terms of *writing* that Husserl can represent geometry as a form of universal knowledge.

Derrida's introduction to Husserl's *Origin of Geometry* poses the question of the proto-geometer who, in a flight of pure thought, on a certain day, in a certain place, created geometry *ex nihilo*. Although the proto-geometer had at his disposal a set of givens of a pre-scientific culture, he did not know of anything like geometry. Husserl invites us to recreate the proto-constitution of geometry via phenomenological introspection. For although geometry was no doubt created in an empirical event, the sense of that creation did not disappear but remains inscribed, as distant sedimentation, in the acquired notion of geometry. Phenomenological retrogression will not tell us how geometry actually did originate, but it will inform us as to how geometry must originate, the supra-empirical requirements for its eruption one day into the pre-geometric world. The a priori of geometry is ahistorical only insofar as it needs no call to fact to establish its existence; but once, in a reduction, the entirety of the empirical world is bracketed, including a history of facts, what remains is the profound historicity of the creation of mathematical ideality. Husserl believed geometry to share constitution by the transcendental ego with the rest of the transcendental world. The crisis of European thought for him was how science and philosophy have forgotten their origins, and built unfounded conclusion upon conclusion. Only phenomenology could purge science and philosophy, restore them to their proper course and check their headless proliferation. Only phenomenology was capable of descending the layers of sense deposited by science, of which geometry is paradigmatic, and by illuminating its origins, relocate its *telos*.

The instauration of geometry is a beginning of philosophy. Geometry commences when morphological ideality, which is linked to empiricism, to factuality, to all that is non-phenomenological, is disrupted by a *pure thought*, the first thought which can truly be called philosophical. This pure thought transgresses the entirety of the natural world and deposits truth as ideality. It is the first philosophical gesture if by philosophy we mean, as Husserl thought, the systematic description of pure possibilities that subtend any possible real world. It is absolutely essential that the purity of the first geometric thought be rigorously maintained; it must proceed from nothing, from non-geometry, and by a passage to the limit produce geometry as an ideal possibility.

Here Derrida begins his interpretive itinerary. How are we to understand a pure thought and a passage to the limit? If before this pure thought geometry as such did not exist, how can a passage to the limit both create it and recognize it as geometry? Derrida points to a surprising silence of Husserl's part here. In his most concrete formulations, Husserl associates a passage to the limit with the idea in the Kantian sense, with the prescription of complete givenness for a content which itself is infinite. We are thus invited to think of the proto-geometer's flight of pure thought as being under the authorization of the Kantian idea. If we are to understand the former, we should subject the latter to phenomenological analysis. But here we reach an impasse. The content of a

Kantian idea is the sole phenomenological object to be "screened from vision," so to speak. Althought the idea, the completion in consciousness of an infinite series, produces ideality as that which is visible, its content, that of which it is the idea, is an intention deprived of the possibility of fulfillment by intuition. The content of the idea, precisely because it is infinite, is deprived of phenomenality; yet paradoxically, because the idea alone allows for the crystallization of pure facticity into objectivity, it is an absolutely essential condition for phenomenality in general. Husserl never stopped considering the *noema* as a manifold of perspective in temporal flux whose unity as the same X is indubitable precisely because of the presence of the Kantian idea. The idea is therefore not one phenomenological tool among others but the guarantee of a relation to objectivity in general, the guarantee of temporal integrity within the fundamental levels of pure consciousness.

Derrida strikes at the structure of the Kantian idea. Husserl was forced to maintain that the jump to geometric ideality must be an absolute break with pre-geometry, one not mediated by anything in the world and therefore one that is not temporally extended (punctuality being the guarantee against spacing, or spatiality in general). Yet, Derrida, argues, *does not the idea, whose presence is essential to intentionality inasmuch as it is the vehicle for the constitution of the content of consciousness, function by anticipating that content before it is constituted as a noema?* The Kantian idea is the anticipation of that ideal content which guides the initial passage to the limit and allows the proto-geometer to recognize geometry when he creates it; the idea is the extraordinary agency by which intentionality creates ideality by having it already "in mind."

It is a passage, and therefore temporal, but an unheard of temporality. For the logic of the idea demands a re-examination of the concept of origin, of a first-time. *The proto-geometer's initial flight, because it was mediated by the idea, was of necessity guided by the presence of something like geometry. We are led to the unthinkable conclusion that ideality precedes its own protoconstitution.* But it is not ideality in the full presence of itself that precedes its solidification in consciousness as a phenomenological object, but a trace of ideality that is structurally implicated in any primordial constitution. The strange temporality of the idea, which places effect before cause, can be called temporality only by a metaphor which has no ontic grounding. Similarly, the trace of the object which precedes its consitution is no longer conceivable as a being within the limits of phenomenological ontology. Both are metaphors without reference.

Phenomenology is the intimate relation of an ego to its outside via intentionality. This relation is always to an object, to a phenomenon available for vision. If the pure ego, in its self-transcendence towards a world of phenomena, must constitute that world through a non-reducible delay, the delay inherent in the historicity of the idea, we may draw two types of conclusions. First our confidence in the punctuality of the instant, which as Husserl never ceased to believe, is the form which ultimately situates the invariability of the ego, is irreparably shaken. Second, the non-phenomenal, the pure contingency of the infinity of time and space, has been introduced into the interiority of phenomenology. *That of which the idea is an idea, the ontological in the non-phenomenological sense of the word, is a structural component of phenomenality in general.* To say that the idea is that which makes a phenomenology possible implies that phenomenology is radically precluded from thinking itself phenomenologically. Yet philosophy can never be anything more than phenomenology; the ontological question which reverberates past the limits of phenomenology is only recuperable incompletely as vision. The non-phenomenal of which Derrida speaks is not a content provisionally shielded from vision, a content whose eventual elucidation is a horizonal task of philosophy, but a content whose unknowableness is absolute and yet indispensable to thought as philosophy.

A desire for scientificity appears recurrently in Husserl's work: he always hoped to institute a purely logical, therefore univocal, language whose self-effacement would inscribe phenomenology without distorting it. A large portion of *Origin of Geometry* is devoted to that language which the proto-geometer must have already had at his disposal before he created geometry. For although Husserl always maintained that the ego's work was essentially silent, that pre-expression is independent of expression, in *Origin of Geometry* his stance appears to undergo a subtle change insofar as he argues that objectivity can only be constituted by intersubjectivity, that only a community of monads can assure the ideality of the object. The name of this communal guarantee is language.

Had geometry been created by a non-speaking subject, if such a thing is possible, it would have died with him and therefore been a purely empirical and contingent event. Only if the proto-geometer can express his discovery can its ideality be protected, and even then it faces peril. For there is no assurance that its transmission will be accurate, that the ideality of its sense will not be impaired by its passage from one subject to another. Only the inscription of geometry into written language will ultimately safeguard its integrity. Writing does not merely reproduce an already present ideality, it produces ideality as that which is infinitely repeatable as same. Derrida draws two conclusions: 1) the pre-geometric culture must have already mastered speech and writing before geometry could have been created. 2) If we substitute for geometry ideality in general, the creation of ideality from non-ideality, then it follows there could never have been an initial creation of ideality; for if, according to Husserl's own formulations, the pure ideality of language is necessary not as an adjunct to but as an absolute requirement for the constitution of ideality, then a certain kind of ideality, that of language, must have been at play before ideality as such first appeared.

Husserl never devoted himself to the problem of a transcendental language because language is not an object whose phenomenological explication is a possible task, but a content which, because it is itself internally involved in the mechanism of the Kantian idea, is phenomenologically off-limits. The conclusions of *Origin of Geometry* appear to concern only ideality. Language was anterior to ideality, the bastion of phenomenological security, the silent pre-expressive stratum of consciousness, that which retained the possibility of origination, punctuality, self-presence. Husserl refused to think of the transcendental ego as anything but pre-expressive: language was a supplement, a non-productive addition to pre-linguistic sense whose sole function was to mirror the underlying stratum. Derrida contaminates the transcendental ego with non-primordiality. His critique erodes the unshakable barrier phenomenology erects between the two parallel egos, the transcendental ego which does not need language because its self-perception is immediate and apodictic, and the psychologistic ego, in its pre-reduction mundaniety, is always alienated from itself. The strict maintenance is essential to phenomenology for it is the condition of the possibility for an entire gamut of parallel concepts which form the scaffolding of phenomenology: expression and pre-expression, indication and expression, non-ideality and ideality, intersubjectivity and subjectivity, transcendent world and transcendental ego, etc. Husserl's insistence on the impossibility of any seepage between these is for Derrida the preservation of being as presence. He wants to bring to light a certain non-presence which torments phenomenology from within, by introducing an ineradicable nonprimordiality into the nucleic transcendental ego that irreparably taints its mastery over self and object with an irredeemable loss of control. The prohibition against the blurring of Husserl's essential distinctions is transgressed by the internal logic of the law which institutes and maintains them. Located within phenomenology is the seed of its own destruction.

Derrida finds that the irreducible proximity of language to primordial thought is something which eludes by nature every phenomenal or thematic actuality.[39] And related to this, he finds that the legitimate scope of Husserl's phenomenological reductions reaches its limit with the uncovering of the intertwining of *arche* and *telos* in the historicity that is announced by the sense of every fact. Derrida amplifies Fink's observation that Husserl does not pose the problem of a transcendental language and his wonder at whether, "if, after the reduction, one can still have at his disposal a *logos* in the same sense as before."[40] Derrida does so by calling attention to the consistently unthematized assumption, *the unthought axiomatic*, operative in Husserl's post-reductive descriptions, regarding the phenomenological transparency of the natural sense of the factically embodied language that he must employ in order to make and maintain the non-factical distinctions puitatively uncovered by those very descriptions.

Thus despite what one commentator has characterized as the "bewildering labyrinth of the most diverse inter-textual references,"[41] Derrida's critique centers on Husserl's failures both to pose the question of "transcendental discourse" and in his failure to pose the question regarding the ideal constituting capacity and transparency of factical language. These failures create a tension in Husserl's thought which in turn generates an unwarranted tendency toward idealization, yielding the result that "phenomenology cannot be grounded as such in itself, nor can it indicate its own proper limits."[42] Derrida's criticism here is not without problems: he follows Ricoeur's analysis and over-reads Husserl's "principle of principles" to intend to mean "implicitly that [the immediate presence of the thing itself in person] means: of the phenomenally defined or definable thing, therefore the finite thing."[43] There is also the conspicuous absence of any consideration by Derrida of the problematic of "reflection" in Husserl's phenomenology in general, with respect to the reduction. Overall, however, this is a criticism from which Husserlian phenomenology has yet to fully recover.

The key insight by Derrida is that language functions to render intrinsically problematic the project of the pure (and therefore univocal) descriptive tracing of the references at issue. For Husserl language is assigned tacitly a constituting function with respect to objective ideality, ideality whose meaning or sense is, in principle, accessible to all and not simply the protogeometer. The problems are with what language assumes with regard to the constitution of objective ideality in Husserl's analyses. Husserl has failed to provide an analysis of the phenomenological origin of language.[44] Inasmuch as for Derrida Husserl is very conscious that at bottom the problem of geometry's origin puts the problem of the constitution of intersubjectivity on par with that of the phenomenological origin of language, the omission of an analysis of the latter is of more than programmatical concern. In the absence of such an analysis, Husserl's account of the instituitive origin of objective ideality must necessarily involve decisions about the relation of language and ideality that are not accounted for, i.e., grounded, phenomenologically. This in turn triggers the problem that Husserl's decisions regarding language in the constitution of intersubjective ideality are based on a phenomenologically unwarranted assigning of privilege to the sign as it functions as a sign-signifier or sign expression.[45] This sets into question phenomenology's manifesting any capacity to ground itself.

Derrida's Critique of Husserl in *Speech and Phenomena*

Derrida presents *Speech and Phenomena* as offering arguments proving the internal incoherence of Husserlian phenomenology by tracing a series of exclusions which systematically haunt Husserl's project, beginning with the exclusion of indication from expression, and leading through the exclusion of representation from present meaning to the exclusion of past and future times from temporal presence. Two of the targets are Husserl's phenomenological account of internal time-consciousness, and the distinction between the indicative and expressive functions of signs. Derrida's argument again is that such an account betrays phenomenological principles by trafficking in an unaccounted for metaphysical presupposition of presence.[46]

The parameters of the first argument should be familiar enough. The ground of Husserl's project of phenomenology is consciousness. The root of all presence and the source of all evidence is self-consciousness as self-presence. Temporal immediacy, simultaneity, is a necessary condition, even a defining condition, of evident presence. Derrida argues that Husserl requires a temporal present that is simple, a punctual instant, in order to ground a self-presence which needs no mediation by signs, and this punctual now phase provides just such an original present, a present not constituted in a synthesis of differences. His critical point will be that no simple, punctual instant is possible, and if such is the case, then the project of phenomenology is flawed from its beginning.

The punctuality of the now as self-identical is the source-point for the self-evidence of presence, yet it can only be so through a contradictory relation with retention. On the one hand, the authority of the present absolute perceptual source can be maintained only in contrasting continuity with retention as non-source, non-perception. But, on the other hand, the retentive phase must remain within the present's sphere of absolute certainty in order to maintain a foundational continuity. According to Derrida, Husserl needs both claims to get simple self-identity and temporal continuity. Both are self-presence, and therefore, also, the presence of objective meaning that is recognizably the same through reiterations. Derrida treats this retention as a re-presentation of the now absent *prior* now phase. Within the so-called living present, there is a necessary indicative function, an essential retentive pointing to what is absent. That is, within the present there is an essential and primordial nonpresence.

> "Self-presence must be produced in an undivided unity of [an instanteous] temporal present so as to have nothing to reveal to itself by the agency of signs." [47]

Thus for something to be present it must be absolutely self-contained. It must not point beyond itself to any further logical, temporal, or spatial context. Nor can the present be a dependent moment on some greater whole, for then again, it must point to or indicate something beyond itself.

The gist of Derrida's argument is to show how the metaphors of voice as self-presence, the equation between genuine, authentic sense and the image of a consciousness pictured as ideally coinciding with its own expressive intent. This structures each and every move by which Husserl attempts to validate the findings of phenomenological inquiry. Language, truth, and logic are all construed as finally dependent on the validating content of intentional activity identified with pure self-presence. Despite Husserl's attempts to criticize traditional metaphysics, for Derrida metaphysics' finest hour is represented by Husserl. The "return to the things themselves" is precisely this ultimate effacement of metaphysics in the act of its predominance. The "principle of principles," that which guarantees the truth of the things themselves is an essential metaphysical one: the presence of presence to itself.

Consistent with this is Husserl's constant relegation of writing, merely graphic convention, to a realm of lifeless signification, articulated through a series of supposedly self-evident contrasts and exclusions. Most important is the cardinal distinction between expressive and indicative signs, a second area of Derrida's critique of Husserl in *Speech and Phenomena* that has drawn a great deal of attention. The former are conceived as bearers of a self-present meaningful intention which serves to authenticate their manifest sense. The latter are devoid of this expressive potential, existing merely as empty signs or arbitrary tokens of a purely conventional character. Husserl is obliged to maintain this distinction in view of his phenomenological appeal to intentionality as source and guarantee of meaning. Derrida seeks to show, however, the extent to which Husserl's arguments fail to preserve this distinction between expressive and indicative signs, but point to the conclusion that language can only be conceived in terms of an arbitrary signifying network devoid of all original expressive intent.

Derrida's specific argument is that in order for there to be a proper understanding of logic, since that discipline is concerned only with the meanings expressed by linguistic signs, Husserl must argue that a proper understanding of logic requires that one distinguish between the *indicative* function which signs, including linguistic signs, can have, from the *expressive* function which only linguistic signs can have. Derrida argues that Husserl fails to separate expressive from indicative functions. Indeed, anyone's attempting to do so would fail, because expression is a species of the genus "indication" and that what Husserl calls "essentially occasional expressions" turn out to play an essential role in the expressive function itself. Derrida is seeking to convict Husserl of Platonism: because he fails to ask the question of the "structure of the sign in general" Husserl takes the full presence of expression to be possible in isolation from the absence involved in indication. Thus Husserl's project is impossible from the start, as his pure logical grammar must study expression in its purity, independent of indication, and since expression cannot be separated from indication, the entire project is compromised.

> Husserl's whole enterprise—and far beyond the *Investigations*—would be threatened if the *Verflechtung* [interweaving] which couples the indicative sign to expression were absolutely irreducible, if it were in principle inextricable and if indication were essentially internal to the movement of expression rather than being only conjoined to it, however tenaciously.[48]

Essentially occasional expressions are those whose concrete meaning is a function of the occasion of their use, in contrast to objective expressions, for which the circumstances of their utterance do not determine the meaning expressed.[49] Husserl distinguishes expression from indication, and then appeals to soliloquy to show that expressions can function even when they exercise no indicative function. He acknowledges the two are "interwoven" in communicative speech, but that they are always distinguishable, and that in inner speech, *im einsamen Seelenleben*, there is expression but no indication.[50] Yet Husserl himself speaks of indication in analyzing occasional expressions;[51] and when he admits that we are removed from the ideal that objective truths in themselves should be expressed by means of objective meanings, this seems to confirm Derrida's prediction that such indicative adherences will continually reappear, and getting rid of them will be an infinite task.[52]

Satirical or not, this is a solid objection. Wherever we find expressions such as *I, here,* and *now,* the meaning of these expressions is "carried off into indication whenever it animates real intended speech for someone else."[53] Derrida's example is with the expression "I" which should express an ideal meaning which is independent of all realized relation to an object.[54] Husserl is committed to the claim that the expressive function of "I" should not essentially involve indication, but Derrida's analysis contradicts this. Husserl states that in solitary speech, where we to find expressions free from being interwoven with the indicative function, the meaning of "I" is essentially realized in the immediate idea of one's own personality.[55] But the word "I" "has the character of a universally operative indication" of the fact that "each speaker has his own I-presentation, and thus his own individual concept of "I.""[56] Fulfillment thus seems essential to the speaker's meaningful use of "I" and the word thus functions indicatively. Husserl seems caught in contradiction. He had previously built his account of meaning on the refusal to identify meaningfulness with the realized relation to an object, yet he now claims that the word "I" has its normal meaning only when its meaning is realized. Whereas before he had insisted on the ideality of meaning, he now claims that "I" has an ever new meaning depending on who utters it.[57] Derrida draws the conclusion:

> *Husserl's premises should sanction our saying exactly the contrary.* Just as I need not perceive in order to understand a statement about perception, so there is no need to intuit the object I in order to understand the word I. The possibility of this nonintuition constitutes the *Bedeutung* as such, *the normal Bedeutung* as such.[58]

Derrida attributes to Husserl the claim that expression and indication are mutually exclusive but conjointly exhaustive species of signs, since to function signitively is either to express or to indicate, but not both, and that the two types of signification differ in that what is signified expressively is made present through the signification, whereas what is signified indicatively is made visible as absent, or outside, or transcendent.[59] Had Husserl considered the essence of signification, he would have seen that all signitive functions are mediated by the outside, the transcendent, and thus by what cannot be fully present. Since he is later unable to avoid including both indication and absence from expression, he will be forced to admit that any locution that expresses a meaning must necessarily, at the same time, indicate something else. Language is always caught up in structures of convention or pre-existent sense which effectively bar any appeal to self-present intention as the locus of meaning. Communication is only possible, indeed, by virtue of the fact that language can be detached from its original expressive intent and still possess meaning as part of the generalized economy of signs. Husserl conceives language on the model of face-to-face communicative utterance, and extension of the metaphor which not only privileges the temporality of constant presence but those of inner speech above the detours and vagaries of writing. Moreover, as Derrida goes on to show, writing is coextensive with the realm of indicative signs which pose such a threat to Husserl's undertaking. On the one side speech bears its traditional connotations of life giving presence, naturalness and immediacy. On the other stands writing with its associated properties of absence, difference, and exteriority. What Derrida brings out is the extent to which images of writing, the functions of indicative language, invade the grounding metaphors of Husserlian phenomenology.

As with the other objections, there are of course possible responses to this. Derrida seizes upon the multiple possible meanings of *Verflechten* to emphasize not just an interweaving but an irreducible entanglement to which Husserl need not be committed. That indicative and expressive funtions of linguistic signs are *interwoven* need not entail that it is impossible to *untangle* the two functions. His argument also ignores Husserl's own developments and reconsiderations in his thinking regarding these points, a complexity with regard to other thinkers of which Derrida is extremely aware and does not deserve the hyperbolic conclusions drawn. Also, Derrida's way of advancing these arguments is maddening to the analytically trained. He constantly makes provisional conclusions, marked by conditional syntax. Long series of rhetorical questions imply the rhetorical force of their tacit replies. When the anticipated answers are supplied, and the subjunctives become *pro forma*, the chain of argument appears as if magically justified. Such scorched-earth rhetorical maneuvers and dazzling conclusions strike many as mere posturing, for some almost a criminal continuance of the historical injustices Husserl's thinking has already suffered.

Husserl provides Derrida with a paradigm case of an essentially Heideggerian critique of presence. If Husserl talks of first-hand seeing, the things themselves, presence in the flesh, fulfilled meanings, the principle of principles, Derrida continually shows these to be promises that cannot be kept. The perceptual object, contrary to Husserl's repeated claims, is not a pure presence, not primordially and corporeally present in person, but precisely a complex interplay of presence and absence. Derrida's is a more merciless and comfortless criticism, but both Heidegger and Derrida are engaged in competing deconstructions of Husserl's project. To read Derrida's engagement with Husserl too much simply in terms of arguments would be to make the same mistake as to read Derrida's engagement with Heidegger in terms of arguments. That despite tendentious and even misreadings of Heidegger, he gets it right. Derrida attributes to Heidegger positions that simply are not to be found on Heidegger's pages, but the point, as is often said, is to reveal the unspoken secret which lies hidden within the texts, much as Heidegger himself did with any number of metaphysical thinkers. Until the Derridean and Husserlian scholarly camps realize that Heidegger is at the center of their dispute, their exchanges over Derrida's Husserl interpretations will languish in crippling misunderstandings impossible to overcome.

Derrida's Husserl critique reveals neither a clinical refutation nor an embarassingly onanistic indulgence. Stylistic divides and score-settling agendas continue to mar the scene. These Heidegger-fueled French thinkers in general, however, and Derrida in particular, were perfectly right to appropriate phenomenology, which belongs to nobody, not even Husserl, in either its letter or inspiration. The points of rupture between the positive scientific phenomenological project and the displacement of its possibilities toward other paths, these *detours in philosophy*, always trouble some and gratify others. Such detours are to be interpreted not as a regression, but as full of promise. Restless thinking, fashioning new questions, will always seem insolent to be so exacting over such displacements. Who could remain unmoved by intrepid returns of thinking, which will fascinate the thinker even as they discourage the orthodox? If their questioning is not perfunctory, they will demonstrate an acuity in line with the requirements of the piety that must crown, in the word of Heidegger, thinking worthy of the name.

XIV. Winch and the Charge of Relativism

The year 2004 marked the fortieth anniversary of the publication of Peter Winch's celebrated paper 'Understanding a Primitive Society.' Winch's work exercised a profound impact across a range of intellectual disciplines, including philosophy, sociology, anthropology, and political theory. Winch's paper is typically understood as the quintessential statement of relativism: different cultural groups, at different times and places, have their own peculiar conceptions of 'reality'. These different realities are frequently incommensurable with each other, such that (some of) what is 'reality' for a member of a 'primitive society' is illusion and error for the modern Western individual, and perhaps vice versa as well. In a word, Winch was perceived as completely abandoning the notion of reality entirely and reducing it into as many different, incommensurable, realities as there were different systems of socially functioning beliefs and practices. In a famous line from Winch's article, he expressly states, after all, that "[R]eality is not what gives language sense. What is real and what is unreal shows itself in the sense that language has."[1] Winch's critics, numbering in the hundreds, including such luminaries as MacIntyre, Gellner, Popper, Apel, and Habermas, have subjected his ideas to at times scathing critique, arguing that a pernicious relativism follows inexorably from his ontological and epistemic relativism.[2] Because 'what is real' can only be known and understood in the light of rules and criteria internal to, and constituitive of, some functioning, on-going form of social life, it is not permissable to evaluate or criticize aspects of that reality by reference to any external criteria of evaluation. I will argue however that most of the criticisms against Winch have fundamentally misunderstood his philosophical goals, and careful comparison with some well-chosen German philosophers can help us see those misunderstandings more clearly.[3]

Too often the "charge of relativism" is simply a populist rhetorical strategy to ingeniously exploit the general public's fascination with embarassment and ridicule when attacking a philosophy perceived as dangerous. Philosophers usually treat any whiff of it with schoolboy contempt. Many seem to regard the slightest nod to relativism as a sign of the modern world's abdication of reason and moral decay, on a par with drive-by shootings and acts of terror. Until quite recently in analytical circles the incoherence of relativism was almost an article of faith, and a routine pit-bull-like public display of its incoherence obligatory. Only in the past decade has there been a marked change in the perception of the problem of relativism and the solutions offered, in part because it was accepted (unwillingly) that the lightning-quick charges of self-refutation had not managed to deliver the death-blow for which it was devised. Nozick echoed these sentiments when he indicated: "For some time now, I have felt uncomfortable with the quick refutation of relativism, a favorite of philosophers and one that I had often used in conversation."[4] Similar concern surrounds how the epithet of fideism functions in various debates regarding Wittgenstein and the philosophy of religion exclusively as a term of abuse, despite how Wittgenstein himself never claimed to be a fideist, nor has any of those thinkers typically labelled "Wittgensteinian fideists" have ever claimed that Wittgenstein was a fideist or that they were themselves fideists. The term fideist, like relativist, "becomes a convenient, and highly misleading, label under which to assimilate, and at the same time rather effortlessly cast suspicion upon, the work of a number of different philosophers."[5]

We ought not to entirely ignore the logical puzzles of self-referentiality seized upon by our analytical colleagues; but neither ought we to permit the entire validity of our inquiry to rest on whether it can avoid a paradox, as though, like Oedipus, we could not find our way without first solving riddles. Adherents to such thinking of course lined up to take their obligatory shots at Winch's article, ignoring Winch's own repeated protests to the contrary regarding relativism, not to mention his own work on the complex of issues surrounding it. One could even read Habermas' monumental *Theory of Communicative Action* as largely a response to the "threat" posed by Winch's thoroughgoing critique of the idea of an epistemically privileged (Western-scientific) conception of universally valid rationality. Habermas' central project is an attempt to work out a universal theory of rationality that is both normative, in the sense of being able to assess the cognitive adequacy of different world-views, and an explanatory reconstruction of the developmental process which has brought about the 'rationalization' of the modern Western world. Writing squarely within the tradition of the Frankfurt school of critical theory, Habermas hoped that his theoretical endeavor would provide the desiderata of a new foundation for a contemporary critical theory of modern industrial society.[6] Comparison to Habermas will give us a view to a kind of Kantian impulse against which Winch's thinking can be set in relief.

Habermas' Kantian roots show themselves in what might be called his metaphysical approach to social, political, moral, and epistemic problems. By this is meant that his characteristic method is to seek to divine, through philosophical analysis, "the rational content of anthropologically deep-seated structures" which generate the complex empirical phenomena of social, political, and psychological life. These structures can only be known through a kind of transcendental reconstruction. For example, Habermas's theory of communicative action claims to identify the implicit, pre-theoretical knowledge and competencies, the abstract rules, mechanisms, and steering media which structure individual consciousness, the inner-subjective life-world, and the social system. On this foundation he then builds a critical normative moral and political theory, the normativity of which derives solely from the alleged facticity of the aforementioned structures and processes allegedly underlying language, communication, argumentation, and social evolution. By contrast, Winch adopts what might be called a descriptive approach to social, political, moral, and epistemic problems. The descriptive approach emanates from Wittgenstein, who is vehemently opposed to philosophy theory and explanation. Winch's approach is exemplified in 'Understanding a Primitive Society' where he refuses to engage in metaphysical evaluation of the rationality or cognitive adequacy of alien practices and beliefs. It is precisely this attitude which has attracted heated criticism, but which has in my view not been properly understood. Perhaps some clarity can be displayed by following Winch along two fault lines, the first being that of the adoption of Wittgenstein's quasi-phenomenological descriptive method, and the second with regard to the idea of "forms of life," each of which I will seek to examine in turn.

Any reading of a text, as hermeneutical theorists such as Gadamer have persuasively argued, necessarily contains certain 'prejudices' or 'background' assumptions which ineluctably shape the direction of that reading. It is just this background assumption which animates many of Wittgenstein's most acclaimed expositors and commentators. For example, according to Baker and Hacker, the task of the Wittgensteinian philosopher is to arrive at a correct conception of the harmony between thought and reality. Winch on occasion also adheres to this positivistic quest to distinguish sense and nonsense once and for all. However, while Wittgenstein's earlier Tractarian philosophy clearly was centrally concerned with distinguishing sense from nonsense, on my reading his later work wholly repudiated this quest. Wittgenstein came to relinquish the very idea that philosophy could, or should, claim to reveal 'the way things really are.' In opposition to metaphysical readings of Wittgenstein, one should take entirely seriously the descriptive approach that he commends, an approach famously encapsulated in #109 of the *Investigations*:

[W]e may not advance any kind of theory. There must not be anything hypothetical in our considerations. We must do away with all explanation and description alone must take its place. And this description gets its light, that is to say its purpose, from ... [our] problems.[7]

By this Wittgenstein primarily means philosophical theory and explanation. This is a form of philosophy—the overwhelmingly dominant one—whose theoretical practice is modelled on the scientific mode of explanation:

Philosophers constantly see the method of science before their eyes, and are irresistibly tempted to ask and answer questions in the way science does. This tendency is the real source of metaphysics.[8]

For Wittgenstein this method of science can be seen in the attempt to uncover hidden mechanisms, powers, states, processes, and structures which are assumed to generate, and hence explain, phenomena such as consciousness, language, meaning, and so forth. Another core element of this picture of philosophical explanation is its Kantian mode of inference, much as what we briefly described with regard to Habermas, whereby it is asserted that things must be this way or that, as dictated by the requirements of the philosopher's a priori metaphysical scheme. This mode of explanation manifests in such questions as: what must be the case, at the deepest level of reality, in order for linguistic communication, or at least the philosopher's picture of what is involved in linguistic comminication, to be possible?

Winch's approach to thinking runs counter to this impulse on many fronts. In the philosophy of social sciences and anthropology, his efforts seek to display the phenomena under investigation through the particular examples addressed. Through this approach Winch preserves the phenomena in question against the craving for homogeneity and a presumption of theory which seeks to transmute them into autonomous rational enterprises. This is prevalent in Winch's underrated views on ethics, as well, in which he works against the presumption of ethical theorists laying claim to an ultimate criterion to determine the content of morality. Far from being an "armchair analyst" of human cultural diversity, or some British intellectual "on safari," one of the main aspects of Winch's 'Understanding a Primitive Society' is in illustrating the fallacy of the assumption that we possess, in any armchair from which we might sit or safari from where we might hunt, all we need to understand the rationality of cultures other than our own.[9]

In 'Understanding a Primitive Culture,' Winch first of all praises the descriptive perspicuity of Evans-Pritchard's ethnography, in which the latter goes "a very great deal further than most of his predecessors in trying to present the sense of the institutions he is discussing as it presents itself to the Azande themselves." However, Winch then goes on to object that Evans-Pritchard vitiates this sense with his insistence that while Zande individuals reason in a manner that is logically and psychologically no different to that of Western individuals, nevertheless the 'social content' (the concepts and categories available for individual thought and experience) of Zande witchcraft and magic does not 'accord with objective reality.' And objective reality, for Evans-Pritchard, refers to the basic structure of reality revealed to us Westerners by modern science (basically a disenchanted naturalistic universe governed solely by cause-and-effect relations). Evans-Pritchard asserts that 'objective reality' contains no such thing as witches and supernatural causes: 'Our *body of scientific knowledge and logic are the sole arbiters of what are mystical, common sense, and scientific notions.*'[10]

Winch argues that this is an ethnocentric prejudice, predicated on a question-begging deployment of the concept 'accordance with objective reality.' He maintains that the idea of an 'objective reality' independent of the conceptual system through which that reality is known is spurious. Hence we cannot judge that our body of scientific knowledge does, and the Zande system of magic and witchcraft does not, accord with objective reality, for the simple reason that the former defines for us what objective reality indeed is. Winch points out that Evans-Pritchard presents the notion of objective reality as an unproblematic statement of fact, as the way things really are. Winch disputes this, insisting, on the contrary that certain metaphysical claims are embodied in the notion of objective reality. Evans-Pritchard claims to know a priori what reality consists of independently of sensory experience and scientific investigation, and his conception of objective reality is therefore logically no different from the Zande conception of reality. Neither science nor logic can test or prove Evans-Pritchard's notion of objective reality because it is presupposed by any actual or scientific inquiry.

We must first of all re-sheathe the many blades brought to bear on Winch's anthropological knowledge.[11] Contrary to the manner in which he has often been represented, Winch does not claim to provide a superior anthropological account of or insight into the Azande. Nor could he, given that he does not claim to know any more about Zande practices than what is reported in Evans-Pritchard's magisterial study. Nor does Winch question the basic validity of Evans-Pritchard's ethnographic observations. But he does question that evaluative framework within which Evans-Pritchard presents his account of Zande life. For Winch, it is not a question of the adequacy of Evans-Pritchard's account of Zande life as such, but rather the adequacy of evaluating the sense and rationality of that way of life in terms of criteria internal to Western scientific instrumental reason. In evaluating Zande life thus, Winch believes that Evans-Pritchard makes it difficult for the Western reader to see any sense or coherence in Zande beliefs and practices. In general Winch wants to problematize our taken-for-granted cognitive commitment to the scientific (metaphysical) form of explanation and understanding.

The core issue for many of Winch's critics is the possibility of adopting a critical stance towards the desirability and rationality of different forms of life. Consider this remark by Winch:

> We start from the position that standards of rationality in different societies do not always coincide; from the possibility, therefore, that the standards of rationality current ... elsewhere ... are different from our own.[12]

This sends pulses racing with its suggestion of relativism. What may seem irrational by our standards may well be rational by a different set of standards. That would seem to preclude any criticism and, possibly, even any understanding, of the ideas and values of another culture. But Winch also writes:

> We should not lose sight of the fact that the idea that men's ideas and beliefs must be checkable against something independent—some reality—is an important one. To abandon it is to plunge straight into a protagorian relativism, with all the paradoxes that this involves.[13]

But although it is generally assumed that Winch sought to legislate against such critical evaluation, he did state, quite unequivocally, that his argument does not entail

> "accepting as rational all beliefs couched in magical concepts or all procedures practised in the name of such beliefs. This is no more necessary than is the corresponding proposition that all procedures 'justified' in the name of science are immune from rational criticism."[14]

And in a later article, Winch reiterates that he had never argued, "absurdly, that ways in which men live together can never be criticized as in any sense irrational." One of the main purposes of his article 'Understanding a Primitive Society," Winch explains, had been to point out that there are 'more kinds of criticism than one.'[15] Winch's argument is that instead of simply assuming that we as social inquirers know what we mean by such locutions as the "cognitive adequacy"[16] and validity of belief claims belonging to alien cultural systems[17] we should on reflection find such notions deeply problematic. Just because we have some conception of the cognitive adequacy and validity of our own epistemic practices, we cannot simply employ this notion to pave over with asphalt the paths of access to radically different ways of life. Critics have missed the fundamental orientation of the article, namely, that Winch is less interested in what we can discover about Zande magic and witchcraft than what we can learn about ourselves—our own prejudices, through learning about their and others' way of life.

Further analogy with Gadamer is relevant here. Gadamer famously argues in *Truth and Method* that even before I interpret a text or grasp the meaning of an object, I have already placed it within a certain context, approached it from a certain perspective, and conceived of it in a certain way.[18] There is no neutral vantage point from which to survey the 'real' meaning of a text or object; even a scientific approach to an object places it within a certain context and takes a certain attitude towards it. A great deal of the work involved in Gadamerian hermeneutic analysis is constantly investigating how one's own interpretive stance constitutes a necessary constriction of possible interpretive modes. The meaning of any object is co-determined by one's own circumstances, life-relations, expectations. Against the medieval idea of god-like perspective Gadamer emphasizes the reciprocal illumination and obfuscation that he claims is part of all understanding. He denies that there can ever be one correct or absolutely exhaustive way of understanding either one's own or another's text, and argues that any understanding necessarily ignores certain features of a text in its very focus on and clarification of others.

In the application of this general approach to that of cultures, Winch wants to remind us that reflecting on the problems involved in trying to understand a primitive society is that perhaps our own way of life and dominant cultural institutions make less sense to us than we unreflectively assume. Winch's position does not entail that 'alien cultural systems' can only be understood in their own terms[19] or that the realm of human action can only be understood in terms of the concepts and conventions of the actors.[20] He does not claim that we must jettison all the concepts and categories constituitive of our form of life in order to understand Zande beliefs and practices, as if in some gesture of absolute alterity. If this were really the case, there would be no understanding at all. Winch argues instead that cross-cultural understanding is indeed possible but depends on identifying institutions or practices in our culture which bear some affinities with those in the culture we wish to understand. But this in turn requires the constant clarification activity of the practices of our own culture. What is required is to 'find ways of thinking in our own society that will help us to see the Zande institution in a clearer light'[21] which in turn first requires that we see our own situations in such a light.

With Winch, Gadamer would hold that such "hermeneutic interpretation' can never lay claim to a final, authoritative position on its subject-matter. As Gadamer put it:

> In this domain [of historical science] one must see the 'result' of the happening of interpretation not as much in progress, which exists only in partial aspects, as in a process opposed to the decline and fall of knowledge: in the revival of language and the re-aquisition of the meaning that is spoken in and through tradition. This is a dangerous relativism only from the standard of an absolute knowledge that is not ours.[22]

For Gadamer, the rationality of the tradition cannot be measured against an ideal of either absolute knowledge, complete enlightenment, or Habermasian constraint-free consensus; it is to be evaluated instead within a practical context, as that degree of knowledge, enlightenment, and openness of which we are capable at a given time. In contrast to Habermas' counterfactual norm of an ideal speech situation, Gadamer makes use of the way in which prejudices are overcome and ideologies revealed in the continued course of the tradition itself. Such revelations do not follow linear paths toward transparency. Since each revelation is simultaneously the closing of other options, Gadamer stresses the finitude and fallibility of our knowledge. Sociological maturity and responsibility follows not from the possession of a "theory" of society but rather from an awareness of our hermeneutic situation or historical horizons and hence an awareness of otherness.

Winch's perspective, in sharing such finitude and fallibility, is rightly called a kind of analytical hermeneutics.[23] His critique of Evans-Pritchard is not that the famed sociologist illegitimately seeks to understand the Azande through the medium of Western concepts; rather, similar to Gadamer's hermeneutic critique of early century positivism, Evans-Pritchard fails to put his own perspectives sufficiently into play and be open to any possible enrichment of his own point of view. Just as Gadamer argued that positivism's objectivity, attained through scientific method, is no more adequate than the prejudices it presupposes, so too Winch holds that such prejudices are as much thresholds as limits, in that they form perspectives from which a gradual development of our knowledge becomes possible in the first place. Evans-Pritchard fails to adequately acknowledge the prejudices of his own perspective. There is no objectivity that would lift us above such situatedness. Nonetheless in coming to an understanding with others we can learn how to amend some of our assumptions. Evans-Pritchard claims to evaluate the 'rationality' of Zande witchcraft and magical practices in terms of their 'accordance with culturally independent objective reality'. But in fact he is evaluating witchcraft and magic through unacknowleged analogy with central institutions and practices peculiar to Western society.

Both Gadamer and Winch, then, in their own ways, work against the reification of fixed interpretive perspectives, and the attempts to posit 'objective' methodologies or 'theories' that regulate our engagement with some phenomena. A similarity can be found between Winch's criticism of Evans-Pritchard and Gadamer's critique of Dilthey's employment of the Cartesian method of doubt in the human sciences, in which Gadamer opposes the entrenchment of a fixed mode of investigation that constricts the scope of the inquiry.[24] So too does Winch frequently cite how "our own conception of what it is to be rational is certainly not exhausted by the practices of science."[25] Both are fundamentally hermeneutic moves with respect to how any inquirer is a finite cultural being whose understanding is shaped by formed vantage points and perspectives. Because of this, an inquiry is effective the degree to which it involves a process of disclosing the fore-meanings and pre-judgments that derive from these perspectives.

Gadamer's work against the presumptions of *method* and Winch's against the presumption of *theory* also yield tremendous ethical implications. Since the nature of the selfhood of the hermeneutic thinker is part of the historical reality that comes into play in understanding, hermeneutics precipitates a transformation in the very modes of being of the self. For Gadamer there is an ethical dimension to hermeneutic inquiry that is lacking in the natural sciences. So too for Winch, because one cannot attain to either complete self-transparency nor objective overview of absolute knowledge, such a hermeneutic descriptive approach ought to trigger the recognition of a similar yet inassimilable other and engender a kind of recognition in the heterogeneity of the human. This requires the continual testing of our own prejudices, a reflexive questioning based upon a serious and open encounter with an other not one's own. It involves recoiling back upon one's own inquiry-standpoint and a disclosure of prejudgments that may become subject to transformation. It also involves, in Winch's case, a painstaking openness to ethical examples, and the resistance to thinking that all moral possibilities involving courses of action surrounding such examples must conform to some theory undergirding all of the examples.

Failure to attend to such differences risks procedurally reifying prejudgments to where they harden into fixed prejudices, an uncritical privileging of perspectives which ossify viewpoints and impede understanding. The failure to even be able to see the legitimacy of alternative perspectives is not to be mistaken for possession of an absolute truth; instead it is perhaps a kind of repression or confusion, and the prejudgments inherent become fixed and work covertly to produce misunderstandings. The permanent demand that differences, socio-cultural or moral, be always and inevitably subsumable under some higher synthesis is not illustrative of what is to count as rational or moral, but is instead illustrative of the "poverty of our own lives."[26]

Urbanizing the Wittgensteinian Province Regarding Other "Forms of Life"

It is well known that access to the uniqueness of Winch's thought is difficult, because so much of the undergirding for his thinking presupposes knowledge of Wittgenstein, similar, perhaps, to how much of Aquinas must be understood by prior reflection on Aristotle, or Gadamer's reliance on Heidegger. In reading many of Winch's works, one happens upon the Wittgensteinian background fairly quickly. Elsewhere the influence is more subtle. Often being able to see the dynamic at work within a hermeneutic controversy requires stepping back and taking detours that spell out the confusions. Of course it is easier to blur all subtle distinctions or influences and dismiss controversies *en passant*. Such a move seems characteristic for the Czech anthropologist Ernst Gellner, a figure for whom any detour from the destruction of all things Wittgensteinian would seem to have been a wasted trip.[27] Gellner repeatedly claims that Wittgenstein and Winch are relativists for whom, for example, the world-view of Frazier is just as good as the world-view of the savages whose rituals he studied. This just is not true, since according to both Wittgenstein and Winch, the world-view of Frazier is much inferior to the world-view of the savages, since Frazer continuously mistakes the savages' symbolic statements for empirical ones.[28]

For Gellner, "Forms of life" is taken in the most extreme fideist conception possible, as self-contained language games, literally window-less monads which can be invoked in justifying any political, social, or religious perspective whatsoever. Never mind that Wittgensteinian language games can be criticized, rejected, or condemned in any other Wittgensteinian language game. This is actually the perfect negation of Winch's and Wittgenstein's views. One of Winch's achievements was to argue persuasively that it is the fundamentally *non-self-validating character* of Wittgensteinian language-games that demonstrates the sense of what Wittgenstein really meant about validation, namely that language games need arbiters, but that whatever arbitrates them does not happen to be philosophy. Gellner does not have the slightest idea that on the other end of his reading of Wittgenstein as some sort of transcendental relativist, there is an alternative reading which posits a near naturalizing view of language games being something common to all human beings. The point is precisely to highlight the ineliminability of nature as against convention. Further detour seems necessary to set this other reading into relief.

Much of the literature critical of Winch's famous article on primitive cultures speaks little to the influence, for example, of Wittgenstein's own remarks on Sir James Frazer's classic study of primitive magic and religion, *The Golden Bough* (1890). Wittgenstein read *The Golden Bough* and wrote a series of remarks about it in his notebook in the early 1930's. A further set of notes and marginalia about Frazer was written later in 1948.[29] Frazer had sought to explain the mode of succession for the priesthood of Diana at Nemi, near Aricia, in antiquity. Wittgenstein makes numerous harsh remarks about Frazer's methodology. Frazer's account of the magical and religious views of mankind is *unsatisfactory*.[30] His explanations of the primitive practices that he recounts are *misleading*.[31] His explanations are even *cruder* than the meaning of those practices themselves.[32] All Frazer does is to make those savage rites plausible to people who *think as he does*.[33] But he is imprisoned in such an impoverished spiritual life as to make it impossible for Frazer to conceive of a life different from that of England of his time. He cannot imagine a priest who is not basically a present-day English parson with the same *stupidity and dullness*.[34] Frazer's overall efforts are methodologically inadequate, but in place of his historical enquiries, Wittgenstein does not offer alternative empirical methods of investigation. "The very idea of wanting to explain a practice—for example, the killing of the priest-king—seems to me wrong."[35] In its place, he insists as he does in his general philosophical methodology, that "here one can only describe."[36] Most of Wittgenstein's criticisms turn on the fact that Frazer's account of the magical and religious notions of primitive societies make them appear as mistakes, at times resting on false empirical beliefs. Frazer as well merely makes a practice plausible to people who think like he does, blind to the symbolism of ritual and are lacking in, or lack awareness of, the ceremonial impulse to give expression to what is awesome, wondrous, terrible, or tragic in human experience. Instead Frazer thought that primitive man was impressed by the forces of nature because he could not explain them.[37]

Winch rejects Evans-Pritchard's instrumentalist assumptions regarding Zande magic in a way reminiscent of Wittgenstein's arguments against Frazer. Their juxtaposition is far from capricious, as Winch, in a footnote, states that Wittgenstein's comments on Frazer helped his own interpretation.[38] Furthermore, both Wittgenstein and Winch make similar complaints about the respective targets of their criticisms; both Frazer and Evans-Pritchard are accused of interpreting the mystical practices of other cultures as if their role were similar to that of science and technology in Western society. Wittgenstein rejects Frazer's key thesis that the practitioners of primitive magic and ritual seek the kind of prediction and control of natural phenomena associated with modern science. Winch criticizes Evans-Pritchard for characterizing Zande mystical notions as false, a move that Winch claims unfairly assumes the universal applicability of the epistemological criteria associated with Western science.

It is thus a fairly simple thing to see in Winch's work an attempt to "urbanize this Wittgensteinian province" with regard to its ramifications for attempts at understanding social life. I would cast the net wider, however, in saying that Winch's goal was to develop more fully the sense of some of Wittgenstein's most basic terms. When, early in Winch's 'Understanding a Primitive Society' is the remark that "this essay will pursue further some questions raised in my book *The Idea of a Social Science*," we should take Winch very seriously on this front, as everything said in the 1964 paper is prefigured in the 1958 book. This in turn then requires us to first take seriously the degree to which Winch's thinking revolves around Wittgenstein's idea of there being "forms of life." Winch, in the second chapter of his book, indicates the close relation between understanding the nature of social phenomena and elucidating the concept of forms of life.[39] This soon begets very complex problems, however, as entire industries of fog have blanketed this phrase with layers of meanings. It will help us to first see what Wittgenstein might have meant by such a phrase, and then see how forms of life are related to the recognition of language games, and how Winch's work in his famous paper is an exploration and extension of these parameters.

It is well known that Wittgenstein makes only five references to "form of life" in the *Philosophical Investigations*.

(A) It is easy to imagine a language consisting only of orders and reports in battle.—Or a language consisting only of questions and expressions for answering yes and no. And innumerable others.—And to imagine a language means to imagine a form of life. (#19)

(B) Here the term "language-game" is meant to bring into prominence the fact that the speaking of language is part of an activity, or of a form of life. (#23)

(C)"So you are saying that human agreement decides what is true and what is false?"— It is what human beings say that is true and false; they also agree in the language they use. That is not agreement in opinions but in form of life. (#241)

(D)Can only those hope who can talk? Only those who have mastered the use of a language. That is to say, the phenomena of hope are modes of this complicated form of life. (If a concept refers to a character of human hand-writing, it has no application to beings that do not write). (p. 174).

(E) It is no doubt true that you could not calculate with certain sorts of paper and ink. if that is, they were subjected to certain queer changes—but still the fact that they changed could in turn be got only from memory and comparison with other means of calculation. And how are these tested in their turn?

What has to be accepted, the given, is—so one could say—forms of life. (p. 226).[40]

These are the primary references to forms of life. Many more of Wittgenstein's writings are usually cited in analyses of the concept, especially those from *On Certainty* relating to the idea of world-picture.[41] One of the questions that is to be raised, however, and certainly with regard to Winch's application of these ideas to the phenomena of the social, is that of the number of human forms of life—is there just one form, or are there multiple other possibilities? Notice for example how only one of our passages expressly refers to forms in the plural. The importance of this question for epistemology derives from the fact that without at least the possibility of multiple forms of life the notion is of no use to relativism. If there is only one form of life, then the idea of using it as the context in which different, perhaps conflicting forms of knowledge and truth are grounded obviously falls flat. This in turn casts light on Winchian sorts of applications, as just what is at issue is whether or not, when confronted with the Azande, we are indeed being confronted with another form of life. So it is important to figure out just what Wittgenstein is saying in these passages, and that is no simple task.

The first passage (A) has the famous line that "to imagine a language means to imagine a form of life." At first blush, this could be taken to mean that speakers of Spanish, French, and German indeed have different forms of life. Given the fluid transactions and interchanges between speakers of these languages, however, it is hard to see what more the statement could then be saying than that speakers of different languages speak different languages. Consideration of the following passage from *Zettel* helps clarify the point being made:

> ... "language" is for us a name for a collection, and I understand it as including German, English, and so on, and further systems of signs which have more or less affinity with these languages. (#322)[42]

One obvious interpretation of this is in its apparent extension of the concept of language from the common languages to the whole field of semiotics, the application of this *Zettel* passage to #19 of *Philosophical Investigations* would seem to radically limit the number of possible forms of life. "Language" would come to mean any humanly recognizable language, and so imagining this language would not imply a plurality so much as coming to recognize the distinctively human form of life.[43] The epistemological issue was put forth famously (if infelicitously) in Davidson's classic essay "On the Very Idea of a Conceptual Scheme." In order for some alternative conceptual scheme even to be recognized as a language we must be able to translate it into our own language. If we cannot, then we have no reason to consider it as a language. On the other hand, if we can translate it, then we cannot say that it is really an alternative conceptual scheme. The conclusion seems to be that conceptual-scheme relativism, while attractive at first sight, proves on closer examination to be unintelligible.[44] This way of putting the issue reinforces the situation that there is but one single form of human life, and that the different possible forms of human life considered by Wittgenstein are really not possible for us. Rather, they only offer enlightenment about our own form of life, but nothing really with which we can make an airtight comparison. We cannot grasp different forms of life and in so far as we do grasp putative different forms, they are not alternatives *to* us so much as they are alternatives *for* us.[45] Wittgenstein suggests frequently in his later writings that there may be people fundamentally different from 'us': for example, people who price wood by the area it covers on the ground, or who continue the series '+2' beyond 1000 with 1004, 1008. Such people may be considered as sharing a different form of life. But these putative alternatives to our form of life are to be understood (so the argument goes) not as real empirical possibilities, but as devices designed to highlight our own situation—they show us "how we go on." If we do really understand these different forms of life then they are not really alternatives, and if we fail to understand them then they are nothing to us.

The initial problem with such an interpretation of the passages in question is that it ignores Wittgenstein's express point in #19 where he says that "it is easy to imagine a language consisting only of orders and reports in battle" and "*innumerable others.*" How can this multitude of possible languages square with the limited number of languages envisioned in the *Zettel* passage? Again, the initial response argues that in fact it is not easy to imagine such languages, not really. We can imagine that such languages exist, but the more we try seriously to imagine what they are like, the less we sometimes grasp them, and the more prone we then are to misunderstand them or project our own categories in order to absorb them. How could there be a language consisting only of orders and reports in battle? How could people with such a language live? We cannot really imagine. On this reading, such pretend or quasi-transcendental possibilities might help us to learn something about ourselves and our limits, but cannot inform us about possibilities beyond those limits. So when the first part of #19 speaks of "innumerable languages" to imagine which is to imagine a form of life, these are not real possibilities for us. The only language we can really imagine are those so closely related to our own that they are comprised in the "collective" mentioned in *Zettel* #322. There is not a difference being absorbed, as the corresponding form of life would therefore just be ours, namely that of humankind.

I tend to think this Quinean take on the issue glosses over important gradations of complexities of which Winch was trying to make sense. By 'forms of life' Wittgenstein means little more than a suggestion of naming for the kinds of practices having no more fundamental practices against which they can be judged. It is here where we get into some very complicated, and at times not very explicit, equivalences in the literature between 'forms of life' and 'language games.' Those who believe there are indefinitely many forms of life do so because they consider them to be much the same as language games, whose multiplicity no one doubts.[46] The list of language games that Wittgenstein provides in #23 of the *Investigations* is quite clearly to be taken as an enumeration of forms of life. The Hintikkas do not even seem to see the issue as problematic, replacing 'form of life' with 'language-game' without considering the changes worthy of mention.[47]

Black's reading best accounts for the close connection between 'forms of life' and language-games which as well explains their differences.[48] Black argues that language-games were initially introduced to emphasize the rule-governed nature of discourse, but that as Wittgenstein's thought developed he became increasingly unsatisfied with the idea that rules explain use. Wittgenstein moved away from the narrow conception of 'game' explained by its constituitive or formal rules or grammar, towards an ever broader conception which came to include more and more of the context of the language. According to Black, Wittgenstein never fully developed this new idea, which explains the paucity of references to *Lebensform* in the late writings. Black's argument is that Wittgenstein realized that language-games were not designed for what he now wanted them to do but he never really worked out just what that was. This highlights the fact of development in Wittgenstein's thought even through and beyond the *Investigations*. And it suggests that this development lies in the direction of trying to find a solution to the inability of rules to constrain action, a direction which leads to an increasing emphasis on context.

Winch's urbanization tracks along a similar trajectory. His discussion of other cultures is an exploration of a particular example of imagining the social contexts of another culture. It is important to note that, when Wittgenstein says that "to imagine a language means to imagine a form of life," what is meant by "imagine" here is not to be taken over-cognitively. That is, the sorts of structures we are talking about are not forms through which the human mind must see itself, because they are not forms of understanding. They are more like lived possibilities. The task of grasping such possibilities is at once more immediate and more tangible that that of imagining. Part of what is involved includes being able to carry on a practice and being able to participate in it, in a context of congruent spontaneous reactions to other people. Converts to the Shakers, for example, could whirl and shout in the Shaker manner in part because they possessed the human attunement to the experience of being in a proximity to God expressible through such movement. Similarly, Evans-

Pritchard became able to remark that he found in the Azande witchcraft practices that he learned to carry on as satisfactory a way of running his own home as any of which he knew.[49] This is so because he could share in the structure of those practices of trying to get the world right and of intervening in it to accomplish particular ends and shared the human recognition that life is subject to contingencies which alter one's original projects. Once someone embodies these attunements, practices, and attitudes, learning to participate in further practices that express or instantiate them rests on their possession.

An analogy might be helpful here, although one which we ought not press too far into service, with Heidegger's account of the existential structures of Dasein in *Being and Time*.[50] Heidegger's existentials are necessary conditions of being human, exist in every form of life, and so condition every empirical orientation. These forms of everyday life however are not formed or shaped or organized by the existentials but exhibit them because those forms are simply variations on the existentials. Thus any relation to others, those of isolation, indifference, empathy, or hatred, is a variant of being-with others, and any mode of selfness, whether it be tradition-directedness, other-directedness, inner-directedness, or autonomy, is a variant of the impersonal mode of selfhood. This is the sense in which existentials condition actual concrete life. Like awakening and falling asleep, they are its most widely applicable features. Concrete modes of existence are only modifications of them. They are the deepest, most common and most pervasive structures of being human. These existentials do not make us what we are; they simply describe the most general features of our lives. They are not categories in the kantian sense of being constitutive forms of the being of physical objects. Rather, they are the constituitive forms of being human. They are not "forms of understanding" and so do not concern merely the mind; rather, they are lived, forms of existing, and they govern the emergence or the happening of human reality.

Winch's appeals to "limiting conceptions" in 'Understanding a Primitive Society' hold a similar office. The idea that human beings share "forms of life" and that understanding other sociocultures rests on these commonalities, the embracing of common needs, emotions, ends, interests, and instincts; common actions, reactions, and practices; and common facts of life together with similar physical environs. Just as Heidegger was steering between the Platonic metaphysical conceptions of "universals" and the reductionism of the biological sciences with regard to understanding human reality, so too is Winch. The rationale behind his move again lies in an interpretation of Wittgenstein, according to which human actions and practices are conceived of as expressing these "existentials," in the circumstances in which they occur. A commonality, in emotions of sadness, frustration, and fear, the goals of safety, nourishment, shelter, are to be located neither in the biological facts nor metaphysical clouds of theory, but in the practices themselves.

Both Winch and Evans-Pritchard circle around such structures. Grasping that the Zande were consulting an oracle in order to determine whether witchcraft had a hand in recent misfortunes did not resolve all Evans-Pritchard's bafflement. He dissipated much of the remaining opaqueness by surmising that the Azande were out to unravel the causal nexus. In conjecturing this, Evans-Pritchard rested his understanding of the Zande on an existential structure, namely, the practice of getting the world right, and also of intervening in it in order to influence it. Such critics as Winch and Wittgenstein might be right that anthropologists have sometimes misinterpreted this or that practice as an instance of these general types. Surely however, it is erroneous to deny these types of practices of any organized group of human beings. In any event, Evans-Pritchard achieved understanding of the Azande practice of killing and gutting fowl by bringing it under this "lived-structure of experience."

Winch's rival account relies on similar frameworks. Winch argued that the Azande practice should be understood as expressing an "attitude toward contingencies ... which involves recognition that one's life is subject to them," more specifically, which involves recognition that life can continue even when one is let down by things that one finds important. Such an attitude, dare we say it, is an "existential structure of dasein." It is hard to imagine any mode of animate life that lacks this recognition as even a minimally organized human existence. Contrary to the almost constant charge of relativism levied against him, Winch makes explicit reference to such structures in his essay. For example, he cites three "limiting notions"—birth, death, and sexuality—"that are inescapably involved in the life of all known human societies in a way which gives us a clue where to look, if we are puzzled about the point of an alien system of institutions."[51] These limiting notions are existential structural circumstantial phenomena by reference to which what, why, and what people are about in doing certain things can be appreciated.[52] Winch's remarks very late in 'Understanding a Primitive Society' on how the temporal structure of death conditions a great deal of human activity similarly parallels Heidegger's famous existential of being-towards-death.

These lines, as well as the references to Vico, apply to participations in forms of life. The tissues of congruous reactions that are being treated as forms of life comprise the structures of the practices that people take over during their lifetime. What Winch is doing is fleshing out Wittgenstein's working through specific examples of understanding different sociocultures, identifying those "existentials" at work and defending their status as frames with which we have enough in common to begin thoughtful comparison and orientation in those practices. Once we understand this, the relationship between Winch's own work and the "rationality debates" that it inspired can only be seen in an ironic light.[53] Winch was simply not interested in the thought experiments invented by Davidson regarding the project of radical translation and interpretation, worrying as he did about the epistemic possibility of there being any kind of intercultural understanding at all. Perhaps this is why Winch is so often falsely accused of denying the possibility of such intercultural understanding. In as much as he held that there are always comparable lived possibilities between human communities, he never bothers with the skeptical concern of a completely untranslatable language of the kind dismissed by Davidson. Instead he is concerned only with the partial difficulties of translation generated by the conceptual differences between cultures.

Winch would surely say that the problem with these arguments is that the concept tends to over-unify the characteristics which go toward making up a form of life. Perhaps "like-mindedness" can be more or less shared, more or less stable. If so then the "transcendental" objection loses its punch, for it relies on being an all or nothing thing. Either we share the subjectivity of the group or we do not. What such an argument assumes, however, is a kind of unified subjectivity. The assumption that to adhere to a form of life is to share a particular kind of subjectivity is the key step in the 'transcendental' objection to multiple forms of life. Winch tried to address these difficulties under the rubric of rules—that to understand a practice is being able to imagine what it is like to carry it out. Later Winch interpreted this to possess such an attitude is to be prepared to react to another person in particular ways under certain contingencies, and to do so. To understand people, in a sense commensurate with the possession of this attitude, is to participate in the ways people react to one another under certain shared contingencies.

These are articulations of a dimension of a human being that at one time was called mind, but which after Heidegger are labeled existentials, and later by Winch an "attitude towards a soul." These are not merely cognitive understandings but the articulation of a dimension of human life about which more can and must always be said, and what is said recalibrated from the position which we happen to occupy. These *"seelische"* conditions must be approached by working through specific examples of understanding different sociocultures, identifying them at work, and recognizing their similarities while at the same time resisting their theoretical articulation. What this does is reveal those points by which human understanding and different forms of social life become possible.

Many have found in the work of "Wittgensteinians" extremely helpful compliments to European philosophy, providing as they do mechanisms for dispelling the confusions which often surround hermeneutic controversy which manifest themselves in language and go very deep into human life. Dissolving deep rooted perplexity is a very great thing to have done, but cannot occur in the absence of good intentions, or running roughshod over an opponent with relativism charges. The best detours alert us to how miscommunications which fueled the debates in the first place will not be continued to be mystified or ignored. What results is an illustration that one may well be able to use the techniques of ordinary language to clarify the conceptual confusions in hermeneutics just as, for example, thinkers such as Wisdom, Dilman, Winch and Rhees worked to clarify conceptual confusions in ethics and the social sciences.

XV. The Mimes of Sophron and Gadamer's *Philebus*

Reading Gadamer's discussion of the *Philebus*[1] suggests at first a gap between what in fact Plato intends to say in the *Philebus* and what Gadamer interprets him to be saying. This is no small task to establish, since one is faced with establishing what in fact Plato *is* saying in the *Philebus*.[2] Centuries of scholarship have commented on the dialogue's obscurity. There is dispute even as to whether or not the dialogue is ultimately about ethics, epistemology, or metaphysics. Socrates and Protarchus are seemingly having an important discussion on pleasure, and it is certainly Plato's most sustained treatment of that topic. But the dialogue quickly morphs into extended and difficult treatments of "one-and-many" problems regarding monads, instructions for procedures of inquiry methodology, a general analysis of "everything that exists" in the universe, and a classification of "knowledges" according to their accuracy and purity. The Neoplatonic commentators had already surmised that the dialogue was about a great deal more than just pleasure, and worried over its impact on the theory of Forms. Contemporary stylometric analyses have yet to definitively place the dialogue in any chronological order with regard to other dialogues, despite its having been written with the criticisms of the *Parmenides* in mind.

An additional coat of complexity to be added (before perhaps stripping the interpretive layers) is the testimony of Aristotle in regard to the *Philebus*, as many scholars have assumed that Aristotle had accurately reported Eudoxus' views on pleasure and that these views are what Plato is responding to in the *Philebus*. Indeed, one can count at least 5 major scholars (Gosling, Sayre, Schipper, Bury, Hackforth) as enlisting Aristotle to help decipher obscure passages in *Philebus*, such as his testimony (in *Metaphysics* 987B15) and elsewhere that the ontology of the *Philebus* includes intermediate mathematical objects. Each scholar subsequently draws a different conclusion from Aristotle's interpretation, but the point is that all begin their arguments with the assumption that Aristotle has accurately reported a Platonic dialogue.[3]

This in turn becomes no small issue, as it portends an entire approach to how one reads all of Plato's dialogues, opening on to a path which holds that the dialogues are not philosophical treatises at all but more like Aristotle's reference to them in the *Poetics* (1447B9-11) as items to be classified with the "mimes of

Sophron and Xenarchus."[4] This claim in effect classifies Plato's works as works of something other than philosophy. Indeed, so this line continues, no dialogue may be said to represent some "doctrine" of Plato. If one wants to know what Plato believed, an unimpeachable source provides us with more direct information about Plato's thinking than Plato himself ever put down in 20 years of writing: this source is Aristotle, who spent twenty years at the Academy, and heard what Plato himself actually said.

Thus Plato never expressed his "philosophy" in writing. If the *Seventh Letter* is to be believed, he was emphatically against such a procedure. Plato never actually speaks in any of his dialogues, so even if the dialogues did represent, in some sense, Plato's philosophy, one could never be sure that any given speaker represents Plato's own voice in the dialogues. Socrates surely is not Plato's mouthpiece, since he does not even appear in all of the dialogues (*Laws*), he is not always the main speaking character of a dialogue (*Timaeus* and *Sophist*), he sometimes gets humiliated in a dialogue (*Parmenides*), he sometimes maintains contradictory positions during a dialogue [*Meno*, where he alternately tells us that virtue can be taught (89c), that virtue cannot be taught (89e), that virtue does not come by nature (89a) and that virtue does come by nature (100b)], he seems to change his mind part way through some dialogues (*Protagorus, Cratylus*), not to mention his persistent claims in dialogues that he does not know anything.

Quick and easy references to "Plato's philosophy" thus stagger to the finish line. Indeed, the use of expressions such as "Plato said that love is X" or "The *Symposium* sets forth Plato's views that love is Y" are extremely questionable. Plato uses *philia* for love in the *Lysis* and the *Phaedrus*, but uses *eros* for love in the *Symposium*. In the entire corpus of Aristotle, we find not one single word on what Plato thought about either *eros* or *philia*. Hence on the view that we should look only to Aristotle for Plato's "philosophy," we can only conclude that we simply do not know what is Plato's theory of love. So too the time honored (and eternally anthologized) notions that Plato held to a "recollection theory" of epistemology or a "two-world" metaphysics. Aristotle wrote an entire treatise on the topic of memory, and nowhere in it, or anywhere else, does he give the slightest mention of a "theory of recollection" attributable to Plato. Plato's "theory of Forms" fares somewhat better on this analysis, since on this front Aristotle has a great deal to say in relation to Plato's thinking, especially in his *Metaphysics*. This has no small relevance to the *Philebus*, as in relation to it Aristotle attributes to Plato an entire mathematical theory in Books A, M, and N of the *Metaphysics*. But nowhere does Aristotle criticize Plato for locating his Forms in some other world or supernatural dimension. Indeed, he correlates

Plato's Forms with his formal and material causes—locating both of these Platonic notions within *this world* as causes. In Chapter ix of Book 1 of the *Metaphysics*, Aristotle cites 14 criticisms of Plato, none of them accusing Plato of setting up another reality opposed to this one. If Aristotle is correct, then those who claim a two-world view for Plato are at variance with the man who spent twenty years in daily contact with Plato. Once again, much of the "theory" does not correspond to any explicit discussion in the dialogues. As a result, many scholars have compounded the problems by either dismissing Aristotle's testimony, piecing together the views by presumed connections with other dialogues, or, in a very unfortunate move, conjecturing that these features are a part of something they call Plato's "Unwritten Doctrine."

The reason for this prolonged stage-setting is that it puts us in a better position to see what Gadamer is doing in relation to the *Philebus*, how easy it is to misconstrue his philosophical hermeneutics in relation to Plato and Aristotle in general, and how much benefit might be derived from paying greater attention to it. And while Gadamer is guilty of some of the aforementioned sins, (such as writing on Plato's unwritten dialectic), very preliminarily, it can be suggested that he is both forwarding an interpretation of *Philebus* which reconciles its various interpretive dilemmas, as well as very much "portending an entire approach" to how one reads all of Plato's dialogues. Indeed, Gadamer is giving a first version of an entire hermeneutic theory in relation to any text, and to human understanding in general. In this connection the importance for Gadamer of Heidegger's lectures on Aristotle during the 1920's cannot be underestimated, and how doing hermeneutics as a kind of phenomenology is central. For it seems Martin Heidegger can as well be added to that list of scholars "aristotelianizing" Plato, and what I seek to show is that Gadamer is involved in a complex movement akin to pulling Plato back from the Aristotelianism through which Plato has previously been interpreted; more specifically, Gadamer would like to retrieve the model of practical philosophy (*phronesis*) that was conceived by Aristotle, but in a certain sense would like to infuse that model with the spirit of universal dialogical openness that he finds portrayed, in an exemplary manner, in the Socrates of the *Philebus*.

Thus Gadamer's work on the *Philebus* is at once an enactment of phenomenological hermeneutics as applied to a platonic dialogue, and an illustration of the proximity of such hermeneutics to *phronesis*. Gadamer was no slouch as a Greek scholar (good enough to have passed the state examination for philology under the tutelage of Paul Friedländer), and from the beginning, his work on the Greeks was guided by his interests in the Greek conception of

practical philosophy. Gadamer's *Habilitationschrift* had its genesis in a question
concerning Aristotle's ethics. Thus *Plato's Dialectical Ethics* remains a work that
centers on the questions of ethics, of the good for human life. This issue
announces itself explicitly in the title of Gadamer's later study *The Idea of the Good
in Platonic-Aristotelian Philosophy*, which Gadamer himself refers to as a kind of
provisional conclusion to the work undertaken in his work on the *Philebus*.[5] At
the same time and in a way reminiscent of the young Nietzsche, it is a turn away
from the dominant philological approach of the day, as exemplified by the Jaeger
school. In the third preface to his book on the *Philebus*, Gadamer mentions how
Werner Jaeger's school in Berlin had at the time reached such a "point of
refinement" to where many Aristotelian terms no longer required translations in
scholarly discussions. Such could only be seen as a sclerosis to one interested in
hermeneutics. As Gadamer puts it:

> Did that not involve an evasion of the real task of expressing by means of one's own
> linguistic materials, employing the conceptual potential of those materials, the way in
> which, in Greek thought, the things themselves, the facts of the matter, presented
> themselves? So I tried to lay aside all scholarly knowledge for once and to take as my
> point of departure the phenomena as they show themselves to us.[6]

Gadamer's *Philebus* interpretation also is inextricably woven together with
Heidegger's phenomenological appropriations of Aristotle in his now famous
lecture courses from the 1920's. Heidegger's Aristotle lectures seem to have
provided both the positive methodological model for Gadamer's efforts in
relation to the *Philebus*, and also a provocation to resist Heidegger's insistence
upon reading Plato through the eyes of Aristotelian critique, providing a
resistance against which Gadamer was able to develop his own interpretation.
In these lecture courses, in which Gadamer participated as a student, it became
apparent just how difficult it is to lay bare one's presuppositions so as to
approach Aristotle phenomenologically. For several semesters Heidegger
conducted seminars later to be called *Phenomenologische Interpretationen zu Aristoteles*
seeking to indicate the hermeneutic situation out of which such interpretations
could proceed, which he came to describe with the phrase "hermeneutics of
facticity." This phrase refers to the self-address of factical life—life's attempt to
catch itself in the act, as it were, of interpreting, interpretation directed at that
which is doing the interpreting. The task would be to strive to bring about
factical life's own self-articulation as far as possible in the face of its own
inescapable situatedness, and since such situatedness would include the very
language and concepts historically employed in such analysis, it would be co-

extensive with the project of the de-structuring of the history of ontology. To some extent, then, what Heidegger presents in his *Phenomenologische Interpretationen zu Aristoteles* concerning philosophical methodology, later developed extensively in *Being and Time*, is as well taken up by Gadamer implicitly in his work on the *Philebus*.[7]

However, it can also be said that Gadamer turns Heidegger's Aristotle against Heidegger's Plato, who took the author of the dialogues to be the decisive step toward metaphysical thought's obliviousnessness to Being, the most famous expression of which occurs in Heidegger's wartime "Plato's Doctrine of Truth," but can also clearly be seen in his lecture course on Plato's *Sophist* during the winter semester of 1924-25.[8] Very early in this lecture course, and in a way similar to our earlier list of *Philebus* scholars, Heidegger is enlisting the Stagirite as the "guiding line" which will insure the correct path of access to Plato's thought. Thus the initial Gadamerian question becomes: what is missed by such a reading that might be taken as authentically Platonic? While it is not the case that Heidegger does not realize the implications of his hermeneutical approach, or that he does not know what he is missing in appropriating Plato's thought the way he does, and that Gadamer's work on the *Philebus* is not a critique of Heidegger, (it was after all written under the direction of Heidegger), it is nonetheless a bold move by the young Gadamer, a movement in a direction away from the guiding line of Aristotle and toward a genuine encounter with Plato's thought.

While Heidegger sees Plato as of monumental significance in western thought, though the ancient thinker's work is marked by the confusions and unclarity which accompany all such radical and foundational thoughts, he seems to have had little regard for Platonic dialectic, even calling it a "genuine philosophical embarassment" in *Being and Time*.[9] He is also clear in his lecture course on the *Sophist* that dialectic is marked by basic deficiencies. Thus part of what Gadamer is seeking to do in his *Philebus* work is to illustrate how Heidegger in his own way remains committed to reading Plato through Aristotle, and that reading Aristotle from a Platonic point of view, and releasing the guiding line, would bring us into a clearing in which Plato's own thinking would no longer be classified among the mimes of Sophron but would finally and actually be allowed to emerge.

Gadamer first and foremost regards Plato's mode of philosophizing as determined most decisively by the experience of human finitude, which leads Plato to identify philosophy with dialectic. Equally significant is how Plato regards philosophy as an ethical matter. In the 1931 preface to *Plato's Dialectical Ethics*, Gadamer recasts the book's title as a question:

> The title does not promise an answer: rather it poses a question: in what sense Plato's dialectic poses, and in general can pose, the problem of ethics. I do not assert that Plato's "ethics" is dialectical; rather, I ask whether and in what way Plato's dialectic is "ethics."[10]

This reversal suggests that the very activity of philosophy itself, dialectic, constitutes ethics, and, as Gadamer will come to develop, the ethical claim of dialectic should be understood in connection with its opposition to sophistry. No philosophical claim can avoid its own collapse into dogmatism without the laying bare of all presuppositions, the examining of all prejudices, the willingness and openness to grow, that in Plato's eyes constitutes the greatest transgression against the philosophical life, and as well the greatest danger within the ethical and the political realm. "Plato's philosophy" crosses the finish line after all, but not as an ethical doctrine, nor as an articulation of *arete* by means of the concept, nor in the form of expressions such as "Plato said that ethics is X" but as protreptic, as *bildungsroman*, as a movement from one place to another. In its own provisional character, what is happening *through* the texts, more than what is said *in* them, directly reflects this fundamentally Socratic sense of the finitude of human existence.

Plato's Dialectical Ethics opens with Gadamer's distinguishing Plato from Aristotle in three ways. First, Plato's conviction that human knowing is always an imperfect striving toward perfection, namely the idea of the Good, marks his project as fundamentally privative, oriented toward that which always surpasses it. That is, Plato's analysis of human possibilities is something to which pure theory is added only as something extreme and never fully attainable. Secondly, Aristotle's is a fundamentally theoretical orientation in ethics, where with Plato the dialectic just *is itself* ethics, and thus marked by a radical provisionalness, intertwining as it does with the very thought that it addresses. Plato is not subject to the presumption of theory because dialectic is not at a conceptual remove but is constituitive of the very activity of philosophizing itself. Third, for Gadamer, Aristotle's critique of Plato does not do justice to what is in fact encountered in the dialogues, not in the sense that Aristotle somehow failed to grasp Plato's thinking, which is absurd, but that his presumption of theory, his orientation in the language of the concept, could only ever achieve a flattening out of the expressive density and multiplicity which belongs to life itself, and which is present in Plato's artistry. The point is that something is of course gained, but something fundamental also is lost, in the "conceptual clarity" Aristotle brings to the Platonic text.

The culmination of the interpretation of Platonic dialectic in his book on *Philebus* can be taken to suggest that the problem of dialectic in Plato is in large measure the problem of ground. According to Gadamer's usage, to ground something means to give a ground for it, to articulate in *logos* the reason or cause, in Greek the *aitia*, for its necessarily being the thing that it is. This is the basis for what Gadamer calls "scientific inquiry," the process which exhibits a thing's necessarily being that way. For example, a condition of ill health may be recognized as undesirable by everyone, but most will not have any real understanding of the condition, and call it by different names and suggest all different manner of remedies. For such people the condition, as it were, lacks a ground. The plurality of aspects that constitute the condition are not gathered together and understood in any unitary respect. However, someone who understands the ground for the condition, someone who knows the cause that necessarily establishes this condition as being just the condition that it is and none other, will be in a position to bring about or to prescribe a remedy that will restore health. The Platonic name for this process of discerning a unitary *eidos* from out of a sensible manifold and establishing its ground is dialectic.

For example, Gadamer's comment about what takes place near the beginning of the *Philebus*: the question about which has a greater share of the good life, *hedone* or *episteme*, "means, from the start, that it is necessary to bring out what manifold of phenomena is embraced in a unified way in the one thesis and the other."[11] In other words, one has to agree on a unitary starting point which can then be interrogated further as to its proper ground. Yet, in a way, this starting point is already a ground, in that dialectic must take this unity as its guide and commit itself to disclosing nothing other than what belongs to it. The more serious question, then, is that dialectic must allow itself to be guided by that which it is itself called upon to determine—namely, the thing itself. The thing itself must be allowed to, as it were, ground itself, to show itself in the full depth of its being grounded. Initially, the object of dialectic must first appear as ungrounded, as not yet having a ground, since it is itself what is to be grounded. This is the initial unity that must be agreed upon before dialectic is to begin (which Gadamer often refers to in the *Philebus* book as the *Sache*). There would also seem to be a sense in which the *Sache* already contains its ground. It is not that determining the ground of something is an operation that is performed upon it; rather, the thing itself prescribes what can and cannot be said about it, including, most of all, that which necessarily belongs to it and makes it what it is. The grounding of the thing thus takes the form of a disclosure, or a clearing, of the ground that already belongs to the thing. The aim of dialectic is nothing other than a hermeneutic enactment of *zu den Sachen selbst* in terms of letting the *Sache* ground itself. Thus the problem of the ground must arrive at and confront the issue of self-grounding, and one of the issues in the *Philebus* for Gadamer seems to be whether the forms of knowing, which seem to be largely understandable in terms of *techne* and *episteme*, are adequate to this problem of self-grounding.

Thus the opening sections of the book on *Philebus* are dedicated in large part to showing that dialogue, properly understood, is something like the ground of dialectic, that dialogue is the manner in which the dialectical process of grounding takes place. Only through being submitted to a proper testing in dialogue can the proposed ground be confirmed in its necessity as the true ground; and only an appropriately attuned dialogue, one that really listens to the facts of the matter, can first effect the proper securing of the *Sache*. The very essence of the dialectical is to let the *thing speak itself*,[12] and this understanding remains decisive for Gadamer throughout his work, since in the penultimate section of *Truth and Method* Gadamer indicates that in dialectic "it is the thing itself that asserts its force,"[13] and that "there is something resembling dialectic in hermeneutical experience: an activity of the thing itself, an action that, unlike the methodology of modern science, is a passion, an understanding, an event that happens to one."[14] What we see in Gadamer's *Philebus*-considerations are an initial conceptualization of how the thing comes to speak, in a way proper to it, and asserts itself as it is, holds its ground, and offers up the sort of resistance, in the midst of the swirling flux of language, that would permit it to speak against something, and which served as a response to the sophists rushing flood of words, detached from their stabilizing connections to the things themselves. Can it be that, free of the Aristotelian guiding line, this is what Plato was really about, how it is possible to emerge from the stream and hold fast in the current as a kind of grounding which is at once a self-grounding and the emerging of the thing itself?

Gadamer's specific de-aristotelianizing of Plato concerns Heidegger's lecture courses on Aristotle, including the remarks on Aristotle Heidegger supplies in his lecture course on the *Sophist*. In book 6 of the *Nicomachian Ethics*, Aristotle provides an analysis of what are commonly called the intellectual virtues, the various modes of *aletheuein*, the disclosure or unconcealing of the world that is accomplished in human speaking (*legein*). This represents a key moment for Gadamer's own thought. For Aristotle, the self-showing of beings is accomplished most directly in terms of *nous*, the direct apprehension or perception of beings by the intellect. This pure noetic insight is then articulated in terms of the four main ways it can be carried out: *techne*, *episteme*, *phronesis*, and *sophia*. These articulations are then distinguished and ranked according to what Heidegger in the *Sophist* lecture course identifies as two main criteria: first the character of the beings they disclose, and second their comportment with respect to the *archai*, the origins and causes of those beings.

In his book on *Philebus*, Gadamer begins to expose the false security of technical-theoretical knowing. For what these forms or habits of knowing do not ask about is how the *eide* to which they look are first able to appear. In them the question of ground is pursued only to a certain point, and then abandoned at the axiomatic limits of the science. Mathematics, for example, does not question beyond its fundamental presuppositions, its axioms. And the artisan, for her part, does not ask about the nature of what is to be produced, but only about the means by which to produce it. As Plato writes in book 10 of the *Republic*, the nature of the pattern itself must be prescribed by those who use the product, not by those who make it (601d). At bottom, then, the ultimate ground of any technical-theoretical knowing is taken simply for granted as given, and cannot be investigated from within the confines of the particular craft or science itself. In his *Philebus* study Gadamer also argues that this ground is in fact constituted by just that form of dialectical thinking first embodied by Socratic dialogue. Everything the Greeks call science has the character of shared substantive understanding (*sachliche Verständigung*)—which arises from out of human conversation and agreement.

A better translation of this phrase might choose a word other than "substantive," since the suggestion that Socratic dialogue is guided by some independent "substance" standing apart from language, such that the success of *sachliche Verständigung* could be measured by its agreement with such a substance, is the last thing Gadamer would want to convey. Better would be to keep before us the idea that the word "substantive" indicates an orientation towards the disclosure of whatever is at issue, not referring to a pre-given metaphysical substance. Also *Verständigung* suggests but does not entail a sharing between people. This ambiguity preserves Gadamer's intent that language essentially entails a give and take of living, spoken dialogue, and retains the suggestion of a "between" in which understanding takes place. This means for Gadamer that the fundamental unit of meaning in language is not the individual statement but conversation, with its distinctive play of question and answer. Thus Gadamer is referring to a process of coming to an understanding, in contrast to the Greek *nous*, that is suggestive of a back-and-forth movement or process of disclosure.

This process holds as much for Aristotelian *episteme* and *techne*, which he calls *apodeixis*, or "showing from," as for Platonic dialectic. Since both the Platonic and Aristotelian forms of *Wissenschaft* have their essential origin in Socratic conversation, Gadamer's larger claim emerges, namely that there is a fundamental continuity between socratic conversation, platonic dialectic, and Aristotelian *apodeixis*.

Dialectic is thus the continuous middle term between dialogue and *apodeixis*, even though the former depends manifestly on agreement with others, where the latter, being essentially a monological form of discourse, would seemingly depend on the self-evident necessity of demonstration. This is Gadamer's reply to Heidegger's attempt to construe dialectical thinking as an inferior method of disclosing beings that would be overcome by genuine *theoria*. Dialectic is not a method at all for Plato, but a way of living a human life, one which has a fundamental connection with ethics and which in itself reflects human finitude. In arguing for a dialogical basis for the Greek conception of science in general, Gadamer wants to show that dialectic is not merely one possible method for carrying out the philosophical enterprise, but rather is the very enactment (*Vollzug*) of philosophy itself. In challenge to Heidegger's aristotelianizing perspective that subsumes dialectic to *techne* and *episteme*, Gadamer is moving toward a recovery of an understanding of *theoria* which is itself a form of dialectical *praxis*. Once *theoria* is disentangled from the modern prejudice that opposes "theory" to "practice," it is possible to articulate the dialectical basis of all forms of theoretical discourse.

This is why Gadamer begins his book on *Philebus* and dialectical ethics with an extended consideration of science. Properly understood, as *sachliche Verständigung*, it is scientific discourse alone that can be construed as ethics, thus indicating that Plato opposed dialectic to sophistry on ethical grounds. When speakers engage in discourse which is scientific, when they engage in *shared substantive understanding*, they find themselves bound together in the solidarity of that common pursuit. This is the result not of their adherence to some pregiven set of rules, such as those prescribed by the scientific method, or the mutual observance of some ethical code for scientific professionals, but a unity which emerges out of a shared subordination to the project of the highest things disclosing themselves. In this solidarity is formed, if you will, a hermeneutic community, the common experience of whom is defined in large part by the common language of the participants in the shared disclosure of things themselves.

We suggested earlier that Gadamer is not only forwarding an interpretation of *Philebus* which reconciles its various interpretive dilemmas, as well as sketching out an entire approach to how one should read all of Plato's dialogues, but he is also giving a first version of an entire hermeneutic theory in relation to any text, and to human understanding in general. Insofar as such scientific discourse must respond to the demand to be substantive (*sachlich*), it necessarily entails a reference to what Plato thinks under the heading of the idea of the good, and this in turn discloses the need for a unique kind of ground. This ground is understood by Gadamer as a universal ontological principle which provides the formal structure for whatever comes to be, and is able to be understood. We might, at least in some small way, make good on the first of these claims to a greater degree, by pointing out how Gadamer's elaboration of the dialectical structure of scientific speaking and the continuity of dialectic and *apodeixis* reconciles some interpretive puzzles at the textual level of the *Philebus* itself.

As is well known, Socrates and Protarchus are arguing over which psychic state or condition promotes the good life, pleasure or knowledge. The hedonistic position that pleasure is the good for all living beings (11a) is one that Protarchus has taken over from "*kalos*" Philebus, who has withdrawn from the discussion (11c). Philebus is represented as a dogmatic person who "shall always think that pleasure is the victor" (12a) and, after entrusting his position to Protarchus, washes his hands of the argument (12b). He will later on break into the discussion only to complain that he does not understand (18a-d), or to fallaciously protest against Socrates (22c) or complain that the significance of intelligence is being overplayed (28b). The only time Philebus does try to enter the argument (27e) he plays into Socrates' hands by admitting that pleasure is indefinite. Of course Protarchus is often not the best interlocutor either: at the beginning he recognized no distinctions whatsoever among pleasures; Gadamer refers at times to his responses having fallen short of the level of insight that the discussion has reached. Even Socrates' worries that he is making a fool of himself (23d1-5), hesitates to go into details (24e4-5), and seems to misquote the god of the divine method differently in 23c9-10 than in 16c9-10. Such are not incidental but an expression of the dialogic prerequisites for shared substantive understanding, "prepared from the very beginning by the steps explicitly taken to ensure the partner's suitability for substantive argument."[15]

The profound difficulty that characterizes Socratic dialogue is that it seeks to let itself be guided by a subject matter of which it does not yet have a clear understanding. It can do so only by submitting all substantive claims to an impartial, anonymous testing in which no particular individual but only the thing itself is to be judge. Such testing requires a substantive rigor that excludes all purely external intrusions, as well as the contingent but aimless to and fro movement that characterizes sophistical techniques of disputation. Where the sole aim is refutation and superiority, the discussion is not motivated by the issue in question. Indeed, since the entire aim of sophistic discourse is to overcome and thereby exclude the other person from the conversation and convert dialogue into monologue, *sachliche Verständigung* depends from the outset on the dialogical securing of the subject matter. When Socrates presses Protarchus (13a7-b5) for the identical feature in pleasures which makes him call them all good, we incline to the essentialist call for those things whose presence in all the many X's guarantees that we might rightly call them all X's. That Socrates also calls them "monadic" also implies that they exist, as opposed to coming to or passing away from existence. This implies that answering the question, what is the good, is not merely an ethical question, but also has ontological ramifications.

The meaning of the dialogue however is not in its specific arguments so much as in its display of how such arguments are begotten. The jockeying is exemplary of how evidentness requires substantive assent freely given in response to what is substantive in the speech of the other, which can only happen under conditions of openness. Protarchus admits pleasure is generic like colors, but then retreats on the assumption that no progress can be made along such lines that have pleasure to be like intelligence in that they both seem to be one and many. Socrates in turn narrows the discussion by excluding those one-many issues that involve generation and corruption. Such adjustments underscore the necessary constituitive role of the other. Philebus' participation precludes a shared scientific understanding of the subject matter as his perspective rules out that the other has anything to say to him. The process of testing requires that one place value on different perspectives, since it is only in this space of difference that the issue in question can be secured. That Socrates employs the language of division of the fourfold is not necessary (20c4-6), but then proceeds *as long as Protarchus agrees* (23c5), points to how both parties adjust in the dialogic context. When one no longer seeks the assent of the other, shared understanding is no longer a possibility. The discourse can no longer properly be called scientific, since the subject matter will not have been fixed in place.

The *Philebus* then pushes the one-and-many problem to the next level. Against Protarchus' contention that all pleasures are alike, Socrates points out that, on the contrary, pleasures not only differ from one another, but can even be in opposition (12c-e). The same holds true for knowledge (13d-14b). The source of difficulty is in understanding how one thing, pleasure or knowledge, can at the same time have many different and even opposite forms, again the famous problem of the one and the many, but this time applied to Forms. The contrast Plato is drawing is between a Form as a self-identical, immutable, timeless, and unified entity on the one hand, and on the other, a Form which differs from, and even opposes, other Forms, including those which are its parts. Socrates' reply to Protarchus at *Philebus* 12c-e mirrors what he said to Meno (in *Meno* 74b-76a) namely that regarding *Arete* there is one Form "over" the many sensible manifestations of it. Protarchus has the opposite problem of insisting that, e.g., all pleasures, as pleasures, are alike. So Socrates must stress that even if pleasure as a genus or kind is one, it can have many different and even opposing species, or parts. Yet exactly how any genus, Form, or monad can contain many, even opposite, parts, and still remain unified, is not clear. This, as all Plato fans know, replays the dilemma of participation from the *Parmenides* (131a-131c), namely, that either each part participates in its own part of the whole or each part participates in the whole Form, resulting in the form becoming separate from itself. Either disjunct leads to problems, since if each part participates in the whole of the form, then the Form is not the same as itself and would forfeit all self-identity. But that each sensible has its own part is also unacceptable as it would entail the denial of the universality of Forms, since *that* part would be unique to *that* sensible, and if this were so, then the Form would depend upon the sensible in which it is substantiated for its existence and character, triggering a complete reversal of standard Platonic ontology. How does a Gadamerian analysis of the *Philebus* address these *aporiai* in regards to the existence and ontological status of the Forms?

The real problem of the one and the many shows up with pure unities, such as the good or man as such. As pure they cannot be divisible. The problem seems to find its solution in the theory of the mixture, presented in the *Parmenides*, but just as *aporia*, not as a *euporia*. In the context of the *Philebus*, the immediate concern is to deal with the one-and-many problem as it applies to pleasure and knowledge. It might be reasonable at this point for traditional scholarship to infer that since the *aporiai* are about Forms and that the nature of pleasure and knowledge involve these puzzles, then the proper analysis of pleasure and knowledge also will involve Forms. But this does not mean that both pleasure and knowledge themselves *are* forms, only that an understanding of them requires something *like* them. Thus the exact ontological status of pleasure and knowledge are open questions at the outset of the dialogue—we have no reason to affirm or deny that pleasure and knowledge are themselves

Forms. Before this gets determined, more needs to be said about the *aporiai* and how best to approach them.

How best to approach them is through living a human life. Gadamer's whole point has been that Plato presented philosophy not as a doctrine or theory so much as a form of human existence. The life represented by Socrates reveals the fundamental character of human Dasein. Thus both the doctrine and the practice of philosophy as originally presented by Plato are essentially ethical. Gadamer at this time is challenging the Heideggerian thesis that Greek ontology "understands Being as something present at hand in the present" [*gegenwärtig Vorhandenes*].[16] One of the main elements of this line of thinking is that the Greeks (with Plato being the foremost Greek in this sense) did not understand (or perhaps no longer understood) being in terms of the revealing-concealing movement of *aletheia*, but instead had begun to regard being as itself "a" being. One of the things lost in this way of thinking is the possibility of understanding being in terms of temporality, *kinesis*, and difference. Instead, being is understood as being present-at-hand, available, disposable. That is, being is understood as having a fixed essence, thought in terms of presence, that can be disposed over, so that to know something is to have disposition over it. One need not, as did Heidegger, go back to the pre-socratics to locate an original, pre-theoretical opening of human existence—it was right there in Plato all along.

As this is an early work, Gadamer does not push this as far as will later Heideggerians. Although the outcome of the debate between knowledge and pleasure, or as the argument shifts around 63e, between reason and pleasure, firmly sides with reason, this is not found to be the primary good for humans; that place is reserved for the Good itself, introduced into the argument fairly late in the game (60b) and weakly defined throughout. What is clear is that the superiority of the Good is established by its qualities of autonomy and the power of self-sufficiency and perfection. (67a). The standard by which the virtues are judged in the *Philebus* turns out to be self-sufficiency; the Good, as the only wholly self-sufficient thing, is judged to be the highest of them. If we link *phronesis* to the Good, as Plato wants, we admit that another standard of self-knowledge is self-sufficiency, the "presence" of which would surely be the target of later scholars.

Regardless, Gadamer's *Philebus* provides an important early sketch of the way Gadamer understands the dialogical structure of ground. Insofar as it is the other person who alone warrants the truth that shows itself in a dialectical discussion, the ground that is thereby displayed can be seen to have a fundamental dialogical character, secured, but in always only a provisional sense, in and through a substantive disciplined discourse. This dialogical conception of "scientific knowing" represents an initial attempt on Gadamer's part to break from Heidegger's dogmatically Aristotelian reading of Plato. As his *Truth and Method* will emphasize, the being of what is understood is not something other than the appearance by which it becomes manifest. A dramatic play only properly exists when it is being performed. Only in the *Vollzug* of performance, which encompasses the conversation-like interplay between the performers, the text, and the audience, does the play fully and meaningfully come into its own.

What is true of the play is true of all conversation and all understanding. What is understood is only understood as it presents itself. Just as Plato in the end may have been correct in banishing the poets from the *Republic*, not because their task was inferior but because exile is the proper condition of poetry, so too the classification of Socrates together with the mimes of Sophron might not be entirely inappropriate after all, escaping as it would the framework of *techne* imposed on his thinking by Aristotle. The Platonic dialogues are not philosophical treatises but character studies, scenes from human lives, with characters individualized by name, differences in temperament, in background, in interests, in outlook, in style of speaking, even occasionally in dialect. Some conversational participants are boys, some young men, some middle aged, some old. Some are sophists, rhetoricians, soldiers, politicians, poets, rhapsodes, soothsayers, physicians. Some are aggressive and some passive. Some are enthusiasts and some are cynics. Some are straightforward and some are ironical. Since the philosophical arguments are interwoven with the character traits, interests, and daily activities of different types of men, the platonic dialogues are philosophical mimes which attend rigorously to the problematic character of grounding itself. What emerges is an understanding of dialectic that neither falls prey to infinite regress of grounds, nor simply stops with some arbitrarily named ground. Platonic dialectic calls for a notion of ground capable of turning back upon itself, of grounding itself. As Gadamer was to later argue, "the critique of poetry (in the *Republic*) is simultaneously a justification for Plato's writing."[17] Socrates does not in fact ban *all* poetry from his city—"songs in praise of good individuals" withstand his criticisms. The song of praise in the form of poetic play is shared language, the language of common concern. Where no such shared substantive understanding exists, a *philosophical discussion* about the true state becomes the only true praise.[18]

Despite the enduring legacy of Platonism, then, the basis of Greek science for Gadamer is not some changeless *eidos*, forged in the vault of heavens and handed down by divine dispensation; the true Promethean fire is dialectic itself, which alone secures these guiding images and patterns and gives to them their binding certainty. By setting into question the persistance of the Aristotelian standpoint that imputes to Plato an unwavering adherence to a certain metaphysics of presence, Plato's true thinking could be allowed to emerge in its most proper sense, and understood as a science of the good.

XVI. Poetry and Founding in Rilke and Heidegger

While several authors have explored Heidegger's readings of poets, few have done so in the appropriate way.[1] Most have addressed Heidegger as a *critic* of poetry, and look at the import of poetry from the point of view of Rilke and Hölderlin scholarship in order to demonstrate how Heidegger misconstrues them. The criticisms levied against Heidegger thus have more to do with how he reads them to his own ends at the expense of the poets themselves. These critics see such a strategy as criminal in general, and measure the worth of interpretations merely in terms of a zero-sum game wherein traces of instrumentality are grounds for exclusion. The critics invariably identify what are taken to be interpretive blunders in Heidegger's dialogue with poets, and object to what are variously regarded as Heidegger's phenomenologically unwarranted totalizing, or his violent projection of the history of being upon texts that resist the closure such a vision entails, or his idiosyncratic interpretation based on an arbitrary selection of texts. Of the many poets Heidegger has addressed, from Hölderlin and Träkl, to Mörike and George, many critics take his readings of Rilke to be the most problematic.

Heidegger addresses Rilke in "What Are Poets For?" more or less upon the heels of two lecture courses on Hölderlin (from the winter of 1941-42), and the summer of 1942 as well as some brief remarks on Rilke in courses on Parmenides (winter 1942-43), and Heraclitus (summers of 1943 and 1944). Fully convinced by 1946 of Hölderlin's singular import for European culture, Heidegger turns to Rilke in order to determine whether he is a poet of the same rank, or rather, in order to argue that he most likely is not, insisting that Rilke's poetry remains bound to a metaphysics of subjectivity, much as he did in the lecture course on Heraclitus in which he claimed that Rilke is a poet "in whom the age of completed subjectivity poetizes itself to its end." In *What are Poets For?* Heidegger repeats the claim in different guise, claiming that Rilke's angel is "metaphysically the same" as Nietzsche's *Zarathustra*.[2]

Heidegger's reading revolves around an "improvisational poem" Rilke inscribed in a gift copy of *The Notebooks of Malte Laurids Brigge* and later enclosed in a letter sent to his estranged (even abandoned) wife, Clara. Heidegger also concerns himself with what he terms the ground words of Rilke's poetry, words that, we are led to believe, carry the key to Rilke's corpus, words whose interplay make up the author's principal figures, and the ones that characterize the being of the poem. Heidegger however sifts through letters and other poems, thereby supplementing his discussion when other materials complement and enrich his reading. In fact he resorts to this so often that one can hardly claim that the essay is primarily a reading of the improvised verses, even though he proceeds as if he were doing just that. Rather, Heidegger's central concern is Rilke's corpus, and thus his interpretive work really concerns the meaning and relation of the ground words, not the sixteen lines of any particular poem. This is evidenced by Heidegger's reliance upon the figures of the angel, Orpheus, and the poet, none of whom are named in the cited lines. Moreover, he assumes certain identities that the lines in question do not authorize, for example that the "nature" mentioned in the first line is the same as the "primal ground" invoked in the fourth. Given a more general reading of Rilke, however, the connection is not unwarranted.

Despite the steady stream of opposition to his approach, I remain sympathetic to what Heidegger is doing. In his *Contributions to Philosophy*, Heidegger writes "The one who seeks being, in the ownmost overflow of seeking power, is the poet who 'founds' being."[3] What this means remains obscure, but much of the opposition to Heidegger's readings of poets neglects looking at this matter of *poetic founding*. Just exactly what Heidegger is doing with Rilke can best be seen by detailing first of all an account of what Heidegger in general is looking for out of poetry. This can be spelled out along three trajectories; first, by reminding us of how Heidegger's thinking about language is connected to his concerns about global technology; second, that technology constricts writing in its most intimate levels; and third, that his conception of language can be seen when set in relief against other, more traditional conceptions of language. Only then will we be in better position to return to his specific remarks about Rilke.

I.

It has been said that to first and best understand a thinker is to ask what it is most of which he or she is afraid. Such a question is not difficult either to ask or to answer with Heidegger. His works are permeated by a deeply embittered vision of the ruins of modernity to the extent that he wrote in a spirit of desolation about the gods having abandoned the earth. As a thinker he did not shrink back from thinking through to its deepest depths the unfolding horizon of a culture of pure technicity. More than Marx who remained wedded to the biblical dream of proletarian redemption, more than Nietzsche who countered the nihilism of the will to power with the possibilities of reclaimed human subjects as their own dancing stars, Heidegger is both prophet and doomsayer of an even more extreme technological age.

There is a peculiar completeness to the leveling accomplished in this age in which the "gods have fled." Even the dominant subjectivity Heidegger once diagnosed as characteristic of modernity disappears into a kind of general availability of things to be ordered. There is no first being that grounds all the rest. There is no hand-wringing about the momentousness of this happening. Everything is humming along and creepily functional. This for Heidegger is the culmination of the west's metaphysical drive: the meaning of reality is pure available presence. There are no hidden dimensions that are anything more than a lack of information. Everything is in plain view, humans included: humanity just belongs within this universal ordering and is not its source. Humanity acts within possibilities and a mode of temporality that solicits and challenges it to further activity. He calls this phenomenon *das Gestell*, all of the nuances of which are difficult to capture in translation.[4]

In its ordinary meaning *Gestell* signifies frameworks that hold things ready: bookcases, racks, holders. Etymologically it contains the prefix *ge-* which can mean a collectivity (as in *Gebirge*, "mountain range," from *ge-* and *Berg*, "mountain"). This is followed by the root word *stell*, "to put or place." Thus *Gestell* could mean a collection of things having been put in their place. He elsewhere defines the word as the bringing together of all the modes of *stellen*, with the additional connotation of "putting a demand on," in the sense of there being a standing order.[5] The word also carries an almost military meaning, seen in the compound *Gestellungsbefehl*, a mobilization order or a standing ready. The various English translations are as plural as the many meanings Heidegger seeks to convey: an enframing, a composite, an imposition. We will refer to it as the sense of the *total installation of being*, the idea that being itself is prestructured as an ontology of ready-made objects called to attention to serve the slightest whims of human beings.[6]

The later Heidegger wavered between being hopeful and being unremittingly pessimistic about this state of affairs. The total installation of being is thought to be a nihilism so dark that it lacks the light even to see itself as darkness and instead conceives itself as Enlightenment or the convenience of high "living standards." At times his thinking is quite clear on the negative point about human incapacity in this regard, that any such effort to think through the situation only produces new forms of technical objectification. At other times his thinking is quite unclear about how we might escape from the interlocking systems of technological thought and practice in which our lives are enclosed. In places, the only hope he offers lies in the possibility that the danger by which humanity is threatened may come to be understood as the danger that it is. One of the ways by which to escape the *Gestell*, however, is to reflect on what poets bring to word.

> Long is the destitute time of the world's night. To begin with, this requires a long time to reach to its middle. At this night's midnight, the destitution of the time is greatest. Then the destitute time is no longer able even to experience its own destitution. That inability, by which even the destitution of the destitute state is obscured, is the time's absolutely destitute character.[7]

If his thinking could dismiss as illusory the pretension that humanity has mastery over technology, claiming instead the opposite that human beings are set in place as a condition for the possibility of the development of technology, that is because there is already something different at work in Heidegger's own writings. This total installation affects us immediately and overall, but it is not the last word. There is a possibility that our experience of being challenged within technology could turn us toward something else. Heidegger wants to locate this installation in the place where it is made possible. The installation of technology is not ultimate; something more primal speaks through it. The epoch of technology is complete in itself, but there must be something more to say than just describing all the myriad structures of its installation in our air-conditioned nihilism. Heidegger says: "What we experience in the total installation as the constellation of man and being through the modern world of technology is a prelude to what is called the event... In the event the possibility opens for us of overcoming the simple dominance of universal imposition in a more original happening."[8]

Because the modern world presents everything as open to view and available to understanding, because it takes nothing to be hidden that cannot be revealed by getting more facts, we are ironically in a better position to recognize the conditions that make any world possible. If we think everything has been made present and available, then nothing remains hidden or beyond our world to account for it. In this situation, we can recognize that there is nothing to ground our world but its happening, the happening of a world. There is only the emerging, the event, the coming into unconcealment, the clearing that opens a space for humans to live a certain way of being human. Recognizing this is "emancipatory"—we can know the limits of our world and can refuse to accept as ultimate any of the grounds or measures or principles it offers.

In other words, because of the dominance of the total technical installation of being, which plays out and levels out the metaphysical impulse to search for causes and grounds, we are especially situated to experience the event on its own. But this is the most dangerous of situations, for that which most threatens is also the necessary key to overcome that threat. What is disturbing of course is that it is not far from this view to a view which holds that the greater the threat, the better chance there is of recognizing it. Surely this is a lynchpin of the later Heideggerian dynamic, the ironic notion that technology dominates us, yet it is only through the most extreme forms of such domination that we can even see the domination. Just how we are led to an understanding of the event is the motor for Heidegger's thinking regarding poetry and the poets. He variously considers art, poetry, everyday things, and eventually language in general as ways through which non-technological being may yet be manifested or "founded." It is thus important to remember the degree to which Heidegger's work on Rilke is as much about global technological metaphysics as it is about this or that line of Rilke's poetry.

II.

The plight of language in the *Gestell*, as words are transformed by the universal availability of the technological world, is that metaphorical creativity becomes incidental and superfluous, which is to say its responsiveness is seen to reside outside the fully manageable and calculable world. This complete transparency is truly for Heidegger a darkening, the culmination of the western tradition that equates truth with lucid typification of things and the world as resources for consumption. Heidegger repeats this view that the essential nature of language is increasingly encroached upon by the contemporary technological disposition inasmuch as language is regarded as information or the vehicle of information. In his short work on Hebel, Heidegger raises his fears about the connection of machine apparatuses with language:

> The language machine regulates and adjusts in advance the mode of our possible usage of language through mechanical energies and functions. The language machine

is—and above all, is still becoming—one manner in which modern technology controls the mode and the world of language as such. Meanwhile, the impression is still maintained that man is the master of the language machine. But the truth of the matter might well be that the language machine takes language into its management, and thus masters the essence of the human being.[9]

That Heidegger determines the way in which the technological drive to master and facilitate every process would eventually move into the most intimate areas of thought, certainly into the expression of thought in writing, is a prognosis that has proven astute, as a brief detour through the historical background of word processing will show.

Word processing was originally developed and used by data processors who developed the first text-writing programs as handy aids to their central work of writing programs for data handling. The original text editors used by programmers in their data-handling work were programmer-oriented editors on mainframe computers. The writer-programmer uses symbological references to text rather than the direct, interactive manipulation of text on CRT or video monitor. These text editors did not so much manipulate text as apply the reasoning of algorithmic programming to the process of writing. Such roundabout use of the computer for writing had less to do with word processing than with the application of information processing techniques to the construction and editing of texts. Here a first major step was made: natural language was interpreted as a standard code, edited, and transmitted so as to reappear in its natural-language form. The encoding of letters in the ASCII (American Standard Code for Information Interchange) computer code not only permitted the transmission of natural-language at electronic speed; encoding natural language on computers makes possible a new approach to language as directly manipulable. Data-handling techniques for number-crunching or high-speed manipulation of quantified routine information were applied to natural language communication.

Heidegger's was no mere premonition of such an eventuality. Latent in his thought on total installation is the potential for technology to implement a world-language of electronic communication networks through the interpretation of natural languages in mathematical-technological terms. This is connected with his claim of how the contemporary world is intelligible only as the extreme development of the trend toward rational typification and systematic organization pushed forward by modernity. Logic is the foundation of the systematic thinking which can become the basis for a homogeneous world language. But the logic meant here is not the traditional Aristotelian logic which organizes and evaluates inferences occurring in natural language. Rather, logic here is a network of symbols equally applicable to electronic switching-circuitry as to assertions made in natural language; logic in this sense can become an underlying digital language to be used for the transmission and communication of natural language. Just as geometrical axioms are no longer bound to the domain of real circles, physical figures, but are operable with contrary postulates, so too modern logic is free of any naturally given syntax.

In his work on Leibniz, Heidegger analyzed the logic of Leibnizean rationalism as the precursor of modern calculative thinking which goaded forth technological metaphysics. The logic of total systematic management was present already in the logical principles of such founders of modern rationality as Leibniz. Leibniz's plan for a symbolic logical calculus of total analyticity was the forerunner of contemporary formalism of all computer logic, and Leibniz himself, besides developing the binary logic, worked on some primitive models of a computational engine. Heidegger's treatment of modern logic in Leibniz was prescient—the Leibnizean logic of binary digits has become the basis of the encoding of language, thus creating a qualitatively different level of typification.[10]

Writing converted to ASCII is fundamentally different as a phenomenon from handwritten manuscript. Digital reproduction of writing is as different a phenomenon in form from typewritten, printed language as digital audio reproduction differs from phonograph recordings and oxidized tape recordings. When a phenomenon has been digitized, it has been transmogrified into a new form, a form that can be controlled by human beings with a precision beyond previous forms of reproduction. *Digital* is derived from the Latin *digitus*, or "finger." The fingers are the primordial counters, the first servants of human calculation. When something is digitized, it is interpreted as a sequence of numbers, numbers that have a precision that cannot be experienced directly in the original phenomenon, though the original phenomenon may have in itself a certain kind of precision that cannot be reduced to quantities or numerical relationships. Once a phenomenon has been digitized, it can be treated, as can all mathematical entities, as a series of relationships and proportions. The relationships between the wave lengths of acoustical phenomenon can, for example, be calculated and modified, while at the same time the fundamental relationships between the wave lengths can be preserved. Wave lengths that have been digitized can be manipulated so as to improve upon the recorded phenomenon. For example, recordings of the ocean may never sound really like the ocean until they have been interpreted digitally as quantities and then altered variously until the audio reproduction sounds real, like the ocean itself should sound. The impossibility of removing the flaws of the recordings of the original ocean sounds gives way to the creation of the real ocean sounds through digital manipulation. Phenomena that have been digitized are new creations at the fingertips of human beings. Controlling phenomena as we experience them is itself a new kind of experience. The digital phenomenon is one facet of a totally administered environment; the digits on which we count the world we experience come through electronic manipulation to be the world we experience.

The temporal mood of total control and simultaneity is characteristic of the total and now digital installation. This mood develops into modern technology over several centuries as modernity develops. In his work on Leibniz, Heidegger shows how the logic of formal systems is the modern continuation of the *visio Dei* in medieval Scholasticism. Leibniz strove from his *De arte combinatoria* of 1666 to base the deductive capacity of human reasoning on a universal logistical calculus of human science. The logistical calculus was to foster a *characteristica universalis*, a universal grammar to promote the complete deductive formalization of all rationality and scientific justification. The temporality Heidegger finds in Leibniz's analytical formalism is the all-at-once simultaneity of total presence. The epistemological-ontological model behind the logic of Leibniz is the *visio Dei*, the deity's omniscient intuitive cognition which was put into the philosophical tradition by the Aristotelianizing Scholastics. It is the knowledge of God, at least in its temporalizing simultaniety, that serves as a model for human cognition in the modern world as projected in Leibniz.[11]

The temporality of modern logic is at work in computer writing. The word is under siege in the systems of electrified codes. The rhythmic tempo of technical installation is instantaneous simultaneity, the logic of a total management with everything at disposal. The freedom of human *ingenium* must be mastered to fit the tempo of such imposition. The ease and intuitive freedom of writing within such systems masks the revealing-concealing processes intrinsic to the truth of the world. Electronic writing moves language further into the mode of information exchange. Language is increasingly treated as information and is processed by the techniques of information management. Treated as information, language becomes a transparent vehicle for what is already determined. In-formation is already formed by the network of involvements in which it is exchanged, taking place in a world presumed to be already formed. The informational mode of language leads to the curtailing of the human ability to call things freshly into the world, to name or address things poetically.

III.

Today poets write on electronic screens. No one would think of hand writing their texts. Yet such is a very recent conceit. Calligraphy does not stand in the mainstream of the symbolic element of Western writing as it does in the far east. Western alphabetic symbols serve to inscribe, roughly and approximately, the phonetic contours of spoken language, leading many to the conclusion that written symbols cannot be considered apart from their vocalization. As such the visual symbolization of language appears merely to serve as notation for the spoken word. But this subservient role does not exhaust the ontological dimension. For many centuries before instrumental thinking dominated, a cultural premium was placed on writing by hand—and its high esteem was both due to the purely functional value of inscription as a means of communication or as an aid to memory. The scribal hand was related to the spoken words as a repository of speech; but more important, the scribe was from early on respected as the vessel of a higher transcending activity. Writing and reading conferred special status on the few who mastered the skills. The status was not based on power or convenience or efficiency or economics. Someone who possessed the skills was deemed closer to a higher realm of thought than was found in everyday existence—even if the person was of low standing and even if the scribal hand was primarily in the service of another.

The epitaph for Xantias, for example, a stenographer for his Roman master in an early Roman settlement in Cologne in the second century A.D., exhibited in the Roman-Germanic Museum in Cologne, next to the Cologne Cathedral, illustrates how the scribe, a mere 16 year old boy, was regarded as dwelling close to the Muses. If ancient Greece and Rome attributed noble leisure to the scribal hand, the Jewish-Christian stream of Western civilization applied far greater solemnity to the skills of working with the book. The conception of the sacred book (Bible itself meaning *ta biblia,* or group of books) connected literacy with a special entry to revealed truths through contact with the sacred book. Christians invented the book, or codex, although the Christians who invented it had not yet become the powerful institution known as the Church. Groups that were later declared heretical played an important role in creating a sacred literacy through the copying of books. [A prime example might be the semi monastic ascetic community of Egyptian gnostics who lived a frugal existence at the edge of an oasis between Cairo and Luxor. In the fourth century A.D. they created a sacred library of religious texts known today as the Nag Hammadi Library. The community supported itself largely through a strong literary business. Its library was later buried by a group of unorthodox monks shortly after the Paschal Letter of Bishop Athanasius of Alexandria in 367 A.D. which urged the expulsion of heretics and their books from the Pachomian Christian monasteries in the area. The library was unearthed in 1945]. Because of the notion of the word of God, the natural universe as a whole became a book in which the believing eye reads what the hand of the creator wrote. Much has been made of the Renaissance shift from God's book of nature to the modern effort to examine or read nature directly, the finding of information in nature. The sacred book was the center of institutionalized religious life, and the transmission of its contents was an apostolate for those who administered the books as well as for those who promoted the Gospel by copying sacred texts.

The cult of books in the Christian west, far from being the exclusive concern with proclamation [*kerygma*], was also essentially contemplative. Manipulation of the inscribed symbols as manuscript—both terms containing as a component the Latin word for hand—was a special kind of handiwork. Not only handy for the missionary apostolate of an expanding Christianity, the cult of the book was at the same time the cultivation of a transcending state of mind, a distanced and composed contemplative attitude. During barbarian onslaughts, it was the monastic tradition that preserved books. Monks and dedicated ascetics used the book to preserve states of awareness beyond the mundane routines of necessity. The personal care and contemplation given to books in monasteries were more than a merely subjective piety and more than the religious zeal for processing information for propagating the faith. Books in the medieval period were far from indifferent receptacles of information. Reading was a practice in the strict sense of the term. Active reading was a practice in the strict sense of the term, a discipline and a way of life, connected with prayer and the transformation of the spirit.

In the same lecture course in which he later addresses Rilke, Heidegger comments at length on how the basis for handwriting has to do with the primordial embodiment of human awareness.

> Human beings "act" through the hand; for the hand is, like the word, a distinguishing characteristic of humans. Only a being, such as the human, that "has" the word [*mythos, logos*] can and must "have hands." Both prayers and murder happen through hands, as do gestures of gratitude and salutation, oaths and summoning, but also the "work" of the hands, "handwork" and equipment. The handshake seals the bond of association. The hand unleashes the "work" of ravaging devastation. The hand

becomes present as hand only where there is disclosure and concealment. The animal has no hands, nor are hands derived from paws, claws, or talons. Even in moments of desperation the hand is never merely a "claw" with which the human being "crawls." The hand has only emerged from and with the word. The human being does not "have" hands, but the hand contains the essence of the human being because the word, as the essential region of the hand, is the essential ground of being human. The word as something symbolically inscribed and as thus presented to vision is the written word, that is, script. As script, however, the word is handwriting.

It is not by chance that modern man writes "with" the typewriter and "dictates"—the same word as "to invent creatively" [*Dichten*]—"into" the machine. This "history" of the kinds of writing is at the same time one of the major reasons for the increasing destruction of the word. The word no longer passes through the hand as it writes and acts authentically but through the mechanized pressure of the hand. The typewriter snatches script from the essential realm of the hand—and this means the hand is removed from the essential realm of the word. The word becomes something "typed." Nevertheless, mechanical script serves as a mere transcription for preserving handwriting or where typewritten script substitutes for "print." When typewriters first became prevalent, a personal letter typed on a machine was regarded as a lapse of manners or as an insult. Today, handwritten letters slow down rapid reading and are therefore regarded as old-fashioned and undesirable. Mechanized writing deprives the hand of the dignity in the realm of the written word and degrades the word to a mere means for the traffic of communication. Besides, mechanized writing offers the advantage of covering up one's handwriting and therewith one's character. In mechanized writing all human beings look the same.[12]

Here Heidegger sees a primary connection of thought and gesture in that both are tied to living in a specific, physically conditioned environment. He sees the connection between thinking and bodily orientation broken by the intervention of mechanical devices in those cases where the devices usurp the primary connection of thought and gesture as they are rooted in the physical environment. He focuses on the typification process brought about through the modern rationalist model of standardized intelligibility, which underscores the qualities of repetitious, formal specifications and instant clarity and certainty. Now computers have made mechanized typewriting obsolete. The hand is drawn once again into a nonmechanical, nonimprinting process. The writing action of word processing is related again to personal bodily gestures, such as pointing and moving things, but the actions are done in an already typified element. Direct hand-movements are no longer simply replaced by an industrial-mechanical mode of action; the gesturers of word processing operate in a typified environment but do so in ways that have left behind the industrial machine with its cumbersome but efficient mediation of human actions. The electronic element shifts the personal quality of action onto another level. Formulation can establish impersonality while achieving a directness undreamt of with typewriters. It becomes possible to treat the entire verbal life of the human race as one continuous, anonymous code without essential reference to a human presence behind it, which neither feels it must answer to anyone nor necessarily await an answer. Textual database searches conceal as well as reveal what is learned. The Boolean search operations help hone our intentions and thought impulses as they begin to seek something. What is possible with the computer's logic defines what is sought. The computer hones down our intentions and impulses in the sense of making them narrower or at least different from spacious meanderings. As more is revealed more accurately with greater control, lost is the thought process that does not happen to dovetail with the power of computerized writing.

IV.

Heidegger's specific contribution to our understanding of what poets are for consists then of a unique, evocative, and comprehensive description of technological experience as a process originating in the metaphysics of enframing, the total organization and installation of being driven forward by the animating energy of directionless will. It assumes the form of a theory of civilization which, beginning with the basic assumption that technology cannot be understood solely in the language of the technological itself, traces the genealogy of planetary technicity to its ancient roots in a way of being that comes to represent human destiny. As human destiny, technology can neither be refused nor simply affirmed because of its inextricably ambivalent nature. Left unquestioned, technological experience reduces life to a standing reserve in which the being of every conceivable thing is stockpiled in the unconditional service of the will to technique. Coming home to the neglected questions of how to move through and beyond the empire of planetary technology is "what poets are for."

In Heidegger's famous 1936 essay "Origin of the Work of Art," we are told that to comprehend the essentially poetic character of all art we need the "right concept of language." This "right concept" will demand of us a surmounting of the traditional functional and linguistic approaches to language.[13] Language understood as a vehicle of communication, or as an object of linguistic science, although containing its own legitimacy, is not really the language of the poetic. Language as communication is the verbal and written exchange designed for the imparting of information. This is language approached in terms of its function and viewed as an instrument for defining, explaining, deducing, and drawing inferences pertinent to objectifiable matters of fact. The linguistic and metalinguistic approaches to language are of the same cloth as in the instrumental approaches to language. In the science of linguistics, language becomes an object with a complex of morphemes, parts of speech, and syntactical and semantic rules. Language understood in this way is an especially complicated and powerful tool, making possible the improvement of numerous cooperative practices that constitute human culture.

This "right concept of language" might be more clearly seen when set in relief against two powerful and opposing accounts of linguistic meaning, the account of language-as-representation and the account of language-as-expression. The first of these accounts came fully into its own in the seventeenth century, with the Lockean "Way of Ideas" and the Cartesian epistemological revolution. The second account is in romantic revolt against the first and can be found initially in the work of Herder and Humboldt, and later, perhaps, Nietzsche.[14] For Heidegger, both accounts are lacking.

According to the representationalist account of language, language is, whether directly or indirectly, a "show" of what is going on in the soul. How does language reveal what is going on in the soul's inner landscapes? By way of a system of signs. A sign is an agreed upon mark, a conventional designation, standing for something that exists independently of it. Here is a passion or idea; there is its sign. Thus anxiety and the word "anxiety" are not at all the same: the first is, say, a passion common to all human beings, and the second is a word of a particular language, namely English. Everyone knows what anxiety is, but not everyone knows what the English word "anxiety" means. And one could just as well use another sign altogether to designate that same passion. Calling it "anxiety" is neither better nor worse that calling it "*Angst.*" The sign is doing its work so long as it is understood by its audience.

In this way the linguistic sign becomes interpreted as a pure name, a kind of proper name with which the passion (or whatever is being so represented) is conventionally associated and that can be used, in virtue of that association, to refer to it. The sign thus becomes the representative, a handy substitute, for the thing itself. Language can then be understood, it seems, as an ordered system of such representatives. When these individual representatives are combined in particular, conventionally specified (i.e., grammatical) ways, the result is a true or false representation of a relationship among the passions that those representations represent.

Locke and Descartes accept and extend this attractively simple account of language-as-representation. Both take language to be the outer (public, "physical") expression of the inner (private, "mental") landscapes of the soul, and incorporate a philosophy of mind that builds in representation, understood to take place by means of the mechanism of natural resemblance, at the most fundamental level of mental operation. Both Locke and Descartes erect their views upon a family of metaphors for the basic cognitive power of human beings, that the mind is, in Rorty's famous phrase, the mirror of nature; it is a passive medium that reflects, well or ill, the reality that stands before it. These natural reflections of reality were called ideas, and it was assumed that, like the images appearing in an actual mirror, our ideas are the more or less accurate copies of the things that originally cause them to appear to us. At bottom, mind is a quasi-mechanical reflection. As a result of their "natural" resemblance-relations to reality, our ideas are, on this account, representatives -- the inner mental image becomes the deputy, the substitute, for the physical thing itself. All thought, all cognition. occurs in the medium of the idea thus defined. All beliefs about the world are on this account simple or complex constellations of these "natural" representatives. Thus we think, truly or falsely, about the world, but that intentional connection of thought to reality is possible only because the universal medium of thought, the idea, has an immediate "natural" connection of resemblance to the reality that caused it to appear.

Language, the medium in which thinking is made public, is for Locke and Descartes simply an artificial iteration of the essentially representational structure of mind itself. Words are the names of ideas. As ideas represent or resemble reality, so spoken words represent or name or designate ideas. Spoken language is thus the representation of a representation, the artificial sign of a natural sign; written language is merely another step in the same direction, the sign of a sign of a sign. While Descartes and Locke do not agree on how all ideas actually come to be present to consciousness, (whether some are innate, as Descartes believed, or whether all come through experience, as Locke held), and while Locke stresses much more than does Descartes the conventionality of words, the ways they come to be connected to ideas through our own decisions and associations, both agree that language, written or spoken, is a system of designative representation founded on the "natural" resemblance of idea to object.

Thus the representationalist account of language rests upon a philosophy of mind that builds in a form of "natural" representation, of "natural" intentionality, as the basic structure of human consciousness. It is the "natural identity" of idea and object that is supposed to underwrite our original linguistic designations of reality, connecting word to world -- common sign to particular thing -- through the necessary medium of the resembling idea. These immediate designations make possible all subsequent linguistic representations. When this notion of "natural" mental representation began to collapse in the eighteenth and nineteenth centuries, some new account of language was therefore demanded. Its criteria of adequacy were set by the criticisms that demolished the philosophical foundations of the earlier account, criticisms which we will not now review.

With this, then, the charm of the representationalist philosophy of language disappears as well. For all its simplicity and attractiveness, language-as-representation required some trope of quasi-mechanical isomorphism to make it go. Because such tropes so decisively failed to live up to their promises, a new philosophy of mind was required, and with its advent, a new account of language began to emerge in the late eighteenth century. Heidegger calls this new account language-as-expression, and finds it most clearly developed in the work of the linguist Humboldt, but there are other, even more powerful, versions in play. As the name suggests, one may summarize this account as the view that language is the fundamental activity of human self-expression.

The essentials of the expressionist conception can be grasped by starting with its emphasis on human activity, an emphasis largely absent from representationalist accounts of mind and language. Rather than stressing, in Cartesian fashion, the essential passivity and receptivity of human consciousness, the expressionist conception of mind makes the recognition of will central. Human life is essentially purposeful activity in a social context, and all forms of human consciousness, even the most abstract, must be understood as forms of that activity. Mind is not some preexistent, independent spectator of one's life activity and social relationship; rather, mind is the expression of that active and communal life itself.

It is difficult to say, with the precision and economy required here, what "expression" means, and for the present purposes it will not be necessary to trace this notion all the way through the daunting complexities it generates in Hegel, who was its great champion. The fundamental idea is nevertheless clear: mind shows itself as certain complex and complicated forms of human activity. The presence of mind is constituted by particular sorts of social practices and "products," not by some metaphysically distinct substance; and the relationship of mind to these constitutive "products" -- i.e., to sentences, buildings, works of art, theological systems, political institutions, etc. -- is not like the relationship of an approaching storm to a falling barometer but more like the relationship of, say, disappointment to the frown that shows it. Disappointment is made evident not by or through language but in it.

Expression then is embodiment. It is the appearance, the immediate and inseparable presence, of mind in some medium. The embodiment of disappointment in the frown of my editor when told of the project's delay is neither accidental nor indirect. The frown and the 'feeling' are not two genuinely independent things, which just happen to have become associated with each other. The frown *is* the disappointment, essentially. It is only with practice and instruction that one learns how artificially to separate the reality of disappointment from its sign, as in cases of pretense.

Ceteris paribus, then, the mind is present only as embodied or expressed in some medium. Mind is not an independent, incorporeal substance that just happens to attach itself to some physical gesture or construction, but is human activity of a certain level of complexity necessarily embodying itself in some medium of expression. It is not the mirror of nature -- it just *is* nature: natural activity grown complicated enough to have become self-reflective, activity so complex and sophisticated that it can cast off exterior expressions or embodiments of itself. Thinking, then, is nature's self-expression, not its representation from someplace outside.

This expressionist philosophy of mind leads invariably to a corresponding philosophy of language. In this account, language is the fundamental medium of self-expressive mind. It is the basic "material," the fundamental social practice, in terms of which human beings embody their intelligence. Embody is the correct word here, rather than encode or represent. Language is conceived here not as a fixed and orderly set of conventional designations used to construct representations of an antecedent and independent world; rather, it is the activity itself of world-creation through human self-expression. Indeed world and language are not, as in the representationalist account, two separable items; they are not fact and its picture. They are one. World first of all shows itself -- expresses itself, embodies itself -- in the language that human beings use in their relations to one another. Without language there is no human world at all. In this way language becomes an essential feature of human spiritual development. It is the medium in which human beings create a habitable world to live in together.

Nietzsche is the other great champion of this approach to language, as he accepts the failure of representationalism as a philosophy of mind and language. For Nietzsche, the human being is a locus of creative will to power, not a camera or mirror of what there is. There is no serene, Cartesian knowing subject to gaze placidly upon reality. The basic activity of consciousness is not representation but interpretation, where interpretation is an act of force, the introjection of meaning into some plastic material. Interpretation is embodiment, in other words. Even rationality is not a style of representation according to the final order of things; it is the expression of a way of schematizing experience in the sense of fundamentally practical interests, that has come to be built into our language and practices.[15] The defining excellence of a higher humanity is not some alleged capacity for grasping secure metaphysical truth, as Plato and Descartes both believed. Rather, it is our creative power to push through, again and again, our own ends of self-mastery and control. It is our capacity to be active, self-defining, self-interpreting individuals, not thoughtless and reactionary members of the herd.

Language thus for Nietzsche is a means of expression.[16] A language is not an impersonal and objective photographic medium; on the contrary, its vocabulary and idiom are always the expression of a particular and quite specific way of seeing -- i.e., interpreting -- what there is. As such a means of expression, moreover, it always embodies a "relationship", not a "fact," not an "essence-in-itself." As noted, the representationalist account of language construes the proposition, the basic unit of language, as a kind of picture, as a "true" or a "false" reflection of some independently existing state of affairs. There are the things-in-themselves, says the representationalist; here is their recapitulation in words. But for Nietzsche the proposition is a "means of expression"; it is a sign -- or better, a symptom -- of a particular state of the will to power in relation to what confronts it. Language expresses; it does not represent reality, external or internal, any more than the symptom "represents" the disease.

V.

Heidegger's views on language, we can finally say, are a response to this choice between language-as-representation and language-as-expression. In keeping with his remarks on technology, however, he does not challenge the correctness of these traditional views.

No one would dare to declare incorrect, let alone reject as useless, the identification of language as audible utterance of inner emotions, as human activity, as a representation by image and by concept. The view of language thus put forth is correct, for it conforms to what an investigation of linguistic phenomena can make out in them at any time.[17]

All the empirical and conceptual data available from linguistic study favor some form of representationalism or expressionism. Nevertheless these perfectly correct accounts of language are seriously inadequate. Despite their antiquity and comprehensibility they never bring us to language "as language". Their very progress obscures the primordial truth of language on which all such conceptual correctness about language is parasitic.

We do not wish to assault language in order to force it into the grip of ideas already fixed beforehand. We do not wish to reduce the nature of language to a concept, so that this concept may provide a generally useful view of language that will lay to rest all further notions about it.[18]

Heidegger thus casts about for that which forces our thoughts about language so inexorably into this bind. The answer is that, for all their differences, both language-as-representation and language-as-expression agree in the assumption that language is essentially a human instrument adapted to human purposes. We speak a language. Language is our creation, a human invention, and it is used by us to further our own purposes: communication, science, art, grocery shopping, whatever other purposes communication serves.

From the representationalist perspective, this assumption certainly seems correct. If the essence of language is an orderly system of conventional designations by means of which our ideas can be represented, then what is language but an instrument for human communication? One can see this assumption very clearly at work in the seventeenth century attempts to "improve" language by increasing its precision and carrying power. What was Leibniz's if not the deliberate development of a perfect language, the *characteristica universalis*, which would make possible the fully adequate representation of all our ideas? Language is here clearly understood to be a human instrument, and one that, like any tool, can be self-consciously refined and adapted.

The expressionist perspective is much the same, of course. We are creatures who strive to flourish, it says, and we congregate to serve that end. Thus there naturally arise among us various cooperative practices, various systems of coordinated human behavior, that help us defend ourselves against dangers and to further our goal of life-in-abundance. On this account, language is just another system of cooperative human behavior; it is another form of human self-expression aiming at human good. Like farming, a language is a set of normative practices whereby the will to power embodies itself in order to push itself through. The expressionist will admit, of course, that a language is an especially complicated and powerful form of self-expression, since the extraordinary degree of cooperation and coordination it affords makes possible the improvement of all the other cooperative practices that constitute human culture. Indeed language even makes possible its own development: the invention of new and more powerful languages adapted to specific ends. In all of this one clearly sees language understood as a tool in service to the end of human flourishing.

Heidegger wants to get behind the linguistic "humanism" he finds common both to language-as-representation and to language-as-expression. Certainly human beings naturally and urgently speak, and certainly that speaking is often directly or indirectly in aid of our various purposes. But for Heidegger our speaking is simply not a primordial or essential speaking; language speaks more primordially than we. And to truly experience language we cannot look merely to everyday speech, to the speech of the crowd:

> If we must, therefore, seek the speaking of language in what is spoken we shall do well to find something that is spoken rather than to pick just any material at random. What is spoken purely is that in which the completion of the speaking that is proper to what is spoken is, in its turn, an original. What is spoken purely is the poem.[19]

VI.

Armed as we are now with this background, we can return to Rilke, and Heidegger's concern that Rilke's poetry does not manage to resist technological metaphysics, that it cannot transform our technological partitioning of the happening of being, although reflection upon Rilke's efforts can be instructive in what it takes for poetry to reach back into its own ground and engage being in its own coming to be. In the essay "Language" (delivered in 1950) Heidegger chose a short poem by Trakl, "A Winter Evening," as an example of that pure speaking or language to which the philosopher must learn to listen.

> Speaking occurs in what is spoken in the poem. It is the speaking of language. Language speaks. It speaks by bidding the bidden, thing-world and world-thing, to

come to the between of the difference. What is so bidden is commanded to arrive from
out of the difference into the difference....The difference lets the thinging of the thing
rest in the worlding of the world. The difference expropriates the thing into the repose
of the fourfold. Such expropriation does not diminish the thing. Only so is the thing .
Such expropriation does not diminish the thing. Only so is the thing exalted into its
own, so that it stays world. To keep in repose is to still. The difference stills the thing,
as thing, into the world.[20]

Let us see if now this can be understood. Rilke's poetry is similarly understood
as first of all a "naming." It names the opening, it names the venture, it names
the unshieldedness. One may seem on familiar philosophical ground here if one
understands the speaking of the language in the poem in this way: that, like the
poem, all language begins with naming, that words and the world first hook up
with one another through individual or communal acts of object-baptism.
Perhaps language can be understood as an orderly system of names, or that
naming is the fundamental semantic tie. One hears the echoes of language-as-
representation in such conceptions.

Such conceptions, however, fail to do justice to language as such, although
such accounts of linguistic meaning would not be incorrect. They fail to do
justice to language because to name is not merely to attach pre-existing labels to
objects already present to hand, as I might now name my shirt "Bill". That sort
of naming depends upon a prior ability to recognize my shirt as a distinct and
redefinable object and upon a stock of already available name-words
recognizable as such. It is already parasitic upon or laden with a great deal of
what Heidegger calls more primordial naming. It is that more primordial
naming that gets covered over in representational accounts of language. To
understand the poem, and language itself, as an original act of naming, one
needs a deeper understanding of what it is to name something at all.

Primordial naming for Heidegger is "calling." By this he means, to bid
something to come into nearness.

> This naming does not hand out titles, it does not apply terms, but it calls into the
> word. The naming calls . . Thus it brings the presence of what was previously uncalled
> into a nearness.[21]

To call something to come close implies that, before the calling, the thing called
was not close. It was not already there like my shirt called "Bill" was already
there as an object represented to my consciousness. To call into the word is
always an act of revelation. It first shows the thing to us by naming it. Such

primordial naming cannot rely upon a catalog of names already in place -- that stock is called into being only through the call of primordial naming itself. Language does not preexist this call; rather, it is in this first naming that language as we know it comes originally to be. To call this way is always to call into the distance, as it were, and what is named in the poem is called only into nearness, not to full presence-at-hand like the shirt. What is truly called into the word as present remains also at the same time removed.

What naming calls from absence into nearness is a "thing," only now understood in the full reverberances began in the essay on art, modified in the essay on technology, and brought home in the remarks on the fourfold.

> What does the first stanza call? It calls things, bids them to come.....It invites them in, so that they may bear upon men as things.[22]

A thing is not something that exists on its own, something essentially separable from other things. In the language of the art-essay, the thingly character of the thing does not consist in its being a represented object, nor can it be defined in any way in terms of the objectness of objects; on the contrary, without its correlative world the thing cannot be what it is. For Heidegger it is always "thing-world" and "world-thing," or, as he says elsewhere, a thing gathers its world.

With the discussion having moved to language, one might now have better occasion to think "words" instead of things and "a language" instead of world. Imagine that one has been living outside one's native land -- say, living in China -- and one day as one is walking in the woods, far from any tourist areas, lost in one's thoughts, one suddenly hears reference to the "Cleveland Indians." Those words, "Cleveland Indians", immediately gather to one the language of their utterance. Suddenly one is in English, and one waits for other words in the same family ("no pitching", "last place") to make their appearance. One listens for the familiar rhythms and inflections. In a flash one hears the whole of one's native language. The words "Cleveland Indians" are not mere sounds, mere heard objects or representations to one's consciousness. They are of course words and thus always and already the words of a certain language that makes them intelligible as the words that they are, (just as it is the case, as Heidegger struggled to express in the art-essay, that things are always and already things of a certain world). Without the language they gather, words would not be words at all. But to gather the language is to gather the world of those words as well.

"Cleveland Indians" heard unexpectedly on a Chinese mountainside brings one not just English, but home: father, Saturday afternoons, love and pain.

So it is that the things named in the Trakl poem -- snow, the vesper bell, the well-laid table -- gather a world. By "thinging," by appearing there as the things that they are, these things "carry out world." They bring near the referential totality within which they are what they are. And the world borne by things is now not the traditional technological one; it is not a collection of mental or physical objects or experiences.

VII.

That a thing can gather a world in the same way a word gathers its language is understood when one returns to Heidegger's example in "Building Dwelling Thinking" of a bridge over a stream. The bridge, a human artifact, was not always standing there, connecting the banks and allowing the traffic to pass unimpeded. When the bridge was built, certainly the "physical" and the economic, as well as perhaps the aesthetic and the social circumstances of the neighborhood changed. There is now a new "physical object" at such-and-such a location; it is now easier and cheaper to transport one's goods to market; people now have something to admire and be proud of; and so on. But is this not merely a rather lyrical way of stating some quite ordinary facts?

What the building of the bridge allows us to see is not just another single thing, namely the bridge itself; rather, it allows us to begin to see the relationships among all the things that are there, but relationships we are inclined to forget or ignore. A given relationship thus shown is what Heidegger has meant by the world of the thing. For as language is a set of synergistic relationships among words, relationships that create words qua words that then in their turn create the relationships themselves, so world is a set of such relationships among things. The bridge gathers a world. It becomes the point from which distances are computed. It becomes something to be defended against natural and human enemies, thus showing one those enemies and reminding one of one's own capacities for violence and neglect. It becomes a way to the other bank, reminding us of the benefits and burdens of commerce with those on the other side. The bridge focuses attention on a radiant whole; it reveals relationships, it strikes resonances, that show one one's place within that whole. It gathers to itself and to us in that gathering a world.

These relationships that the bridge reveals are not merely "accidental" or "psychological" ones. That are not just associations we human beings happen to have made. The bridge gathers those constitutive facts of human life; it is what it is, in other words, only because of them. It simultaneously reveals and depends upon them. The human landscape is essentially, one wants to say, a place of locality, commerce, aggression and defense, trust and mistrust, and the bridge "speaks" all these things. Indeed it makes sense to build these bridges only because these things are true.[23]

The question poses a big problem for the advocates of language-as-expression. Those views again are committed to the view that language is just a "product" -- an "expression", of a particularly complex form of life, namely that of human life. They must, therefore, somehow argue that the established differences (e.g., the norms) originally necessary to language are, either consciously or unconsciously, human "products" too.

But they could only be human products if one can ignore the first horn of the dilemma just examined. To get language going, on the conscious human product model of linguistic norms, one would need to be able to note a difference before one had any public system of description available within which the difference could be noted. This would be a difference existing altogether outside a system of representation, a private language, if you will, and this after Wittgenstein appears to be a senseless notion. But what of the claim that these linguistic norms just arise unconsciously out of complex forms of human interaction? This seems to be no more than to say that they arise; their nature and genesis remain as mysterious as ever. The appeal to the human factor does no work at all, it is void of all substantial content. It is similarly void then to think of language as a form of "human" expression, and with that the metaphor of expression loses whatever power it had as well.

A similar problem arises for the language-as-representation camp. If language is conceived as a holistic system of signs used by us to represent facts to others, how did that system of signs originate? Accounts of their origin put them in the same dilemma, for if "consciously" established, such norms commit one to the possibility of a private language, and if established "unconsciously" the account of their origin is void of explanatory power altogether. The representationalist account falls to the ground, it seems, independently of its familiar epistemological problems.

Heidegger's insight is the recognition that the things primordially named in the poem are related to one another in a world that grants them. The mysterious part/whole relation is just that: mysterious. It is dif-ference, the necessary condition for language, prior to any system of description. It is that primordial "activity" of "differing" by means of which things and world, word and language become possible both in their interpenetration, their intimacy, and in their separation. There must be some primordial articulation of things into a world, of words into a language. Those differences must be opened up and maintained as differences in order that language be at all. And that opening up and keeping open cannot originally be done by human beings.

Thus nothing can be said directly about this *ereignis*. It cannot become its own object of scrutiny, since any such scrutiny would have to be linguistic and thus presuppose and employ the very dif-ference it is trying to capture and explain. One remains in the possession of exactly that which one wants to distance and possess. The speaking of language, its ability to speak of anything at all, must remain mysterious and ungrounded. The worlding of the world and the thinging of the thing are equally impervious to philosophical explanation. The answer to the question of why there is difference is dif-ference, and that is an answer only in a highly attenuated sense.

In the masterful poem "language speaks" directly by naming, by bidding the things of the world to come close, to disclose themselves as the things that they are in a way free of technological metaphysics. Heidegger calls this, curiously, a happening unto itself. Whatever authority is at work here rests with poetry itself, with the measure it provides. Heidegger is insistent in the denial that any subjectivity dictates what comes to pass in the language of the poem qua measure, whether it be that of the poet, the critic, or the philosopher. What he says of Hölderlin in another context is instructive in this regard:

> This poet's poetizing does not revolve around the poet's own ego. What has for a long time hindered modern, contemporary human beings, who think in terms of self-consciousness and subjectivity, from hearing this poetry is simply this: The fact that Hölderlin poetizes purely from out of that which, in itself, essentially prevails as that which is to be poetized. When Hölderlin poetizes the essence of the poet, he poetizes relations that do not have their ground in the subjectivity of human beings.[24]

What has happened here is that we are in the position of not knowing what to say about language. We are maneuvered out of the theoretical attitude with respect to language. We are further than ever from getting a fix on it. We cannot ask what it is, for the whole grammar of proposition making has been displaced by a discourse without the copula: things thing, world worlds, stillness stills, and all of this occurs when language speaks. And we are far from knowing any of what exactly happens, for what happens does not occur for the benefit of our experience. Yet this occurrence provides a measure, as it were, not from beyond its own borders.

VIII.

In the later reflections of language, Heidegger frequently discusses the faltering of language by way of the meaning of *"Zeigen"* (showing) that is radically irreducible to a representational and "technological" concept of language. It is precisely this digitilization of the relation between language and things which is subverted by the "showing" of the originary word that occurs in the poetic. The faltering of language, at which Heidegger says reflection on the nature of language arrives, is to be understood as a "showing"; but rather than fall back into a metaphysical concept of language as a sign for something, this "showing" subverts both our usual referential way of understanding the word-thing relation and our own relation to language itself. To experience language as *"Zeigen,"* or as *"Sage"* (originary saying) means that language is not a mere faculty of man. It ceases to be something with which we as speaking human beings have a relation; it is instead the relation of all relations, the universal medium through which anything becomes meaningful at all. Language is *"Zeigen"* not by being an instrument for showing things; rather, *"Zeigen"* means *"Erscheinen lassen"*—that is, to "make appear."

The happening of language occurs in a poet when the language of their poetry addresses being at the precise point where its own being presents itself as poetry. Rilke's poems are not devices, they cannot posit theses or assertions that aim to represent being. Those efforts ignore how their own saying is an event of being, attending instead to that which is to be represented or posited or asserted, thereby failing to comport themselves in an original fashion. Thus Rilke's ground words, in concert with one another, engage precisely this happening, through engaging their own being at its point of origin, the site wherein there comes to be a poem. Now the question that must be asked is: *how* do the ground words of Rilke's poetry manage to reach back into their own ground and engage being in their own coming to be?

In order to transform our technological partitioning of the open into a kind of praise for things, Rilke turns toward poetry as a mode of comportment. On Heidegger's reading, such a turn requires that one *venture* the play of language in the venture that is one's life. Taking up the threads from this term used by Rilke, Heidegger says: "the more venturesome cannot be the ones who merely say. The saying of the more venturous must genuinely venture or risk the traditional saying. The more venturesome are such only if they are sayers to a greater degree."[25] Poets risk their linguistic inheritance in their saying, venturing past it, perhaps using it in a new way, as Rilke does in the cases of the angel and Orpheus.

> There is a saying that fits itself into the traditional saying, without, however, reflecting upon language, whereby it would become just another object. This entry into the traditional saying characterizes a saying that follows after something to be said solely in order to say it. That which is to be said should be, then, what, in its essence, belongs to the province of language.[26]

Heidegger is addressing the point wherein language comes to pass as language. He is addressing the site wherein the speaking of language is gathered. Poets venture language in an exceptional fashion the degree to which poetic language is gathered as language into poetry. This is the furthest thing imaginable from technological writing where language is an object of theoretical concern to be digitally mastered and re-mastered. Rather, the path concerns a saying that enters into an inherited way of speaking. If one looks up words in a dictionary, the word will stand as a mere signifier, a stand in for some event that it purportedly represents. Within the poem the words are more than signs. They are figures and they address as such, departing, in their repetition, from the roles to which they are bound in ordinary or technological usage.

In Rilke's case, this move away is significant. Traditional sayings are not merely repeated for the sake of something else. Rather, they are repeated simply in order to say, as something to be said. Those who prove more venturesome in their saying thus are poets who fit themselves into traditional figures but retune them as figures of poetry through and through, as pure song.

It is in this pure song that the province of language is breached. Poetic figures are taken and presented as such, and they are not expected to be anything else. They are not tools for analysis or communication. Their nature as poetry, as language, is thus highlighted in a gesture toward the province of language. If the poetic figure was sufficient unto itself, we would never catch a glimpse of the province of language. Rather, that site would recede behind the figure appearing as something complete unto itself, much as the essential site of things seems to do. But insofar as the poetic figure appears as a repetition of a traditional saying, the poetic figure appears as something said again, thus underscoring the event of its saying. It is this poetic emphasis that opens for us the province of language, the site wherein language occurs.

But an exposure of the precinct of language is not all that occurs in the language of those who prove more venturesome. Within their own repetitions of traditional sayings, in offering "something to be said," as a figure of poetizing and nothing more, Rilke's poetic figures also sing of their own ground. They reach back, recoil upon the ground of that saying, carry it into their song, and thereby poetize poetry as well. They are thus not just poetic figures but also figures of poetizing. Initially one has a traditional saying that is repeated or re-said as a figure of speech or poetry, as an instance of language. The language does not rest with this repetition. Instead it returns in a saying of its own ground and figures it. In Rilke's case, it is a figuration wrought through figures such as nature, the open, the draft, the angel, and so on.

Rilke's ground words are examples of traditional sayings repeated as poetic figures in his poems. They are taken from extra-poetic contexts and presented as poetry. As poetic figures they do not lie still, however. Rather, they also poetize the grounds of poetry: they not only expose the precinct of language insofar as it arises within the language of the poem, but they also figure it. And in figuring the precinct, they also figure their own saying, that saying that they underscore and throw into relief in being poetic figures. By setting themselves and their saying within the grounds they figure, they draw that ground into the language of the poem. It is not the case, therefore, that the language of the poem somehow drags the precinct of language from some supposed far side of language into its own saying. Thus it is not the case that the language of the poem represents its own ground. Rather, it says those sites by allowing them to manifest themselves in and through the work.

IX.

What began with a reflection on Rilke has brought us a great distance. A good deal of the scholarly address to Heidegger's thinking about Rilke is cast too much in terms of propositional refutations. Rilke remains ensconced in metaphysics because his imagery remains oblivious to its own commitments to a metaphysics of presence, as in his emphasis on nature, and how in its venturing it is similar to Nietzschean will, and its correlate in subjective consciousness. Rather than focusing too much on the "argument" of whether or not Rilke indeed achieves, as much attention should be shed on what is occurring in his poetry which Rilke very nearly achieves. If we now ask "what are poets for?" we need not, at least not necessarily, subject the work of art to some kind of utilitarianism. One could always ask what are the consequences of the writing and the reading of poems, but if we pose the question in this way, we will suppose that our sense of the wherefore of poetry must arise beyond the language of the poem, lying instead in the priorities of a cost-benefit analysis. Heidegger is asking instead to attend to what the poetry tells us. If one does that, we will not need to subject poetry to some external measure, such as the public good. Rather, we will ask: what is found there already in the poem?

One finds within the language of some poetry, after arduous reflection, poems of poetry that provide a measure capable of grounding being and orienting our lives. A possible dwelling in which the basic manner of human existence comes forth on its own. "Poetizing is the original admission of dwelling."[27] That which brings us into relation with the dimension of presencing wherein we dwell, wherein we find measure in a non-enframing way, comes to pass in poetry. Poetry holds a measure for human life. Poetic appraisal takes place when the language of the poem arranges and establishes the dimension or an open by tracking that opening within the poem's own language. Figures of poetry figure their own ground. Poetic dwelling takes place in the language of poetry, when poetry tracks its own language back into the scene wherein it first speaks as poetry. This however is not to be read as Heidegger merely elevating "poems about poetry" at the expense of other kinds of poems. How many contemporary poets have reacted in exhaustion with regard to yet another poem about language! But what we are seeing with regard to Rilke is more severe than this. In appearing as something said, poetic figures are called upon to indeed accentuate their status as language. However, they probe and provoke the grounds of their own figurative status. The poetry toward which Heidegger is pointing marks both the site wherein it originally occurs as well as the clearing of the open that the occurrence requires, doing so within the folds of its own figures.

Today, in a destitute time, poets must write against the writing which becomes a wireless game with accelerated technical consciousness moving at the speed of injurious neglect. When language figures the ground of its own saying, it summons things to names, but in such a way that calls our attention to the clearing of an open dimension in which things and humans can yet be summoned to measure in the measureless acceleration of biogenetic invention and digital being. Poetry that returns the language of the poems to the dimension of presencing that they figure recasts all things, persons, and events according to the measure they provide. Two more passages will seal our understanding of writing the grounding.

Poetry is founding. The effectual grounding of what endures. The poet is the grounder of being. What we call the real in the everyday is, in the end, unreal.[28]

The poet's saying is not only foundation in the sense of a free bestowal, but also in the sense of the firm grounding of human existence on its ground.[29]

Poets ground being through their poetry, insofar as their poetic figures both invoke and expose the dimension wherein beings occur, including themselves. Poetry does not provide one more substratum for being out of which the meaning of being is mined, or that constitute being out of formless matter. Instead through a language of originary occurrence, poetry throws into relief the happening of things, an event wherein an open dimension is cleared and arranged, a happening within which beings and the worlds to which they belong come to pass. Such a happening stalls the technical destining we face, as it enables us to experience ourselves at the point of originary occurrence. It frees us from the habits that blind us to the drama that underwrites what appears to just be there. Some poetry figures the being of poetry and writing, which in turn exposes us to the deepest dimensions of being. They take the everyday and return it to us. When the gods have fled into the encrypted codes of technology, poetry nevertheless provides a measure for being, beings, and human beings, one that remains attuned to its own place within the dimension it exposes, should it dare to venture so much.

XVII. Winch's Encounter with Melville

There are generally three philosophical themes surrounding Winch's analysis of Melville's *Billy Budd* which are of interest to us. The first is the general notion of the universalizability of ethical concepts. The second is the general role of examples of moral theory derived from literature. Third, after a consideration of these, we would want to say there is a parallel of the kinds of confusions at work in the presumption of theory with regard to moral philosophy and those with regard to literary texts.

Winch's discussion of the plausibility of universalizability is now famous.[1] He used Sidgwick's formulation, though he thought something similar was central to many Kantian accounts in moral philosophy. The universalization principle is paraphrased as the following: «if in certain circumstances I judge an action right for a third party, A, then I am committed to judging the same action right for any other third party, B, given circumstances not relevantly different.»[2] Accepting the principle entails that if we judge an action or decision right, then it is right for anyone who is not relevantly different. This formulation is entirely from a third person perspective on judging whether A and B are in relevantly different circumstances. The third person could be anyone, as could be A or B.

Winch presses the application of the principle from a *first* person perspective. Put this way, the principle transposed would say that if I think that an action is right for me in some circumstance, then I ought to judge it right for anyone else in circumstances not relevantly different. It follows from accepting this principle that if someone chooses a different action than mine in similar circumstances, I should judge them not right but wrong. Winch argues against this principle. He focuses on a situation confronted by Captain Vere, commander of the H.M.S. *Indomitable* in Melville's *Billy Budd*. His summary of the story:

> Billy Budd, a foretopman of angelic character, is impressed into service on the *Indomitable* from the merchantman *Rights of Man* on the high seas. He is persecuted by the satanic masters-at-arms of the *Indomitable*, Claggert, in a campaign which culminates in Claggert's falsely accusing Billy, before Vere, of inciting the crew to mutiny. In the stress of the situation, Budd is afflicted with a speech-impediment which prevents him from answering the charge. Frustrated, he strikes Claggert, who falls, strikes his head and dies.

The difficult dilemma concerns how to deal with Billy. On the one hand, as a Naval officer, Vere is required to administer justice as specified by the military code. Military justice demands capital punishment for Billy. On the other hand, Vere thinks Billy «innocent before God,» by which we are to take it that natural justice demands his acquittal. Thus the dilemma admits no compromise between the opposite demands of military and natural justice.

The dilemma for Vere is deep, not merely a formal conflict between conflicting sources of justice. Vere's obligation to uphold military justice is deeply held and moral, not a formality. It stems from his oath of loyalty as an officer and from his sense of what military company demands. Similarly, Billy's innocence before God is no less compelling to Vere for whom the demands of natural justice are plain – demands alive in his and his fellow officers' sense of propriety. Winch characterizes the situation thus to prevent the dilemma from appearing as merely a conflict between one's public role and one's private conscience; or between one's commitment to institutional justice and one's inclinations. Vere's dilemma is intrinsically moral because the demands of justice on both sides are for him moral. Winch says, «I have laboured these points because it is important to my purposes to establish that Vere is faced with a conflict between two genuinely moral 'oughts', a conflict, that is, *within* morality.»[3]

Within either military justice or natural justice taken separately, it is perhaps clear what Vere ought to do. However, Vere faces the question outside either narrower context, but still within morality. This is crucial, since we could grant that the universalizability principle could be applied within military or natural justice. The example focuses on the universalizability principle's applicability to a broader conception of moral questions, rather than focusing on arguably different notions of justice or value. If the principle holds in this broader sense, then any judgment (like Vere's) against Billy carries a further commitment to thinking that those who would acquit him judge wrongly. Vere finds against Billy. Winch claims that he (Winch) could not have found against Billy in conformity with military justice, but that he does not think that Vere acted wrongly. That is, Winch denies the applicability of the universalizability principle to this moral question.

As the Wittgensteinian tradition has long taught, when words become untethered from their usual moorings, they take on new meanings. Initially it seems to make sense in ascribing a modal character to discourse concerning the word *ought*. Consider the following statement: «The plane leaves in 30 minutes, but it is just a short walk down the concourse, so you ought to make it in time.»

Such an expression seems to describe some necessary transitions from how things are now to another state. Ordinarily, such injunctions apply generally. For anyone relevantly similar, one is warranted in asserting that such an injunction applies to them. Unless there is a basis for an exception from the general, such as an injury, we take the *ought* to apply as much to you as to me. The scope of such injunctions is not arbitrary, rather they apply to anyone in similar circumstances. The assertion the warrant justifies is independent of those to whom it applies. In this way it seems similar to causal necessity.

However, there are differences in ethics, as there the use of «ought» does not of itself entail a commitment of a kind claimed in the universalizability principle or consequent upon laws of causality. It admits of exceptions. Winch does not judge Vere wrong, though Vere decides the opposite of what Winch finds it right to do. Winch is not saying it is too difficult to judge or that he cannot judge because the facts of the situation are unclear. He and Vere are trying to find the right thing to do in the same situation. They accept the same facts *ex hypothesi*, and are aware of all the details of military justice. Winch grants that innocence and military duty are as important for Vere and him. Winch's position does not entail that there is no right or wrong thing for Vere to do. There are answers to the question of what is right for Vere to do. This is precisely why Vere agonizes over the dilemma, *because* he is seeking the right answer. If he believed that whatever he did would be right, then his agonizing would not command our sympathy.

The claim here is that what I decide is right for me to do can be different from what you decide is right for you, though the considerations in deciding used are the same. There is no single correct interpretation in this situation, as such would be a «view from nowhere.» It is a claim instead for always a view from somewhere, and from somone, for a kind of subjectivity because it opens the possibility that remaining differences should be sought in our individuality, rather than further decision making considerations. It is not a claim about what specifically makes a decision right. The point will depend on answering the question of why in this situation Winch's «finding out the right thing to do» does not include finding out that Vere's doing otherwise is wrong. Vere too is trying to find out what is right. Such an encounter with Melville is an enactment of the task of finding out, not a display of what is found. Winch discusses «finding out» as follows:

A man in a situation like Vere's has to decide between two courses of action' but he is not merely concerned to decide to do something, but also to find out what is the right thing for him to do. The difficulty is to give some account of what the expression 'find out' can mean here. What I have suggested is that the deciding what to do is in a situation like this, itself a sort of finding out what is the right thing to do; whereas I think that a writer like Sidgwick would have to say that thje decision is one thing, the finding out quite another. It is because I think that deciding is an integral part of what we call 'finding out what to do' that I have emphasized the position of the agent in all this.» [4]

Winch's is an attack on what has been called the *presumption of theory* in ethics,[5] the idea that we can abstract from the concrete individuals' lives some feature, and then say that *it* (the abstract rational theory) contains *the* criteria of what is rational or worthwhile in a human life and what is not. An analogy might be with Kierkegaard's *Either/Or*. The issue in that text is that Kierkegaard wants to guide us away from the idea that what we find important, the ways we make sense of our lives, are underpinned by some sort of extra-lived necessity such that this is all that could be important or make sense to anyone. Along these lines Winch is maneuvering us into an essentially Kierkegaardian position. In deciding I aim to determine the right thing to do. The right thing is what it is possible for me to do or what I must do. The term Winch uses to capture the deliberative elements of these situations is moral modalities.[6] It is the unique aspect of these which reveal the «somewhere» from which such judgments can be made, and the subsequent inapplicability of universalization principles.

Kierkegaard thought typical justifications in religious thought took the form of doctrinal postulates supported by rational argument, all too reminiscent of the structure of an objective scientific theory. Just as such an approach tends to trivialize religion by casting it in the language of historical facts and propositions, so too with ethical life. Again, the justifications proffered are likely to be misunderstood or adapted to a conceptual framework intrinsically inimical to ethical life. Kierkegaard of course had Kant or Hegel in mind, but again the insight applies in general to the craving for the universalizability of moral concepts. *Either/Or* was an attempt to *portray* aesthetic subjectivity rather that *theorize* about it. The point is for the reader of *Either/Or* to, when he decides rightly, find something out about himself. What it does not entail is what is right for others to do in similar situations. In some cases I understand, in finding out, what is right for me to do because it is what I must do. Understanding what I have found out *just is* understanding what I must do. The

Billy Budd case is one such case. In other cases, perhaps, I come to understand what is possible for me to do.

Works of literature exhibit the requisite fullness to such moral modalities. In the typical ethics class you will look at examples, and apply theories to those examples distended from lived life. (10 men in a lifeboat – what do you do?) Such examples simply do not carry with them the existential weight. Taking them seriously presupposes that what is characteristic of the ways in which we express our moral concerns can be examined quite apart from any consideration of the *lives* of those involved, and what it is about those concerns that make them important *to* those involved. Indeed, it is something which «shows itself» in the explanation of the issues involved. Kierkegaard does not even attempt to *say* what moral action is: instead he *shows* us what it is by portraying various cases in all their existential light. Philosophers want to tidy up all this heterogeneity with abstract concepts and systems. But ethics is in no need of such philosophical support, any more than is literature.

The confusion in people such as Sidgwick or Kant is in examining the logical structure of different modalities to specify as the logical form of moral argument *that* form which is characteristic of all of them. The tendency is to «theorize» by way of some universalizability principle. But part of Winch's point, it seems to me, is to wean us away from the idea that there *is* any such form, or that theories are even necessary in ethics, and away from the presumption in wanting there to be a theory there at all. Instead one must, as it were, wait on the possibilities put before us. Like Kierkegaard, Winch is not advocating them so much as he is *showing* lived-differences. Seeing differences is just as important as seeing similarities between moral points of view. That there can be differences is an important insight into human ethical life. As Wittgenstein points out, there is a deep resistance to the recognition of differences in ethics:

> In considering a different system of ethics there may be a strong temptation to think that what seems to us to express the justification of an action must be what really justifies it there, whereas the real reasons are the reasons that are given. There are the reasons for or against this action. 'Reason' doesn't always mean the same thing; and in ethics we have to keep from assuming that reason must be really of a different sort from what they are seen to be.[7]

So too for Winch, when one has found out what one must do, in response to a question as to what is the object of one's understanding of what one has found, one can only respond by giving a restatement of the considerations that led to this discovery. And these considerations are expressible only in terms of the ideas and concerns which moved the decision in the first place, namely the situation itself. I express my understanding of what it is I must do in this situation by doing it.

I might press certain Kierkegaardian themes a bit further. One of the great critical insights in Kierkegaard is how it is possible to hallucinate sense when one employs a religious vocabulary. For Kierkegaard to see whether someone is a Christian is not merely a matter of finding out what sort of propositions she assents to or what sorts of justifications she is prepared to supply for those propositions or beliefs. It is more a matter of looking to the way in which her conception of herself as a Christian informs her life. Almost everyone in the Denmark of Kierkegaard's day thought of himself as a Christian, yet Kierkegaard thought no one was, and that most of his countrymen suffered from the illusion that they were Christians, calling this state pejoratively: *Christendom*. If the truth of Christianity is *lived*, then the risk is that people will use Christian-sounding words without their actually meaning anything by them. If we confine ourselves to the claim that a kind of lived religious background is the necessary condition for the employment of certain religious concepts, it will be by no means clear whether such a background is in place, since it is not something which can be determined simply by looking at the sort of vocabulary people employ. One must try to learn of the intelligibility of religious concepts employed, by inhabiting the *world* of those words. The words must have some world, some existential accompaniment for their words to have meaning. It is not as if the words have zero meaning, or are world-less. The problem is that these same words can be used in contexts in which they take on different meanings. The issue is not the words used but the concepts expressed by those words, and the problem is that such words can often be used without expressing a religious concept at all.

So, following Kierkegaard, just as a religious concept is only able to have its sense within the context of a certain sort of life, so too can works of literature help us illustrate the strange phenomenon of concepts surviving outside the frameworks of life that made them intelligible in the first place. Consider 40-somethings use of the word "album." We still use that term to refer to collections of music by various bands, even though it is largely a thing of the past. Even though I presently use that concept, there is no sense to be made in using that concept apart from its relation to sets of practices in which that concept has its life. Kierkegaard discovered among the citizens of Christendom something similar with respect to the word Christian and a whole host of other religious concepts; they wanted such words both to express a concept which applies to their lives as they presently lead them and to retain a feature of the concept which no longer intelligibly applies. But of course the recognition of this requires an ability to see the possibility of there being alternatives at all. There can be a kind of "Christendom" with regard to texts as well.

Kierkegaard and Winch are not providing us *examples* which await our moral judgments. They are presenting examples *of* people making moral judgments. The presumption of theory was in thinking that the either/or simply awaits systematic ordering to be determined by criteria some theory possesses. I think Kierkegaard presents these subjectivities with an eye to getting his reader to see what he (the reader) *does* want to say about them. There are no general rules which can determine in advance what one *must* say about them. What Winch is doing with Melville's story is providing an account of how decision-making can amount to finding out something about one's own subjectivity, namely, what it is possible for one to do here and now, without in so doing finding out what *anyone* could do. If in decision-making one need not find anything about anyone besides oneself, then there is no basis for a claim that in deciding I always commit myself to universal judgments about what anyone else similarly placed should do. To the extent that decision-making is individual, it is free from any universalizing constraints, however proper. The universalizability refuted can then be seen to have been a consequence of general ideas about reason. Thus the point of Winch's insights is to display one's ability to discern what is possible for oneself.

What Winch's critics have assumed is that the story of Billy Budd is supposed to directly provide a kind of counter-example to the universalizability principle; that this story shows clearly and unambiguously that two agents in a given situation might reach different moral judgments and both be correct. It has then been argued that Melville's story does not show this at all. So, Winch's critics argue variously: that Vere in fact made the wrong decision, or that Vere made the right decision, the decision that anyone in his situation should reach, or that we just do not know what it is like to be in Vere's situation and so cannot judge his action either way.[8] But Winch does not intend this example to show *directly* that the universalizability principle is false. It is not what the example shows but what his response to the story shows which is important here. Winch is drawing our attention to the way in which *he* reaches a judgment about Vere's decision.

In what I want to say next, of course I run the risk of turning around and generalizing precisely in ways we have just cautioned to avoid. But I want to develop the idea that there is a similarity between an impoverished view of what is at work in conceptual life and an impoverished view of what is at work in a text. This is not to make of Winch a full-blown hermeneutic literary theorist, as he leaves so much unsaid, and perhaps rightly so. But the posture of his readings, and his relation to those readings, is very different from the textual poverty that is normally at work in the analysis of the use of examples in moral philosophy taken from literature. Such examples are problematic because there are important differences between appreciating literary depictions of problems and facing them oneself. This is not to say that problems have to be ours before we can learn from them.

I want to say that Winch's is a fundamentally hermeneutic gesture, in both its ethical and its interpretive import. For thinkers like Nussbaum or O'Neill, scenes from literature are initial data awaiting further assessment by way of a conceptual alignment which has somehow become lost.[9] But, as Cora Diamond puts it, understanding a concept is not just a matter of knowing how to grasp things under a concept, it is being able to participate in *life-with-the-concept*.[10] Literature helps us to think in this way. Its myriad contexts portray the worlds that open up in and as a text. Great works of literature «world» in Heidegger's sense of the term. They show us something about human life which has nothing to do with our choosing to evaluate things one way or another. Literature shows, displays, the *life-with-the-concept*. Philosophers destroy this sense when they say: «this» is what it is like to use these concepts, for that itself is a use, a philosophically reflective use, of the concepts. Philosophical reflection is itself a form of moral reflection.

Kierkegaard's insight was that the meaning of religious concepts is connected to the conditions of intelligibility which must obtain in applying those concepts. His work "shows" how people continue to employ certain words but are no longer able to use them to express the concepts which those words formerly expressed, and that this loss is due to the loss of the existential religious framework in which those concepts formerly had their life. Something like this is at work in Winch's encounter with Melville. Absent the *world* in which such concepts operate, they are prone to hallucinate a meaning where there is none. The manner in which concern reflects itself in one's life is not pertinent to the establishing of universalizable actions or even precise arguments. The truth of such concepts often involves an essential reference to the character of the subject's concern, an internal connection. The meanings of those terms cannot be severed from the lives in which they operate, and the common experiences of human life that surround them, such as joy and sorrow, hope and despair. If the philosopher wishes to give an account of something like justice-concepts he must begin with a description of the contexts in which these concepts have their life. There can be no general justification or universal application of such concepts, any more than there could be of prayer, and the confusion is in thinking that there was a need for philosophical justification at all.

Just as there was a kind of kinship between Winch and Kierkegaard, so too I see a kinship between Winch and Ricouer. Ricouer concurred with Gadamer that interaction with texts provide a dynamic basis this process was ill-presented by the personification of the text as a conversation partner. The necessary condition of a dialogue is the presence of the interlocutors to one another. Such presence is not merely some condition of proximity, but also serves to contextualize the conversation in such a manner so as to provide a referential matrix for interpretation. The referential situation provided by the emergent disclosure of meaning through statements and responses provides the focus and the stimulus for continuing the dialogue.

For Ricouer the problem was not simply that the immediate presence presupposed by the dialogical model of understanding is unattainable in hermeneutic inquiry. In addition, the model of presence was too limiting and constraining to encapsulate the improvisational complexity of the textual encounter. An orientation towards presence suppresses the world of the text, and serves to limit arbitrarily the possibilities of meaningful disclosure. The notion of a text as a «thou» remains conditioned by the model of human presence. By contrast, Ricouer's more consistent development of a disclosure model of hermeneutics avoided the reliance upon an authorial subject as the basis for the truth of the text. «Insofar as the meaning of a text is rendered autonomous with respect to the subjective intention of its author, the essential question is not to recover, behind the text, the lost intention, but to unfold, in front of the text, the world which it opens and discloses.»[11] I see Winch's gesture as on the threshold of something like this. The hermeneutic encounter with the text of *Billy Budd* is not analogous to a dialogue with a personified Thou but is rather a process in which linguistic disclosure of a text opens different worlds of meaning before readers.

Winch's encounter with *Billy Budd* is not simply a medium between two subjects or a substitute for the authorial partner in a philosophical conversation. The text is the source of a disclosive practice that supersedes and transforms the subjectivity of both author and reader. Literary examples are not merely the mediation between two otherwise autonomous and unchanging subjects; rather, literary textuality is *constitutive* of modes of subjectivity. The meaning disclosed by the world of the text transcends the subject and challenges the interpretive frameworks of understanding derived from the manner in which «being» is disclosed to the subject. The transformative effect of such a hermeneutic gesture is the potential clash of disclosed worlds.

Gadamer's critique of method is similar in its opposition to methodological objectivism which represents the imposition of fixed methods that lack reflexive openness. The aim of objective knowledge in the natural sciences requires a consciousness maximally transparent to itself, one without any alien forces influencing it unawares toward a given conclusion. Such self-transparency is predicated upon the methodological controls that minimize the role of the observer. Gadamer was, after all, also in the non-universalizability business. The hermeneutic inquirer is a finite cultural being whose understanding is shaped by historically formed vantage points and perspectives. Winch's in it's own way is a hermenutic gesture in that he acknowledges the fore-meanings and prejudgments that derive from such perspectives. As Gadamer once put it, «the possibility that the other person may be right is the soul of hermeneutics.»[12]

The ethical dimension of hermeneutics might be economically understood in terms of a kind of improvisation. Our moral lives are such that we do not approach situations with a script, and we come to understand others as also unscripted. The value of improvisation is when confronted with differences. When faced with novel circumstances we must extend the application of our moral concepts. Such an extension calls us to ourselves in our moral lives. Moral improvisation is meant to reflect the notion that morality requires a kind of flexibility that is at odds with strict, systematic, theoretical frameworks. Moral thought does not go on in a situation with fixed, given possibilities, the alternatives then being something for which no one has responsibility for, except insofar as one has by one's previous actions brought into existence certain fixed elements of the situation. The notion of improvisation signals an entirely different view of what is involved in the moral life. The idea of possibilities as fixed in advance and built into the situation locates the moral agent's responsibility and his freedom in a quite different place from where one sees it if one takes the capacity for improvisation as esssential in any account of our moral life.

In musical improvisation, there is no predetermination. There is no definite thing that the musicians are going to play, as if some structure were there waiting to be discovered by the players of which they were unaware. What the musicians will play is undetermined in the sense that there is no fact of the matter about what will be played, no set of notes waiting for discovery, prior to the actual playing. Winch's hermeneutic gesture offers something like this, a display of the ethical space that allows room for plurality and differences which mark the possibility for subjectivity. The idea is mostly brought out in the context of moral dilemmas where we are inclined to say that there is no single correct interpretation – each choice brings with it a kind of balance of gain and loss. We might choose one course over another in light of other commitments without, thereby, being committed to thinking that others should make this choice. Without claiming that all situations are like this, it might be the case that many ethical decisions are underdetermined in the sense that what we choose to do flows out of prior commitments, plans, intentions.

The crux of Winch's argument is that a person's moral judgment in such cases may turn on what is personally morally possible for them. Such moral modalities are inextricably linked to interpretive modalities. Many such modalities are already operative at the level of the text itself, one of which is Melville's discussion of Admiral Horatio Nelson prior to the introduction of Vere. These chapters depict Nelson as being good in a way that seems to contrast pointedly with Vere. Lester Hunt has generally spelled out three contrasts between Nelson and Vere.[13] First, Nelson and Vere differ with respect to an important trait of character. The contrast appears prominently in the passage in which Melville replies to a criticism of Vere from individuals who hold a utilitarian perspective, from the «Benthamites of war,» as he calls them. These critics fault Nelson for having chosen, during the battle of Trafalgar, to stand high on the quarterdeck of the *Victory*, wearing his dress uniform and medals. Nelson was fatally wounded in the battle, unable to insure that his dying instructions, to anchor the fleet against possible storms, were followed. They were in fact reversed by his successor, with considerable loss of life resulting. Melville replies that this charge applies the wrong standards to the assessment of Nelson's conduct. With respect to prudence, Nelson is vulnerable to criticism, but with respect to the greatest virtue of a military man, he is not.

The virtue that Nelson is faulted for lacking is however one that Vere seems to have in abundance. Indeed, Vere's speech to the officers is a brilliant example of utilitarian prudence, aimed entirely that achieving what is deemed to be good on balance. Hence the first difference between Vere and Nelson is the difference between a character that is dominated by prudence and one that is dominated by virtue that loves something to excess. The further difference involves the way Nelson died, and his «ornate publication of his person» on the quarterdeck of the *Victory*, which was the subject of the utilitarian criticism of him for excessive self-exposure. In this respect Vere is once again the direct opposite of Nelson. Vere consistently evinces not self-disclosure but, on the contrary, a pronounced self-reserve. «(W)hen nothing demanded his paramount action, he was the most undemonstrative of men.»[14] Someone seeing him for the first time on a ship might have taken him for a «discreet envoy» rather than a sailor.[15] This discretion is apparent in the way he manages the affairs of the ship. Soon after the surgeon confirms Claggert is indeed dead, Melville comments on how Vere operates «to guard as much as possible against publicity.»[16] Vere maintains complete secrecy through the entire drumhead court proceedings. Vere's secrecy involves him in the sacrifice of one of the fundamental values of a liberal society: respect for the reason and will of individuals. His justification for secrecy is that the people (meaning the ship's company) lack the intelligent responsiveness necessary to qualify them in participation of the discussion.

Vere's policy of secrecy cost Billy his life, and his reputation. The very point of Melville's narrative, as announced in its subtitle, is to unmask the events on the *Bellipotent*, to destroy the secrecy inaugurated by Vere. Melville is the anti-Vere, and the text proffers an alternative to the lingering damage he has done. Whereas Vere has promoted secrecy, Melville promotes the opposite value, one he has explicitly associated with Nelson: publicity. Melville's «inside narrative» further undermines Vere's reasons for secrecy. Vere claims his secrecy was necessary because the people on the ship lacked the capacity to comprehend and discriminate. The note on which the story ends reveals that he was wrong about this: they have comprehended and discriminated essentially the same fact that the officer of the marines has comprehended: that in some ultimate sense Billy is an innocent person.

The third comparison with Nelson is connected with the execution aboard the *Bellipotent*. In the same year with this story, Melville says, Nelson, at the time a mere Rear Admiral, was removed from his ship by his superior, and placed in command of another, the *Theseus*, because the *Theseus* had taken part in the Great Mutiny, and the mood of its crew was thought to be still in a dangerous state. He seemed the best available officer to deal with such an explosive situation. The reason was not that he was a stern disciplinarian, for he was not one to «terrorize the crew into base subjection,» but rather «to win them, by force of his mere presence and heroic personality, back to an allegiance if not as enthusiastic as his own yet as true.»[17]

The same sort of power, to prevent chaotic violence by one's mere presence, is attributed to Billy Budd by the captain of the *Rights of Man* as Billy is being removed from his ship to serve on Vere's. Before Billy came aboard, he says, his forecastle was a «rat-pit of quarrels» but Billy changed all of that. «Not that he preached to them or said or did anything in particular, but a virtue went out of him, sugaring the sour ones.»[18] Nelson and Billy, on Melville's showing, have something in common: they are both able to solve a certain problem, and they are able to do so by their presence alone. That sort of problem is essentially the sort that Vere faces after the death of Claggert: what he fears is precisely an outbreak of violence. The contrast between his solution and the sort of solution Nelson and Billy represent comes to the surface. Discipline cannot get any more severe than executing someone who is not morally deserving of death. Vere's solution is quite literally the one Nelson avoids: to terrorize the crew into a state of subjection. He maintains power by use of fear.

The world of the text confronts us with lived-differences. What we have is an either/or with regard to Nelson and Vere. Melville's work depicts (at least) two schemes: an overflowing love of glory, shiningly revealing itself to the world, and lifting human beings toward its own level through its mere presence, is a way in which a naval vessel can be commanded. There is also the course of prudent calculation of social utility that devises a plan that combines stealth and coldly brutal severity. Winch decides which is the best course for him. We are to follow his lead in deciding which is best for us. In announcing his disagreement, Winch is acknowledging difference. By the sheer act of such acknowledgement, by the force, as it were, of *its* mere presence, there is an admission of otherness, of the possibility of different perspectives. This possibility is one which has us acknowledge not merely the world of the text but the need for an un-universalizable, that is to say, improvisational response. The announcement of Winch's subjectivity, after all, is also that of Vere's, and Vere's pointing to his buttons and Nelson's wearing his medals are modalities with which we grapple.

What is crucial for Winch is that when he says he could not convict a man innocent before God he is not referring to some weakness or psychological incapacity, but a kind of genuine moral limit. To approach such a limit is to decide what one's own moral life is about. Winch's position is expressive of his moral character. His essay compliments the melville text in what it calls us toward. What it is he says he cannot do here is not an indictment of what others could do. While it is something short of «thanking God for Captain Vere,» it is a display, at least in part, of what is required in the founding of a particular moral character. We come to understand from this what it is to have a moral identity in terms of such limits and the ideas that are involved in them. Winch's objection to their universalizability is then that our moral identities, our distinctive moral characters, may properly differ in this sense. The problem with universalizability is that such a view may well require a violation of one's ownmost moral character. And it would be wrong to take the blindness to be a matter of philosophers and literary theorists going on as if we had lost concepts which we have not lost at all, recoverable only by theory. Indeed they were perfectly happily there for everyone else, including the philosopher, and the literary theorist, when they are not theorizing, but allowing the text to emerge and form into and out of the moral integrity of our lives.

Notes

Notes to Chapter Two

[1] Martin Heidegger, *Beitrage zur Philosophie (Vom Ereignis)*. *Gesamtausgabe* Band 65. Klostermann: Frankfurt am Main, 1989. p. 344.

[2] Heidegger, *Contributions to Philosophy (from Enowning)* Translated by Parvis Emad and Kenneth Maly. Bloomington: Indiana University Press, 1999. p. 241.

[3] Heidegger, *Being and Time*. Translated by John Macquarrie and Edward Robinson. New York: Harper and Row, 1962.

[4] Heidegger, "Platons Lehre von der Wahrheit." 1942. In *Wegmarken*, pp. 109-144. Frankfurt am Main: Klostermann, 1967. "Plato's Doctrine of Truth." Translated by John Barlow. In *Philosophy in the Twentieth Century*, vol. 2, 251-270. New York: Random House, 1962.

[5] Paul Friedländer, *Plato*, Volume 1, translation by Hans Meyeroff. 2nd edition. Princeton: Princeton University Press, 1969.

[6] Rudolph Carnap, "Überwindung der Metaphysik durch Logische Analyse der Sprache," *Erkenntnis*, 2, (1931). Translated as "The Overcoming of Metaphysics through Logical Analysis of Language," by Arthur Pap in *Heidegger and Modern Philosophy*. Edited by Michael Murray. Yale: 1978, pp. 23-24.

[7] Heidegger, *Was Heisst Denken?* Tübingen, Germany: Niemeyer, 1971. *What is Called Thinking?* Translated by Fred Wieck and J. Glenn Gray. New York, Harper and Row, 1968. *Schellings Abhandlung uber das Wesen der Menschliche Freiheit*. Tubingen: Niemayer, 1971. *Schelling's Treatise on the Essence of Human Freedom*. Translated by Joan Stambaugh. Columbus: Ohio University Press, 1985. *Erlauterungen zu Hölderlins Dichtung*. Frankfurt: Klostermann, 1951. "*Hölderlin and the Essence of Poetry*," translated by Douglas Scott, in *Existence and Being*. Chicago: Henry Regnery, 1949, pp. 233-291.

[8] Heidegger, *On Time and Being*, translated by Joan Stambaugh. New York: Harper and Row, 1972. p. 24.

Notes to Chapter Three

[1] An excellent source for this motif in Sartre is Philip Watts, *Allegories of the Purge*. Stanford: Stanford University Press, 1998.

[2] Michael Scriven, *Politics and Culture in Postwar France*, p. 49. See also George Steiner, "Sartre: The Suspect Witness," in The Times Literary Supplement, 3 May 1991, pp. 3-5. Watts, P. 62. For additional facts of Sartre's wartime biography, see Annie Cohen-Solal, *Sartre: A Life*. Translation by Anna Cancogni. New York: Pantheon Books, 1987. Simone de Beauvoir, *The Prime of Life*. Translation by Peter Green. New York: World Publishing, 1962.

[3] Sartre, *What is Literature? and Other Writings*. Ed. Steven Ungar. Cambridge: Harvard University Press, 1988, p. 251. Quoted in Watts, p. 68.

[4] Ibid., p. 252.

[5] See Watts, op. cit., pp. 67-73.

[6] Sartre, What is a Collaborator? *Situations III*. Paris: Gallimard, 1949, pp. 43-61.

[7] Scriven, p. 41-62. See P. Daix, *J'ai cru au martin*. Robert Laffont, 1976, p. 340, n.1. D. Craute, *Communism and the French Intellectuals 1914-1960*. London: Andre Deutsch, 1964, p. 151.

[8] L. Casanova, *Le Parti communiste, les intellectuels et la nation*. Editions Sociales, 1949, p. 9. Sartre refused the Nobel Prize for literature in 1964 on the grounds that he did not wish to "become a spokesperson or a western bourgeois cultural institution."

[9] Sartre, *Critique of Dialectical Reason*, Volume II. Gallimard, 1985, p. 45.

[10] Sartre, "Sartre parle des maos," interview with Michel-Antoine Burnier. *Actuel*, February 28, 1973, p. 76.

[11] Sartre, *Avant-propose aux Maos en France de Michele Monceaux*. Gallimard, 1972, pp. 329-330.

[12] See F. Noudelmann, "Sartre et l'inhumain," *Les Temps Modernes*, No.s 565-6. Sept. 1993, pp. 48-65.

[13] de Beauvoir, *La Ceremonie des adieux*. Gallimard, 1981, p. 44. See also Sartre, *Archives Organization de la Radio-Television Francaise*, 4 December 1974.

[14] Alan Stoekl, *Agonies of the Intellectual: Commitment, Subjectivity, and the Performative in the 20th Century French Tradition*. Lincoln: University of Nebraska Press, 1992, p. 104-121 ff.

[15] Sartre, *Nekrassov*. Gallimard, 1956.

[16] Jean-Paul Sartre, *Critique of Dialectical Reason. Vol. I: Theory of Practical Ensembles*. Translation by Alan Sheridan-Smith. Edited by J. Ree. Paris: Gallimard, 1960: NLB, 1976.

[17] Ibid., p. 256.

[18] Ibid, pp. 270-276.

[19] By the late 1950's it was apparent none of the European countries could hold on to their African colonies much longer. In November 1960 De Gaulle announced limited freedoms for Algeria after terrorist activity by the FLN (Front de Liberation Nationale Algeria). The French-Algerian generals did not take it so well, however. They created the Organisation de l'Armee Secrete (OAS) which went about assassinating Muslims and European sympathizers, counting on terrorism to delay settlement in Algeria. Their trademark weapon was plastic explosives. Thus both the OAS and the FLN were involved in terrorist activities. Sartre was friends with Frantz Fanon, a Martinican doctor, writer, and member of the provisional revolutionary government of Algeria and arch supporter of counter-violence, since colonialism had depended on violence. After De Gaulle has entered into negotiations between the OAS and the FLN, both parties tried to assassinate him, and so too Sartre. He was known to be on the list for assassination by the

OAS. On November 1, 1961, Sartre gave a speech and participated in demonstrations by French intellectuals at the Place Maubert when plastic explosives were thrown at his podium. While living in a flat on the 42 Rue Bonaparte, Boulevard Saint-Germain in January 1962, a plastic bomb exploded destroying his apartment. In March, when Sartre gave a lecture on Algeria in Brussels, bomb warnings reduced the size of the crowds. To escape what was now an incredibly dangerous situation for him in Paris, Sartre and de Beauvoir travelled to the Soviet Union and Cuba for a year. See the chapter aptly titled "Kill Sartre" in Ronald Hayman, *Sartre: A Life*. Simon and Schuster. New York, 1987, pp. 381-393.

Notes to Chapter Four

[1] Maurice Blanchot, "Affirmation (Desire, Affliction)" in *The Infinite Conversation*. Minneapolis: University of Minnesota Press, 1993, pp. 106-122. The text was originally published in two parts: "Simone Weil et la certitude," *La nouvelle revue Francaise* 55(1957), pp. 103-113, and "L'experience de Simone Weil," *La nouvelle revue Francaise* 56 (1957) pp. 297-310.

[2] Martin Heidegger, *Being and Time*. Translation by John Macquarrie and Edward Robinson. New York: Harper and Row, 1962.

[3] Maurice Blanchot, *The Writing of the Disaster*. Translation by Ann Smock. Lincoln: University of Nebraska Press, 1986. See also Blanchot, "Literature and the Right to Death," in *The Gaze of Orpheus*. Translation by Lydia Davis. Barrytown, N.Y.: Station Hill Press, 1981.

[4] Exodus 33:20.

[5] Simone Weil, *Notebooks of Simone Weil*. Translation by Arthur F. Mills. New York: Putnam, 1956, 211. See Miklos Vetos's chapter "Time and the Self," in his *Religious Metaphysics of Simone Weil*. Albany: SUNY Press, 1994, pp. 120-123. Vetos makes interesting reference to Heidegger and Weil on death (pp. 156-58) but does not consider the later Heidegger's views concerning language, which would bring him, along with Blanchot, into greater connection with Weil.

[6] Simone Weil, "The Iliad as a Poem of Force," in *The Simone Weil Reader*. Edited by George Panichas. London: Moyer Bell, 1977, pp. 153ff.

[7] Weil, *Notebooks*, 252-3.

[8] Simone Weil, *On Science, Necessity, and the Love of God*. Translation Richard Rees. Oxford: Oxford University Press, 1968, 188.

[9] Simone Weil, *Waiting for God*. Translated by Emma Craufurd. New York: Harper and Rowe, 1951, p. 135.

[10] Simone Weil, "Human Personality," in *Simone Weil: An Anthology*. Edited by Sian Miles. New York: Grove Press, 1986, pp. 49-78.

[11] For a discussion of Weil's use of language, see the essays in *The Beauty that Saves: Essays on Aesthetics and Language in Simone Weil*. John Dunaway and Eric O. Springsted, editors. Mercer University Press: Macon, GA, 1996.

[12] Simone Weil, *The Need for Roots*. Translation by Arthur F. Wills. New York: Putnam, 1956, pp. 25-6.

[13] Simone Weil *Lectures on Philosophy*. Translation by Hugh Price. Cambridge University Press, 1978, p. 76.

[14] Weil, "The Power of Words," in *The Simone Weil Reader*, p. 271.

[15] Weil, *Notebooks*, 234.

[16] The best philosophical discussion of this aspect of Weil's thought remains Peter Winch, *Simone Weil: The Just Balance*. Cambridge University Press, 1989.

[17] Weil, *Notebooks*, 120.

[18] Blanchot, *Infinite Conversation*, p. 120.

[19] Blanchot, *Infinite Conversation*, p. 108.

[20] Blanchot, *Writing of the Disaster*, p. 23.

[21] Blanchot, *Infinite Conversation*, p. 119.

[22] On this theme in Simone Weil, see Rowan Williams' "The Necessary Non-existence of God" in *Simone Weil's Philosophy of Culture: Readings Toward a Divine Humanity*. Edited and Introduced by Richard H. Bell. Cambridge: New York, 1993.

[23] Death and its implications for language are further explored by Blanchot in his novel *L'Arret de mort*. Paris: Gallimard, 1948. *Death Sentence*. Translation by Lydia Davis. New York: Station Hill Press, 1978.

[24] Blanchot, *Infinite Conversation*, p. 115.

[25] St. Augustine, *On Christian Doctrine*. Translation D. W. Robertson, Jr. New York: MacMillan, 1958, I.6.

[26] Heidegger, "Origin of the Work of Art," in *Basic Writings*. Edited by David Farrell Krell. New York: Harper and Row, 1977. In *Existence and Existents* Levinas analyzes certain modes of existence, fatigue, laziness, insomnia, in which individualized consciousness is dispossessed by the incumbency of the *il y a*, deliverance from which appeared to Levinas in the form of an ethics. See Levinas, *Existence and Existents*. Translation by Alphonso Lingis. The Hague: Martinus Nijhoff, 1978.

[27] On this point see Derrida, *Aporias*. Translation Thomas Dutoit. Stanford University Press, 1993.

[28] A reference to Deuteronomy 24:17 that permeates Levinas' work.

[29] Levinas, *Totality and Infinity*. Translated by Alphonso Lingis. The Hague: Nijhoff, 1969, p. 80. Levinas' and Blanchot's works intersect each other on many levels, having had a close friendship for 60 years.

[30] Levinas, *Totality and Infinity*, p. 60.

[31] Levinas, *Totality and Infinity*, p. 62.

[32] Levinas, *Totality and Infinity*, p. 195.

[33] Exodus 33:20-23.

Notes to Chapter Five

[1] Representative of this trend might be texts such as *Phenomenology and the Theological Turn: The French Debate*, by Dominique Janucaud, et.al. New York: Fordham University Press, 2000; and John Caputo and Michael Scanlon, eds., *God, the Gift, and Postmodernism*. Bloomington: Indiana University Press, 1999; Robyn Horner, *Rethinking God as Gift: Marion, Derrida, and the Limits of Phenomenology*. New York: Fordham University Press, 2001.

[2] Kant, *Von einem neuerdings erhoben vornehmen Ton*, in *Werke*, Vol. VI, Cassirer: Berlin, 1912-1922, pp. 487, 495.; James, *Varieties of Religious Experience*. New York: Modern Library, 1929, p. 370. See Kevin Hart, *Trespass of the Sign: Deconstruction, Theology, and Philosophy*. Cambridge: Cambridge University Press, pp, 207-240.

[3] Marcel Mauss, *The Gift: The Form and Reason for Exchange in Archaic Societies*. Translation W. D. Hall. London: Routledge, 1990.

[4] Georges Bataille, "La Notion de depense," (1933), in *La Part maudite*. Introduction by Jean Piel. Paris: Editions de Minuit, 1967. The essay is also in Bataille, *Oeuvres completes* Vol. 1: Premiers Ecrits, 1922-1940. Edited by Denis Hollier. Paris: Gallimard, 1970. pp. 300 ff.

[5] Sartre wanted to distance himself from any mystical approximation of philosophy because it risked association with "contemplative" thought which was divorced from the political. Bataille's mysticism seemed to advocate to Sartre a retreat from the world into interiority, a rejection of reason as the basis for moral action, and an almost treacherous embrace of experience irrespective of ethical consequences. In claiming that Bataille "had not understood Heidegger," it is interesting to see Sartre trying to exculpate Heidegger from the same charges of contemplation and mysticism in his *Existentialism is a Humanism* (1947). His review of Bataille is on some front a rehearsal for his defense of existentialism as a philosophy of commitment and responsibility. That Heidegger repudiated Sartre's efforts would seem to confirm Habermas' contention that Bataille and Heidegger are in fact in great proximity to the mystical.

[6] Jean-Paul Sartre, "Un nouveau mystique," in *Situations I*. Paris: Gallimard, pp. 143-188. Hereafter NM. This is one of the most important of Sartre's essays not yet to be translated. Translations are my own. Sartre's interpretation must be understood in the context of the spirit of the purge before the end of the war, and the self-appointed critical task of determining collaborators and clearing the old destructive influences on French letters. See again Philip Watts, *Allegories of the Purge*. Stanford: Stanford University Press, 1998.

[7] Ibid., NM, p. 174.

[8] Ibid., NM, p. 150.

[9] Ibid., NM, p. 184.

[10] Ibid., NM, p. 166. Vainement M. Bataille tente-t-il de s'intégrer à la machinerie qu'il a monté: il reste dehors, avec Durkheim, avec Hegel, avec Dieu le Père.

[11] It was not only Sartre who saw in Bataille's a specifically *Christian* mysticism. Gabriel Marcel also saw in Bataille an escapable desire for a return to God. See Marcel, *Homo Viator*. Trans. Emma Craufurd. Glouster, MA: Peter Smith, 1978. In spite of reservations about their conclusions, Bataille does not conceal his admiration for the writings of Dionysius the Areopagite, Jakob Boehme, Nicolas of Cusa, Meister Eckhart, Saint John of the Cross, Saint Theresa of Avila, Saint Catherine of Siena, Angela of Foligno, as well as many other, mostly western and Christian, mystics.

[12] Sartre, NM, op. cit., p. 151.

[13] Ibid., NM, p. 152. " la communication qu'il veut établir est sans réciprocité. Il est en haut, nous sommes en bas. Il nous délivre un message: le reçoive qui peut. Mais ce qui ajoute à notre gêne, c'est que le sommet d'où il nous parle est en même temps la profondeur abyssale de l'abjection.

[14] Derrida, "From Restricted to General Economy: A Hegelianism without Reserve," in *Writing and Difference*. Translation Alan Bass. London: Routledge, 1978, pp. 251-277. *Donner le temps: 1. La fausse monnaie*. Paris: Galilee, 1991. *Given Time: 1. Counterfeit Money*. Translation Peggy Kamuf. Chicago: University of Chicago Press, 1992.

[15] Hegel, *Phenomenology of Spirit*. Translated by A.V. Miller. Oxford: Oxford University Press, 1977, 19.

[16] Derrida, "From Restricted to General Economy: A Hegelianism without Reserve," in *Writing and Difference*. Translation Alan Bass. London: Routledge, 1978, pp. 271.

[17] Bataille, *The Accursed Share, Vol. I*. Translation by Robert Hurley. New York: Zone Books, 1991, p. 25.

[18] Derrida, *Donner le temps: 1. La fausse monnaie*. Paris: Galilee, 1991. *Given Time: 1. Counterfeit Money*. Translation Peggy Kamuf. Chicago: University of Chicago Press, 1992. (Hereafter GT).

[19] Derrida, GT, 27-28. See Derrida, *Aporias*. Translation by Thomas Dutoit. Stanford: Stanford University Press, 1993. See also Derrida, "Sauf le nom." Translation by James P. Leavey Jr., *On the Name*. Edited by Thomas Dutoit. Stanford: Stanford University Press, 1995, pp. 35-85.

[20] Derrida, GT, p. 12.

[21] Ibid., p. 14.

[22] Ibid., p. 26-27.

[23] The chip has no real life function. Most programming information is not generally available a month in advance, and even if it were, why would someone need to tape a month's worth of television programs, and who could remember the appropriate times to insert the new blank tapes?

24 Heidegger, *Being and Time*, op. cit., p. 26, 255, 464.

25 Martin Heidegger, *The Basic Problems of Phenomenology*. trans. Albert Hofstadter. Bloomington: Indiana University Press, 1982, p. 10.

26 John Macquarrie, *Heidegger and Christianity*. London: SCM Press, 1994, p. 60. Heidegger, "Letter on Humanism," in *Basic Writings: Martin Heidegger*. rev. ed. by David Farrell Krell. London: Routledge, 1993, pp. 217-265.

27 Derrida, GT, op. cit., p. 20.

28 Heidegger, "Time and Being," *On Time and Being*. Translation Joan Stambaugh. New York: Harper and Row, 1972, pp. 1-24.

29 Heidegger, *What is Called Thinking?* Translation J. Glenn Gray. New York: Harper and Row, 1968, p. 126.

30 Heidegger, *Being and Time*, op. cit., p. 327.

31 Ibid., p. 286.

32 Heidegger, *What is Called Thinking?* Translation J. Glenn Gray. New York: Harper and Row, 1968, p. 143.

Notes to Chapter Six

1 Heidegger, *On Time and Being*, translated by Joan Stambaugh. New York: Harper and Row, 1972. p. 78.

2 Heidegger, *Platon: Sophistes*. Marburg lecture course WS 1924-25. Edited by Ingeborg Schüssler, 1992.Vol. 19, *Gesamtausgabe*. *Plato's Sophist*, trans. By Richard Rojcewicz and Andre Schuwer. Bloomington: Indiana University Press, 1997, p. 8.

3 Martin Heidegger, *The Basic Problems of Phenomenology*. trans. Albert Hofstadter. Bloomington: Indiana University Press, 1982, p. 232.

4 Aristotle, *Parts of Animals*, 640a15ff).

5 Aristotle, *Eudemian Ethics*, 1216b26ff.

6 Aristotle, *Post. Analytics* 93a15-28

7 Heidegger, *Aristotle's Metaphysics 1-3: On the Essence and Actuality of Force*. Translation by Walter Brogan and Peter Warnek. Bloomington: Indiana University Press, 1995, (GA 33) pp. 374-75.

8 Aristotle, *Categories* 3b10-12.

9 Aristotle, *Categories* 2b29-31.

10 Aristotle, *Metaphysics*, 1003b23ff.

[11] Heidegger, "Aristotle-Introduction" (1922), *Phenomenological Interpretations of Aristotle: Indication of the Hermeneutical Situation.* Translation Michael Baur, *Man and World* 25 (1992): 355-93, p. 387.

[12] Aristotle, *Physics*, 200b12.

[13] Aristotle, *Physics*, 185a12ff., 192b32-35, 201a8.

[14] Aristotle, *Physics*, 191a25ff.

[15] Aristotle, *Physics*, 192b10ff.

[16] Aristotle, *Physics*, 201a10ff.

[17] Aristotle, *Physics*, 194b27.

[18] Heidegger, "On the Essence and Concept of *Phusis* in Aristotle's *Physics* B, 1." In *Pathmarks.* Edited by William McNeill. Cambridge: Cambridge University Press, 1998, pp. 217-218.

[19] Heidegger, *Aristotle's Metaphysics 1-3: On the Essence and Actuality of Force.* Translation by Walter Brogan and Peter Warnek. Bloomington: Indiana University Press, 1995, (GA 33) pp. 85.

[20] Ibid., p. 181.

[21] Aristotle, *De Anima.* II. 1.

[22] Aristotle, *De Anima*, 412a20ff.

[23] Aristotle, *De Anima*, 429a15-17.

[24] Aristotle, *De Anima*, 429b3-431a1.

[25] Aristotle, *De Anima*, 431b16-18.

[26] Aristotle, *Metaphysics*, 1003a34.

[27] Aristotle, *Metaphysics*, 1042a23.

[28] Aristotle, *Nichomachian Ethics*, 1139aff.

[29] Heidegger, *Platon: Sophistes.* Marburg lecture course WS 1924-25. Edited by Ingeborg Schüssler, 1992.Vol. 19, *Gesamtausgabe. Plato's Sophist*, trans. By Richard Rojcewicz and Andre Schuwer. Bloomington: Indiana University Press, 1997, p. 19ff.

[30] Aristotle, *Nicomachian Ethics*, 1139b12-18.

[31] Heidegger, *Platon: Sophistes.* Marburg lecture course WS 1924-25. Edited by Ingeborg Schüssler, 1992.Vol. 19, *Gesamtausgabe. Plato's Sophist*, trans. By Richard Rojcewicz and Andre Schuwer. Bloomington: Indiana University Press, 1997, p. 16.ff.

³² Heidegger, *Gesamtausgabe*. Frankfurt: Klostermann, 1975. Vol. 61: *Phänomenologische Interpretation zu Aristoteles. Einführung in die phänomenologische Forschung* (1985), p. 62. Trans. by Richard Rojcewicz. *Phenomenological Interpretations of Aristotle*. Bloomington: Indiana University Press, 2001.

³³ Ibid., GA 61, pp. 164-65.

³⁴ Heidegger, "Aristotle-Introduction" (1922), *Phenomenological Interpretations of Aristotle: Indication of the Hermeneutical Situation*. Translation Michael Baur, *Man and World* 25 (1992): 355-93, p. 377.

³⁵ Aristotle, *Nicomachian Ethics*, 1141a20ff.

³⁶ Ibid., 1178b10-16.

³⁷ Ibid., 1178b20ff.

³⁸ Ibid., X.7.

³⁹ Heidegger, *Platon: Sophistes*. Marburg lecture course WS 1924-25. Edited by Ingeborg Schüssler, 1992.Vol. 19, *Gesamtausgabe. Plato's Sophist*, trans. By Richard Rojcewicz and Andre Schuwer. Bloomington: Indiana University Press, 1997, p. 39.

⁴⁰ Heidegger, *Being and Time*. Translated by John Macquarrie and Edward Robinson. New York: Harper and Row, 1962, p. 318.

⁴¹ Aristotle, *Nicomachian Ethics*, 1134b18-35.

⁴² Aristotle, *Politics*, 1332a4ff.

⁴³ Aristotle, *Nicomachian Ethics*, 1098b27-30.

Notes to Chapter Seven

1   Alphonse de Waelhens, preface to Merleau-Ponty, *La structure du comportement*. Paris: Presses Universitaires de France, 1947. *The Structure of Behavior* (trans. Alden Fisher). Boston: Beacon Press, 1963.

2   Martin Heidegger, *The Basic Problems of Phenomenology*. trans. Albert Hofstadter. Bloomington: Indiana University Press, 1982.

3 Alphonso Lingus, *The Community of Those who have Nothing in Common*. Bloomington: Indiana University Press, 1994; *The Imperative*. Bloomington: Indiana University Press, 1998.

4 Edmund Husserl, *Cartesian Meditations: An Introduction to Phenomenology*. Trans. D. Cairns. Dordrecht: Kluwer, 1993.

5 Martin Heidegger, *Being and Time*. Trans. Macquarrie and Robinson. New York: Harper and Row, 1962.

6 Emmanual Levinas, *Time and the Other*. Trans. Richard Cohen. Pittsburgh: Duquesne University Press, 1994, p. 93.

[7] Emmanual Levinas, *Time and the Other.* Trans. Richard Cohen. Pittsburgh: Duquesne University Press, 1994, p. 59/72.

[8] Ibid., p. 75.

[9] Ibid.

[10] Emmanual Levinas, *Time and the Other.* Trans. Richard Cohen. Pittsburgh: Duquesne University Press, 1994, p. 77.

[11] Ibid., p. 92.

[12] Heidegger, *Zur Sache des Denkens*, *On Time and Being.* Trans. Joan Stambaugh. New York: Harper and Row, 1978, p. 24/25.

[13] Heidegger, *Zur Sache des Denkens*, *On Time and Being.* Trans. Joan Stambaugh. New York: Harper and Row, 1978, p. 15/20.

[14] Ibid., p. 20.

[15] Heidegger,"The Nature of Language," in *Unterwegs zur Sprache*. Pfullingen: Verlag Gunther Neske, 1959; *On the Way to Language.* Trans. Peter Hertz. New York: Harper and Row, 1971, p. 108. (German pagination added). (hereafter Owl)

[16] Ibid., Owl 105, Uzs, 211.

[17] Ibid.,Owl 108, Uzs, 215.

[18] Ibid., Owl 107, Uzs 214.

[19] Heidegger,"The Nature of Language," in *Unterwegs zur Sprache*. Pfullingen: Verlag Gunther Neske, 1959; *On the Way to Language.* Trans. Peter Hertz.New York: Harper and Row, 1971, US p. 211/OWL p. 104. (German pagination added).

[20] Heidegger, *Vorträge und Aufsätze*. Pfullingen: Verlag Gunther Neske, 1954p. 218; *Early Greek Thinking.* Trans. Krell and Capruzzi. New York: Harper and Row, 1976, p. 76.

[21] Levinas, *Totality and Infinity: An Essay on Exteriority.* Trans. Alphonso Lingus. Pittsburgh: Duquesne University Press, 1969, p. 66, 173.

[22] Levinas, *Collected Philosophical Papers*, edited and translated by Alphonso Lingus. The Hague: Nijhoff, 1987, p. 119.

[23] Maurice Blanchot, *The Work of Fire.* Trans. Charlotte Mandell. Stanford: Stanford University Press, 1995, pp. 323-324.

[24] Heidegger, *Poetry, Language, Thought.* Trans. Albert Hofstadter. New York: Harper and Row, 1971, p. 207/30.

[25] Heidegger,"The Nature of Language," in *Unterwegs zur Sprache*. Pfullingen: Verlag Gunther Neske, 1959; *On the Way to Language*. Trans. Peter Hertz. New York: Harper and Row, 1971, US p. 211/OWL p. 104. (German pagination added).

[26] Heidegger, "Letter on Humanism," in *Basic Writings*. Trans. Krell. New York: Harper and Row, 1977, pp. 189-242.

Notes to Chapter Eight

[1] Nietzsche, Letter to Schmeitzner. 13 February 1883. *Briefwechsel: Kritische Gesamtausgabe*. Berlin: De Gruyter, 1967–). Hereafter KGB, III/1:327.

[2] Characteristic of this approach are works such as F. A. Lea, *The Tragic Philosopher: A Study of Friedrich Nietzsche* (London: Meuthen, 1957); R.J. Hollindale, *Nietzsche: The Man and his Philosophy* (Baton Rouge: Lousiana State University Press, 1965); Eugen Fink, *Nietzsches Philosophie* (Stuttgart: W. Kohlhammer, 1973). The most detailed defense of this approach is Lawrence Lampert, *Nietzsche's Teaching: An Interpretation of Thus Spake Zarathustra* (New Haven: Yale University Press, 1986.)

[3] Characteristic of this approach are works such as Kathleen Higgins, *Nietzsche's Zarathustra* (Philadelphia: Temple University Press, 1987); "Reading Zarathustra," in Solomon and Higgins, eds., *Reading Nietzsche* (New York: Oxford University Press, 1988); Daniel W. Conway "Solving the Problem of Socrates: Nietzsche's Zarathustra as Political Irony," Political Theory 16, no. 2 (1988), pp. 257-280; Robert Pippin, "Irony and Affirmation in Nietzsche's Thus Spoke Zarathustra," in Gillespie and Strong, eds., *Nietzsche's New Seas: Explorations in Philosophy, Aesthetics, and Politics* (Chicago: University of Chicago Press, 1988); and Gary Shapiro, "Festival, Carnival, Parody," in *Nietzschean Narratives* (Bloomington: Indiana University Press, 1989).

[4] Nietzsche, Letter to Köselitz, 30 March 1884, KGB III/ 1: 491.

[5] On this point see Paul Loeb, "Conclusion of Nietzsche's Zarathustra," in International Studies in Philosophy, 32:3, p. 137.

[6] Nietzsche, *Ecce Homo*, Kauffmann translation. (New York, Vintage Books, 1968), "Books," Z:4.

[7] Nietzsche's letters are worthy of derridian suspicion on this front. Nietzsche's plans for two further parts to Zarathustra might have been a ploy intended to attract a publisher to Part IV (see Letters to Koselitz, 14 February, 1885, KGB III/3:11-12 and 14 March 1885 KGB III/3:21) or a ploy intended to mislead his sister (see Letter to Elizabeth Nietzsche 15 November, 1884 KGB III/ 1: 557).

[8] Nietzsche, *Thus Spoke Zarathustra*. Kaufmann translation. Viking Press, New York, 1966, III, 14.

[9] Ibid., III, 15.

[10] Ibid., III. 16.

[11] As mentioned by Lampert, op. cit., p. 287.

[12] Ibid.

[13] Ibid., p. 289. Citing Nietzsche's 1888 letters to Brandes and Fuchs (KSB 8:228, 374) Lampert develops Kaufmann's suggestion (in *The Portable Nietzsche*, New York: Viking, 1968, p. 344) that Nietzsche intended Part IV as a "Zwischenspiel" between the whole of Parts I-III and additional Zarathustra parts that he did not write (Lampert, pp. 288-89, 313 n.8). The interpretation I am defending accounts for this point.

[14] Ibid., p. 287.

[15] Nietzsche attempted to retrieve all distributed copies so that Part IV might be published "after a few decades of world-historical crises—wars!" (Letter to Koselitz, 9 December 1888, KGB III/1 5: 514-515).

[16] Nietzsche, Letter to Overbeck. *Sämtliche Briefe*: Kritische Studienausgabe. Berlin: de Gruyter, 1986) Hereafter KSB, 6:455.

[17] Nietzsche, KSB, 7: 46.

[18] Cited on the back cover of the original edition of *Beyond Good and Evil*. Cf. William Schaberg, *The Nietzsche Canon: A Publication History and Bibliography*. Chicago: University of Chicago Press, 1995, pp. 123-24.

[19] Nietzsche, *Birth of Tragedy* (1872). Kaufmann translation. New York: Vintage Press, 1966.

[20] Nietzsche, *Ecce Homo*, op. cit, ("Wise" 4).

[21] Cf. Higgins, *Nietzsche's Zarathustra*, pp. 203-04; Shapiro, *Nietzschean Narratives*, pp. 100, 123.

[22] Paul Loeb ingeniously reconstructs these times sequences in "Conclusion," op. cit.

[23] Nietzsche, *Birth of Tragedy*. op. cit., Section 14, p. 91.

[24] Ibid., p. 90.

[25] A nice discussion of the relation between the novel and dialogue can be found in Marie Jaanus Kurrik, *Literature and Negation*. New York: Columbia University Press, 1979, p. 133-4.

[26] Nietzsche, *Birth of Tragedy*, op. cit, p. 90.

[27] Kurrik, op. cit. p. 135.

[28] Georg Lukacs, *Theory of the Novel*, Anna Bostock translation. Cambridge: MIT Press, 1983, p. 46.

[29] This is, of course, quite in contrast to Lukacs' later Marxist views on the novel.

[30] Lukacs, Ibid., pp. 70-74.

[31] Ibid., p. 56.

[32] Kurrik, op. cit., p. 135.

[33] Ibid.

34 Nietzsche, Letter to Koselitz, KSA 7:1 (109).

35 Nietzsche, *Birth of Tragedy*, op. cit., p. 7-8.

36 Editions of these Greek plays are numerous. While the most famous translations of the satyr plays remains Shelley's, the best is probably Roger Lancelyn Green's *Two Satyr Plays*. Penguin Classics, 1957.

37 Kurrik, op. cit.

38 Nietzsche, *Thus Spoke Zarathustra*, p. 178.

39 Ibid., p. 315.

40 An excellent discussion of the narration shifts can be found in Rudolph Kuenzli, "Nietzsche's Zerography," in *Why Nietzsche Now?* (Bloomington: Indiana University Press, 1981), pp. 99-105.

41 Nietzsche, *Zarathustra*, op. cit., p. 318.

42 Ibid.

43 Nietzsche, *Zarathustra*, op. cit., p. 298.

44 Ibid., p. 217.

45 Ibid., p. 197.

46 Ibid., p. 188.

47 Nietzsche, *Genealogy of Morals*. 3, 3, p. 99. *War dieser Parsifal überhaupt ernst gemeint? Man könnte nämlich versucht sein, das Umgekehrte zu muthmassen, selbst zu wünschen—dass der Wagner'sche Parsifal heiter gemeint sei, gleichsam als Schlussstück und Satyrdrama, mit dem der Tragiker Wagner auf eine gerade ihm gebührende und würdige Weise von uns, auch von sich, vor Allem von der Tragödie habe Abschied nehman wollen, nämlich mit einem Excess höchster und muthwilligster Parodie auf das Tragische selbst.* As Roger Hollinrake has shown in *Nietzsche, Wagner, and the Philosophy of Pessimism* (London: George Allen and Unwin, 1982, Part IV of Zarathustra is designed as a parody of Wagner's Parsifal following the parody of Wagner's tragic Ring trilogy (and preliminary evening, Das Rheingold). Hollinrake dismisses this as merely a reference to H. v. Wolzogen's *Die Trägodie in Bayreuth und ihr Satyrspiel*, Leipzig 1877, which makes reference to Nietzsche in the first sentence.

48 *Genealogy of Morals*, Ibid. *So wäre es, wie gesagt, eines grossen Tragikers gerade würdig gewesen: als welcher, wie jeder Künstler, erst dann auf den letzten Gipfel seiner Grösse kommt, wenn er sich und seine Kunst unter sich zu sehen weiss—wenn er über sich zu lachen weiss.* Translations my own.

49 Zarathustra's consecration of laughter in Part III. *Diese Krone des Lachenden, diese Rosenkranzkrone: ich selber setzte mir diese Krone auf, ich selber sprach heilig mein Gelächter. Keinen Anderen fand ich heute stark genug dazu.* [This crown of laughter, this crown of roses: I myself have set this crown on my head, I myself have sanctified my laughter. I have found no other strong enough for this today.] (18) When Zarathustra says: *So lernt doch über euch hinweg lachen.* (20) Learn to laugh at yourselves, I take it to be a trenchant comment on Luke 6:25, transcribed in a note of 1884 as "der Fluch auf die, welche lachen (the curse on those who laugh N-A., VII, 2:25 (50). In Pliny the Elder's *Natural*

History, VII, xvi., 72, it says: *Risisse eodem die quo genitus esset unum hominum accepimus Zoroastren,*" translated by H. Rackham in the Loeb edition as "It is recorded of only one person, Zoroaster, that he laughed on the day he was born." Nietzsche puns on Horace when he inscribed on the title page of the Case of Wagner: "*eridendo dicere severum*" (laughingly to say what is serious). Horace's original *ridentum dicere verum, quid vetat*, Satires, I. 24. (What forbids us to tell the truth, laughter?).

[50] Excellent discussions of the parodic elements of the poetry of *Gay Science* are Reinhold Grimm, "Antiquity as Echo and Disguise," in *Nietzsche Studien*, Vol. 14, 1984, pp. 202-248; and Sander Gilman, "Braune Nacht—Nietzsche's Venetian Poems," in *Nietzsche Studien*, Vol. 1, 1972, pp. 247-260.

Notes to Chapter Nine

[1] Two thoughtful summaries of pre-twentieth century manifestations of this phenomenon are Arthur Herman, *The Idea of Decline in Western History*. New York, Free Press, 1997, and Patrick Brantlinger: *Bread and Circuses: Theories of Mass Culture as Social Decay*. Ithaca: Cornell University, 1983.

[2] Excellent discussions of this movement can be found in Jeffrey Herf, *Reactionary Modernism: Technology, Culture, and Politics in Weimar and the Third Reich*. New York: Cambridge University Press, 1984), and Michael Zimmerman, *Heidegger's Confrontation with Modernity: Technology, Politics, Art*. (Bloomington: Indiana University Press, 1990).

[3] Oswald Spengler, *Der Untergang des Abendlandes: Umrisse einer Morphologie der Weltgeschichte. The Decline of the West*. (Atkinson translation). New York: Alfred A. Knopf, 1937.

[4] Stephen Dray, s.v. "Spengler, Oswald," *Encyclopedia of Philosophy*, vol. 7, edited by Paul Edwards (New York: MacMillan, 1967), p. 529.

[5] Spengler's reading of Nietzsche is more nuanced that either Thomas Mann or Martin Heidegger gives him credit for. See John Farrenkopf, "Nietzsche, Spengler, and the Politics of Cultural Despair," in *Interpretation*. Vol. 20, No. 2 (Winter 1992-3), pp. 165-185.

[6] Nietzsche, "Vom Nutzen und Nachteil der Historie für das Leben," in *Unzeitgemässe Betrachtungen*, 1874; *Werke: Kritische Gesamtausgabe*. eds. G. Colli and M. Montinari. Berlin: Walter de Gruyter, III: 1, pp. 241-330.

[7] Oswald Spengler, *The Decline of the West*. (Atkinson translation). New York: Alfred A. Knopf, 1937, Volume II, p. 435. (Hereafter Spengler, DW).

[8] For excellent philosophical summaries of Spengler, see Jeffrey Barash, *Martin Heidegger and the Problem of Historical Meaning*. Dordrecht: Martinus Nijhoff, 1988, pp. 151–155ff; John Farrenkopf, "The Transformation of Spenger's Philosophy of World History," in *Journal of the History of Ideas*, 52:3 (July-September, 1991), pp. 463-485, and Arthur Herman's chapter on Spengler in *The Idea of Decline in Western History*. New York, Free Press, 1997, pp. 221-256.

[9] Spengler, DW, p. 37, 38.

[10] A summary of the standard devastating criticisms of Spengler by historians can be found in H. Stuart Hughes, *Spengler: A Critical Estimate*. Scribner's: New York, 1962.

[11] Spengler, DW, p. 25.

[12] Ibid., p. 34.

[13] Ibid., p. 26.

[14] Dray takes it to be a complete confusion on Spengler's part. See Dray, Spengler, op. cit., p. 528.

[15] Michael Pauen, *Pessimismus: Geschichtsphilosophie, Metaphysik und Moderne von Nietzsche bis Spengler* (Berlin: Akademie Verlag), 1997, p. 181.

[16] Mann praised Spengler's work as the product of enormous erudition in his "Von deutscher Republik," (1923) *Gesammelte Werke*, Vol. 11. Oldenbourg: S. Fischer Verlag, 1960; but years later, after the nightmares of Nazism, famously denounced Spengler as Nietzsche's "clever ape" in his *Nietzsches Philosophie im Lichte unserer Erfahrung*. Berlin: Suhrkamp, 1948. Weber even debated Spengler in December 1919 before students at the University of Munich, as cited in Herman, op. cit, p. 244. To his credit, Spengler resigned his position on the board of directors of the Nietzsche Archive in 1935, disgusted with the manipulation of Nietzsche's ideas into ideological support for Nazism. See Anton Mirko Koktanek, *Oswald Spengler in seiner Zeit*. Munich: C.H. Beck'sche Verlagsbuchhandlung, 1968, p. 459ff.

[17] The list appears in Wittgenstein, *Culture and Value*, edited by von Wright and Nyman. Oxford: Blackwell, 1980, p. 19e. Both Drury and Bouwsma address Wittgenstein's references to Spengler, in M. O'C. Drury, "Conversations with Wittgenstein," in *Ludwig Wittgenstein: Personal Recollections*, edited by Rush Rhees. Totowa, NJ: Bowman and Littlefield, 1981, p. 128, and O.K. Bouwsma, *Wittgenstein: Conversations 1949-1951*. Indianapolis, IN: Hackett, 1986, p. 34. Monk, Toulmin, von Wright and Cavell have all acknowledged Spengler's influence on Wittgenstein.

[18] Drury mentions this exchange with Wittgenstein in Drury, op. cit., p. 128. The remarks are elaborated further by Wittgenstein in *Culture and Value*, op. cit., p. 14e. Von Wright develops possible philosophical connections in "Wittgenstein in Relation to his Times," in *Wittgenstein and His Times*, edited by Brian McGuinness. Chicago: University of Chicago Press, 1982. See also William James Deangelis, "Wittgenstein and Spengler," in *Dialogue*. Vol. 33, 1994, pp. 41-61.

[19] Spengler, DW, p. 40.

[20] Ibid., p. 358.

[21] Ibid., p. 45.

[22] Ibid., p. 45-46.

[23] Wittgenstein, "Philosophy: Sections 86-93 of the so-called "Big Typescript" (Catalogue Number TS 213), translated and incorporated within the anthology of Wittgenstein's writings entitled *Ludwig Wittgenstein: Philosophical Occasions*. Edited by James C. Klagge and ASlfred Nordmann. Indianapolis: Hackett, 1993, p. 161.

[24] Heidegger, "Phenomenology and Transcendental Philosophy of Values," in *Gesamtausgabe*. Frankfurt: Klostermann, 1975. Vol. 56/57: *Zur Bestimmung der Philosophie* (1987), pp. 130-135.

25 See Heidegger, *Gesamtausgabe*. Frankfurt: Klostermann, 1975. Vol. 61: *Phänomenologische Interpretation zu Aristoteles. Einführung in die phänomenologische Forschung* (1985), pp. 79-89.

26 Spengler certainly believed in the possibility of deductive rigidity in historical reasoning. See Heidegger, *Gesamtausgabe*. Frankfurt: Klostermann, 1975. Vol. 63: *Ontologie (Hermeneutik der Faktizität)* (1988). *Ontology (Hermeneutics of Facticity)*, trans. John van Buren. Bloomington: Indiana University Press, 1995, pp. 35-57.

27 Heidegger, *Gesamtausgabe*. Frankfurt: Klostermann, 1975. Vol. 61: *Phänomenologische Interpretation zu Aristoteles. Einführung in die phänomenologische Forschung* (1985), p. 74.

28 See S.F. Bonner, *Education in Ancient Rome* (London: Metheun, 1977), p. 56f., c.f. also p. 208f. Heidegger uses the Latin phrase elsewhere. See Heidegger, "Brief über den Humanismus," in *Wegmarken*. Frankfurt, Germany: Vittorio Klostermann Verlag, 1967, p. 176. Trans. Krell, "Letter on Humanism" in Heidegger, *Basic Writings*, ed. Krell. New York: Harper and Row, 1977, p. 224-5.

29 Karl Löwith, "Les implications politiques de la philosophie de l'existence chez Heidegger," *Le Temps Modernes* 2 (1946): 343-360. Hans Georg Gadamer, *Introduction to Heidegger's Der Ursprung des Kunstwerkes*. Stuttgart: Reclam Verlag, 1977, pp. 102-104.

30 Heidegger, *Gesamtausgabe*. Frankfurt: Klostermann, 1975. Vol. 26: *Metaphysische Anfangsgründe der Logik im Ausgang von Leibniz*, p. 177; Trans. Michael Heim, *Metaphysical Foundations of Logic*. Bloomington: Indiana University Press, 1992, p. 141.

31 Barash, op. cit., p. 148-49.

32 Ibid., p. 150.

33 See Heidegger, *Gesamtausgabe*. Frankfurt: Klostermann, 1976. Vol. 9: *Wegmarken*, "Anmerkungen zu Karl Jaspers Psychologie der Weltanschauungen," pp. 1-44.

34 Heidegger, *Gesamtausgabe*. Frankfurt: Klostermann, 1975. Vol. 61: *Phänomenologische Interpretation zu Aristoteles. Einführung in die phänomenologische Forschung* (1985). Trans. by Richard Rojcewicz. *Phenomenological Interpretations of Aristotle*. Bloomington: Indiana University Press, 2001.

35 Heidegger, *Gesamtausgabe*. Frankfurt: Klostermann, 1975. Vol. 61: *Phänomenologische Interpretation zu Aristoteles. Einführung in die phänomenologische Forschung* (1985). Trans. by Richard Rojcewicz. *Phenomenological Interpretations of Aristotle*. Bloomington: Indiana University Press, 2001, p. 56.

36 Spengler, DW, Vol. II, p. 48.

37 In the memorable phrase of Michael Zimmerman, to which my discussion is greatly indebted. See his "Ontological Decline of the West," in *A Companion to Heidegger's Introduction to Metaphysics*. Edited by Richard Polt and Gregory Fried. New Haven: Yale University Press, 2001, pp. 185-205.

38 Heidegger, *Gesamtausgabe*. Frankfurt: Klostermann, 1975. Vol. 29/30: *Die Grundbegriffe der Metaphysik: Welt-Endlichkeit—Einsamkeit*, p. 111. *The Fundamental Concepts of Metaphysics: World, Finitude, Solitude*. Trans. W. MacNeill and Nicholas Walker. Bloomington: Indiana University Press, 1994.

[39] Heidegger, *Nietzsche*. Pfullingen: Neske Verlag, 1961, 1: p. 360.

[40] Heidegger, "Anaximander Fragment," in *Early Greek Thinking*. Krell and Capruzzi translation.. New York; Harper and Row, 1975, p. 17.

[41] Heidegger, *What is Called Thinking?* J. Glenn Gray translation. New York: Harper and Row, 1968, p. 29.

[42] Heidegger, *Gesamtausgabe*. Frankfurt: Klostermann, 1975. Vol. 54: *Parmenides* , edited by Manfred S. Frings, 1992, p. 82, 168. *Parmenides*. Translation by Andre Schuwer and Richard Rojcewicz. Bloomington: Indiana University Press, 1992, p. 56, 113.

[43] Ibid., GA 54 p. 82-83; *Parmenides*, p. 56.

[44] National Socialist scholarship on Nietzsche was enormous. Some of the most prominent include *Nietzsche und die Nationalsozialismus*. Munich: Zentral Verlag der NSDAP: 1937, by Heinrich Härtle; Ernst Horneffer, *Nietzsche als Vorbote der Gegenwart*. Düsseldorf: A. Bagel: 1934; Richard Oehler, *Friedrich Nietzsche und die deutsche Zukunft*. Leipzig: Armanen, 1935; Friedrich Würzbach, *Nietzsche und das deutsche Schicksal*. Berlin: Bondi, 1933; Alfred Baumler, *Nietzsche: Der Philosoph und Politiker*. Leipzig: Reclam, 1931.

Notes to Chapter Ten

[1] Anderson, "Mathematics and the Language Game," *Review of Metaphysics*, Vol. 11 (1958), pp. 446-58. Dummett, "Wittgenstein's Philosophy of Mathematics," *Philosophical Review*, Vol. 68 (1959), pp. 324-348. Paul Bernays, "Comments on Ludwig Wittgenstein's Remarks on the Foundations of Mathematics," *Ratio*, vol. 2 (1959), pp. 1-22.

[2] G. Kreisel, "Einige Erläuterungen zu Wittgensteins Kummer mit Hilbert und Gödel," in P. Weingartner and J. Czermak (eds.) *Epistemology and Philosophy of Science: Proceedings of the 7th International Wittgenstein Symposium* (Vienna: Hölder-Pichler-Tempsky, 1983), pp. 295-303; Review of Wittgenstein's Remarks on the Foundations of Mathematics," *British Journal for the Philosophy of Science*, Vol. 9 (1958). pp. 135-158.

[3] Hao Wang, *Reflections on Kurt Gödel*. Cambridge, MA: MIT Press, 1987, p. 49.

[4] Wittgenstein, *Zettel*, Edited by G.E.M. Anscombe and G.H von Wright. Translation by G.E.M. Anscombe. Basil Blackwell, Oxford, 1981, #463, p. 82e.

[5] Wittgenstein, *Philosophical Investigations*, edited by G.E.M. Anscombe, R. Rhees, translated by G.E.M Anscombe. New York: Macmillan Co., 1953, p. 1.

[6] *Wittgenstein's Lectures on the Foundations of Mathematics: Cambridge, 1939*, Edited by Cora Diamond. Ithaca: Cornell University Press, 1976, p. 239.

[7] G.H. Hardy, *A Mathematician's Apology*. Cambridge University Press, Cambridge, 1967, pp. 123-124.

[8] Wittgenstein, *Remarks on the Foundations of Mathematics.* Edited by G.H. von Wright, R.Rhees, G.E.M.Anscombe. Translated by G.E.M. Anscombe, revised edition. MIT Press, Cambridge, 1978, VII. 41.

[9] *Wittgenstein's Lectures: Cambridge, 1932-35.* Edited by A. Ambrose. Chicago: University of Chicago Press, 1982, p. 127.

[10] *Wittgenstein's Lectures on the Foundations of Mathematics*, pp. 167-168.

[11] *Wittgenstein's Lectures: Cambridge*, p. 124-125.

[12] *Wittgenstein's Lectures: Cambridge*, p. 99.

[13] *Wittgenstein's Lectures on the Foundations of Mathematics*, 286. (My emphasis)

[14] Nicholas Gier, *Wittgenstein and Phenomenology.* SUNY Press, Albany, 1981; Herbert Spiegelberg. "The Puzzle of Wittgenstein's *Phänomenologie* (1929?) (with supplement 1979), in Spiegelberg, *The Context of the Phenomenological Movement*, Nijhoff, The Hague, 1981, pp. 202-228; Spiegelberg, "One More Supplement," *Journal of the British Society for Phenomenology*, Vol. 13, (1982), pp. 296-299. Merrill and Jaako Hintikka, *Investigating Wittgenstein.* Blackwell: Oxford, 1986. Jaako Hintikka, *Selected Papers, Vol. I.* Kluwer, Dordrecht, 1996. Paul Ricouer, "Husserl and Wittgenstein on Language," in *Phenomenology and Existentialism*, ed. E.N. Lee and M. Mandelbaum. Baltimore: Johns Hopkins, 1967. Pp. 207-217.

[15] Wittgenstein, *Philosophical Remarks.* Translated by. R. Hargreaves and R. White. Oxford: Blackwell, 1975.

[16] Quoted by Hintikka, op. cit., from MS 107, p, 176, Dated October 22, 1929. See Wittgenstein, *On Color.* Translated by McAlister and Schättle. Oxford: Blackwell, 1977, I, Sec. 53.

[17] *Wittgenstein's Lectures on the Foundations of Mathematics*, p. 247].

[18] *Wittgenstein's Lectures on the Foundations of Mathematics*, p. 251.

[19] See Rudolph Carnap, "Autobiography," in *The Philosophy of Rudolph Carnap.* P. A. Schilpp (ed), 1963, p. 53. Also Eckehart Kohler, "Godel and the Vienna Circle: Platonism versus Formalism," in *History of Logic, Methodology and Philosophy of Science*, section 13 (Vienna Institute for Advanced Studies). S.G. Shanker, "Wittgenstein's Remarks on the Significance of Godel's Theorem," *Gödel's Theorem in Focus.* S. G. Shanker, ed. London: Croom, Helm, 1988.

[20] Wittgenstein, *Philosophical Investigations*, 129.

[21] *Remarks on the Foundations of Mathematics*, p. 68.

[22] see Heidegger, *The Piety of Thinking.* Translations, notes, and commentary by James G. Hart and John Maraldo. Indiana University Press, Bloomington and London, 1976.

[23] *Remarks on the Foundations of Mathematics*, p. 78.

[24] Ibid.

25 see D.Z. Phillips, *Faith and Philosophical Enquiry.* New York: Schocken Books, 1970, p. 104. See also Phillips' *The Concept of Prayer.* Routledge and Kegan Paul, London.

26 Wittgenstein, *Lectures and Conversations on Aesthetics, Psychology, and Religious Beliefs*, edited by Cyril Barrett. University of California Press, Berkeley, 1967, p. 72.

27 Wittgenstein, *Culture and Value.* Translated by Peter Winch. Basil Blackwell, London, 1980, p. 72.

28 *Ludwig Wittgenstein and the Vienna Circle*, 1931: p. 196.

29 Wittgenstein, *Philosophical Investigations*, p. 125.

30 Wittgenstein, *Philosophical Grammar*, edited by R. Rhees. Translation by A.J.P Kenny. Basil Blackwell, Oxford, 1974, p. 290.

31 *Ludwig Wittgenstein and the Vienna Circle: Conversations recorded by Friedrich Waismann*, B.F. McGuiness (ed.), J. Schulte and B.F. McGuiness translation. Basil Blackwell, Oxford, 1979, p. 119.

32 Wittgenstein, *Tractatus Logico-Philosophicus*, D.F. Pears and B.F. McGuinness, translation. Routledge and Kegan Paul, London, 1961, 2.2–2.05; 4.46–4.461.

33 *Ludwig Wittgenstein and the Vienna Circle*, p. 131.

34 *Ludwig Wittgenstein and the Vienna Circle*, p. 119.

35 *Ludwig Wittgenstein and the Vienna Circle*, p. 149.

36 Wittgenstein, *Lectures and Conversations on Aesthetics, Psychology, and Religious Beliefs*, p. 53-56.

37 *Ludwig Wittgenstein and the Vienna Circle* [1929]:35 / CAM I [1930]: 19.

38 *Remarks on the Foundations of Mathematics*, VII, #15.

39 *Ludwig Wittgenstein and the Vienna Circle*, 198-199.

Notes to Chapter Eleven

1 "Was ist Metaphysik?" Reprinted in *Wegmarken,* 2nd edition. Frankfurt: Klostermann, 1978, pp. 103-121. "What is Metaphysics?" translated by David Farrell Krell, in Martin Heidegger, *Basic Writings,* 2nd edition. London: Routledge, 1993, pp. 93-110. An earlier translation by R. F. C. Hull and Alan Crick appears in *Existence and Being*, by Martin Heidegger. South Bend: Regnery/Gateway, 1979, pp. 325-369.. Rudolph Carnap, "Überwindung der Metaphysik durch logische Analyse der Sprache," *Erkenntnis*, 2 (1931), translated by Arthur Pap, "Overcoming Metaphysics through the Logical Analysis of Language," in *Heidegger and Modern Philosophy.* Ed. by Michael Murray. New Haven and London: Yale University Press, pp. 23-34.

2 Immanual Kant, *Critique of Pure Reason.* Translation of first (A) and second (B) German editions (1781, 1787) by P. Guyer and A. Wood. Cambridge: Cambridge University Press, 1997, A50/B74.

[3] Ibid., A15/B29.

[4] Ibid., p. A271/B327.

[5] Ibid., p. A138/B177.

[6] Michael Friedman, "Overcoming Metaphysics: Carnap and Heidegger." In *Origins of Logical Empiricism*. Ed. R. N. Giere and A. W. Richardson. Minneapolis: University of Minnesota Press, 1996, pp. 45-79. See also his *Parting of the Ways: Carnap, Cassirer, Heidegger*. Lasalle, Il.: Open Court Press, 2000.

[7] Heidegger, *Kant and the Problem of Metaphysics*. trans. Richard Taft. Bloomington: Indiana University Press, 1990.

[8] Paolo Parrini, *Knowledge and Reality: An Essay in Positive Philosophy*. Dordrecht: Kluwer Academic Publishers, 1998, p. 19. Hempel, "Problems and Changes in the Empiricist Criterion of Meaning." In *Semantics and the Philosophy of Language*, ed. Leonard Linsky. Urbana: University of Illinois Press, 1952, 163-185.

[9] See Carnap, (1950) "Empiricism, Semantics, and Ontology," in *Revue internationale de Philosophie* 11:20-40; Reichenbach, "The Verifiability Theory of Meaning," *Proceedings of the American Academy of Arts and Sciences*, Vol. 80, 1951. *Contributions to the Analysis and Synthesis of Knowledge*, 46-60. Boston: American Academy of Arts and Sciences.

[10] Michael Inwood, "Does the Nothing Noth?" in *German Philosophy since Kant*. Edited by Anthony O'Hear. New York: Cambridge, 1999, pp. 271-291.

[11] Heidegger, *Sein und Zeit*. Tübingen: Niemeyer, 1927; 7th ed. reset, 1953; 15th ed. 1979; 16th ed. 1986. *Being and Time*. Macquarrie and Robinson translation. New York: Harper and Row, 1962, p. 187. (Pagination from the German edition).

[12] Ibid., p. 266.

[13] Ibid., p. 262.

[14] Ibid., p. 285.

[15] "What is Metaphysics?" translation by R. F. C. Hull and Alan Crick, *Existence and Being*, by Martin Heidegger. London: Vision, 1949, pp. 339.

[16] Ibid.

[17] Caputo, John. *The Mystical Element in Heidegger's Thought*. Athens: Ohio University Press, 1978.

[18] Meister Eckhart: *The Essential Sermons, Commentaries, Treatises, and Defense*. Ed. Edmund Colledge and Bernard McGinn. New York: Paulist Press, 1981, p. 184: 5b.

[19] Ibid., p. 199: 52.

[20] For recent overviews of the central figures of the Kyoto school, see James Heisig, *Philosophers of Nothingness: Essay on the Kyoto School.* Honolulu: University of Hawaii Press, 2001; Michiko Yusa, *Zen and Philosophy.* Honolulu: University of Hawaii Press, 2002.

[21] Keiji Nishitani, *Religion and Nothingness.* Trans. by Jan Van Bragt. Berkeley: University of California Press, 1982.

[22] Keiji Nishitani, "God and Absolute Nothingness," in *Collected Works.* Tokyo: Sobunsha, 1986-95, Vol. 7, pp. 70ff. Eckhart's work was derivative of 13th century religious women's mystics, beguinal figures such as Mechthild of Madgeburg and Marguerite Porete. The beguines were semireligious women who devoted themselves to prayer and mutual exhortation without taking formal vows. These views were most influentially disseminated in Christian mystical theology by the anonymous sixth-century author known through the Middle Ages as Dionysius the Areopagite. Dionysius distinguishes two modes of naming God: the cataphatic, in which names are positively attributed to the divine, and the apophatic, in which all attributes are "unsaid" or denied in order to mark the illimitability of God's being. Dionysius the Areopagite is the apostle Paul's Athenian convert, named in Acts 17:34. The probably Syrian monastic author of the texts known under his name was part of a religious circle, many members of which took pseudonymous names from the New Testament. Throughout the middle ages, however, his work was believed to be that of Paul's convert and therefore to date from the first century. See Pseudo-Dionysius, *Complete Works.* Trans. Colm Luibheid. New York: Paulist Press, 1987.

Notes to Chapter Twelve

[1] David Roberts, *Art and Enlightenment.* Lincoln: University of Nebraska Press, 1991; Jurgen Habermas, *Philosophical Discourse of Modernity.* Trans. by Frederick Lawrence. Cambridge, MA: MIT Press, 1987. "Modernity—An Incomplete Project." *The Anti-Aesthetic.* Trans. by Seyla Ben-Habib. Edited by Hal Foster. Port Townsend, WA: bay Press, 1983, pp. 3-15; Lambert Zuidervaart, *Adorno's Aesthetic Theory.* Cambridge, MA: MIT Press, 1991; Peter Uwe Hohendahl, *Reappraisals: The Shifting Alignments in Postwar Critical Theory.* Ithaca: Cornell University Press, 1991; "Adorno Criticism Today." *New German Critique.* 19.2 (1992): pp. 3-15; James Martin Harding, *Adorno and a Writing of the Ruins: Essays on Modern Aesthetics and Anglo-American Literature and Culture.* Albany: SUNY Press, 1997; Max Paddison, *Adorno's Aesthetics of Music.* New York: Cambridge University Press, 1993.

[2] For a complete history, see Rolf Wiggerhaus, *The Frankfurt School: Its History, Theories, and Political Significance.* Trans. by Michael Robertson. Cambridge, MA: MIT Press, 1995.

[3] Theodor Adorno, (with Max Horkheimer). *Dialektik der Aufklärung. Philosophische Fragmente.* Amsterdam: Querido, 1947. *Dialectic of Enlightenment.* Trans. John Cumming. London: Verso, 1979.

[4] Adorno, *Minima Moralia.* Translated by E. F. N. Jephcott. New York, Verso, 1974, p. 50.

[5] Hegel, *Aesthetics: Lectures on Fine Art.* Trans. by T. M. Knox. Oxford University Press, 1998, p. 11.

[6] Novalis [Friedrich von Hardenberg]. *Das Allgemaine Brouillon: (Materialien zur Enzyklopädistik 1978/99). Schriften.* Vol. 3. Ed. Richard Samuel. Stuffgart: W. Kohlhammer, 1983; "Die Christenheit order Europa. Ein Fragment." *Werke, Tagebücher und Briefe Friedrich von Hardenbergs.* Vol 2. Eds. Hans-Joachim Mähl and Richard Samuel. Munich: Hanser, 1978, pp. 729-750; Schiller, Friedrich. "Über die ästhetische Erziehung des Menschen in einer Reihe von Briefen."

Philosophische Schriften I. Nationalausgabe. Vol. 20. Ed. Benno von Wiese. Weimar: Böhlaus Nachfolger, 1962, pp. 309-412; Schiller, "Über naive und sentimentalische Dichtung." *Philosophische Schriften I. Nationalausgabe*, Vol. 20. Weimar: Bölhaus Nachfolger, 1962, pp. 413-503.

[7] Michael Jones, "Twilight of the Gods: The Greeks in Schiller and Lukacs," in *The German Review*, 59 (1984): 49-56; E.M. Butler, *The Tyranny of Greece over Germany*. Cambridge: Cambridge University press, 1935.

[8] Full translation: *Es waren schöne glänzende Zeiten, wo Europa ein Christliches Land war, wo eine Christenheit diesen menschlich gestalten Welttheil bewohnte; Ein großes gemeinschaftliches Interesse verband die entlegensten Provinzen dieses weiten geistlichen Reichs.* "*They were beautiful radiant times, when Europe was a Christian land, when one Christianity occupied this part of the humanely formed world; oner great communal interest connected the most widespread provinces of this broad spiritual empire*" *(732)*. Lukacs also makes reference to Novalis's contention that all philosophy is an expression of transcendental homelessness, manifesting the desire always to be at home. [from Novalis's *Allgemeines Brouillon (Materialien zur Enzyklopadistik)* 1798/99, #857: "*Die Philosophie ist eigentlich Heimweh—Trieb überall zu Hause zu seyn.*" (434)

[9] [*Was jedoch fehlt, ist der ursprünglich poetische Weltzustand, aus welcham das eigentliche Epos hervorgeht*]. Hegel's discussion of the novel hardly exceeds one page in length, but captures powerfully how the novel form because it was the favorite of 19th century bourgeois writers, and a gold mine for the sociological approach of Marxist criticism of the 20th century.

[10] Georg Lukacs, *Theorie des Romans: Ein geschichtsphilosophischer Versuch über die Formen der großsen Epik*. Frankfurt am Main: Luchterhand, 1988. *The Theory of the Novel: A Historico-Philosophical Essay on the Forms of Great Epic Literature*. Trans. Anna Bostock. Cambridge: MIT Press, 1971. p. 41/32.

[11] Nicholas Vazsonyi, *Lukacs Reads Goethe: From Aestheticism to Stalinism*. Columbia, SC: Camden House, Inc, 1997.

[12] Adorno, "Nachtmusik" (1929), *Moments Musicaux: Neugedruckte Aufsätze, 1928 bis 1962*. Frankfurt am Main: Suhrkamp, 1964, p. 62.

[13] Adorno, "Die Idee der Naturgeschichte" (1932). *Gesammelte Schriften*, 23 Vols. Edited by Rolk Tiedemann. Frankfurt am Main: Suhrkamp, 1970, p. 357. For a more complete discussion of the complex relation between Lukacs and Adorno, see Susan Buck-Morss, *The Origin of Negative Dialectics*. Sussex: Harvester Press, 1977, pp. 44-62.

[14] Walter Benjamin, *Ursprung des deutschen Trauerspiels*. Berlin: Rowohlt (Frankfurt am Main), 1963; *Origin of German Tragic Drama*. Trans. by John Osborne. London: Verso, 1977, p. 28.

[15] Ibid., pp. 28-29.

[16] Ibid., p. 34.

[17] Adorno, *Negative Dialectics*.Trans. by E. B. Ashton. New York: Continuum, 1973, p. 163. The original reads: "*konstellationen allein repräsentieren, von aussen, was der Begriff im inneren weggeschnitten hat ... Indem die Begriffe um die ... Sache sichj versammeln, bestimmen sie potentiall deren Inneres.*"

[18] Adorno, *Asthetische Theorie*. Ed. Gretel Adorno and Rolf Tiedemann. Frankfurt am Main: Suhrkamp, 1970. *Aesthetic Theory*. Trans. by C. Lenhardt. New York: Routledge and Kegan Paul, 1984. p. 201.

[19] Ibid., p. 66, 399, 169, 503.

[20] Adorno, "Noten zur Literatur," 1958ff., 1974. Vol. II. *Gesammelte Schriften*. Suhrkamp: Frankfurt, 1970ff, p. 572, note 22.

Notes to Chapter Thirteen

[1] Derrida, *Edmund Husserl's "L'Origine de la géométrie,"* Paris: Presses Universitaires de France, 1962. *Edmund Husserl's Origin of Geometry: An Introduction*. Translated by John Leavey. Boulder, CO: Nicholas Hays Ltd, 1978; Derrida, *La voixet le phénomenè*. Paris: Presses Universitaires de France, 1967. English translation by David Allison: *Speech and Phenomena*. Bloomington: Indiana University Press, 1973; *Writing and Difference*. Translated by Alan Bass. Chicago: University of Chicago Press, 1978.

[2] Derrida, "The Time of a Thesis: Punctuations," trans. Kathleen McLaughlin, in *Philosophy in France Today*. ed. Alan Montefiore. Cambridge: Cambridge University Press, 1983, p. 39.

[3] Newton Garver, "Preface to Derrida," *Speech and Phenomena*. Translation by David Allison. Bloomington: Indiana University Press, 1973, p. ix.

[4] Richard Rorty, "Two Meanings of Logocentrism," in *Redrawing the Lines*. Edited by Reed Way Dasenbrock. Minneapolis: University of Minnesota Press, 1989, p. 207.

[5] David Wood, "Beyond Deconstruction?" in *Contemporary French Philosophy*. Edited by A. Phillips Griffiths. Cambridge: Cambridge University Press, 1987, p. 182.

[6] Hans-Georg Gadamer, 1989c, 95. "Letter to Dallmayr," in *Dialogue and Deconstruction*. Edited by Diane P. Michelfelder and Richard E. Palmer. Translated by Richard Waite and Richard E. Palmer. Albany: SUNY Press, pp. 93-101.

[7] J. Claude Evans, *Strategies of Deconstruction: Derrida and the Myth of the Voice*. Minneapolis: Minnesota University Press, 1991, p. 169.

[8] Alan White, "Reconstructing Husserl: A Critical Response to Derrida's Speech and Phenomena," in *Husserl Studies*, Nijhoff Publishers, Dordrecht. Volume 4, 1987, pp. 45-62.

[9] Rorty, "Deconstruction and Circumvention," in *Critical Inquiry* 11:1984, p. 22, n.12.

[10] Depp, "A Husserlian Response to Derrida's Early Criticisms of Phenomenology," in *Journal of the British Society for Phenomenology*, Vol. 18, No. 3 (October, 1987), pp. 226-244.

[11] John Searle, "Reply to Louis H. Mackey," in *New York Review of Books* 31/1 (1984), p. 48.

[12] Kevin Mulligan,"How Not to Read: Derrida on Husserl," *Topoi*, 10 (1991), pp. 199-208.

[13] Scanlon, "Pure Presence: A Modest Proposal," in *Derrida and Deconstruction*. Edited by Lester Embree and William McKenna. Athens: Ohio University Press, 1991.

[14] Recent anthologies include Leonard Lawlor, *Derrida's Interpretation of Husserl, The Southern Journal of Philosophy* XXXII (supplement), 1994; McKenna and Evans, *Derrida and Phenomenology.* Dordrecht: Kluwer, 1995; overviews include Hobson, 1998, 43-53 Howells, 1998 6-28. More recent and more thoughtful Husserlian analyses are in Burt C. Hopkins, "Transcendental Ontologism and Derrida's Reading of Husserl," *Philosophy Today* (Spring, 1996), pp 71-79; J.N. Mohanty, *Phenomenology: Between Essentialism and Transcendental Philosophy.* Evanston: Northwestern University Press, 1997, pp. 62-76. Whole books include Lawlor, *Derrida on Husserl: The Basic Problem of Phenomenology.* Bloomington:Indiana University Press, 2002; Paola Marrati-Guenoun, *La Genese et las trace,* Dordrecht: Kluwer, 1998. Timothy Mooney's response to Mulligan is in *Philosophy Today,* Vol. 27 (3), Fall, 2003, pp. 305-321. A recent and fairminded review of the literature comes from Joshua Kates, "Derrida, Husserl, and the Commentators: Introducing a Developmental Approach," in *Husserl Studies,* 19 (2003), pp. 101-129.

[15] Quoted in Evans, *Strategies of Deconstruction: Derrida and the Myth of the Voice.* Minneapolis: Minnesota University Press, 1991, p. xi.

[16] Husserl, *Philosophie der Arithmetik.* Edited by Lothar Eley. The Hague: Martinus Nijhoff, 1970.

[17] Frege, *Die Grundlagen der Arithmetik.* Stuttgart: Reclam, 1987.

[18] Husserl, *Logische Untersuchungen.* Tübingen: Max Niemeyer Verlag, 1968. *Logical Investigations.* Translation by J. N. Findlay. London: Routledge, 1970, First Investigation, Section 26. Where comparison is helpful, I provide German/English pagination.

[19] Husserl, *Ideen zu einer reinen Phänomenologie und phänomenologischen Philosophie.* Translation F. Kersten. *Ideas Pertaining to a Pure Phenomenology and to a Phenomenological Philosophy.* Collected Works. Vol. 2. The Hague: Martinus Nijhoff, 1982.

[20] Heidegger, *Gesamtausgabe.* Frankfurt: Klostermann, 1975. Vol. 20: *Prolegomena zur Geschichte des Zeitbegriffs (1979).* Trans. by Theodore Kisiel. *Prolegomena to the History of the Concept of Time.* Bloomington: Indiana University Press, 1992

[21] Ibid., p. 37.

[22] Ibid., p. 46.

[23] Ibid., p. 60.

[24] Ibid., p. 47.

[25] Husserl, *The Idea of Phenomenology.* Translation by Alston and Nakhnikian. The Hague: Martinus Nijhoff, 1964, p. 7.

[26] Heidegger, *Prolegomena,* op. cit., p. 113.

[27] Ibid.

[28] Ibid., p. 107.

[29] Ibid., p. 102-108.

30 Ibid., p. 110.

31 Ibid., p. 113-114.

32 Heidegger, *Gesamtausgabe*. Frankfurt: Klostermann, 1975. Vol. 24: *Die Grundprobleme der Phänomenologie (1975)*. Trans. by Albert Hofstadter. *The Basic Problems of Phenomenology*. Bloomington: Indiana University Press, 1988.
33 Heidegger, *Prolegomena*, op. cit., p. 264.

34 Ibid., p. 56.

35 Sartre, *Situations I*. Paris: Gallimard, 1947, pp. 31-35. Translation Joseph P. Fell, "Intentionality: A Fundamental Idea of Husserl's Phenomenology," in *Journal of the British Society for Phenomenology* 1-2, 1970, pp. 4-5. See also Sartre, *Being and Nothingness*. Translation Hazel E. Barnes. New York: Washington Square Press, 1953; *Transcendence of the Ego: An Existentialist Theory of Consciousness*. Translation Forrest Williams and Robert Kirkpatrick. New York: Hill and Wang, 1960.

36 Edmund Husserl, *Idees directrices pour une phenomenologie*. Translation Paul Ricoeur. Paris: Gallimard, 1950.

37 Merleau-Ponty, *Phenomenology of Perception*. Translation Colin Smith. London: Routledge, 1962.

38 Levinas, *En decouvrant l'existence avec Husserl et Heidegger*. Paris: Vrin, 1974; first edition 1949, with editions in 1967.

39 Derrida, *Edmund Husserl's "L'Origine de la géométrie,"* Paris: Presses Universitaires de France, 1962. *Edmund Husserl's Origin of Geometry: An Introduction*. Translated by John Leavey. Boulder, CO: Nicholas Hays Ltd, 1978, p. 70.

40 Derrida, Ibid., p. 69n.

41 Rudolf Bernet, "On Derrida's "Introduction to Husserl's Origin of Geometry," in *Derrida and Deconstruction*, edited by Hugh J. Silverman. Hew York: Routledge, p. 139.

42 Derrida, op. cit., p. 140.

43 Ibid., p. 138. See Paul Ricouer, "Husserl and the Sense of History" in *Husserl: An Analysis of His Phenomenology*. Translated by Edward Ballard and Lester Embree. Evanston: Northwestern University Press, 1967, pp. 143-174.

44 Derrida, Ibid., p. 79. cf. Husserl, *Origin of Geometry*, p. 358.

45 Ibid., p. 92n.

46 Derrida, *La voixet le phénomenè*. Paris: Presses Universitaires de France, 1967. English translation by David Allison: *Speech and Phenomena*. Bloomington: Indiana University Press, 1973, pp. 27, 33, 48, 60.

47 Derrida, Ibid., p. 60.

48 Derrida, Ibid., . p. 27.

[49] Husserl, *Logische Untersuchungen*. Tübingen: Max Niemeyer Verlag, 1968. *Logical Investigations*. Translation by J. N. Findlay. London: Routledge, 1970, First Investigation, Section 26. Where comparison is helpful, I provide German/English pagination.

[50] Ibid., II.1, 24/I, 269.

[51] Ibid., II.183/I, 316.

[52] Derrida, op. cit., p. 27.

[53] Ibid., p. 94.

[54] Husserl, op. cit., II. 1, 37-38 / I, 280-282.

[55] Husserl, *Logische Untersuchungen*. Tübingen: Max Niemeyer Verlag, 1968. *Logical Investigations*. Translation by J. N. Findlay. London: Routledge, 1970, II. 1, 82 / I, 316, quoted by Derrida in *Speech and Phenomena*, 94n/106n.

[56] Ibid.

[57] Ibid., II. 1, 82 / I, 315.

[58] Derrida, *La voixet le phénomenè*. Paris: Presses Universitaires de France, 1967. English translation by David Allison: *Speech and Phenomena*. Bloomington: Indiana University Press, 1973. p. 107/96.

[59] Ibid., p. 22, 43.

Notes to Chapter Fourteen

[1] Peter Winch, "Understanding a Primitive Society," in *Understanding and Social Inquiry*. Ed. by Fred Dallmayr and Thomas McCarthy. Notre Dame: University of Notre Dame Press, 1977, pp. 159-188, p. 162. Hereafter "UPS."

[2] See E. Gellner, *Cause and Meaning in the Social Sciences*. London:Routledge, 1973; Karl Popper, "Winch on Institutions and *The Open Society*," in P.A. Schilpp (ed.) *The Philosophy of Karl Popper, Volume II*. La Salle, IL: Open Court, 1974, pp. 1165-74. K.O. Apel, "Universal Principles and Particular Decisions and Forms of Life," in *Value and Understanding*, R. Gaita (ed.). London: Routledge, 1990, pp. 72-101. Habermas, *Theory of Communicative Action*, Vol. 1. Cambridge: Polity Press, 1991. A helpful summary of the scholarship can be found in Colin Lyas, *Peter Winch*. Tedington: Acumen, 1999.

[3] No doubt a maneuver that would have sent my old professor's teeth a-grinding, but probably less so than the continued charges that he was a moral relativist, or an arm-chair anthropologist, or an inadequate phenomenologist of religious practices.

[4] Robert Nozick, *Invariances: The Structure of the Objective World*. Cambridge: Harvard University Press, 2001, p. 15. Quoted in Maria Baghramian, *Relativism*. Routledge; London, 2004, p. 137.

[5] Richard Amesbury, "Has Wittgenstein Been Misunderstood by Wittgensteinian Philosophers of Religion?" *Philosophical Investigations*, Vol. 26, No. 1, January 2003, p. 48.

[6] Habermas, *The Theory of Communicative Action. Volume 1: Reason and the Rationalization of Society.* Trans. by T. McCarthy. Boston: Beacon Press, 1984.

[7] Wittgenstein, *Philosophical Investigations.* Oxford: Blackwell, 1968.

[8] Wittgenstein, *The Blue and Brown Books.* Oxford: Blackwell, 1972, p. 18.

[9] This language comes from Berel Dov Lerner's criticism of Winch in *Rules, Magic, and Instrumental Reason.* London: Routledge, 2002, pp. 108ff. (Hereafter RMI). For a response to all such attacks against Winch, see D. Z. Phillips, "The Presumption of Theory," in his *Interventions in Ethics.* Albany: SUNY Press, 1992.

[10] Winch, "UPS," op. cit., p. 165. quoted by Winch, with his italics.

[11] Lerner remarks: "We are never informed how Winch, whose experience of primitive cultures has been limited to the wilds of London, Swansea, and Illinois, developed this sensibility, while Evans-Pritchard, the patron saint of participatory observation, remained imprisoned in his western parochialism." RMI, p. 111.

[12] Winch, "UPS," op. cit., p. 175.

[13] Winch, "UPS," op. cit., p. 161.

[14] Winch, Ibid., p. 163.

[15] Winch, *Trying to Make Sense.* Oxford: Blackwell, 1987, p. 207. In the first edition of *The Idea of a Social Science* Winch admittedly used many formulations that have led to his philosophy being read as relativist, but he retracted most of these formulations explicitly in the preface to the second edition (Winch, *The Idea of a Social Science and its Relation to Philosophy.* London: Routledge, 1990, ix-xviii). And after the notorious passage in which Winch calls both science and religion "nonlogical" he emphasizes that this way of putting matters is misleading if taken by itself, because it ignores "the overlapping character of different modes of social life. (pp. 100-101. A related discussion of Wittgenstein as anti-relativist is Hilary Putnam's Gifford Lecture "Wittgenstein on Reference and Relativism" in *Renewing Philosophy.* Cambridge: Harvard University Press. 1992, pp. 158-179.

[16] J. Habermas, *Theory of Communicative Action*, Vol. 1. Cambridge: Polity, 1991, p. 58-59.

[17] A. Giddens, *Central Problems in Social Theory.* London: MacMillan, 1979, pp. 251-252.

[18] H. G. Gadamer, *Wahrheit und Methode.* Zweite Auflage. Tübingen: J.C.B. Mohr, 1965; *Truth and Method.* Translation Garrett Barden and John Cumming. New York: Seabury, 1975.(

[19] A. Giddens, *New Rules of Sociological Method.* London: Hutchinson, 1976, p. 49.

[20] H. Pitkin, *Wittgenstein and Justice.* University of California Press, 1972, p. 250.

[21] Winch, "UPS," p. 180.

22 Gadamer, "Replik," in *Hermeneutik und Ideologiekritik*, K.O. Apel, ed, et al. Suhrkamp: Frankfurt, 1977 p. 299.

23 Roy Howard, *Three Faces of Hermeneutics*. Berkeley: University of California Press, 1982, pp. 35-86.

24 Gadamer, *Wahrheit und methode*. Zweite Auflage. Tübingen: J.C.B. Mohr, 1965; *Truth and Method*. Translation Garrett Barden and John Cumming. New York: Seabury, 1975.(TM, 211–WM 225).

25 Winch, "Comment" (Response to Jarvie), in *Understanding and Social Inquiry*. Ed. by Fred Dallmayr and Thomas McCarthy. Notre Dame: University of Notre Dame Press, 1977, p. 208.

26 Winch, "UPS," p. 183.

27 Gellner's assault on Wittgenstein can be found in *Words and Things. An Examination of, and an Attack on, Linguistic Philosophy*. London: Routledge & Kegan Paul, 1979, and is continued in Gellner, *Language and Solitude: Wittgenstein, Malinowski and the Hapsburg Dilemma*. Cambridge: Cambridge University Press, 1998.

28 See W.W. Sharrock and R. J. Anderson (1985), "Criticizing Forms of Life. *Philosophy* 60: 394-400.

29 'Remarks on Frazer's "Golden Bough"', tr. J. Beversluis, in C. G. Luckhardt (ed.), *Wittgenstein: Sources and Perspectives* (Ithaca, NY: Cornell University Press, 1979, pp. 61-81. It is to be remembered that these remarks are incomplete and never intended for publication.

30 Ibid., p. 60.

31 Ibid., p. 65.

32 Ibid., p. 69.

33 Ibid., p. 60.

34 Ibid., p. 65.

35 Ibid., p. 61.

36 Ibid., p. 63.

37 Ibid., p. 67.

38 Winch, "UPS," p. 188.

39 Winch, *The Idea of a Social Science and its Relation to Philosophy*. Second edition. London: Routledge, 1990, p. 42.

40 Wittgenstein, *Philosophical Investigations*. Third edition. Trans. G. E. M. Anscombe. New York: MacMillan, 1958. (All pages numbers are to this edition).

41 Wittgenstein, *On Certainty*. Oxford, 1969.

[42] Wittgenstein, *Zettel.* Oxford, 1967.

[43] Newton Garver defends this interpretation. See N. Garver, "Form of Life in Wittgenstein's Later Work," *Dialectica* 44. 1-2 (1990), pp. 175-201.

[44] Donald Davidson, "On the Very Idea of a Conceptual Scheme," in *Inquiries into Truth and Interpretation.* Oxford: Clarendon, 1984, pp. 183-198.

[45] Bernard Williams defends a version of this argument with regard to Wittgenstein. See Williams, *Ethics and the Limits of Philosophy.* London: Fontana, 1985.

[46] Such as: Steven Hilmy, *The Later Wittgenstein.* Oxford: Basil Blackwell, 1997; and Jaako Hintikka and Merril B. Hintikka, *Investigating Wittgenstein.* London: Basil Blackwell, 1986.

[47] Ibid., p. 218.

[48] Max Black, "*Lebensform* and *Sprachspiel* in Wittgenstein's Later Work." *Wittgenstein and his Impact on Contemporary Thought.* Proceedings of the Second International Wittgenstein Symposium. Eds. Hal Berghel et a. 2nd ed. Vienna: Hölder-Pichler-Temsky, 1980, pp. 325-331.

[49] Winch, "UPS," p. 162.

[50] Heidegger, *Being and Time.* Trans. John Macquarrie and Edward Robinson. New York: Harper and Row, 1962.

[51] Winch, "UPS," op. cit., p. 183.

[52] Ted Schatzki, in an otherwise brilliant article, mistakenly insists on referring to these as "universals." See Schatzki, "Human Universals and Understanding a Different Socioculture," *Human Studies.* Kluwer Academic Publishers, 26: 1-20, 2003.

[53] Such as those anti-relativistic arguments of the kind collected in B. R. Wilson, ed., *Rationality.* Evanston: Harper and Row, 1970, and J. M. Hollis and S. Lukes, eds., *Rationality and Relativism.* Cambridge, MA: MIT Press, 1982.

Notes to Chapter Fifteen

[1] Hans-Georg Gadamer, *Platos dialektische Ethik* in *Gesammelte Werke.* Tübingen: J.C.B. Mohr, 1986, Band V. *Plato's Dialectical Ethics: Phenomenological Interpretations Relating to the Philebus.* Trans. By Robert M. Wallace. New Haven: Yale University Press, 1991.

[2] Plato, "Philebus." *Collected Dialogues of Plato.* Edited by Hamilton and Cairns. Bollingen Series: Princeton University Press, 1980, pp. 1086-1150.

[3] J.C.B. Gosling, Plato: *Philebus.* Oxford: Clarendon Press, 1975. K. Sayre, *Plato's Later Ontology.* Princeton: Princeton University Press, 1983. E.W. Schipper, *Forms in Plato's Later Dialogues.* The Hague: Martinus Nijhoff, 1965., R. Hackforth, *Plato's Philebus.* Cambridge: Cambridge University Press, 1962. R.G. Bury, *The Philebus of Plato.* Cambridge: Cambridge University Press, 1897.

[4] Sophron, of whom we have many fragments, was a Sicilian mime-writer of the 5th century b.c., probably 430-360b.c. Mimes were writers who would represent some scene of everyday life or a

representation of some familiar type of character. Their work was marked by the imitation, by voice or by gestures, of any situation or any character familiar enough to the onlookers, much like the topicality of Seinfeld observational humor. We know that Sophron's mimes were referred to as poems, but were not in meter but rhythmic prose They were also in the broad "Doric" dialect of Syracuse with many touches of local color in their wording. They were also classified into men-mimes and women-mimes, and composed as dialogues made up of question and reply. Plato never mentions Sophron by name, but scholars trace some of Plato's scenic moments to Sophron, such as that of the appetitive parts of the soul being like a leaky jar set forth in the *Gorgias* 493a-c, with the reference to some "clever Sicilian" being Sophron; and *Republic*, V, 451 c reference to men and women-drama, a reference to Sophron. The external testimony to Plato's acquaintenance with Sophron is extensive. Duris of Samos (340-270b.c.) mentions that Plato "always had Sophron in his hands." Duris is generally trusted by scholars, as he studied under a follower of Plato, Theophrastus, in the Lyceum at Athens. Timon of Phlius (320-230b.c.) expressly states that Plato "cultivated the mimetic art in writing his dialogues" from Sophron. Valerius Maximus, Quintilian, and Diogenes Laertius also all mention Sophron in relation to Plato. John M.S. McDonald's authoritative work *Character-Portraiture in Epicharmus, Sophron, and Plato* (Sewanee, Tennessee, 1931) concludes that Plato's own aptitude for mimesis was stimulated by Socrates and strengthened by an appreciative reading of the clever old Sicilian, Sophron.

5 Gadamer, *The Idea of the Good in Platonic-Aristotelian Philosophy.* Trans. P. Christopher Smith. New Haven: Yale University Press, 1986.

6 Gadamer, PDE, xxxii.

7 Heidegger, *Phänomenologische Interpretationen zu Aristoteles: Einführung in die phänomenologische Forschung.* (Freiburg lecture course of WS 1921-22. Edited by Walter Bröcker and Käte Bröcker-Oltmanns. Gesamtausgabe. II. Abteilung: Vorlesungen, 1919-1944. Frankfurt: Klostermann, 1975, Volume 61.

8 Heidegger, *Platon: Sophistes.* Marburg lecture course WS 1924-25. Edited by Ingeborg Schüssler, 1992.Vol. 19, *Gesamtausgabe. Plato's Sophist,* trans. By Richard Rojcewicz and Andre Schuwer. Bloomington: Indiana University Press, 1997. "Plato's Doctrine of Truth," trans. John Barlow, in William Barrett and Henry D. Aiken, ed., *Philosophy in the Twentieth Century.* New York: Random House, 1962, Vol. 3.

9 Heidegger, *Being and Time.* Macquarrie and Robinson trans. New York: Harper and Row, 1962, p. 22.

10 Gadamer, PDE, xxv.

11 Gadamer, PDE, p. 16.

12 Gadamer, PDE, p. 44.

13 Gadamer, *Truth and Method,* p. 464.

14 Ibid., p. 465.

15 Gadamer, PDE, n. p. 105.

16 Gadamer, PDE, p, 34.

17 Gadamer, "Plato and the Poets," in *Dialogue and Dialectic*, trans. P. Christopher Smith. New Haven: Yale University Press, 1980, p. 58.

18 Gadamer, "Plato and the Poets," in *Dialogue and Dialectic*, trans. P. Christopher Smith. New Haven: Yale University Press, 1980, p. 66.

Notes to Chapter Sixteen

1 Beda Allemann, *Hölderlin und Heidegger*. Zurich: Atlantis Verlag, 1954; Marc Froment-Meurice, *That is to Say: Heidegger's Poetics*. Translated by Jan Plug. Stanford: Stanford University Press, 1998.; Paul Bove, *Destructive Poetics*. New York: Columbia University Press, 1980; Gerald Bruns, *Heidegger's Estrangements: Language, Truth, and Poetry in the Later Writings*. New Haven: Yale University Press, 1989; Christopher Fynsk, Heidegger: *Thought and Historicity*. Expanded ed. Ithaca: Cornell University Press, 1993; Andrzej Warminski, *Readings in Interpretation: Holderlin, Hegel, Heidegger*. Minneapolis: University of Minnesota Press, 1987; Veronique Foti, *Heidegger and the Poets: Poesis, Techne, Sophia*. Atlantic Highlands. N.J.: Humanities Press International, 1992.; Michel Haar. *The Sounds of the Earth: Heidegger and the Grounds of the History of Being*. Translated by Reginald Lilly. Bloomington: Indiana University Press, 1993.

2 Heidegger, "What are Poets For?" in *Poetry, Language, Thought*. Translated by Albert Hofstadter. Harper and Row, 1971, p. 134.

3 Heidegger, *Contributions to Philosophy (from Enowning)*. Translated by Parvis Emad and Kenneth Maly. Bloomington: Indiana University Press, 1999, p. 9.

4 Heidegger, "Origin of the Work of Art," in *Poetry, Language, Thought*. Translated by Albert Hofstadter. Harper and Row, 1971, p. 84.

5 Heidegger, *Vier Seminar*. Frankfurt am Main: Klostermann, 1977, p. 129.

6 Heidegger, *Vier Seminar*. Frankfurt am Main: Klostermann, 1977, p. 129. For other translations, see William Richardson, "Heidegger's Way Through Phenomenology to the Thinking of Being." In *Heidegger: The Man and the Thinker*, edited by Thomas Sheehan. Chicago: Precedent, 1981, p. 66n.24; Theodore Kisiel, translator's note, Werner Marx, *Heidegger and the Tradition*. Evanston: Northwestern University Press, 1971, p. 176n, Joseph Kockelmans, *On the Truth of Being: Reflections on Heidegger's Later Philosophy*. Bloomington: Indiana University Press, 1984, pp. 229, 237; Gianni Vattimo, *Le avventure della differenza*. Milan: Garzanti, 1980; and David Kolb, *The Critique of Pure Modernity*. Chicago: University of Chicago Press, 1986, p. 145.

7 Heidegger, "What are Poets For?" op. cit., p. 93.

8 Heidegger, *Identity and Difference*. Translated by Joan Stambaugh. New York: Harper and Row, 1971, p. 36.

9 Hebel—der Hausfreund [Pfullingen: Gunther Neske, 1957]; trans. Bruce Foltz and Michael Heim under the title "Hebel—Friend of the House," in *Contemporary German Philosophy*, vol. 3 [University Park, Pennsylvania State University Press, 1983], pp. 89-101.

10 Heidegger, *The Metaphysical Foundations of Logic*. Translated by Michael Heim. Bloomington: Indiana University Press, 1984.

[11] Ibid., p. 49.

[12] Heidegger, *Parmenides*. Frankfurt: Klostermann, 1982, pp. 118-119; originally lectures given in the winter of 1942-43, vol. 54 of the *Gesamtausgabe*.

[13] Heidegger, "Origin of the Work of Art," op. cit., p. 73.

[14] The distinction is from Charles Taylor, *Human Agency and Language: Philosophical Papers I*. Cambridge: Cambridge University Press, 1985, pp. 215-292.

[15] Nietzsche, *The Will-to-Power*. Edited by Walter Kaufmann. Translated by Walter Kaufman and R. J. Hollingdale. New York: Random House, 1967, #522, #604.

[16] Ibid., #625.

[17] Heidegger, *Poetry, Language, Thought*. op. cit., p. 193.

[18] Ibid., p. 190.

[19] Ibid., p. 194.

[20] Ibid., p. 206.

[21] Ibid., p. 198.

[22] Ibid., p. 199.

[23] See Heidegger, "Building, Dwelling, Thinking," in *Poetry, Language, Thought*. op. cit., pp. 145-161.

[24] Heidegger, *Hölderlin's Hymn "Der Ister."* Translation by William McNeill and Julia Davis. Bloomington: Indiana University Press, 1996, p. 165.

[25] Heidegger, "What are Poets For?" op. cit., p. 137.

[26] Ibid.

[27] Heidegger, "...poetically man dwells..." in *Poetry, Language, Thought*. op. cit., p. 227.

[28] Heidegger, *Hölderlin's Hymn "Germania" and "The Rhine."* *Gesamtausgabe* Vol. 39. Frankfurt am Main: Vittorio Klostermann, 1980, p. 33.

[29] Heidegger, *Elucidations of Hölderlin's Poetry*. Translated by Keith Hoeller. Amherst, N.Y.: Humanity Books, 2000, p. 59.

Notes to Chapter Seventeen

[1] Winch, "The Universalizability of Moral Judgments," in *Ethics and Action*. London: Routledge & Kegan Paul, 1972, pp. 151-170.

[2] Ibid., p. 152.

[3] Winch, p. 158.

[4] Winch, "Universalizability," op. cit., p. 165.

[5] D.Z. Phillips, "The Presumption of Theory," in *Interventions in Ethics*. SUNY Press, 1992, p. 61.

[6] Winch, *op. cit.*, p. 168.

[7] Rush Rhees, *Moral Questions*. MacMillan. D.Z.Phillips,(ed.)

[8] David Wiggins, "Truth and Truth as Predicated or Moral Judgments," in Wiggins, *Needs, Values, Truth*. Oxford: Blackwell, 1987; L. Alweiss, "On Moral Dilemmas: Winch, Kant, and Billy Budd," *Philosophy*, 78, pp. 205-218; K. Kolenda, "Moral Conflicts and Universalizability," *Philosophy*, 50, pp. 460-8; J. Atwell, "A Note on Decisions, Judgments, and Universalizability," *Ethics*, 77 (1967), pp. 130-4.

[9] Onora O'Neill, *The Power of Example*. Vol 61. January 1986; Martha Nussbaum, *Poetic Justice: The Literary Imagination and Public Life*. Boston: Beacon Press, 1995.

[10] Cora Diamond, "Losing Your Concepts," *Ethics*. January, 1988, p. 266.

[11] Paul Ricouer, *Hermeneutics and the Human Sciences*, ed. and trans. John B. Thompson. Cambridge University Press, 1981, p. 111.

[12] See Jean Grondin, *Introduction to Philosophical Hermeneutics*, trans. Joel Weinsheimer. New Haven: Harvard University Press, 1994, p. 124.

[13] Lester Hunt, "*Billy Budd*: Melville's Dilemma. *Philosophy and Literature*, 26 (2002), pp. 273-295. I follow the general parameters of this discussion.

[14] Herman Melville, *Billy Budd and Other Tales*. Introduction by Joyce Carol Oates. New American Library, 1998, p. 21.

[15] Ibid., p. 22.

[16] Ibid., p. 62.

[17] Ibid., p. 20.

[18] Ibid., p. 8.

Index

PHENOMENOLOGY
& LITERATURE

Hans H. Rudnick
General Editor

The focus of this series is on studies using the tenets of phenomenology and its various dogmatic and skeptical evolutions to elucidate and interpret primarily literary works of art in the contexts of aesthetics, ontology, epistemology, axiology, hermeneutics, communication, reader response and reception, and cultural and social theory. Studies of a comparative nature, which straddle and/or combine the disciplines of philosophical and literary studies, are distinctive features of this series. Emphasis is on subjects that may advance the state of the art, set trends, generate and continue discussion, expand horizons beyond present perspectives, or redefine previously held notions. Approaches may center on individual works, authors, schools of phenomenological thought, or abstract notions, including issues of a comparative nature spanning the cultures, languages, and literatures of several nations from the perspectives of world literature and philosophy.

For additional information about this series or for the submission of manuscripts, please contact:

Acquisitions Department
Peter Lang Publishing, Inc.
P.O. Box 1246
Bel Air, Maryland 21014-1246

To order other books in this series, please contact our Customer Service Department:

(800) 770-LANG (within the U.S.)
(212) 647-7706 (outside the U.S.)
(212) 647-7707 FAX

Or browse online by series:
www.peterlang.com